Contagious Idea

Ben Cullen in Dumfries in 1995

Contagious Ideas
On evolution, culture, archaeology, and Cultural Virus Theory

Ben Sandford Cullen

Collected writings
edited by James Steele,
Richard Cullen and Christopher Chippindale

Oxbow Books

Published by
Oxbow Books, Park End Place, Oxford OX1 1HN

© the Estate of Ben Cullen 1990, 1992, 1993, 1995, 1996, 2000
contributors and editors 2000

ISBN 1-84217-014-7

A CIP record for this book is available from the British Library.

This book is available from
Oxbow Books, Park End Place, Oxford OX1 1HN
(T: 01865-241429; F: 01865-794449)

and

The David Brown Book Co
PO Box 511, Oakville, CT 06779, USA
(T: 860-945-9329; F: 860-945-9468)

and

www.oxbowbooks.com

The cover design is taken from a piece of pottery decorated by Ben Cullen.

Printed in England
at the Short Run Press, Exeter

Contents

Preface

Ben Cullen was a great one for questions. Just when you thought, after a couple of hours, that you had explained the origins of modern humans and why anyone would do anything as daft as build a megalithic tomb he would give you that quizzical look and say "Yes, but don't you think that is all upset by ...", and off we would go again. Perhaps it was the Australian in him. Ben came from the country that gave tall poppy syndrome to the world. Under this system no-one is allowed to stand out from the crowd for too long. The academic world in particular wields a very sharp scythe and you had best jump. Ben was therefore exposed at an early stage in his career to strong selection. He was both aware of what would await him if he stayed and well schooled in what was expected of him if he left. Hence the questions. I like to think that once in the UK he saw his role as reversing that much quoted remark of Sir John Lubbock's, tossed out in 1865, that colonisation of the world proceeded "just for instance as the weeds of Europe are now gradually but surely creeping over the surface of Australia". Ben's response was to supply an evolution that Lubbock never knew and colonise the archaeological world with Cultural Virus Theory.

CVT, as this book shows, was Ben's idea. It is the meme of his memory that now assumes an evolutionary trajectory of its own. It remains an untried theory and like all evolutionary processes is up against strong selection. In the trying CVT will almost certainly change, as it would if its meme-master had been here to shepherd it through the evolutionary landscape of academic debate and enquiry. Good theories are open to interpretation and re-interpretation. Darwinian evolution is one of those, as the cottage industry that now surrounds its namesake shows. Darwin's greatest insight, sadly ignored by many archaeologists including his friend Sir John Lubbock, was that essences explained nothing about organisms. A theory of change needs to understand variation. CVT provides us with a way of harnessing powerful biological metaphors, tried and tested with palaeontological and now genetic data, to the parallel domain of culture and its explanation. This is the most exciting interface to be researching: the co-evolution of biology and culture. Ben recognised it early. His potential contribution to the understanding of the co-evolutionary process was great.

ix

He was well-placed to draw on biological metaphors for change and temper them with his time-depth perspective on human culture. The case-studies that he left us with demonstrate an impressive range of knowledge and a willingness to apply new contributions to move the argument on. Co-evolution can be a difficult field to define and an even harder one to illustrate with examples. Terry Deacon[1] captures much of it in his sound-bite explanation of language: "I suggest that an idea changed the brain". Ben might instead have said that the brain caught a cold. And as a result we have been asking questions ever since. I continue to miss his.

Clive Gamble

---

[1] T. Deacon, *The Symbolic Species: the co-evolution of language and the human brain*, (Penguin Books 1997), 322.

Editors' introduction

The papers in this book have been chosen to give the reader a clear and full understanding of Ben Cullen's contributions to archaeological theory. Although Ben's desperately premature death deprived us of the opportunity to see him develop this work further, there is plenty here to celebrate. These papers demonstrate that by the time he reached the age of 31, Ben had already achieved the coherent formulation of a unique, rigorous and highly provocative theory of human culture.

Ben Cullen was born in Sydney, Australia, in 1964. In 1971 his family moved to a rural environment on the mid-north coast of New South Wales, where he attended the local one-teacher school with eleven pupils. Ben's interest in biological and cultural Darwinism began at an early age. When he was seven, his parents were surprised to see a letter 'arrive' in the mailbox addressed to Ben Cullen and with the sender's name – Charles Darwin London – on the back. Somehow a 'contagious idea' had become indelibly inscribed in a young mind.

Ben completed his schooling at Kendall and Wauchope, where he was *dux* of his final year in 1981. He was a talented all-rounder, being an outstanding sportsman at national level, and involving himself in art, music, creative writing and theatre. He studied archaeology and Chinese at the University of Sydney, coming under the influence of R. V. S. Wright and particularly of Roland Fletcher, who encouraged his interest in cultural Darwinism. Ben graduated with First Class Honours, picking up a University Blue in Athletics along the way.

He completed his doctoral thesis in 1993. In 1990 he had been awarded the Greenwell Post-Graduate Travelling Scholarship and had travelled widely in Britain and the USA, discussing and elaborating his ideas in meetings with many prominent evolutionary theorists. In 1992 he moved to England, taking school-teaching jobs and coaching school athletics to support himself while he finished his thesis.

At the time of his sudden death in December 1995, of unknown causes but perhaps due to a cardiac arrhythmia, Ben was a Research Fellow in the Department of Archaeology, Queen's University Belfast. His papers were appearing with increasing regularity in professional books and journals, and it was clear to all who knew him that he was destined, had he lived, for academic success at a very high level indeed.

As these papers record, Ben's intellectual project was the foundation of a rigorous neo-Darwinian theory of cultural change. For such an explanatory framework to be appropriate to human culture, he recognised the need to demonstrate both that cultural traits are inherited by individuals independently of their genes, and that such traits are in some sense particulate in nature. He also recognised that a neo-Darwinian theory of the evolution of cultural traits requires that selection should act on available pre-existing variation which is, in itself, random or undirected. Ben's own distinctive contribution, the 'Cultural Virus Theory', is his solution to the problem of developing a theory of cultural change within these constraints.

In the opening chapters of this book, taken from his PhD thesis, he documents his dissatisfaction with the purported Darwinian basis of some pre-existing frameworks for explaining culture change in archaeology and anthropology. Cultural Evolutionism is rejected as non-Darwinian since it posits both an intrinsic tendency for cultures to evolve towards greater complexity, and a tendency for convergent parallel evolution independent of the constraints of available cultural variation in specific regional and local traditions. Cultural Sociobiology is also rejected, because it assumes that socially learned behaviours can be treated as phenotypic traits contributing to the genetic inclusive fitness of individuals. In Ben's view, this assumption fails to take account of the extent to which cultural transmission can promote the spread of ideas whose persistence conflicts with the priorities of the 'selfish gene'.

Ben recognised two competing models of Cultural Selectionism, the only framework of those he discusses that provides a genuinely neo-Darwinian theory of cultural evolution (seen as a process separate from genetic evolution). In the papers reproduced here, he proposes that the Cultural Selectionism prevalent in American anthropology tends to regard cultural traits as components of the individual phenotype, thus making individual people the units of selection in cultural reproduction. He identifies the basis for this view in the notion that cultural traits have no mechanism of self-replication. His own approach, defined in opposition to this, explores ways in which cultural traits might be seen as self-reproducing entities analogous to viruses; and the appropriateness of this analogy is the most distinctive premise of Cultural Virus Theory.

In these papers Ben takes the view that a human culture is, fundamentally, a set of learned ideas. He proposes that since ideas spread socially without being confined to the routes of transmission of genes, they should be considered not as individual phenotypic traits but as 'viral phenomena'. Each such idea is therefore a 'freelance fragment which needs to "borrow" other organisms' bodies in order to reproduce' (p. 136). One advantage of this perspective is that it encourages us to consider how ideas can come to predominate in a society, when they do not maintain or enhance the genetic fitness of their human hosts. The core of this book consists of Ben's statements of, and defence of, Cultural Virus Theory.

It is clear from his postdoctoral work that Ben was increasingly interested in applying Cultural Virus Theory to the explanation of cultural persistence and change in specific cases (particularly with respect to religious ideas and to art traditions). The papers reprinted in the last section of this book include discussions of the parasitic nature of megalithic religion and of Renaissance art, and introduce new refinements of the Virus metaphor for human culture. These refinements include the application of the concept of eusociality to artefact production systems, and the application to cultural evolution of theories of virulence derived from Darwinian medicine. In this latter refinement, Ben proposes that pernicious ideas which we acquire by vertical transmission (from our parents and other members of the older generation) will tend to reduce our genetic fitness less than those acquired by horizontal transmission (from members of our own generation, and particularly from non-kin). This refinement was undoubtedly part of his response to his critics, when they asserted that Cultural Virus Theory neglects humans' ability to resist the persuasiveness of pernicious ideas. Perhaps, by implication, of all social relationships it is in those of parents and children that we should find the most care taken to avoid transmitting fitness-reducing ideas, and with the most success.

It seems very timely, now that Darwinism is being rediscovered in Anglophone archaeological theory (e.g. Barton & Clark 1997; Lyman *et al.* 1997; O'Brien 1998), to publish these explorations of neo-Darwinian culture theory. Ben Cullen's intellectual project explored, with compelling logic, the consequences of assuming that cultural evolution is a process which is analytically separable from genetic evolution, but which has its own neo-Darwinian dynamic. The papers in this book may well persuade their readers that (as Daniel Dennett puts it) 'a scholar is just a library's way of making another library'. Ideas can indeed spread without maintaining or enhancing the genetic inclusive fitness of their hosts, and Ben invites us to consider the reasons for this 'from the ideas' point of view'. No one who met Ben could come away entirely uninfected by his enthusiasm for such an approach.

The text of the present book is taken from Ben's writings, much of it from his 1993 PhD thesis (Cullen 1993a). In part 1, chapters 1–4 are from the thesis; chapter 5 is from a 1993 paper. All of part 2, chapters 6–8, is from the thesis. In part 3, chapter 9 is Ben's contribution to the 1996 volume *Darwinian archaeologies*; chapter 10 is from a 1995 paper; chapters 11 and 12 are from his contribution to the 'Einstein meets Magritte conference', 1995. (See below, for exact sources.) Since Ben's PhD thesis has been published in full (as Cullen 1996a), and the other and published texts are also available, our aim here has been to provide a succinct account of Ben's ideas rather than to reprint exactly what has appeared before. So we have also not included the text of his early ABC radio talk 'The Cultural Virus', compelling though it is; what it says was superseded by later writing. We have reduced and edited some sections of the thesis, and eliminated some duplications and overlaps; and we have silently corrected occasional slips in referencing (some remain because we cannot resolve them, or because we cannot trace the publication Ben was referring to). Two illustrations implied in the texts we do not have, so the text at each point sets out in words what the diagram would have figured. The overviews that introduce each chapter taken from the thesis are Cullen's; the others are our own.

Ben was a young scholar whose ideas were developing quickly and changing as they grew. We cannot know where his ideas would have taken him, so we have not presumed to guess: this book tries simply to present in good order and at reasonable length that which he had done when he left us.

Published material, other than the PhD, appeared previously as:

Chapter 5, from: The Darwinian resurgence and the Cultural Virus critique, *Cambridge Archaeological Journal* 3 (1993): 179–202.

Chapter 9, from: Cultural Virus Theory and the eusocial pottery assemblage, in H. D. G. Maschner (ed.), *Darwinian archaeologies* (New York (NY): Plenum, 1996): 43–59.

Chapter 10, from: Living artefact, personal ecosystem, biocultural schizophrenia: a novel synthesis of processual and post-processual thinking, *Proceedings of the Prehistoric Society* 61 (1995): 69–90.

Chapter 11, from: Ben's first paper presented to the 'Einstein meets Magritte Interdisciplinary Conference', June 1995, at the Vrije Universiteit Brussel, Belgium. To be published in F. Heylighen, J. Bollen & A. Riegler (ed.), *The evolution of complexity: the violet book of Einstein meets Magritte*. Dordrecht: Kluwer Academic, 1999.

Chapter 12, from Ben's paper presented to the 'Einstein meets Magritte Interdisciplinary Conference', June 1995, at the Vrije Universiteit Brussel, Belgium. To be published in S. Smets, S. Gutwirth & L. Van Langenhove (ed.), *Science and society: the orange book of Einstein meets Magritte*. Dordrecht: Kluwer Academic, 1999.

Acknowledgements

Ben Cullen was generous in his acknowledgements. These are the acknowledgements from his PhD thesis from which much of this book is drawn:

During my candidature I was a very grateful recipient of the Greenwell Post-Graduate Research Fund, which enabled me to undertake a four-month tour of English and American Universities (Cambridge, Harvard, Boston, Chicago, Northwestern, Loyola, Stanford, and Berkeley), gathering data and conversing with many archaeologists, anthropologists, historians, and biologists. It is fortunate that the postgraduate students of the Anthropology Department have this fund at their disposal.

There are several people to whom I am particularly indebted, and who therefore deserve a special mention.

I must firstly extend my warmest gratitude to Roland Fletcher, my supervisor, who has contributed a large amount of time and effort throughout the course of my research. He read and commented upon all drafts, and was always readily available whenever I felt the need to see him.

John Cook must be thanked for his continued interest in my ideas over a long period. Without his perceptive responses and enthusiastic encouragement my time as a Doctoral candidate would not have been as productive, nor as enjoyable.

Stephanie Moser has managed to rebuild my confidence whenever it flagged, and to be there to help whenever a problem requiring a creative solution arose.

Alice Gorman has helped by supplying a lot of perceptive comments and sensitive support at all stages of the project.

John Von Sturmer has provided me with many interesting and helpful conversations about issues of mind and culture, and this has undoubtedly done much to improve the quality of the research.

Neil Maclean has played the devil's advocate in the nicest possible way, listening with great patience and responding with great diplomacy.

He has, as a consequence, enabled me to question and thereby strengthen my arguments.

Thanks are also due to Stephen Shennan, who read and commented on my numerical and data chapters; if any errors remain, they must be considered to be my responsibility.

Daniel Tangri, Greg Wyncoll, John Clegg, Jadran Mimica, Diane Austin-Broos, and John Kelt have all contributed quite a large amount of academic discussion to my research over the years, and their influence on my thinking should not be underestimated. I would also like to thank them for their companionship and personal support during my decade at the University of Sydney.

My thanks must also go to W. W. Howells, G. P. Murdock, and D. White for making a range of cranial and cultural data widely available to other academics; such large bodies of data enabled a far more comprehensive testing procedure than would otherwise have been attempted.

During my candidature I have discussed the various issues of this study with a large number of people from many different disciplines. My sincere thanks are due to all of these people, each of whom either gave up some of their time to discuss certain issues or problems associated with the thesis, or raised an important point during one of my seminars: Ass. Prof. Robert S. Armstrong; Dr Rita Armstrong; Dr Robert Attenborough; Dr Geoff Bailey; Prof. John Ballard; Hugh Barton; Ass. Prof. Jeremy Beckett; Prof. Charles Birch; Prof. Jim Brown; Dr Gavan Butler; Dave Cameron; Dr Chris Chippindale; Sharon Claydon; Grant Chambers; Prof. Grahame Clark; Dr Aedeen Cremin; Christine Cullen; Richard Cullen; Dr George Dales; Dr Richard Dawkins; Lance Day; Gary Dunnett; Prof. Bill Durham; Bill Elwood; Stan Florek; Dr Rob Foley; Prof. Derek Freeman; Peter Gallison; Dan Garber; Patrick Glass; David Gosling; Prof. Stephen Jay Gould; Ian Gollop; Prof. Norman Hammond; Dr Tim Hardy; Prof. Les Hiatt; Dr Catherine Hills; Dr Ian Hodder; Prof. William Irons; Dan Hogg; Ian Hughes; John Huss; Oliver Jones; Quentin Jones; Dr Ian Johnston; Dr Norman Johnston; Jon Kelt; Dr Pat Kirch; Dr Bernard Knapp; Prof. Stephen Knight; Estelle Lazer; Dr Andrew Lattas; Dr Marsha Levine; Dr Lisa Lloyd; Ass. Prof. Fred McDonald; Dr James McGlade; Ass. Prof. Bill Maidment; Prof. Bernard Martin; Niall Marks; Dr Paul Mellars; Barnaby Miln; Dr. Stephen Mithen; Sir Derek Pattinson; Dr Kim Paul; Dr Kate Pretty; Dr Robert Preucel; Prof. Colin Renfrew; Dr Jim Rhoads; Prof. Bob Richards; Dr David Rindos; Prof. Keith Runcorn;

Dr Curtis Runnells; Dr Peter Rowley-Conwy; Dr Eddie Schipper; Dr Jim Specht; Laura-Jane Smith; Dr Mike Smith; Prof. Larry Stager; Dr George Stocking; Dr David Stronach; Robert Tate; Hartmut Tschauner; Dr John Terrell; Dr Robyn Torrence; Prof. Ruth Tringham; Dr Sander Van Der Leeuw; Prof. Michael Walker; Dave Walton; Dr Peter White; Prof. Gordon Willey; Dr Bill Wimsatt; Prof. Richard Wright; and Dr Alison Wylie.

As editors of Ben's book, we thank Michael Shanks, Julian Thomas and Colin Renfrew, who joined us in developing the framework of this book, and other colleagues for varied assistance.

The Crane Child

A baby, a boy, called Michel in the article, was born to a disoriented, possibly retarded teenager, the child of a rape. Until he was about two years old, he lived with his mother in a tenement next to a construction site. Every day she stumbled in and around and out of the apartment, lost in her own madness. She was hardly aware of the child, barely knew how to feed or care for him. The neighbours were alarmed at how Michel screamed, but when they went to knock at the door to ask her to quiet him, often she wasn't there. She would go out at all hours, leaving the child alone, unguarded. Then one day, quite suddenly, the crying stopped. The child did not scream, and he did not scream the next night either. For days there was hardly a sound. Police and social workers were called. They found the child lying on his cot by the window. He was alive and remarkably well, considering how severely he appeared to have been neglected. Quietly he played on his squalid cot, stopping every few seconds to look out the window. His play was unlike any they had ever seen. Looking out the window, he would raise his arms, then jerk them to a halt; stand up on his scrawny legs, then fall; bend and rise. He made strange noises, a kind of screeching in his throat. What was he doing? the social workers wondered. What kind of play could this be?

Then they looked out the window, where some cranes were in operation, lifting girders and beams, stretching out wrecker balls on their single arms. The child was watching the crane nearest the window. As it lifted, he lifted; as it bent, he bent; as its gears screeched, its motor whirred, the child screeched between his teeth, whirred with his tongue.

They took him away. He screamed hysterically and could not be quieted, so desolate was he to be divided from his beloved crane. Years later, Michel was an adolescent, living in a special institution for the mentally handicapped. He moved like a crane, made the noises of a crane, and although the doctors showed him many pictures and toys, he only responded to the pictures of cranes, only played with the toy cranes. Only cranes made him happy. He came to be known as 'The Crane Child'.

And the question Jerene kept coming up against, reading the article, was this: What did it sound like? What did it feel like? The language belonged to Michel alone; it was forever lost to her. How wondrous, how grand those cranes must have seemed to Michel, compared to the small and clumsy creatures who surrounded him. For each, in his own way, she believed, finds what it is he must love, and loves it; the window becomes a mirror; whatever it is that we love, that is who we are.

From chapter three of the novel *The lost language of cranes* by David Leavitt, (Penguin Books 1986).

Part one

The Cultural Virus critique

1
The untried theory

Overview

In this chapter a general background to the study is provided, in two basic parts. Firstly, the problem of the 'untried theory' is introduced and the basic aims of the study are defined in relation to this problem. These research aims are then related to a number of wider debates, some of which are not necessarily or frequently associated with neo-Darwinian theory.

An unusual abstraction

While the origin of evolutionary theory in anthropology is often traced to Darwin (e.g. Renfrew & Bahn 1991: 22; and see White 1959b: 106 for an opposing view), it is very important to distinguish the early theories of cultural evolution from Darwinian and neo-Darwinian theories about the physical evolution of humans. Ironically, although Darwin's special contribution to evolution was the elucidation of *how* evolution had occurred, rather than the fact of its occurrence, this innovation did not carry over into the study of cultural evolution. While the notion of the natural selection of random variation was to profoundly influence research in human physical evolution until the present day, no cultural equivalent of this mechanism was championed by the early cultural evolutionists. Rather, like the 'red-Lamarckians' of the day (Desmond & Moore 1992: 252, 275, 295), it is fair to say that whether inspired by Darwin or not, the early cultural evolutionists 'took the idea and ran with it'. The explanatory frameworks which they produced over the next century were anything but Darwinism, let alone neo-Darwinism; indeed, they resurrected almost all of the philosophical elements which characterise the Lamarckian world-view (see chapter 2). The evolutionary legacy which we inherit today in cultural fields of enquiry has, therefore, very little to do with neo-Darwinian principles, and it is crucial that this fact is brought to the attention of the reader right from the very beginning of the study.

It is also important that the reader bear in mind that this study focuses on a deeper or more general level of explanation than that level which theoretical discourse is most commonly directed at. To use Chomskian language, one might say that this study is concerned not with the specific forms that theories of cultural change take, but with the deep structures behind them. However, unlike Chomsky's 'rich innate endowment' (Mithen 1989: 489), the 'deep structures' of evolutionary theory (general concepts like 'selection' or 'determinism') are obviously not genetically determined.

Selectionism and its alternatives are meta-theories, or theories about theories; they are concerned with the syntactical rules which govern the construction of causal explanations of regional sequences – a handful of background assumptions which are generally more implicit than explicit. To put it another way, evolutionary theories (with some exceptions) provide knowledge of the mechanisms operating in history, but not about the course of history itself, which only emerges in the analysis of a particular case (Shennan 1989: 340). Whether any given explanation of a regional cultural sequence is judged to be neo-Darwinian or Lamarckian depends not upon the presence of certain diagnostic causes or effects, such as duck's feet and water, or ploughs and food shortage. Rather, it depends on the particular manner in which causes and effects are juxtaposed: whether water causes the genesis of duck's feet, or merely selects for them once they appear; and whether food shortage causes the genesis of ploughs, or merely selects for them once they are discovered by happenstance.

When we debate whether to adopt a 'neo-Darwinian' position at the expense of a 'Lamarckian' one, we are therefore not concerned with the specific constituents of a causal explanation, however universal or particular that explanation may claim to be. Strictly speaking we should be concerned only with the *manner* in which any such causal factors are *incorporated into* the explanatory scenario. Thus debates about the very use of Selectionism itself (as distinct from debates about the validity of a particular selectionist explanation of a particular structure) are located at an unusually abstract level of discussion. Theoretical discourse, whether in the organic or inorganic sciences, normally focuses on the level of 'determining *which* causal forces are at work in a particular system', and not at the more general level of 'determining *whether any such forces are selective at all*'.

So most of the theoretical discourse that surrounds, say, the explanation of the tiger's stripes, would tend to concern which aspects of the jungle environment (interacting with which aspects of the tiger's phylogenetic heritage) are most responsible for the stripes. It would be already taken for granted that the final cause or causes of the tiger coat pattern, once ascertained, will be selective in nature, not determinative. Similarly, debates about the forces responsible in the evolution of hominids focus at the level of specific hypotheses about which forces are most pertinent in governing the reproductive success of early hominids. Whether a hypothesis concerns the need for the capacity for language, the advantages of upright posture in avoiding heat exposure on the savannah, or the need for social co-operation, it is taken for granted that these factors can only influence hominid gene pools by causing selection of some kind.

Nor is the situation substantially different in the humanities, although it is not identical, as we shall see. Theoretical debates in cultural fields of enquiry commonly take place below the level of abstraction at which the neo-Darwinian/Lamarckian logical dichotomy occurs. A group of archaeologists or anthropologists debating the relative merits of Freudian and Marxist theory are most likely to argue about which list of causes (for example the social and economic versus the individual and psychological) is most correct. It is usually taken for granted that these causes produce their effect by 'determining' rather than 'selecting for' particular states of mind, and thus the debate takes place within an implicit and largely unquestioned 'Lamarckian' framework. Finally, even theoretical discourse in the inorganic sciences takes it for granted that the causal forces in its desmesne are *not* selective, but rather determinative (or chaotic) in nature. Debates about the causes of earthquakes concern the relative importance of a range of causes, but all of them are assumed to take effect through imparting some direct transformation to a tectonic system, not through causing the differential reproduction of, say, lava at the expense of ash, or *vice versa*.

As in other disciplines, then, many explanations of cultural phenomena are preoccupied with the identification of particular causal factors and local theories, ignoring general theories, in much the same way as many biologists or chemists may ignore the general theories of their domain, in their daily practice. But the similar situations are occurring for somewhat different reasons. If the problems of large-scale theory are ignored by a biologist in his or her daily practice, this may often be because they consider these issues to be *already solved*. But when researchers in cultural fields of enquiry do the same, it may often be because they believe this problem to be *unsolvable*.

Whether we assume the 'Lamarckism versus neo-Darwinism' issue to be solved or unsolvable, the net result is much the same. Very little anthropological research has been directed towards an evaluation of the intrinsic potential of selective logic itself, and more often than not the whole issue has been side-stepped in order to get to the more palpable problems of particular cultural systems. Like biological and inorganic science, the bulk of anthropological research takes place at a problem-oriented level, and theoretical discourse, while moving to a more general level than particular problems, rarely addresses any fundamental universalities. But, unlike biology and physics, cultural fields of enquiry do not have a generally accepted theoretical umbrella which superintends problem-oriented research; there are many theories, but no 'universal co-ordinating meta-theory' as it were, no equivalent of theories such as Quantum Mechanics in Molecular Physics, the Theory of Relativity in Astrophysics, or Natural Selection in Biology.

As a consequence, the humanities are now hindered by a peculiar situation; an overwhelming predominance of locally dependent (rather than universal) theoretical structures. The situation might be described as a curious 'bottom heaviness' exhibited by the greater part of cultural and psychological theories. Compared to the general theories of other disciplines, the general theories of culture are all rather specific. Alternatively, one might say that there is a rich diversity in what is sometimes termed the 'middle-range' level of theory in anthropology and archaeology, in the form of a great deal of discourse concerning the causes or lack of causes of various cultural and psychological phenomena. These are the issues dealt with in the bodies of theory associated with words like Psychoanalysis, Phenomenology, Sociobiology, Functionalism, Structuralism, post-Structuralism, Cultural Selectionism, Marxism, and so on. So many approaches investigate, in some form or another, the nature of certain causes, and the nature of certain effects, and, once they find a strong correlation, they see the link as something self-evident in the correlation. They are thus side stepping the simplest and most general questions of all: what is the nature of these links *between* cause and effect in human behaviour, regardless of which of the particular causes and effects we choose to link? Does a given factor *select* from amongst a range of possibilities generated by the human brain, or does it actually *determine*, or shape directly, the behaviour it causes? Or is there perhaps no link at all? *What is the nature of the link itself?*

Many scholars of cultural fields of enquiry find it difficult to even imagine what is meant by such questions, so accustomed have they become to a dialogue which associates cause and effect without redressing the nature of the causal connection itself. In some cases they may even be theoretically unequipped to envisage a level of theory more general again than the level at which familiar dichotomies such as 'Materialism versus Idealism' or 'Structuralism versus post-Structuralism' (as evoked by Hodder 1989b: 70) seem meaningful.

But the issue of the nature of the causal linkages between the described/interpreted state of a given cultural phenomenon and its imputed cause – in other words, whether these causal linkages are determinative or selective (or whether they are Lamarckian or neo-Darwinian in the strict mathematical or logistic sense of these words) – is indeed more general again than issues of the allocation and redistribution of causal primacy to the various realms of influence represented by different anthropological traditions. To put it another way, it is impossible to place, say, Marxism, Psychoanalysis, or post-Modernism in opposition to either neo-Darwinism or Lamarckism, since this latter dichotomy represents a higher generic category of theory classification. Any particular Marxist causal scenario may be shown to use either Lamarckian or neo-Darwinian causal connections, or a combination of the two, as may, for that matter, any particular psychoanalytic or post-modernist causal scenario. Thus it would be perfectly reasonable to ask a Marxist whether he or she intends to impose a neo-Darwinian or Lamarckian logical structure to their causal account; their answer to this question is by no means self-evident in Marxism itself. Moreover, they are quite free to choose either one, and indeed they cannot avoid the choice. Any understanding of (or solution to) the 'Lamarckism versus neo-Darwinism' problem thus requires some familiarity with an unfamiliar level of discussion. The notion of selectionist logistics itself, as distinct from any particular selectionist scenario, is an unusual abstraction.

A latent orthodoxy

As a consequence, most of the issues which occur at this unusual level of abstraction in cultural fields of enquiry have remained largely unresolved. Yet to a certain extent it may be argued that there is a 'default' acceptance of determinism throughout archaeology, throughout anthropology, and even throughout the greater part of psychology; and this can be thought of as some sort of 'latent Lamarckian orthodoxy' (see also chapters 2 and 6), although it is not always exactly latent. The Spencerian origins of Cultural Evolutionism, for example, are now well known, and Spencer's logic was classically Lamarckian; although this will not be expanded upon here (again, see chapters 2 and 6 for elaboration). And there is further evidence of the pervasive occurrence of a deterministic orthodoxy in behavioural studies, evidence not directly connected to the selective issues of these chapters. To begin with, post-modernist manifestos within archaeology have dismissed all previous views as essentially determinist (Hodder 1985: 1) and Shanks & Tilley (1987b: 56). Then again, at least three of the most influential thinkers of human behaviour (Freud [1962]: 57–65; Marx, in Bottomore & Rubel 1963: 67; and Skinner 1953: 6) all expressed some explicit commitment to determinism. More recently, Edelman (1989: 31–2) has summarised non-selectionist views of perception and categorisation in psychology as falling under two main camps: the 'realists', who constitute a class of determinists, and the 'nominalists' who might be characterised as espousing the opposite view, the simple binary opposite of determinism where categories are not determined by 'reality' at all, being simply a matter of habit, or convention, a matter of the arbitrary allocation of names.

Determinism and chaos are really flip-sides of the same coin, as each is ultimately defined in terms of the absence of the other, rather like Sartre's assertions of the relationship of the perception of an object with the perception of the absence of that object: the intimate relationship between being and nothingness (Sartre 1957 *passim*). Some evidence for their relationship may be found in the fact that where 'human freedom' (randomness in human affairs) is explicitly incorporated into an explanation, it is sometimes quickly 'reabsorbed' back into determinism through some notion of 'self' determinism. This situation can be elucidated from Christian philosophy (Stevenson 1987: 46–8) where free will results in the self-determinism of sin, and from Dawkins's account of human freedom from genes (Dawkins 1989: 201) where we rebel within the statistical constraints of our genes by making our own decisions; our genes 'create' us, but they cannot 'control' us; we are 'free to determine' our own future. Similarly Jean Paul Sartre's basic concept of human freedom (Sartre 1957: 439) makes our existence indeterminate; but we then decide what to make of ourselves, so determining our future. Even Lorenz – who postulates that most animals are for the most part determined by the laws of Natural Selection (although Natural Selection, by definition, cannot determine anything, and it might be argued that he too conveniently forgets the heritage constraints on mutation) – reserves a special freedom for humans and their powers of reason (Lorenz 1963: 258). Yet with these powers of reason we then 'self-determine', taking charge of our future, redirecting our own selective pressures in the right direction. Thus determinism of some kind exists as a background element in many 'freedom' philosophies in cultural and psychological studies, although its presence does not, of course, necessarily 'spoil' the entire theory, or mean that the theory as a whole is determinist.

But as often as not this notion of the 'deterministic' causal structure in cultural fields of enquiry is arrived at by default rather than by reasoned argument; a very large number of archaeologists, anthropologists, and even inorganic scientists are under the impression that the only alternative to determinism is complete randomness, which for some people is no alternative at all. In other words, it is thought that if human behaviour is not determined by 'something', then there is no other way to explain any recognisable patterns encountered in the field of enquiry, other than by some appeal to the simple binary opposite of determinism, namely chaos or randomness. For some this is a disturbing thought. If an archaeologist, anthropologist, or psychologist were to admit to themselves any fundamental doubts about determinism, it might leave them with no viable route to explanation of the phenomena they encounter in their field of enquiry. To declaim determinism might be tantamount to forfeiting a claim to expertise.

The untried theory

The problem with these apparently endless oscillations between determinism and randomness is that Selectionism is rarely given its full dues as a third possibility (in cultural fields of enquiry). It fact, it is more often sold short as being one or the other, with those arguing for determinism dismissing Selectionism as a theory of chance, and those arguing for 'free will' dismissing it as 'genetic' determinism. Thus one may sometimes hear a creationist dismissing evolution as a theory of chance; as being no more plausible than the idea that 'a thousand monkeys bashing away at a thousand typewriters would eventually produce the complete works of Shakespeare' (to be fair, some unusual selectionist viewpoints – such as may be found in Kimura (1983; 1985) and Monod (1974) – do fit this statement more than others). Then, at the other extreme, we find cases where a selectionist position is dismissed as determinist, such as when Dawkins's viewpoint is judged to be such (Dawkins 1989: 331) by Lewontin *et al.* (1984).

A strange conundrum, but it is actually more simple than it seems. Both camps are half right and half wrong. Determinists such as creationists are correct when they say that Selectionism is *not* determinism, but they are wrong when they say it *is* chaos. Conversely, the 'high priests of the left' (Dawkins 1989) are correct when they say Selectionism is *not* about complete freedom, but they are wrong when they say that it *is* about determinism. Selectionism is neither deterministic nor random, nor can it be understood in any but the crudest of terms as something intermediate between the two. Indeed, Wright (1967) has argued (and this is expanded upon in Cullen 1993a: chapter 6) that Selectionism is in fact *qualitatively different* in its implications than any of these three alternatives. And Dawkins's selectionist position, so roundly denounced as determinism by Lewontin *et al.* (1984), includes explicit lists of factors (Dawkins 1982: 31) which act as constraints on adaptation, preventing Natural Selection from acting as a perfect determinant (see also Foley 1985: 225 and Mithen 1989: 484).

Finally, selection constitutes a qualitatively different alternative to determinism and randomness in epigenetic contexts also. Psychobiologists such as Edelman (1989: 30–40), working within the different context of cellular selection in somatic time (the life-time of the individual organism, and therefore in principle concerning purely epigenetic processes), view his 'neuronal group selection' model of perception and generalisation as being unclassifiable in terms of the old 'realist versus nominalist' dichotomy. He clearly identifies the definitive mathematical element of his selective theory which precludes its classification under the old categories: its capacity to deal with the problem of the 'polymorphous set' (Edelman 1989: 31).

So selective logic is clearly considered to be qualitatively different to the logic used by other notions of causality, and believed to be so not just by anyone, but by those who really ought to know (see Cullen 1993a: chapter 6 for expansion). And it appears that this vital element has been lacking in many theories of culture which either call themselves, or else have been thought to be, selective. As a consequence, there is as yet no well-established cultural equivalent of the 'expanded' synthesis of modern evolutionary biology (as defined by Gould 1983). This is the problem of the 'untried theory', as outlined by Blute (1979), and implied by Boyd & Richerson (1985), Dunnell (1980), Freeman (1974), and Rindos (1980) *inter alia*. The problem of the 'untried theory' – the lack of an established, genuinely selectionist explanatory framework for cultural process – is the central problem addressed in this study.

The three basic aims

The three basic research aims all relate to the problem of the 'untried theory'. Put briefly, they are as follows:

1

To bring together the various evidence which demonstrates the existence of the problem itself. Neither Cultural Evolutionism, nor Cultural Sociobiology may be meaningfully viewed as being examples of the untried theory. Neither of these is a selective account of culture as the first is not selective, while the latter is not strictly 'cultural'; i.e. not exclusively concerned with culture itself, but with its effect upon genetic process. And while a number of recently formulated selectionist models of cultural process do exist, they are still fraught with serious logical inconsistencies; moreover, the approach has not been subjected to a large-scale global test aimed at refuting its fundamental premises (see chapters 2, 3, 4, and 5).

2
To devise a formula for a general or global test of Cultural Selectionism, whereby its fundamental neo-Darwinian premises might be refuted, and to perform a preliminary test in order that *the formula itself may be tested*, along with the hypothesis of a selective cultural process. Global variation in human skulls provides us with a prototype of a neo-Darwinian system, as they display the distinctive neo-Darwinian signature of 'phylogenetic heritage constraint'. Can this distinctive signature, some sort of 'cultural heritage constraint' be found in artefacts and/or conceptual structures? It appears that the basic tenets of Cultural Selectionism, the 'untried theory' of cultural evolution, stand up very well to the trial (see Cullen 1993a: chapters 6, 7, and 8; here chapter 6).

3
To devise a new cultural selectionist theory whereby the logical inconsistencies identified in chapters 4 and 5 (Cullen 1993a) might be avoided. Once a systematic critique of existing cultural selectionist models has been submitted (see chapters 2–5), there is an obligation to sketch a series of solutions to the problems of the critique. A theory is developed called the Cultural Virus Theory which allows artefacts, ideas, and behaviour patterns to be modelled as neo-Darwinian individuals, without attributing organismic status to them. Moreover, rather than being viewed as 'traits' of humans, they are viewed as benevolent or malevolent 'parasites'. Modern psychobiology, in the form of Edelman (1989), provides us with detailed models of the 'DNA' of the Cultural Virus, and from these models there is the potential to build an evolutionary 'memetics' for the artefact (see Cullen chapters 7 and 8).

The relationship of the study to general issues of archaeological theory

Although many of the issues associated with the application of selectionist principles to human behaviour are intimately related and often parallel to the issues discussed in debates associated with other theories, these links are not brought out very frequently. A few decades ago, selectionist issues were discussed almost exclusively by selectionists, and as a consequence (what was then) 'biological' anthropology (like any other academic community) developed its own terminology. As long as the issues being discussed were essentially principles of Sociobiology and evolution in the gene pools of human populations, this was no problem at all. However, as neo-Darwinian anthropology has turned its attention more and more to the problems of learned behaviour and the implications of sociocultural transmission, it has become more of a problem than before. Many neo-Darwinian archaeologists are now preoccupied with precisely the same problems as non-Darwinian archaeologists, but the use of different terminologies conceals the fact. Different terminology now acts as an impediment to what might otherwise be a fruitful cross-fertilisation of ideas. It is almost as though neo-Darwinian anthropology (the word anthropology being used here in its widest sense) 'independently discovered' culture as it moved away from hard-line Sociobiology, and as a consequence developed its own terminology for this 'new' phenomenon (culture) without making any extensive references to the established terminology of cultural anthropology. If this gap is ever to be bridged, the equivalence of certain 'neo-Darwinian' and 'non-Darwinian' terms must be recognised, and the common goals of the two approaches clearly outlined.

Given this quasi-isolation between the two academic camps, which are now often inadvertently discussing the same issues using different terminology, it is interesting to compare the prolegomena of 'neo-Darwinian archaeology' used so far and throughout the study, with the 'cognitive map' of 'not so Darwinian' archaeological theory. The aim of this section of the chapter is to briefly indicate some possible links between the two cognitive maps.

First and foremost it is important to bear in mind which general level of archaeological theory debates about selection are best classified under. Put simply, it is the most general level of all. This general level of theory was discussed some time ago by David Clarke – one of the authors involved in inciting much of the current theoretical upheaval in archaeology – who summarised the aims of the discipline as follows (Clarke 1978: 20):

1. First, the definition of the fundamental entities that pervade the diverse material, their elements, structures and patterns, and the processes that operate on them, and the effects of the processes on the entities in the dimensions of space and time. A study in statics and dynamics going beyond particular instances.

2. Second, the search for repeated similarities or regularities in form, function, association, or developmental sequence amongst the particular entities from every area, period, and environment.

3. Third, the development of higher category knowledge or principles that synthesise and correlate the material at hand whilst possessing a high predictive value. The development of increasingly comprehensive and informative general models and hypotheses.

In terms of Clarke's archaeological aims, this study corresponds to the third category of archaeological practice; the development of increasingly comprehensive and informative general models and hypotheses for variation and invariation in the archaeological record. Evolutionary theory represents a subset of the general models used in this area, and the first five chapters could be seen, in Clarke's language, to be a discussion of those general models and hypotheses which concern the processes of natural and cultural history, and the similarities and differences between them.

The second section of the study, however (Cullen 1993a: chapters 6, 7, and 8; here chapter 6), relates much more to Clarke's first two aims, as there the general models of the third are related to the descriptions and interpretations of cultural and ecological data produced by the first two. Using the branch of multivariate statistical analysis known as Principle Components Analysis, I shall explore 'statics and dynamics going beyond particular instances' in two-dimensional graphs of the principal components of large data-sets. From the results Clarke's second category can then be realised, in the form of repeated similarities and regularities – i.e. as a series of principal components analyses of variation, in its different forms. The results of these analyses are then considered in light of the general evolutionary theories of the earlier section. While the first five chapters of Cullen (1993a) are concerned only with the third of Clarke's archaeological objectives, the remainder of the study constitutes a dialogue between all three.

If Selectionism belongs to Clarke's third category of archaeological practice, the development of 'higher category knowledge' or of 'increasingly comprehensive and informative general models', it would presumably also belong to the 'high level theory' category of other cognitive maps of the discipline. But this category is labelled in a variety of ways in different cognitive schemes. In 1988, for example, Schiffer offered a somewhat similar overview of the archaeological discipline to that of Clarke, focusing on a classification of the cognitive tools of research, archaeological theory, rather than on the research objectives themselves (Schiffer 1988: 464):

> Archaeological theory consists of three great realms, each of which is made up of one or more domains. The three realms are social theory, reconstruction theory, and methodological theory. Social theory . . . consists of principles for explaining behavioural variability and change. Reconstruction theory permits human behaviour and environmental conditions of the past to be ascertained. . . . Finally, methodological theory encompasses principles which channel the choice of techniques and methods as well as guide employment of reconstruction theory.

Although the label 'social theory' has the connotation of only those high-level theories which make specific appeals to social forces, it is clear that Schiffer intends the word to denote explanations of cultural change in general, so distinguish them from other kinds of archaeological propositions (Schiffer 1988: 465):

> Social theories function, in the archaeological research process, to explain variability and change in human behaviour. By behaviour is meant [*sic*] human activity at any scale or level of abstraction, from the handiwork of a particular artisan to the rise and fall of complex societies.

In Schiffer's terms, therefore, this study might be seen as treatise on social theory, concerned with the various theoretical frameworks employed to explain variability and change in human behaviour. However, I would emphasise that by no means could all such frameworks be considered 'social'. The word 'social' is a convenient label for the category but it must incorporate a more disparate range of theoretical perspectives for archaeology in general than it incorporates for the social theorist. Schiffer would characterise this body of theory concerned with cultural change and evolution as 'high'-level theory, to be distinguished from 'low'- and 'middle'-range theory (Schiffer 1988: 463):

> Though problematic, the concept of middle-range or middle-level theory is used here. The position adopted is that each hierarchy of archaeological principles contains high-, middle-, and low-level theories. In conformity with the spirit of Merton's formulation, principles within each hierarchy can be related logically. A level of theory (high, middle, low), then, denotes a particular degree of abstraction within one hierarchy of related principles or an analogous degree of abstraction that cross-cuts different hierarchies. Thus, we may regard evolutionary theory as high level and the theory of pedestrian tactic survey as middle or low level without implying that the former subsumes the latter.

So the research objectives of this study could be summarised as an initial five chapters of examination and analysis of high-level theory, with the next chapter as an attempt to translate these theories into middle- and low-level propositions, to arrive at some estimate of their efficacy *vis-à-vis* cultural data, and with the final chapters making certain alterations and additions to one high-level theory (Cultural Selectionism).

Having located selectionist issues on the very general cognitive maps of Clarke and Schiffer, it now remains to pinpoint its location within this general category. For this purpose a series of more local cognitive maps of the general theory category itself will be employed. David Rindos (1989: 1), for one example, has stressed that continued successful practice in any field of enquiry depends as much upon advances in high-level theoretical perspectives as in advances in data collection. A series of such significant steps have occurred in evolutionary theory in the recent decades, the most important legacy of which, according to Rindos, is that of the diachronic approach to the explanation of human culture (Rindos 1989: 1):

> In anthropology, an important conceptual shift occurred during the fifties and sixties when ecological thinking began to influence our descriptions of human culture and cultural change. This shift was initiated in large part by Clark's (1952) economic interpretation of prehistory and refined by Steward's (1955) cultural ecology, approaches entailing a materialistic method linking society to the conditions of life to which all human cultures must adapt. During this same period, cultural evolutionism (White 1959a; Sahlins & Service 1960) was enjoying a resurgence, and although it had little to do with a truly Darwinian account of evolution (Campbell 1965; 1976; Dunnell 1980; Blute 1979), it was significant in stressing that any comprehensive explanation of human culture must be diachronic as well as synchronic.

In this way Rindos provides another and more local conceptual map on which the objectives of this study may be located, with the two halves of this research plan corresponding to the diachronic and synchronic explanations of culture. The initial section concerns the analysis of various diachronic frameworks for cultural process; while the second section concerns the relationship between diachronic cultural perspectives of different sorts and the synchronic spatial patterning they imply. Rindos's own work (1980; 1984; 1985; 1986a; 1986b; 1989) is of course in the same category of archaeological discourse as this study; exploration of what Clarke would term the various 'general synthetic models and hypotheses' and what Schiffer would term 'social theory'. However, as will become clear later, while much discussion of the applicability of evolutionary theory to the archaeological record has been undertaken, discussion seems to concentrate on evolutionary explanation of univariate or bivariate temporal sequences. Yet this study attempts to address the applicability of evolutionary theory to large-scale multivariate patterns in temporal or spatial sequences, rather than limiting the use of models of evolutionary processes to the single dimension of time.

Rindos has also offered a coherent typology of evolutionary philosophy, after Campbell (1965), Freeman (1974), Richerson & Boyd (1978), Blute (1979), and Dunnell (1980), and the terminology of this typology is used in many parts of this study. Significant developments in evolutionary perspectives have occurred since the heyday of the ecological and evolutionist schools, resulting in the emergence of a school of thought which he labels 'Cultural Selectionism'. This school uses neo-Darwinian theory to arrange and analyse topics in cultural fields of enquiry. Unlike Sociobiology, neo-Darwinian models are not evoked in the context of human genetics, but in the context of cultural processes themselves. Similar categories to those of Rindos are used throughout the study where a three-way contrast between Cultural Evolutionism, Cultural Sociobiology, and Cultural Selectionism is used to stress the fact that there are three quite different approaches to culture which are frequently referred to as 'neo-Darwinism', not just one. However as the place of this study with respect to selectionist debates is well covered both above and in chapters 3, 4, and 5, for the time being no further effort need be spent on locating its position on the local 'cognitive map' of Selectionism (to use the convenient term of Murray again). This section of the chapter is, after all, not about the internal 'topography' of our maps of selective issues, but about their relationship of their topography to that of other local cognitive maps in the discipline.

So far, then, the issues of the study have been related to the most general levels of archaeological theory, and (as is expanded upon throughout the study) the more local theoretical maps of other studies of selective issues. Yet there are also parallels with literary debates about issues not normally associated with debates about neo-Darwinian principles. For instance, it appears that there are certain parallels between the agenda of post-processual archaeology (Hodder 1982b; 1985; 1989a) and the new, more culturally oriented Darwinian archaeology, despite unremitting attempts to polarise the two lines of thought (Shanks & Tilley 1987a; 1987b). These parallels are a result of a number of thematic similarities which appear to exist in both post-structuralist and selective metaphysics. Put bluntly, the 'strange selective logistics' outlined above (and in Cullen 1993a: chapter 6) appear to constitute some sort of 'ready-made' solution to post-structuralist prolegomena.

Some of these connections, such as a mutual commitment to active decision making and measures of 'free will', have been very forcefully brought out (Mithen 1989: 487–91). But there are also 'deep structure' similarities between the two philosophical manifestos. The term 'post-structuralism' is used by Hodder to denote the movement from language to text, one of the basic themes put forward by a group of French writers which includes Foucault, Barthes, Derrida and Ricoeur, and ultimately traceable to Saussure's analysis of language (Hodder 1989b: 68). Hodder focuses on that part of the critique of structuralism which emphasises the distance between an abstract language and a particular concrete text written in that language. In structuralism, the structured sets of differences which constitute a language are separated from the actual use of that language via the activity of speech; the dichotomy of *langue* and *parole*. In post-structuralism, while it is still recognised that abstract concepts or rules are used in social discourse, the focus is on the fact that an action – or text – is intended to have some tangible effect on other people. Because of this, the context of an act is as important as what it is supposed to signify; without the appropriate context, the desired effect will be unattainable. Part of the context is, of course, the status and/or social identity of the individual who happens to be performing the act. Hodder offers the following example (1989b: 69):

> Consider, for example, a member of the royal family planting a tree or a politician cutting a ribbon in order to open a new motorway. We can all go around cutting ribbons and planting trees. These acts, when carried out in a formal public setting, do not simply have meaning in relation to an abstract set of opposed signifiers. They also have meaning in relation to their stage setting. For example, it is important in the formal occasion that the ribbon cutter or tree planter is of high status, that reporters and the public are watching, that the institutions that have paid for the motorway or nature reserve have asked the member of the royal family or the politician to be present and so on. In other words the "writing" of "texts" (such as cutting a ribbon or planting a tree) depends on institutional contexts.

The writing of a text 'strategically links structure and context'. There is, moreover, no right or wrong way to read a text, and due to the varying subjectivities associated with each individual reader, texts are ambiguous and polysemous. Hodder adds that each signifier merely signifies other signifiers, such that a cultural model of the universe ultimately consists of an ultimately circular series of signifiers of signifiers. An obvious metaphor for this essentially structuralist sentiment would be a dictionary, where each word or signifier may be looked up, only to have it explained in terms of other signifiers, arranged in a certain grammatical order and so constituting a sentence which provides some clue to the meaning of the original signifier. Each of the signifiers in the new sentence may then be found elsewhere in the dictionary, associated with sentences of further signifiers, and so on. But, as we move in the direction of post-structuralism, there is often more than one meaning for each word, and in such cases it is the context 'which allows us to fix meanings' (Hodder 1989b: 69); in other words, it is the context which allows the observer to identify which meaning – of a range of alternative meanings – is the relevant one for interpretation.

Having laid out his interpretation of a post-structuralist perspective, Hodder goes on to relate it to post-processual archaeology (1989b: 70):

> The move from language to text in post-structuralism side-steps the old dichotomy between, on the one hand, normative, culture-historical, idealist archaeology and, on the other hand, processual, culture-ecological and materialist archaeology, and leads to a post-processual phase in which these dichotomies are broken down. Indeed, it is precisely the relationships between the two sides of these dichotomies that become the aim of the study.
>
> The opposition between adaptational accounts and structuralist accounts which has lead to a recent rearguard reaction on the part of die-hard processual archaeologists (for example, Binford 1982), and which has been followed by the placing of this opposition at the centre of study within post-processual archaeology, can be seen as a trend within this book.

Some parallel can be drawn between the two historical summaries of Rindos and Hodder. Rindos contrasts materialistic cultural ecology with the mentalistic, orthogenetic, and progressivist cultural evolutionists; Hodder contrasts processual, ecological materialism with normative culture history. There are also parallels between the solutions offered by Hodder and Rindos; Cultural Selectionism (as is shown in greater detail in chapter 4) is similar to post-structuralism in that it also combines elements from both sides of the materialist versus idealist dichotomy. Rindos (1985) has offered a typology of selective forces acting within culture (which he terms Cultural Selection 1 (CS1) and Cultural Selection 2 (CS2)), one which recognises the differences between cultural and non-cultural selective constraints, but at the same time this typology provides the basis for an explanatory framework which explicitly relates the two kinds of constraints at another level. Thus, broadly speaking, cultural selectionist perspectives could qualify as post-structuralist conceptions of cultural process in that they are neither exclusively idealist or materialist, ecological or cultural, although they are explicitly processual and in fact more faithfully so than 'processualism' itself, in that they focus more on general mechanisms of change than on synchronic notions of adaptation. This fact leads us to a paradox implicit in current terminology, where post-processual archaeology is in fact more processual than its ever been, particularly in approaches like Cultural Selectionism.

Concluding remarks

It can be seen that the problem of the 'untried theory' relates to a large number of familiar debates and frustrating conundrums, and to a variety of general issues throughout archaeology, anthropology, history, psychology, and, for that matter, throughout the humanities in general. A general overview of these widespread issues has been offered, and it is hoped that this overview will provide the reader with a basic repertoire of terms and phrases which will render some of the more esoteric parts of the study less opaque.

2
Cultural Evolutionism

Overview
There has been a substantial amount of literature written on the Cultural
Evolutionists, and so another analysis of their original works, however
comprehensive, would be practically redundant. In light of this situation a
decision was made to focus not upon the original works, but upon the
Cultural Selectionist critique of the approach. Therefore the aim of this
chapter is to provide a general outline of the modern discourse about
Cultural Evolutionism, and to show that the various arguments of these
debates ultimately lead to the conclusion that the approach is not only non-
Darwinian, but also a coherent, fully Lamarckian orthodoxy.

A case of mistaken identity
The story of Cultural Evolutionism (*alias* Social Darwinism) – of how a
completely non-Darwinian evolutionary theory managed to establish a
reputation for being precisely what it was not – must surely be one of the
great 'myths of misconception' in the history of evolutionary theory.
However, a single chapter could never do justice to this tale, and no attempt
will be made to do so. For the moment, it is enough to say that despite the
existence of some very high-quality 'investigative journalism' which
demonstrated this case of mistaken identity beyond reasonable doubt,
ignorance of the philosophical identity of Cultural Evolutionism persists.

Indeed, many archaeologists and anthropologists are still under the
impression that the 'Social Darwinist' and 'Cultural Evolutionist' schools of
the late nineteenth and twentieth centuries (these include Durkheim 1893;
1895; Morgan 1877; Sahlins & Service 1960; Spencer 1873; Tylor 1871; White
1949; 1959a; 1959b; and arguably even Marx 1867; Engels 1884; and Steward
1955) are either selectionist or, at least, 'selectionesque'. But this is simply
not the case. Even 'Social Darwinism' is now generally accepted as non-
Darwinian by those archaeologists and anthropologists who have researched
the approach. However, here an attempt will be made to add to this and to
show that these schools of thought are much more than just *different to*

selectionist thought. They are actually the *logical antitheses of* a selectionist theory of cultural process, in the same way that Lamarckism is the logical antithesis of neo-Darwinism in biology. Therefore defining a selectionist theory of cultural process must first involve a complete understanding of (and careful avoidance of) the Social Darwinist and Cultural Evolutionist notions of process.

The non-equivalence of the Spencerian and neo-Darwinian evolutionary notions of process has been well articulated by a number of theorists with a range of disciplinary backgrounds, including psychology, archaeology, biology, and social anthropology. Prominent works in this area include Blute (1979), Dunnell (1980), Dunnell & Wenke (1980), Freeman (1974), Leonard & Jones (1987), Peters (1980), Richerson & Boyd (1978), and Rindos (1985), *inter alia*, and they are often referred to throughout this chapter and those which follow. These authors write about the fundamentally non-Darwinian nature of prevailing theories of cultural change, and about the absence of any cultural equivalent of the neo-Darwinian evolutionary synthesis of genetics and Natural Selection.

Since Cultural Evolutionism and neo-Darwinism are so different (although the earliest texts out of which the two traditions evolved are less different – see below), the many trials and uses to which the former has been submitted in cultural fields of enquiry have no implications for the latter; the failures of Cultural Evolutionism have no bearing on the validity of building a neo-Darwinian model to stand in its place. Spencerism has been tried and found wanting, but neo-Darwinism has remained essentially untried during this process.

At this point it must be made known that the words 'Darwinism' and 'Darwinian' are not used literally in modern discussions of processual thought, and for this reason I usually use the term 'neo-Darwinian' in preference to the more common 'Darwinian', in order to differentiate modern Selectionism from Darwin's writings. Modern use of the word 'neo-Darwinian' does *not* mean 'Darwin's theory' (which as a matter of fact strays in and out of what today would be considered Lamarckian and Darwinian world-views), but means rather that at least part of the theory in question bears some structural similarity to Darwin's principle of Natural Selection, with the added philosophical element of some appeal to *random variation*. Consistent definition and identification of a 'neo-Darwinian' theory is thus best done on the basis of the presence of the general principle of selection, which can be defined as *the differential reproduction of intrinsically and blindly generated variation* (see Cullen 1993a: chapter 6 for full description). Theories referred to as neo-Darwinian in this study are simply any theoretical structures in which I have been able to identify the structural component of selection.

Yet, it is important to not that many evolutionary theorists consider the 'neo' addition to the word 'Darwinian' to be unnecessary, and therefore use the word 'Darwinian' whenever they are referring to modern Selectionism. Assertions about the absence of a 'Darwinian' theory of cultural process – assertions about the 'untried theory' – are therefore referring to the fact that there is no 'selectionist' or 'neo-Darwinian' theory of cultural process. The assertions are *not* saying that we have not paid enough attention to *what Darwin said about culture*. The Cultural Selectionism account of culture presented in chapters 4 and 5, and the Cultural Virus Theory of chapter 7, are very different indeed to Darwin's approach to human society, which is more like the Cultural Sociobiology of chapter 3 than either of the above perspectives. So the various assertions about the absence of a Darwinian approach to the purely cultural processes of human society – assertions about the untried theory – should be interpreted as a lack of appeal to selective logistics in explanations of cultural change, rather than as a lack of 'Darwin-like' approaches to culture. More often than not, modern usage of the word 'Darwinism' implies a meaning of 'neo-Darwinian synthesis', rather than, for example, a literal interpretation of *The origin of species*.

The assertions usually take the form of an illustration of how none of the concepts – either those implicit or those explicit in the evolutionary theory of cultural anthropology – really employ a neo-Darwinian conceptual framework. Cultural Evolutionism, the general evolutionary framework most well known in disciplines associated with cultural fields of enquiry, is shown to have a different origin and structure to the explanatory paradigm of modern evolutionary biology, in spite of the fact that the two approaches use similar terminology. Blute, for example, writes (1979: 46):

> We have to be critical of sociobiology's relative neglect of the epigenetic sciences of the individual and, indeed, to reject firmly its implicit contention that there is no order to be found in history, the subject matter of the social sciences, except that imposed upon it by evolving gene pools (Blute 1976). Under the pressure of the challenge, however, a substantial number of social scientists have become acquainted for the first time with the modern neo-Darwinian synthetic theory of evolution and with population genetics and, in doing so, have almost certainly come to realise that sociocultural evolutionism has never been an evolutionary theory in the way in which that theory has been employed in the life sciences.

Freeman (1974) has also expressed this view in responding to assertions made by Marvin Harris in *The rise of anthropological theory* (1968). If one accepts that neo-Darwinian theory has not been given a proper trial in the context of cultural process, then, logically, claims to the contrary must depend upon the mistaken allocation of a neo-Darwinian label to a non-Darwinian discourse. Harris claimed that Spencer and Darwin constituted an evolutionary synthesis, thereby implying that the two approaches share the same conceptual structure, and by inference, the same conceptual flaws. Freeman drew out the pronounced differences between the approaches and thereby refuted the claims of Harris. Like Blute, Freeman concentrates on a suite of pre-Darwinian evolutionary principles present in Spencerian thought (Freeman 1974: 213):

> The lumping together of the evolutionary theories of Spencer and Darwin is, in the light of the evidence, unwarranted, for the theories of Darwin and Spencer were unrelated in their origins, markedly disparate in their logical structures, and differed decisively in the degree to which they depended on the supposed mechanism of Lamarckian inheritance and recognised "progress" as "inevitable".

Given the differential influence of each approach in cultural and biological fields of enquiry, we can conclude from Freeman's position that Darwin has not been as influential in cultural fields of enquiry as some anthropologists may believe. In the concluding section of this chapter I will attempt to push the 'non-synthesis' argument concerning Darwin and Spencer even further by showing that Spencer and Lamarck, on the other hand, may be considered a synthesis. Spencerian and related theoretical influences in cultural fields of enquiry have covertly established a Lamarckian orthodoxy in anthropology which can be contrasted with the neo-Darwinian orthodoxy of the biological sciences. For the time being however, attention will be returned to theoretical analyses which have emphasised the pre-Darwinian structure of Spencerism without necessarily emphasizing any possible synthesis with Lamarck. Given the profound similarity between Spencer and Lamarck, demonstrated in the last section of this chapter, it is curious that Harris (if he had to propose a synthesis at all) did not propose *this* synthesis instead.

Having drawn similar conclusions about the structure of sociocultural evolutionism to Freeman, Blute goes on to say that the use of Spencerian evolutionism as a framework within anthropology does not negate the value of all empirical research done to date in the social sciences. A general theory of cultural process based on selectionist principles may well turn out to be highly compatible with the data amassed by researchers in cultural fields of enquiry. In other words, Blute is not of the opinion that the descriptive information that has been accumulated in anthropology and archaeology is seriously biased towards the Spencerian evolutionist framework. Sociocultural evolutionism is non-Darwinian in theory rather than practice (for Blute), and while there is, therefore, no general theory of cultural evolution that is structurally equivalent to the neo-Darwinian synthesis, this does not necessarily mean that anthropological descriptions compiled under the auspices of the Spencerian paradigm are invalid.

These remarks of Blute's foreshadow an argument which is indirectly employed in chapter 6, where general patterns of cultural diversity are drawn out and submitted as definitive signatures of selective process. Blute implies that it is quite possible that the observations and interpretations amassed in the last century under the auspices of what I would call the 'Lamarckian Orthodoxy' may well exhibit patterns which conflict with that orthodoxy. In chapter 6, an attempt is made to show that a definite pattern of historical continuity (*alias* heritage constraint, or origin and influence dependent similarity), is indeed ubiquitous in cultural data regardless of the philosophical paradigm under which it was compiled.

Having contrasted the structure of evolutionary theory in the two fields of enquiry, Blute goes on to contrast their respective origins, firmly labelling the origin of sociocultural evolutionism as 'pre-Darwinian', via White, Spencer, and Tylor, with the following words (Blute 1979: 49):

> Spencer was a pre-Darwinian evolutionist who borrowed his concept of differentiation from Von Baer, the great German embryologist, and applied it to organic phylogeny as well as to the sociocultural world. . . . He believed that phylogenetic change occurred via the same process as did embryological development. Coherence, co-operation, integration, etc., are its outcome according to this view.

Using this historical and structural distinction, we have on the one hand a pre-Darwinian evolutionary paradigm, based principally on 'generative' or 'deterministic' notions of causality as will be shown later, which dates back through Spencer and Tylor to Lamarck and Von Baer; and on the other hand a neo-Darwinian paradigm, based principally on notions of selective causality, which dates back through population genetics to Darwin.

Returning to the problem of the pre-Darwinian nature of Spencerian philosophy, it can now be pointed out that the problem of the 'untried theory of cultural process' is linked to the profound influence of pre-Darwinian world-views in cultural fields of enquiry. In any case, the pervasive absence of neo-Darwinian approaches to cultural process is largely synonymous with the pervasive presence of Spencerian philosophy, since the two approaches are mutually exclusive.

As some of these assertions which support Blute are presented below, it is worth reminding the reader that since these statements were made, various attempts have been made to remedy the situation. The movement is collectively referred to by Rindos (1985) as Cultural Selectionism, a set of ideas which date back to Campbell (1965), and perhaps earlier, with some notable recent examples including Richerson & Boyd (1978), Cavalli-Sforza & Feldman (1981), Boyd & Richerson (1985), Lumsden & Wilson (1981), Leonard & Jones (1987), and Rindos (1984; 1985; 1986b; 1989). Others include Dunnell (1978; 1980), Dawkins (1976; 1982), Clarke (1978), Clegg (1978a), and Fletcher (1977; 1988) (see chapter 4 for a more complete list). Such attempts to begin building a cultural equivalent of the neo-Darwinian evolutionary synthesis are dealt with in chapter 4, while sociobiological attempts to fill the gap are examined in chapter 3. However, the Cultural Selectionists are of interest here not because of their own ideas, but for their opinions on the nature of Cultural Evolutionism.

Thus the following are a series of assertions from different Cultural Selectionists, each of which supports the conclusions of Blute quoted above. These statements concern the absence of a properly selectionist perspective for cultural process, while some of them also support Blute's dismissal of Sociobiology as a viable candidate for such a theory.

Freeman (1974), for example, as implied already above, contrasts both the structure and origin of the evolutionary theories of sociocultural anthropology and biology. The paper focuses on an in-depth contrast of Spencer and Darwin. As Rindos (1985: 66) later reiterates, both were influenced by Malthus, but in very different ways, with Spencer's evolutionary framework remaining fundamentally Lamarckian (and therefore pre-Darwinian), while Darwin moved decisively in the direction of the modern evolutionary framework which now bears his name. Freeman (1974: 213) quotes one of Darwin's great anti-Lamarckian disclaimers, also quoted recently by Desmond & Moore (1992: 315),:

> ... Darwin's theory made a decisive break with certain of the evolutionary concepts of Lamarck – a point which for this present paper is of prime importance. Of this break Darwin was well aware. In January, 1844, for example, when working on the second "sketch" of his "species theory", he wrote (F. Darwin 1888: 23) to J. D. Hooker: "Heaven forfend me from Lamarck (sic) nonsense of a 'tendency to progression', 'adaptations from the slow willing of animals', &c.!"

Similarly Dunnell, discussing evolutionary theory in archaeology, writes (1980: 37):

if evolution is taken to mean as it does in the sciences, it has yet to be systematically applied in either sociocultural anthropology or archaeology. The approach represented by cultural evolution is a social philosophy directly derived from the tradition of Herbert Spencer and the early anthropologists and is unrelated to Darwinian principles.

Richerson & Boyd, discussing evolutionary theory in sociocultural anthropology, make similar assertions to Blute, Dunnell, and Freeman (1978: 130):

although there is an enormous literature in anthropology and sociology which examines cultural evolution, very little of it is properly within the Darwinian tradition. Oddly enough this comment applies to Social Darwinism and related ideas as well as explanations conceived in opposition to the Social Darwinist.

Rindos, with reference to Dunnell (1980), Blute (1979), and Richerson & Boyd (1978), writes (1985: 66):

Use of the word 'evolution' in the context of social and cultural change is no guarantee that we are speaking of anything resembling Darwinism. Hence, we are beginning to realise that Social Darwinism was not Darwinian, Cultural Evolutionism has yet to speak of evolution, and Sociobiology confounds society with biology.

For a final example, consider these words from Leonard & Jones (1987: 201):

Our criticisms of Cultural Evolution are few, but we feel that they are of consequence. Attributed to Spencer, and built upon primarily by Sahlins, Service, and White (e.g., Sahlins 1960; Sahlins & Service 1960; Service 1962; 1971; and White 1949), among others, the model of Cultural Evolution is demonstrably inappropriate as a scientific archaeological paradigm for several reasons. . . . A model based upon the general selectionist tenets of scientific evolution is more appropriate.

Why Spencerian philosophy has been mistaken for Darwinism

Not all anthropologists agree that Cultural Evolutionism is a Lamarckian or even, for that matter, a non-Darwinian evolutionary framework. Harris (1968), as Freeman (1974) and Dunnell (1980: 41) have pointed out, has asserted that the evolutionary theories of Spencer and Darwin constitute, to some degree, an 'evolutionary synthesis'. In reply to Freeman's rejection of this position, Harris firmly insisted that this was indeed the case (1974: 225):

We know from the autobiographies, notes, and letters of Darwin, Spencer, and Wallace that they independently achieved basically similar interpretations of the natural processes responsible for bio-evolution under the direct stimulation of Malthus's *Essay on population*. That essay in turn can only be understood in the context of the 18th- and 19th-century sociopolitical debate concerning the perfectibility of human nature and the progress of human institutions. . . . That the struggle for existence is not one jot less integral to Darwin's evolutionism than it is to Spencer's or Wallace's must be admitted by all who are familiar with the full title of *On the origin of species and the preservation of favoured races* and its conclusions.

However, this apparent discrepancy between the views of Freeman and Harris is not as fundamental as it might first appear. Each is in fact using a subtly different definition of 'Darwinism' for the contrast with Spencerism. This strange state of affairs can be summed up by the apparently paradoxical axiom 'Darwin's ideas were not all neo-Darwinian' – Darwin was not a typical neo-Darwinian in the modern sense of the word. It is also linked to the fact that Darwin's account of the evolution of humans involved no explicit separation of cultural and genetic evolutionary processes. The two were inextricable aspects of the general fabric of human variation. By this I mean that it is very difficult to maintain the modern 'genes versus culture' distinction in the many accounts of human diversity he provides in *The descent of man and selection in relation to sex*. What would be called genetic or cultural differences in modern anthropology jointly constituted a general biocultural fabric of human diversity for Darwin, as it apparently did for most, if not all his contemporaries. Furthermore, his explanation for that biocultural diversity involves not only the ideas for which he became famous, but also ideas which today would be classified as 'Lamarckian' or 'Spencerian'. Both Lamarckian Progressionism and Lamarckian inheritance of characteristics acquired through changes of habit (two basic principles of the Lamarckian world-view described in the next section of this chapter) appear to occur in Darwin's writings, although absolute progression is often vehemently denounced also. Consider, for example, his discussion of the effects of the use and disuse of human organs (Darwin 1871: 116–17):

> It is well known that use strengthens the muscles of the individual, and complete disuse, or the destruction of the proper nerve, weakens them. When the eye is destroyed the optic nerve often becomes atrophied, . . . bones increase not only in thickness, but in length, from carrying a greater weight. Different occupations habitually followed lead to changed proportions in various parts of the body. Thus it was clearly ascertained by the United States Commission that the legs of sailors employed in the late war were longer by 0.217 of an inch than those of soldiers, though sailors were on average shorter men; whilst their arms were shorter by 1.09 of an inch, and therefore out of

proportion shorter in relation to their lesser height. . . . Whether the several foregoing modifications would become hereditary, if the same habits of life were followed during many generations, it is not known, but is probable.

While Darwin does not exactly commit himself to an 'acquired characteristics' position in this paragraph or the many others similar to it, the publication of such statements in modern evolutionary biology would be both controversial and rare. Progressionism, or orthogenesis, the Lamarckian principle involving an intrinsic life force which propels organisms to become more and more complex as time passes, also seems to be implicit in Darwin's writings from time to time. Although, as we shall see, Lamarck's commitment to this principle was far greater; and although Darwin both dismissed Progressionism and ultimately sowed the seeds of its demise with his principle of Natural Selection, consider the following words (Darwin 1871: 121):

> It will suffice for our purpose to refer to the arrested brain-development of microcephalous idiots, as described in Vogt's great memoir. Their skulls are smaller, and the convolutions of the brain are less complex than in normal men. The frontal sinus, or the projection over the eyebrows, is largely developed, and the jaws are prognathous to an "effrayant" degree; so that these idiots somewhat resemble the lower types of mankind. Their intelligence and most of their mental faculties are extremely feeble.

Darwin also at times refers to a 'series' of animals, arranged as a 'chain of being' from simple to complex, from 'lower' to 'higher', as though our contemporaries actually represent archetypal ancestors, rather than simply being products of a different historical trajectory, as they are seen in modern evolutionary biology. Such concepts would be considered anathema in modern 'neo-Darwinian' discourse, and, ironically, other words from Darwin might even be used to silence anyone who said so. Yet these progressionist concepts are reflected in his persistent use of words such as 'high' and 'low' and 'series' in a way which cannot be simply dismissed as metaphorical. He writes (Darwin 1871: 125):

> Various other anomalies in man . . . have been advanced by different authors as cases of reversion; but these seem not a little doubtful, for we have to descend extremely low in the mammalian series before we find such structures normally present.

That Darwin included (in a very 'Social Darwinist' and thus 'non-Darwinian' way) so-called 'primitive' people or 'savages' in this 'chain of being', this series of contemporary ancestors, is suggested by the following assertion, made several pages later (Darwin 1871: 145):

The belief that there exists in man some close relation between the size of the brain and the development of the intellectual faculties is supported by the comparison of the skulls of savage and civilised races, of ancient and modern people, and by the analogy of the whole vertebrate series.

Consider also Darwin's introductory and concluding remarks of the 'Manner of development' chapter (Darwin 1871: 135):

We have now seen that man is variable in body and mind; and that the variations are induced, either directly or indirectly, by the same general causes, and obey the same general laws, as with lower animals.

Darwin later concludes (Darwin 1871: 155):

As all animals tend to multiply beyond their means of subsistence, so it must have been with the progenitors of man; and this will inevitably have led to a struggle for existence and to natural selection. This latter process will have been greatly aided by the inherited effects of the increased use of parts; these two processes incessantly reacting on each other.

Obviously, none of the above passages taken from Darwin involve an explicit commitment to Lamarck or a Lamarckian world-view, but some readers may be surprised by the similarity of certain phrases of Darwin's and the Spencerian and Lamarckian world-view examined in the previous and next sections (the empirical implications of which are then examined in Cullen 1993a: chapter 7). Others, such as Desmond & Moore (1992: 230, 242) have documented Darwin's exploration of Lamarckian notions very thoroughly. Certainly, the above quoted statements would seem to have a more Lamarckian flavour than equivalent statements in modern neo-Darwinian thought.

It is not surprising that Darwin's writings seem quite different to those of modern Selectionism as he was entirely without recourse to half of the modern synthesis; he had no knowledge of the basic replicators of non-cultural evolution – genes – and no knowledge of the mechanism which produces variation in those replicators – mutation. The net effect of a 'geneless' nineteenth-century biology was a blurring of the lines between 'Lamarckism' and 'Darwinism' (although the two approaches are still quite separable right from the beginning, with painstaking scholarly research such as that displayed in Freeman's paper). One of the by-products of this blurring effect is a great deal of semantic confusion in discussions of nineteenth-century evolutionary biology. Different conclusions about the fundamental nature of the theories of individual biologists working during this period can emerge as a result of purely semantic differences in the conceptual apparatus of modern analysts.

The differences between Freeman and Harris constitute a case in point. While Harris is comparing Darwin's evolutionism with Spencer's evolutionism, and finding a synthesis, Freeman is contrasting neo-Darwinism with Spencerism, or to be more precise, contrasting the neo-Darwinism in Darwin's evolutionism with the Spencerism in Spencer's evolutionism, and finding an antithesis. The evolutionary writings of Darwin and Spencer, which Harris compares, are far more alike than the neo-Darwinian and Spencerian evolutionary frameworks, and therefore Harris's assertion does not refute the fundamental differences between these two perspectives. Darwin's evolutionism, perhaps due to the historical influences of his social context which Harris mentions, contained far more pre-Darwinian philosophy than the modern evolutionary synthesis which traces its origin and identity to his work. Thus Harris needs only to articulate the common pre-Darwinian elements of Darwin and Spencer to support his assertion of similarity. Freeman, and indeed most commentators, contrast the 'neo-Darwinian element of Darwin', namely Natural Selection, with the pre-Darwinian elements of Spencer, to emphasise their dissimilarity. Thus, while there may sometimes be a case to be made for common elements between Darwin and Spencer, the case for corresponding commonalities between Spencer and neo-Darwinian evolutionary biology would be much weaker.

While Harris is probably aware of the above distinction between Darwin's evolutionism (i.e. literally Darwin-ism) and modern neo-Darwinian evolutionary theory, and limits his assertion of equivalence to the actual writings of Darwin and Spencer, others are not so precise.

Yoffee (1979; 1980; 1985; and see also Ross 1987: 37–8 for an identical misrepresentation of neo-Darwinian theory), for example, has made a number of statements which imply a belief in the equivalence of Cultural Evolutionism and modern selectionist thought, statements which Peters (1980) and Dunnell & Wenke (1980) have drawn attention to before. As Peters points out, Yoffee equates concepts of adaptation in the neo-Darwinian synthesis with a definition of adaptation from Rappaport, a definition which sees all adaptation as precipitated by environmental change. Ironically, this does not conform to the neo-Darwinian evolutionary paradigm at all. Yoffee (1979) summarises Rappaport's position as follows: 'Rappaport . . . conceives of adaptation as a systemic cybernetic process which is capable of systemic self-transformation only in the context of directional environmental change (Rappaport 1971: 23)'. In doing so, Yoffee does not misrepresent Rappaport; his mistake is to confuse Rappaport's cultural ecology with modern evolutionary biology.

Yoffee therefore goes on grossly to misrepresent the entire discipline of modern biology, as he is evidently not aware that in neo-Darwinian theory variation is constantly generated independently of environmental change, whether that change is directional or not. Mutation is a ubiquitous and on-going process, a result of the fact that no replication process is perfect. Even a potentially perfect replicator would be subject to the availability of the raw materials used for replication, and may be forced to substitute a new available element for an original element now unavailable. And in most instances, replication can be expected to be even more unreliable than this. Mutation is influenced by the environment in a direct manner, but is not directed by those environmental effects. The direct environmental effects on organisms only affect the likelihood and magnitude of mutation; they do not direct the course of those mutations, and therefore usually do not produce adaptive results.

The main problem which the concept of mutation presents for Yoffee's equation of Rappaport with Darwin, however, is that these small-scale environmental effects on copying fidelity continue to take place regardless of the large-scale environmental effects of natural selection. Even if the environment is very stable indeed, errors in copying fidelity still occur and as a consequence mutations continue to appear. As the current structural *status quo* in any population is never perfectly adapted (see Foley 1985, discussed in Cullen 1993a: chapter 6), it is always possible that a new mutation may be adaptive instead of lethal or neutral, and as a consequence replace the old structure, without any environmental change at all. Thus 'systemic self-transformation' can most certainly occur in the absence of directional environmental change in neo-Darwinian process, and Yoffee's equation of neo-Darwinian theory with any system where such cannot occur is misrepresentation on a grand scale.

Thus it can be seen that the minority of analysts (i.e. Harris, Yoffee, and Ross) who do not distinguish neo-Darwinian theory from other process theories usually do so through misrepresenting selective process, rather than through misrepresenting Cultural Evolutionism.

The few exceptions not withstanding, it is clear that Cultural Evolutionism and modern Selectionism are fundamentally different evolutionary theories. For those readers who may still be in doubt, I point out that even the Cultural Evolutionists themselves were emphatically aware of this fact. Dunnell (1980) established this point very convincingly; White, Sahlins and Service often admitted the links between themselves and Tylor and Morgan, while Carneiro, *inter alia*, connects this tradition to Spencer (Dunnell 1980: 41). Consider this often-quoted paragraph from White, which

Dunnell uses to illustrate his point (White 1959b: 106):

> It would be most gratifying to be able to report, in a paper commemorating the publication of *The origin of species*, that cultural anthropologists had borrowed the concept of evolution from Darwin and that they had employed this concept to establish and enrich their science. Unfortunately, we are unable to make such a report. On the contrary, we must point out that the theory of evolution was introduced into cultural anthropology independently of Darwin and, indeed, of biology in general.

Thus there can be little doubt about generally held views on the structure and origin of evolutionary theory in sociocultural anthropology. The consensus of both the cultural evolutionists themselves, and their cultural selectionist critics, is that this philosophical tradition is non-Darwinian and fundamentally different in explanatory structure to the evolutionary frameworks of modern biology.

Cultural Evolutionism as a Lamarckian orthodoxy

So far, then, all that has really been established is that a large number of neo-Darwinian anthropologists and archaeologists have completely discredited the belief that there is any structural equivalence between Cultural Evolutionism and neo-Darwinian theory. For the main part, this is all that need be established for the purpose of the overall research design of the study. Cultural Evolutionism has been shown not to be the 'untried theory', and now other candidates for the theory will need to be considered.

However, a final illustration of how the Lamarckian paradigm persists in Cultural Evolutionism will, I hope, make the selectionist critique of this position stronger still. Moreover, it is interesting to note the existence of such profound structural continuities in evolutionary theory, as it is easy to over-estimate the degree to which 'new' philosophies manage to escape the old.

Let us accept the conclusions of the above authors concerning the essentially non-Darwinian nature of evolutionary philosophy in cultural fields of enquiry, and concur with them in rejecting Harris's (1968) notion that the ideas of Darwin and Spencer constitute an evolutionary synthesis. However, non-Darwinian evolutionary thought does have sufficient consistency, I believe, to be considered an evolutionary synthesis, it is just that the synthesis is better characterised as a Lamarckian one. In other words Harris is half right; there is a logical synthesis between Cultural Evolutionism and biology, but it is with pre-Darwinian biological philosophy rather than with theory of the neo-Darwinian variety. The most obvious biological equivalent of Spencerism is not neo-Darwinism but its binary opposite, Lamarckism. And not only Spencerism, but a range of other related positions in cultural fields of enquiry can also be shown to be more compatible with a Lamarckian conception of historical process than with a selectionist one. There is, however, enough space to give this only the briefest attention here, and the argument is in any case only employed for one purpose: to impress upon the reader the *degree* to which Cultural Evolutionism is non-Darwinian. It is not just different to neo-Darwinism; it is the theoretical opposite of neo-Darwinism.

In order to present this argument, it is also important to impress upon the reader that the Lamarckian world-view encompasses a great deal more than just 'Lamarckian inheritance' (of the environmental determinist or psychological instructionist sort). While cultural perspectives often include some notion of an environmentally directed or a 'rational' and 'objective' dimension to cultural invention, where such inventions may be passed on culturally from parent to child in apparent accordance with Lamarckian inheritance, there are other dimensions to Lamarckian zoological philosophy. Cultural equivalents of these additional elements of Lamarckian philosophy can also be shown to exist in cultural fields of enquiry, and in this way the full extent of Lamarckian influence can be traced. The aim is to convince the reader of an interesting pattern: an evolutionary concept which is demonstrably non-Darwinian is very often also demonstrably Lamarckian. In other words, the range of evolutionary principles available in the humanities appears to be much more restricted than what might at first appear to be the case.

One element of Cultural Evolutionism has already been linked to Lamarck, and that is the principle of environmental determinism known as 'the inheritance of acquired characteristics', a principle which Darwin disparagingly referred to as 'adaptation from the slow willing of animals'. In modern evolutionary discourse, this is the principle generally being referred to when the word 'Lamarckism' is used.

Freeman (1974 *passim*), and Rindos (1985), among others, have documented Spencer's explicit faith in the principle of acquired characteristics, while Boyd & Richerson (1978), Blute (1979), Dunnell (1980), and Leonard & Jones (1987), as documented in greater detail in section 2.1, have all, in turn, linked the Cultural Evolutionists to Spencer. Dunnell has captured the non-Darwinian nature of the Cultural Evolutionist concept of adaptation in the following words (Dunnell 1980: 49):

In cultural evolution, the role of natural selection is largely usurped by the notion of adaptation. . . . Selection is clearly and unambiguously linked to the materialistic metaphysic. Adaptation, on the other hand, has no such limitation. As a functional concept, it is certainly compatible with a selectionist view of change, but it is no less compatible with a transformational view of change and vitalistic causation.

Even Yoffee (1979: 10, and 1985; see section 2.2) has extensively documented the 'environmentally driven' nature of approaches to cultural evolution, although he mistakenly believes that this is also true of modern evolutionary biology.

As this principle is well known to be Lamarckian in origin, the need to 'prove' its connection with Lamarck (through reiterating this principle in *his* words) is not so urgent. It is the links between other aspects of Cultural Evolutionism (Progressionism and the Typological Approach) and Lamarck which are less well known, so more attention will be directed towards 'proving' these other links, as will soon be seen below. For the sake of those such as Yoffee (1979; 1985) and Ross (1987) however, who have mistakenly attributed environmental determinism to neo-Darwinism and not Lamarck, I offer a brief archetypal summary of Lamarck's variety of adaptationism, and of modern cultural equivalents of the position.

Virtually any quote from Lamarck will confirm that it is his adaptationism, and not the Natural Selectionist sort, which implicitly invokes environmental instruction. The environment instructs, not through physically shaping the bodies of animals, but through physically determining their 'needs'. In struggling to meet these needs, the animals transform their own bodies through the effects of use and disuse. Lamarck expresses this concept in the following words (Lamarck 1809: 107):

> ... the environment affects the shape and organisation of animals, that is to say that when the environment becomes very different, it produces in the course of time corresponding modifications in the shape and organisation of animals.
>
> It is true that if this statement were to be taken literally, I would be convicted of an error: for, whatever the environment may do, it does not exert any modification whatever in the shape and organisation of animals.
>
> But great alterations in the environment of animals lead to great alterations in their needs, and these alterations necessarily lead to others in their activities.'

The powers of necessity are not just capable of enlarging or diminishing animal organs, they are also capable of generating new organs which never existed before, or of erasing obsolete organs altogether. In the latter case, it is the absence of necessity for an organ, not the necessity for its absence, which brings about its disappearance (Lamarck 1809: 108):

> ... that new needs which establish a necessity for some part really bring about the existence of that part, as a result of efforts; and subsequently its continued use gradually strengthens, develops and finally greatly enlarges it.
>
> ... when new needs have altogether destroyed the utility of some part, the total disuse of that part has resulted in its gradually ceasing to share in the development of other parts of the animal; it shrinks and wastes little by little, and ultimately, when there has been total disuse for a long period, the part in question ends by disappearing.
>
> ... and these acquired modifications are preserved by reproduction among the individuals in question.

There are many other examples of similar reasoning throughout Lamarck's *Zoological philosophy* (for example, Lamarck 1809: 118–19, 123, 170). Moreover, a little later in *Zoological philosophy* he is more explicit about how new organs come into being, despite the fact that, put crudely, a non-existent muscle cannot be flexed. How does an animal struggle to fulfil needs with an organ which does not exist? Lamarck states that new organs are spontaneously generated by the animal's inner feelings of need (Lamarck 1809: 112):

> Every new need, necessitating new activities for its satisfaction, requires the animal, either to make more frequent use of some of its parts which it previously used less, and thus greatly to develop and enlarge them; or else to make use of entirely new parts, to which needs have imperceptibly given birth by efforts of its inner feeling.

Cultural equivalents of these ideas also hinge on the concept of the generative powers of 'necessity'. It is almost as though sheer desperation is enough to guarantee the survival of any human individual. Although many readers may be familiar with the modern cultural versions of Lamarckian adaptationism, it is important to point out that it occurs both in a specific form, and in a more general form. At its most general, the principle is embodied by any notion that the environment actually informs or instructs, and thereby directs, the course of inventions. This environmental instruction occurs *during the actual moment of invention itself*. Then, in the more specific form of the approach, these environmentally driven or instructed inventions are then asserted to be inheritable as 'acquired characteristics'. It may be illuminating to add that both the general and specific assertions are interconnected, in that the 'acquired characteristic' inheritance of 'random' inventions is implicitly excluded from the agenda. It is also important to point out that both the general and the specific forms of Lamarckian environmentalism are aspects of the process which is termed 'specific' evolution by the Cultural Evolutionists (Watson & Watson 1969: 14). The cultural evolutionist concept known as 'General' evolution concerns a different aspect of cultural process, that of increasing complexity, and this concept may also be found in Lamarck, as will be shown below, where it is labelled 'Progressionism' or 'Orthogenesis'. For the moment, however, discussion will be focused around Lamarckian adaptation (i.e. 'specific' evolution in Cultural Evolutionist terms), in *both its general and specific forms*.

A cultural equivalent of the Lamarckian approach to adaptation can be illustrated with a simple example. Let us imagine that a group of Neanderthals with a classically Mousterian artefact technology are faced with a survival problem, let us say, a series of attacks from packs of wolves. Let us also say that due to certain aspects of the environment (which must be taken purely on faith for the purposes of the argument), the only effective defence against wolves is some Stone Age equivalent of the modern dog-whistle, which produces a powerful blast of high-pitched noise beyond the upper range of the human ear. A Lamarckian environmental determinist would essentially have to argue that wherever a human group was faced with this particular sort of wolf problem, the dog whistle would appear in the artefact assemblages of the group. In other words, a mind which has never been taught how to make metal, leave alone whistles, leave alone how to produce a sound from them, and even leave alone being shown how this may affect wolves, is somehow capable of conceiving of the dog whistle; and, at that, solely through contemplation of the problem of wolf attacks. This is because, in a Lamarckian system, necessity is truly the 'mother of invention'. It is the stimulus of the problem itself which brings about the very genesis of human awareness of how to make and use the dog whistle. This is why the equivalent philosophical position in psychology is known as *instructionism* (Edelman 1989: 31), as features of the environment are seen to actually shape the part of the mind which will ultimately be used to 'represent' them, i.e. 'instruct' the nervous system in an almost didactic way. Lamarckian notions of perception thus imply a 'voice in the burning bush' telling the brain what should be perceived (Edelman 1989: 32).

In contrast, a selectionist account of perception sees the environment as selecting from within a range of shapes which the mind generates in and of itself, in readiness for a varied environment. Hence Edelman's use of the immune system analogy (Edelman 1989: 17), where pathogens do not inform B-cells as to the appropriate antibodies to manufacture. Rather, a huge variety already exists in the B-cell population, and those B-cells with antibodies which happen to 'match' a particular pathogen then undergo accelerated reproduction.

The widespread nature of cultural Lamarckism

It can therefore be seen that at least one of Lamarck's philosophical concepts is present in twentieth-century approaches to culture. What is less well documented is that the other two well-recognised (and interlinked) non-Darwinian elements of Cultural Evolutionism, 'Progressionism' or 'orthogenesis', and the 'Typological Approach', are also pervasively present in Lamarckian Zoology, and the function of this section is essentially to demonstrate this fact.

Firstly, however, as was done with Lamarckian Adaptationism, I would like to briefly reiterate established opinion on the presence of these philosophical principles in Cultural Evolutionism, before moving on to outline their essential qualities, and to show how similar concepts are employed in Lamarckian Zoology.

The presence of both Progressionism and the Typological Approach in Cultural Evolutionism has been well documented by Dunnell (1980: 37–49), Fagan (1980: 25–31), Freeman (1974: 215), Leonard & Jones (1987: 201), Rindos (1985: 66–8), and implicitly by Yoffee (1979 *passim*; and 1985: 41). Some more recent actual uses of structurally similar concepts include Cohen (1981: 202–6), Lourandos (1983: 81), and Watson & Watson (1969: 145–8). It is well established, then, that Cultural Evolutionists often appeal, either explicitly or implicitly, to some law of absolute progress, propelling cultural systems towards ever-increasing complexity and/or perfection, and that they also use a taxonomic system based on such progression (i.e. the Typological Approach). It is also fairly well established that any concept of *inevitable* progress is anathema to selective explanation, as is discussed in greater detail in Cullen (1993a: chapter 6).

'Progressionism' (see also Cullen 1993a: chapter 7) is a term used in the evolutionary literature to describe notions of change which view either organisms or cultural phenomena as possessing some intrinsic force which drives them towards greater and greater complexity and corresponding perfection. One of the simplest ways to identify progressionist reasoning in explanations of cultural change is to find any use of the word 'devolution' (e.g. Cohen 1981: 206). This word is implicitly Lamarckian, as neo-Darwinian evolution has no intrinsic direction which 'devolution' can turn it away from in the first place. Relatively simple organisms such as bacteria have not remained simple for billions of years due to lack of evolution, or due to some cataclysmic 'devolutionary' event. Actually, the opposite is true; their evolution is *even more rapid* than complex organisms such as the chordates, so much so that the capacity of bacterial populations to adapt with almost lightning speed to antibiotics is a modern legend (Sonea 1988).

It is just that neo-Darwinian evolution, unlike Progressionism, does not necessarily involve increasing complexity, and may, as in the case of bacteria, involve an endless number of mutations and selective substitutions within a genome of fixed size. It is important to note, however, that this rule of 'no necessary increasing complexity' in Selectionism does not apply so reliably at the ecological level. If, for example, we take the whole planet earth as an ecological assemblage, it is generally true that 'life on earth' *as a whole* has proceeded towards greater and greater complexity. Dawkins, for example, has used his concept of the 'Meme' not to develop directions for a general theory of culture (as the Cultural Virus position is used for in chapters 5 and 7), but to illustrate the general tendency of neo-Darwinian systems towards *ecological* complexity (Dawkins 1989: 322):

> The word meme seems to be turning out to be a good meme. It is now quite widely used and in 1988 it joined the official list of words being considered for future editions of *Oxford English dictionaries*. This makes me the more anxious to repeat that my designs on human culture were modest almost to vanishing point. My true ambitions – and they are admittedly large – lead in another direction entirely. I want to claim almost limitless power for slightly inaccurate self-replicating entities, once they arise anywhere in the universe. This is because they tend to become the basis for Darwinian selection which, given enough generations, cumulatively builds systems of great complexity. ... Whether the milieu of human culture really does have what it takes to get a form of Darwinism going, I am not sure. But in any case that question is subsidiary to my concern. ... My purpose was to cut the gene down to size, rather than to sculpt a grand theory of culture.

Of course, even ecological complexity is subject to 'backward' turns, in the form of ecological collapse as a result of natural disasters of various kinds. Yet, in a selective framework, such mass extinctions are not considered to represent 'devolution', but evolution, which, if anything, becomes *more* intense at these times. So, in an authentically neo-Darwinian perspective, all 'devolutions' are just cases of evolution. We can therefore conclude that the mere use of the term 'devolution' implicitly betrays progressionist (and thus by definition non-Darwinian) reasoning.

The Typological Approach (again, see also Cullen 1993a: chapter 7) is a natural corollary of Progressionism, as it is simply a classification scheme based on the gradient of increasing complexity allegedly produced by the latter (see Leonard & Jones 1987 *passim* for a succinct discussion). The familiar Cultural Evolutionist sequence of 'Band, Tribe, Chiefdom, State', or related sequences such as 'Band, Tribe, Chiefdom, Capitalist State, Communist State', all rest upon some notion of necessary sequence, of progress towards some ideal. Progress along the sequence can be hastened or slowed, brought to a halt, inverted, or even reversed; but the sequence itself remains. Moreover, its *fundamental linearity* also remains, and this is why even the 'multilinear' concept of Steward (1955) is still quasi-typological, and quasi-progressionist. In fact, even Lamarck allowed a small number of collateral branches in his linear series (see Elliot's introduction to *Zoological philosophy*, Lamarck 1809: XXVI).

In contrast, a truly neo-Darwinian metaphysic is an infinitely (literally) radiating, branching and sub-branching hierarchy based purely on genealogical descent and local (not absolute) progression (see above and also Cullen 1993a: chapter 6, for related points of discussion). It is therefore (which some post-modernists may be surprised to learn) the ultimate relativism. Selection may be a law, but unlike Progressionism in Cultural Evolutionism or Marxism, it is not a law about the course of history itself. It is a law of divergence, rather than convergence, despite the instances of quasi-convergence which do occur within selectionist systematics. If Selectionism must be considered a law, it is a law about the very indeterminacy of the course of history, and in this sense it is a law which immediately deconstructs (at the level of specific sequences) its own lawfulness; in the same way that the banner of relativism in post-Modernism or Critical Theory ultimately deconstructs itself into just another voice amongst the multitude (Renfrew & Bahn 1991: 430).

As already noted at the beginning of this section, the presence of Progressionism and Typological classification schemes in Cultural Evolutionism has been well documented by Blute (1979) and Dunnell (1980) *inter alia*. However, few archaeologists have pointed out that Progressionism is as much an integral part of Lamarckian Biology as it was part of Cultural Evolutionism. In other words, Progressionism was not something invented by nineteenth-century anthropologists; rather, it was a basic constituent of pre-Darwinian philosophy in general. The importance of this observation is to show that there is nothing particularly 'cultural', leave alone selective, about the idea of necessary progress.

It is also interesting to note that Lamarckian Progressionism is not unlike Lamarckian Adaptationism, in that both processes are driven by the 'feminine goddess' of 'Nature', and that in both cases the basic mechanism by which 'she' takes effect is through affecting the needs of organisms, which arise from increasing complexity elsewhere in the body. Progression in one area leads to more, as the energy of the movement of fluids gradually 'accelerates', thereby providing a series of constraints which complement acquired adaptations (Lamarck 1809: 130):

> if nature had not been able to endow the organising activity with the faculty of gradually increasing the complexity of organisation by accelerating the energy of movement of fluids and hence that of organic movement, and if she had not preserved by reproduction all the progress made in complexity of organisation and all acquired improvements, she would assuredly never have produced that infinitely varied multitude of animals and plants which differ so greatly from one another both in their organisation and in their faculties.

Lamarck later explores a number of particular instances of this orthogenetic 'accelerating movement of fluids', in his discussions of infusorians and polyps (1809: 269) and even mammals (1809: 166). Nearer the beginning of *Zoological philosophy* he introduces the concept with reference to the nervous system (1809: 49).

Progressionism is a universal force, a 'transgenerational developmental ontogeny', an in-built complexity clock which ticks away from the moment each new organismic lineage is brought into being by spontaneous generation. Moreover, just as in Cultural Evolutionism and Marxism (indeed, for Spencer evolution and the ontogeny of the embryo were one and the same thing: Desmond & Moore (1992: 393)) it is not just a course towards greater complexity, but also towards perfection, culminating in the class mammalia (Lamarck 1809: 167). The effects of this clock may be obscured by environmentally generated effects, and thus arrested, reversed or slowed, but the series itself may not be transcended, as we may only travel up or down along the linear dimension, or else remain motionless. Moving outside the series, or 'leap-frogging' over a particular stage, is not allowed (Lamarck 1809: 107):

> the increasing complexity of the organisation of animals from the most imperfect to the most perfect exhibits only irregular gradation, in the course of which there occur numerous anomalies or deviations with a variety in which no order is apparent.
>
> Now on seeking the reason of the strange irregularity in the increasing complexity of animal organisation, if we consider the influence that is exerted by the infinitely varied environments of all parts of the world on the general shape, structure and even organisation of these animals, all will then be clearly explained.

Elsewhere, Lamarck makes it even more abundantly clear that such 'degradations' (akin to the 'devolution' of Cultural Progressionism), produced by the environment, actually exemplify rather than confound the spirit of Progression (see Lamarck 1809: 69 and also 1809: 126). All in all, the appearance of complex forms is ineluctable from the moment the simplest forms appear (Lamarck 1809: 236):

> That, since all living bodies are productions of nature, she must herself have organised the simplest of such bodies, endowed them directly with life, and with the faculties peculiar to living bodies.
>
> 'That by means of these direct generations formed at the beginning of both of the animal and vegetable scales, nature has ultimately conferred existence on all other living bodies in turn.

In this way the orthogenetic forces of Progressionism produce a natural series of animals and plants, the 'Great Chain of Being' which bears a striking resemblance to the Cultural Evolutionist Typological scheme which is now such a familiar part of the Cultural Selectionist critique of that approach (Lamarck 1809: 130–31):

> I have divided into six distinct stages the various modes of organisation recognised throughout the animal scale.
>
> 'Of these six stages of organisation, the first four comprise the invertebrate animals, and consequently the first ten classes of the animal kingdom according to the new order that we are going to follow; the last two stages comprises all the vertebrate animals and consequently the four (or five) last classes of the animals.
>
> 'By this method it will be easier to study and follow the procedure of nature in the production of animals that she has brought into existence; to recognise throughout the animal scale the progress made in complexity of organisation and every where to verify both the accuracy of the classification and the propriety of the rank assigned by examining such characters and facts of organisation as are known.

So incorruptible is the series that Lamarck must argue that stages of different complexity must be necessarily of different age (Lamarck 1809: 35):

> it is not true that Species are as old as Nature, and have all been in existence for an equal period . . . (rather) it is true that they have been formed one after another . . . they have only relative constancy, and are only invariable temporarily.

The two Lamarckian forces of Need and Orthogenesis thus work in concert to produce a rigid series of organisms, divided into six basic stages according to mode of organisation, with the most imperfect at the beginning and the most perfect at the end. The first five constitute the living 'contemporary ancestors' of the last, just as they do in the Cultural Evolutionist series of Band, Tribe, Chiefdom, State. Moreover, each principle is dependent upon the other. Without the capacity to respond to the environment, the overly rigid products of orthogenesis would be robotic archetypes unable to survive any environmental change, while without orthogenetic progression the products of the environment would be so varied and 'degenerate' that no coherent pattern of diversity could ever be elucidated by the biologist.

It is no coincidence, then, that Lamarckian Adaptationism, Progressionism, and Typological systems of classification tend to occur together, whether we are speaking of nineteenth- and twentieth-century anthropology, or eighteenth- and nineteenth-century biology. These concepts are integral parts of the same evolutionary framework. As a consequence, the three non-Darwinian elements of Cultural Evolutionism, which have been so well documented by the Cultural Selectionist critique, should not be viewed as evidence that Cultural Evolutionism is some sort of unique anthropological invention, or as some special theory which was custom made for cultural fields of enquiry. They are not 'cultural anthropology's answer to the tyranny of Selectionism'. Rather, they represent the persistence of an even older naturalistic 'tyranny', an even older biology, in explanations of cultural change. It is fair to say, then, that much of non-Darwinian archaeology is dominated by a Lamarckian orthodoxy of the kind that Selectionism originally faced in nineteenth-century biology, and there is no reason to suppose it is any more appropriate for use in cultural fields of enquiry, than it was in fields of enquiry centred upon non-human animals and plants.

Concluding remarks

It can thus be seen that while the Cultural Evolutionists can legitimately boast of being independent of Darwin, White's claim (1959b: 106) of independence from *biology as a whole* may be somewhat misleading. This second and more exaggerated assertion may well reflect the romantic notion that Cultural Evolutionism is some sort of unique invention, specially designed for the 'unique process' of cultural change. But I have tried to argue that this is not the case, as the three main explanatory elements of Cultural Evolutionism are profoundly similar to the three main elements of Lamarckian Zoology. Ironically, then, Cultural Evolutionism is just as 'biological' as popular belief would have it to be; it just that it is 'biological' in a way that is too ancient for many modern anthropologists to recognise. It is biological, but not neo-Darwinian. To use the approach's own Spencerian rhetoric against itself, one can argue that Cultural Evolutionism is simply the 'primitive contemporary ancestor' of modern evolutionary biology, 'pushed out into the adjacent field of culture', where it has somehow managed to survive. It is simply Lamarckian Zoology transposed into a Lamarckian Anthropology.

3
Cultural Sociobiology

Overview
In the last chapter it was shown why Cultural Evolutionism has not solved the problem of the untried theory. Here it is shown why Cultural Sociobiology can also be dismissed as a potential solution. Although the sociobiological perspective provides an adequate framework for the explanation of human genetic process, it does not do the same for cultural process. The unwarranted assumption that the survival of a particular behaviour pattern is simply self-evident in the survival of its host leads Cultural Sociobiology to violate the fundamental Darwinian principle of adaptive selfishness. In doing this Cultural Sociobiology actually sustains, rather than removes, the Lamarckian orthodoxy of Cultural Evolutionism, since a cultural phenomenon ordered by the imperative of organismic reproduction is thereby 'ordered from without'.

Selfishness and Cultural Sociobiology
While Cultural Evolutionism cannot claim to be neo-Darwinian in either structure or origin, Cultural Sociobiology can legitimately claim to be neo-Darwinian at least in the latter. Moreover, while few Cultural Evolutionists have ever identified closely with Darwin, as shown in the previous chapter with reference to Dunnell (1980: 41), Sociobiology has always had a self-proclaimed neo-Darwinian identity. Cultural Sociobiology, however, falls far short of achieving a neo-Darwinian theory for cultural evolution itself, basically through its refusal to take full account of the differences between genetically and culturally transmitted behaviour. It will be argued throughout this chapter that an implicit Lamarckian explanatory structure for cultural adaptation is used by Sociobiology in concert with an otherwise selectionist approach to human genetics. In other words, Sociobiology's perfectly selectionist approach to human survival and reproduction collapses into Lamarckism in cultural contexts where the survival and reproduction of socially transmitted phenomena should properly be the focus of attention. In this way Sociobiology unintentionally maintains the 'Lamarckian

orthodoxy' of Cultural Evolutionism. Once genealogical independence from genetic inheritance is granted to cultural phenomena, any direct causal influence of genes over cultural evolution must assume the qualities of Lamarckism, since culture is then effectively being 'ordered from without' (see Rindos 1986b for a parallel assertion).

A fundamental difference between culturally and genetically transmitted behaviour is that while any genetic trait must be transmitted downwards in the genealogy of a population, i.e. from parent to offspring, a cultural 'trait' can be transmitted in a much wider array of relationships and directions, including the diagnostic pattern of 'horizontal' transmission (Cavalli-Sforza 1991: 78, Cavalli-Sforza & Feldman 1981). Such transmission includes those from offspring to parent or grandparent, between sibs, from parent's sib to offspring, between cousins, or even between unrelated members of the population (in so doing, it thereby 'deconstructs' its own 'trait-hood', as is discussed in chapters 5 and 7). Furthermore, even parent to offspring cultural transmissions are not 'synchronised' with genetic reproduction. These differences would suggest some more than *ad hoc* amendments to the explanatory frameworks used to explain social behaviour in acultural societies such as eusocial insects (Wilson 1971) or mammals such as mole rats (J. Jarvis & R. Brett, in Dawkins 1989: 314). The difference essentially grants a separate and potentially different genealogy to the behavioural 'traits' and genetic traits, respectively, of a cultural organism; while, on the other hand, the behaviour and genotype of the acultural organism have a synonymous genealogy. This basic point will be developed throughout the chapter and shown to conflict with a basic qualification of selectionist theory made by Darwin himself. By doing this, Sociobiology is thus obliged to take up a Lamarckian explanation for cultural adaptation, and consequently uses essentially the same approach to cultural process as sociocultural evolutionism; a conception of evolution as either internally or externally directed. Later in this study, in Cullen (1993a: chapters 6, 7, and 8; here chapter 6), these two approaches become the pre-Darwinian or Lamarckian null-hypotheses for the multivariate analysis of patterns of cultural variation.

Other writers, many of whom have already been referenced in the previous chapter, have also identified conceptual weaknesses in Cultural Sociobiology. Most of the analyses which detract from Sociobiology do not, however, question the authenticity of its reputed links with the neo-Darwinian synthesis of modern evolutionary biology. Yet some characteristics of Cultural Sociobiology which have already been well documented are incommensurate with properly interpreted Selective principles. Blute (1979), Dunnell (1980), Durham (1990: 193), Lewontin *et al.* (1984), Peters (1980), Rindos (1986b), Ross (1987) and Yoffee (1979; 1980; 1985) have given significant attention to the shortcomings of Sociobiology when it comes to cultural contexts. Similar studies which discuss basically sociobiological principles in cultural 'adaptationism' and 'processual' archaeology include Bray (1973), Hole (1973), Alland (1975), Kirch (1980), and Foley (1985). Bargatsky (1984) has provided a particularly comprehensive analysis. Yet none of the above critiques have, to my knowledge, featured the argument submitted below; that Sociobiology violates its own self-proclaimed neo-Darwinian principle of adaptive selfishness in failing to take full account of cultural transmission.

The initial stage of the argument will be take the form of an ethnographic case-study, Betzig's *Despotism and differential reproduction*. Discussion will then be transferred to the general issues raised by the case-study, and reference will be made to a number of other cultural adaptationist and sociobiological approaches.

Despotism and differential reproduction

In the early eighties, Betzig undertook a comprehensive ethnographic and historical study of social hierarchy in pre-industrial societies. In 1986, this work was published in a book under the above-mentioned title. Using a regional sampling procedure, Betzig covers societies from all areas of the world, with most of them dating to the ethnohistorical period. The incidence of 'despotic' leaders and the corresponding incidence of high degrees of 'reproductive success' form the focus of the world-wide comparisons. 'Despotism' is defined as 'the exercised right of heads of societies to murder their subjects arbitrarily and with impunity' (Betzig 1986: 2), and is used by Betzig as evidence for extreme social asymmetry amongst the rights of the individuals of a given society. 'Differential reproduction' is measured both in terms of historical reports of numbers of wives or consorts, or numbers of actual children. What Betzig seeks to illustrate is that, where an individual finds himself (and most are male) in a position where his social rights are considerably greater than those of his fellows, he will attempt to translate that greater power into greater reproductive success via the acquisition of wives and consorts. In other words, human behaviour is viewed to be exclusively shaped by criteria of reproductive success. This typically adaptationist explanatory structure will be examined in greater detail later in this section; at this early point in the discussion Betzig's data and methodology will be outlined.

Vast numbers of ethnographic accounts make this piece of research interesting and informative to read. In general, Betzig's prediction that the incidence of despotism and differential reproduction will be highly correlated finds ample support in her sample societies. For example, in societies of the Natchez of the lower Mississippi valley in North America, there seems to be just such a correlation. Betzig quotes and paraphrases J. R. Swanton's *Indian tribes of the lower Mississippi Valley* (1911), bulletin 43 of the *Bureau of American Ethnology*, in the following excerpt (Betzig 1986: 50):

> In the lower Mississippi valley, the word despotism is almost always used in the early accounts of the government of the Natchez chief. According to Dupratz, he was "absolute master of the goods and life of his subjects," disposing of them at his pleasure; "his will is his reason" (quoted in Swanton 1911: 106). According to Charlevoix, the relationship between a chief and his subjects could be characterised almost as slavery; as soon as anyone had the misfortune to displease either the Sun or the woman most closely related to him, they were ordered to be killed by the guards. "Go and rid me of that dog" they would say, and be immediately obeyed (in Swanton 1911: 101).

Whenever the chief said anything the subjects had to 'howl' nine times; they also had to howl when approaching or leaving the presence of the chief, when visiting his cabin, when formally saluting the chief, and after every question the chief asked (Betzig 1986: 51). In accordance with Betzig's prediction, such despotic social inequality does translate into unequal access to women and differential numbers of offspring among the Natchez. The chiefs not only had the above rights to impinge upon their subjects lives, but also huge houses with many wives and beds, and they had only to notify a woman's relatives that they desired her and she automatically became one of their wives (Betzig 1986: 74).

Another of Betzig's sample societies is the Mbau of Fiji. Here leaders also have both absolute rights over the fate of their subjects and large numbers of wives. Betzig draws on three sources, D. Toganivalu (1912), M. D. Wallis (1851), and T. Williams (1884). The absolute rights which chiefs held over their subjects included the following (Betzig 1986: 54):

> [There was] the case of the chief who requested a hoe from a subject and, on being refused, took his wife instead; the case of the Mbau chief who, on finding his villagers had cut him fewer reeds than he wanted, had the village burned; and the case of the mere petty thief who, discovering that a man had accidentally injured one of his ducks, supposing it wild, demanded the fingers of four individuals in compensation. . . In general, "Offences, in Fijian estimation, are light or grave according to the rank of the offender. Murder by a chief is less heinous than a petty larceny committed by a man of low rank."

Chiefs had the right to take anything from their subjects. When arbitrating over cases concerning theft, they would at times release the guilty party providing a portion of the stolen goods could be extracted in payment. As evidence for the fact that leaders with these absolute rights also had differential access to women, Betzig offers the single example of the chief Tanoa who spoke of the advantages of polygyny with great emphasis, and was said to have had 100 wives (Betzig 1986: 75).

A more dramatic confirmation of Betzig's predicted correlation was found amongst the Azande of Sudan. Her sources include Brock (1918), Casati (1891), Czekanowski (1924), Lagae (1926), and Baxter & Butt (1953). Death was the punishment for the least indiscretion sustained against the ruler, revoked only if the crime was perpetrated by a member of the upper classes. Common offences such as disloyalty, use of magic against chiefs, committing adultery with the wives of the chief, or treason, usually resulted in instant strangulation at the chief's hands (Betzig 1986: 51 after Baxter & Butt 1953). Mutilation was the only alternative to the death sentence, and in adultery cases the offenders were emasculated, and their hands, ears, and lips were cut off. Often the relatives of newly deceased offenders were required to pay indemnity to the chief in the form of several women. Leaders who possessed these rights invariably used their power to maintain disproportionately large entourages of women. Numbers of wives were dependent on the degree of power held by the man concerned. In Azande society, every man with a position of authority had several wives, even though the vast majority of adult men were either bachelors or monogamously married. According to one of Betzig's sources, Zande chiefs had between 30 and 100 wives, and the king had more than 500 women. Young women were monopolised at an early age, and female children were spoken for well before puberty (Betzig 1986: 74).

Many other societies are offered by Betzig as examples of her 'Darwinian' prediction. Khmer kings in south-east Asia mutilated and killed those found guilty of crimes, while maintaining entourages of up to 5000 women. Leaders in Inca Peru possessed the right to 'murder arbitrarily, and the more powerful position a man occupied the more women he was allowed. Many of the chiefs also went to great lengths to prevent other men from gaining access to their women, often by isolating a household of women from the rest of the community. Fourteen societies were included in the sample with more than half of the leaders having more than 100 wives, and all of them having exclusive access to large numbers of women.

Since Betzig's basic method of assessing the reproductive success of these despotic leaders involved counting women rather than children, the next step in her argument was to demonstrate that these large numbers of women were in fact being maintained, at least indirectly, for the purposes or intention of reproductive success. Were the women in the sample societies being valued for their reproductive ability, or maintained for some other social purpose? Betzig argues that the reason is indeed the former. In support of this assertion she appeals to other cross-cultural studies. For instance, ten cross-cultural studies have arrived at the conclusion that childless couples are more likely to divorce, a statistic from which Betzig concludes that at least some marriages are undertaken partly for the purpose of reproduction. Other studies show that in some societies the payments associated with matrimony are not transferred until the marriage has been 'validated' by the birth of the first child. In such societies brideprice payments are frequently delivered only after the birth of children; and where it is paid before the birth of a child, bridewealth compensation may be demanded in the event of a childless marriage; moreover divorce is often the result of adultery. Betzig finds several other variables affecting marriage breakdown which can be logically related to the ability of women to produce children in her ethnographic sample, concluding that an important motivating factor involved in marriage, and by inference, the multiple marriages of despots, is indeed the desire for children.

Thus, Betzig finds ample confirmation in the ethnographic literature for her predictive hypothesis; yet the sociobiological explanatory structure which lead her to this apparently correct prediction is flawed. I will now focus on the flaws in her explanatory structure in order to demonstrate how her explanation is in fact (arguably) Lamarckian, and how, therefore. the explanation would be untenable within a properly interpreted neo-Darwinian framework.

Do despots reproduce despotism when they differentially reproduce?
One of the basic flaws in Betzig's explanatory structure is that it does not discriminate between individually learned behaviour and culturally transmitted behaviour. The question is never asked whether these two kinds of learned behaviour might be completely equivalent. The assumption of equivalence is implicit throughout the study, but particularly apparent in the chapter where the results of the ethnographic sample are freely compared with a range of animals which do not have the human capacity for culture, including seals, mice, chickens, wasps, and deer (Betzig 1986: 87). I am not by any means suggesting that interspecies comparisons of dominance behaviour would not be very illuminating for this kind of

human behaviour, but simply that a discussion of the cultural component to human behaviour should be an integral part of such comparisons. While each of the animal studies cited by Betzig also describe correlations between dominant social position and reproductive success, no mention is made of the fact that wasps, say, have virtually no capacity for cultural transmission. This dismissal of the significance of cultural transmission is typical of many sociobiological frameworks, and in this case, despotic wasps and despotic humans are explained via an appeal to an utterly homologous explanatory framework. Implications of this denial of cultural process will be drawn out later in this section.

But what leads the author to ignore such an obvious process as cultural transmission in the first place? Betzig readily grants the existence of learned behaviour, as suggested above, and correctly cites certain conclusions of psychological research, which maintain that genetically reproduced structures in the brain mediate the learning process, thereby constraining it (Betzig 1986: 9). There is no doubt that genetics can influence behaviour. This does not, of course, mean that genetics determines behaviour; but Betzig accepts this. Betzig counts genetics mechanisms of behavioural *constraint* as sufficient support for a sociobiological approach to human culture.

Having established some link between genes and behaviour, and thereby the basic heritability of behaviour, the next step taken is the articulation of the Darwinian approach. Betzig uses as her basic definition the Darwinian phrase, that 'heritable traits which promote reproduction will spread'. The reader might care to note at this point the conspicuous absence of any reference to constraints on adaptation (e.g. Foley 1985 after Dawkins 1982), in this Darwinian phrase which Betzig relies upon. The phrase is a simple summary of natural selection or adaptation at the organismic or phenotypic level of biological populations. In no part of the phrase is there any reference to genes or the genotype, to mutation as the source of the variation in heritable traits which must exist in the first place, to random recombination, or to random selective processes such as genetic drift. Nonetheless, as an interpretation of natural selection, this phrase which Betzig has chosen accurately summarises the process adequately.

Thus the two basic premises upon which the sociobiological argument is subsequently built are not unsound in and of themselves. Behaviour is influenced indirectly by genes, and heritable traits which promote reproduction will spread. However, Betzig's avoidance of any distinction between cultural and acultural learned behaviour interferes with the manipulation of these two assumptions.

In manipulating the first premise concerning learned behaviour, the author fails to recognise that the human behaviours which she seeks to explain with the Darwinian framework are not merely learned, but *learned in a very peculiar way*. Learned not only in the dialogue between the individual and the physical world, but also in dialogue with a social environment from which certain concepts may be 'learned' as *fait accompli*. For this reason human despotic behaviour cannot be explained purely as an outcome of individual experience and learning interacting with genetically inherited psychological biases. Human individuals have other sources from which to learn, in addition to individual trial and error; obviously the cultural state of other individuals in the society provides the learning individual with the results of the learning experiences of others. If human behaviour was primarily acultural, as behaviour may well be amongst some of the animal groups to which Betzig compares human societies, a given behaviour pattern could well be explained in terms of a combination of individual learning experience and the genetically constrained capacity to learn from that experience. The typical sociobiological framework would be appropriate in such contexts, with the prevalence of certain behaviour types in a given society explained in terms of the natural selection of those genotypes which constrained the individuals learning in that direction.

Culturally learned behaviour patterns however are not so amenable to the classic framework, since the structure of such behaviour is not simply the outcome of complex interaction between learning capacity and learning process. An individual with the capacity for culture can have whole behaviour patterns transmitted to it, and that behaviour pattern is thereby reproduced within the society. The frequency of such behaviour patterns in a particular community is thus an outcome of individual learning and the reproductive success of genetic capacities, and the reproductive success of that behaviour pattern itself. In the despotism case-study, the lack of distinction between different kinds of learned behaviour therefore neglects the fact that despotic behaviour patterns are not perennially re-emergent simply through the reproductive success of genetic capacity and individual learning experience, they also require maintenance through cultural transmission.

Distinctions within the 'learned behaviour' category are commonly omitted in sociobiological frameworks, in association with the treatment of culture as a dimension of phenotypic plasticity, the order of which is explainable only through an appeal to the order that can be imposed by the genotypic basis to that plasticity. In the case of the behaviour of a human in a position of power, ignoring cultural transmission leaves only one conceptual function for selectionist theory; explaining the reproductive success of the genetic capacity for culture through natural selection of those organisms which possess it. Once a culturally transmitted behaviour pattern is considered to be explainable only via an appeal to phenotypic plasticity, it can be explained in the same manner as any other organismic trait.

Thus three assumptions are bound together in Betzig's explanation of Despotism:

(A) A lack of consideration of the implications of cultural transmission for distinguishing socially learned behaviour from individually learned behaviour; leading to

(B) The general classification of culturally transmitted behaviour along with individually learned behaviour, under the general umbrella of phenotypic plasticity; leading in turn to

(C) The ultimate classification of cultural behaviour as a typical class of organismic traits, and seen (as are all traits in adaptationism) purely as vehicles of organismic reproductive success.

A wider perspective on Cultural Sociobiology

So far attention has been focused on a single case-study within Sociobiology. But Betzig is by no means alone in her use of these assumptions. They are apparent in the work of many sociobiological expositions in addition to the case-study. Flinn & Alexander, for example, expressed the third of these concepts when they wrote (1982: 397):

> [we argue that] cultural traits are, in general, vehicles of genic survival, and that the heritability of cultural traits depends on the judgements . . . of individuals with regard to their effects on the individual's inclusive fitness.

Crook & Crook (1988) reveal their acceptance of these interlinked assumptions in the following quoted paragraph. The key phrases are italicised for more specific discussion below. They write (Crook & Crook 1988: 97, my italics):

> Irons (1979), following the pioneering lead of Haldane (1956), remarked that the most reasonable hypothesis is that behavioural differences shown by contrasting human groups *"are environmentally induced variations in the expression of basically similar genotypes"* and that the ability to vary behaviour in response to environmental differences is itself the prime human adaptation to a social world. [there is] [E]vidence that the social expressions of human phenotypes are often strategic in the sense that they *maintain the inclusive fitness of individuals in ways formally comparable to those without culture.* . . .

In the first italicised phrase, Crook & Crook use a definition of culture which does not distinguish culture from individually learned behaviour in acultural organisms, or even from physical phenotypic alterations by the inorganic environment such as a sun-tanned skin. As mentioned above in the case-study, cultural behaviour is thus classified under the general category of phenotypic plasticity, and the possibility that cultural transmission might make cultural phenotypic plasticity any different to other forms of plasticity is thereby ignored. In the second italicised phrase, cultural plasticity, as part of the phenotype, and like any other plasticity, assumes its typical role; the maintenance of inclusive fitness.

Daly (1982) also employs the above series of sociobiological premises in his approach to culture. Throughout his paper in which the critique is made, a sociobiological viewpoint is presented in which cultural 'traits' are considered to be typical expressions of phenotypic plasticity (1982: 405). All such traits are then viewed to be exclusively shaped by adaptation, as if cultural and genetic 'traits' jointly constitute a coherent organism with a single genealogy (Daly 1982: 406):

> ... all evolved traits of all organisms serve a single goal: the replication of the focal individual's genes (the promotion of inclusive fitness). Fitness-promotion entails both (1) accrual of those resources convertible to fitness – being an effective reproductive competitor – and (2) the conversion itself – being an effective dispenser of benefit to kin, especially but not exclusively offspring, and hence an effective "nepotist". . . . This theory of organismic, including human, nature can provide a heuristic metatheory for many areas of social science.

Other studies in which these interlinked assumptions are either implicit or explicit include Alexander (1979; 1988); Betzig *et al.* (1988); Dunbar (1988); Chagnon (1982): Dickemann (1981); Foley (1985; 1987a), Irons (1988), and Wilson (1971; 1975). Where culturally learned behaviour is discussed at all, it is treated no differently to aculturally learned behaviour, which is in turn approached as a kind of phenotypic plasticity, the expressions of which are seen to be part of the organism. They are then explained, like any other organismic trait complex, via an appeal to genetic adaptation.

Problems with the three assumptions

Thus it can be seen that these three interlinked sociobiological assumptions are by no means limited to the Despotism case-study. And, at first glance, the application of the classic Darwinian phrase 'heritable traits which promote reproduction will spread' to the reproductive success of Despotism, or for that matter, any other cultural reproduced structure, seems fairly straight forward. Despotism (a suite of heritable human traits) will undergo differential reproductive success if it conveys reproductive success to their bearers. Despotic behaviour should be common in those societies where individuals increase their reproductive success by adopting it.

But introduction of the acultural/cultural distinction in learned behaviour poses some problems for this apparently simple application of Darwinian concepts to human behaviour. The fact of cultural transmission threatens Sociobiology by threatening the use of the phrase 'heritable traits which promote reproduction will spread' in the explanatory framework. In a behavioural system where behaviour can be culturally transmitted the phrase becomes too general; a picture is given of a trait which possesses heritability and the capacity to promote reproduction, but it is not clear whether the trait is affecting its own reproduction, or the reproduction of some associated entity. The reverse is also true of the phrase; it is not clear whether the trait's heritability applies to itself or to the genealogy of the associated entities whose reproduction it is affecting. Consequently the phrase 'heritable traits which promote reproduction will spread' requires additional qualification for the set of limiting conditions beyond which it does not apply. Such a qualification can be made simply by inserting the words 'their own' to produce the more specific phrase: 'heritable traits which promote *their own* reproduction will spread'. The reproduction must be that of the heritable traits, not of some other traits or entities. Heritable traits cannot spread through affecting the reproduction of some other organism or trait, unless in doing so they also enhance their own chances of reproduction.

Treating despotism as a cultural learned behaviour, and therefore as simply the outcome of learning capacities and individual experience, leads Betzig to ignore the process through which despotism itself may be reproduced independently of the reproduction of a despot – cultural transmission. Cultural transmission, in turn, makes it possible for despotism to 'escape' the lineage of a despot in a way no ordinary human trait can. To use a very simplistic metaphor, the sins of the fathers may not necessarily be visited upon the sons. This circumstance makes it possible for despotism to exploit the despot, or vice versa, such that patterns of adaptive selfishness become highly complicated and problematic. Darwin considered the problem of exploitation important enough to comment on it in the *Origin of species* (Darwin 1859: 229):

> Natural selection cannot possibly produce any modification in any one
> species exclusively for the good of another species; though throughout nature
> one species incessantly takes advantage of, and profits by, the structure of

another. . . . If it could be proved that any part of the structure of any one species had been formed for the exclusive good of another species, it would annihilate my theory, for such could not have been produced by natural selection. Although many statements may be found in works on natural history to this effect, I cannot find even one which seems to me to be of any weight.

Darwin expounded this rule on a number of occasions (e.g. Darwin 1859: 67, 163). Wallace is equally clear about the principle, for example when explaining how the apparent 'altruism' of edible fruit production in plants is really a strategy for seed dispersal (Wallace 1889: 307):

In the restriction of bright colour to those edible fruits the eating of which is beneficial to the plant, we see the undoubted result of natural selection; and this is the more evident when we find that the colour never appears till the fruit is ripe – that is, till the seeds within it are fully matured and in the best state for germination. Some brilliantly coloured fruits are poisonous, as in our bitter-sweet (*Solanum dulcamara*), cuckoo-pint (Arum) and the West Indian machineel. Many of these are, no doubt, eaten by animals to whom they are harmless; and it has been suggested that even if some are poisoned by them the plant is benefited, since it not only gets dispersed, but finds, in the decaying body of its victim, a rich manure heap.

Any reader who remains in doubt about whether adaptive selfishness is an essential philosophical element in any Darwinian or neo-Darwinian explanation, even in complex displays of altruistic behaviour, might consider any of the basic arguments of Dawkins with respect to this issue (Dawkins 1989 *passim*).

An entity cannot undergo differential reproduction purely on the grounds of promoting the reproduction of some other entity, unless conditions are thereby made more favourable for its own reproduction.

Unless the existence of cultural transmission is denied, we must recognise that human behaviour is reproduced by non-genetic means, and thus reproduced independently of human reproduction. Given that the reproduction of despotism and the reproduction of humans are two separate processes, an explanation of the reproductive success of despotism which relies purely on the observed effect of despotism on human reproduction must necessarily be violating Darwin's tenet. Betzig's scenario requires natural selection to produce a modification in one entity (a culturally reproduced behaviour pattern) exclusively for the good of another (a genetically reproduced animal), with no explanation of how despotism might indirectly propagate itself in the process.

The error is connected to the attribution of false equivalence to both forms of learned behaviour, because if despotism was simply individually learned behaviour and not culturally transmittable, there would be no danger of breaking the above Darwinian premise. In such a society human reproduction would be the only reproductive process, and despotism could only become prevalent through the differential reproduction of human genes or gene complexes which predisposed human individuals towards such behaviour.

It must be stressed that this Darwinian principle does not deny the existence of animal or organism partnerships where only one party benefits; the phrase is not in conflict with commensal or parasitic ecological relationships. As Darwin states above, 'throughout nature one species incessantly takes advantage of, and profits by, the structure of another'. The important difference is that the structure or structures from which one party derives benefit must be already formed in the host party, for some other reason or via some other process. In other words, for the host population, commensal relationships may be formed by preadaptation but not by adaptation, while adaptation would be the basic process by means of which the parasitic population would establish the relationship. The structure from which the parasitic population benefits, therefore, was not formed via natural selection exclusively for the good of another species, but for the good of the population in which the structure exists (ignoring, for the moment, alternative scenarios implied by genetic drift or epigenetic processes in the expanded synthesis).

In its approach to *cultural reproduced* phenomena, Sociobiology breaks this basic Darwinian principle, thereby rendering its claim to Darwinian identity untenable. More specifically Betzig has used an invalid and non-Darwinian interpretation of the phrase 'heritable traits which promote reproduction will spread'. She is explaining the selective viability of one entity (Despotism) in terms of its effect on the reproductive success of another (a human individual). A behaviour pattern is seen to be shaped and propagated exclusively for the reproductive advantage of the animal which exhibits that behaviour, and not seen to be spreading according to its likelihood of being culturally reproduced. Cultural transmission is not denied, but it is nonetheless ignored; consequently cultural 'traits' cannot be distinguished from genetically or environmentally emergent organismic states, and cannot therefore be given different treatment. Men and women are viewed by Betzig as not more than the 'products of natural selection', implying a belief that the only order to be found in history or cultural diversity is that which is imposed by patterns in the human genome (see also Rindos 1986b) (Betzig 1986: 2):

Lord Acton once pointed out that "absolute power corrupts absolutely" (1948: 364), surprising hardly anyone. The perhaps naïve question asked here is, why? The answer investigated follows from Darwin. If men and women are products of natural selection, then the evolved end of their existence should be essentially, very simply, the production of children, grandchildren, and other non-descendent kinsmen.

A little later, Betzig explains how this leads to extreme forms of behaviour in those with absolute power (Betzig 1986: 2):

> The important result, as Darwin pointed out, must be that winners leave the legacy of whatever heritable traits helped in that competition to their children. Among Darwin's (1859) own examples: high giraffes should have evolved long necks (p. 161); orchids should have evolved their spout-shaped lower lips in order to get pollinated (p. 142); cuckoos should have evolved to lay eggs in other birds' nests (p. 190).
>
> 'And men and women should have evolved to seek out positions of strength as a means to reproduction. Power, prestige, and privileged access to resources should be sought, not as ends in themselves, but as prerequisites to procreation.

As suggested near the beginning of the chapter, cultural transmission allows a fundamental decoupling of the genealogies of cultural traits and acultural traits, with the obvious implication being that the reproductive success of a trait could be traced down the wrong genealogy. Humans, even in the most strict and orthodox adaptationist accounts, are not simply the products of natural selection, but also the products of cultural selection, two separate selective processes acting in concert. Betzig has simply dismissed cultural transmission as another body of environmental 'noise' interacting with a range of genetically emergent propensities, when in fact culture is another assemblage of systematically reproduced entities with their own genealogy, one that is quite distinct from the genealogy of the human genome. The ordered patterns which Betzig has encountered in human affairs are not simply the order imposed by the phylogenetic constraints of the human gene pool, but also the order imposed by the phylogenetic or historical constraints implicit in cultural traditions.

Thus Sociobiology's 'environmental' interferences need to be subclassified into cultural and non-cultural categories, corresponding at a more specific level to the distinction between cultural and acultural learned behaviour mentioned above. Lack of awareness of the importance of these dichotomies in human behaviour, while seemingly a denial of common sense in most anthropological circles, is more understandable in an overly literal interpretation of Darwin such as Betzig's. Traditionally, Darwinian theory is considered applicable to organisms and parts of organisms, and its applicability to culture (unamended) demands the classification of cultural entities as one or the other; i.e. either whole organisms, or parts of organisms. A view which maintains human behaviour as simply the product of learning and experience, and therefore as the outcome of those parts of the organism associated with learning, can simply classify cultural entities as parts of organisms, and focus all discussion of evolutionary process on the gene pools associated with the organism. However, given that cultural transmission adds a new replicative process to evolution in human behaviour, such misplaced focus leads to the discussion of the structure of one class of entities purely in terms of the reproductive success of another class; anathema in a selective framework.

The collapse into Lamarckism

In the quote from Darwin presented above, a 'complete annihilation' of his theory was predicted in the event of the finding of a structure in one organism formed exclusively for the good of another organism, and that such could not have been formed through natural selection. Therefore, the explanation of cultural structures purely in terms of the good of the genetically emergent structures of organisms presumably implies some processes other than selection to be operating in culture itself. Correspondingly, the sociobiological explanatory framework, through its avoidance of discussion of cultural selection, implies that the processes of transformation by means of which the cultural system serves as 'man's extrasomatic adaptation' are something other than selective.

To put this somewhat convoluted argument another way, a sociobiologist who intends to continue breaking this Darwinian principle, and to see cultural entities as formed exclusively for the good of human individuals, must find a mechanism other than natural selection for this process, or else deny the validity of Darwin's assertion that 'such could not have been produced by natural selection'. The latter alternative is not a real option, as it would require taking up the basically untenable position that reproductive success in one system could automatically propagate structures in another.

Thus, ironically, a sociobiologist must take the first option, and espouse a Lamarckian notion of cultural process (if that process is to be directed exclusively by human reproductive criteria) since neo-Darwinian process by its very nature cannot be exclusively directed by anything, let alone by criteria of reproduction in a separate system of inheritance. The cultural system cannot serve human adaptation without being a system of

Lamarckian adaptation. Evolutionary processes which are externally directed are basically 'Lamarckian' processes, and as a consequence some sociobiologists simultaneously advocate a Lamarckian approach to culture, and a neo-Darwinian approach to the effects of that Lamarckian system on human genetic evolution. Consequently, assertions of the selective or neo-Darwinian nature of human evolution, and the fundamentally Lamarckian or deterministic nature of cultural evolution, often occur in the literature as part of the same theoretical position.

This brings us to the fundamentally Lamarckian nature of the sociobiological conception of cultural change and cultural adaptation. While Sociobiology may legitimately see itself as attempting to introduce Darwinism into human affairs, the introduction was, apparently, never intended for human *cultural* affairs. The approach seeks to apply Darwinian principles to anthropology exclusively in the context of human genetic evolution, and the explanation of other parts of human society in terms of this process. This double standard for genetic and cultural process is widespread in many applications of biological theory to sociocultural anthropology, and in many speculative comparisons of biological and cultural evolution. The juxtaposition of Darwinian genetics with Lamarckian cultural systems occurs not only in Cultural Sociobiology, as will be seen below, but also occurs when 'regular' biologists briefly compare cultural process with the one which they know best. Spuhler, for example, has stated (1984: 13):

> Clearly, the mode of inheritance for cultural behaviour is fundamentally different: by transmission of gametes in biology and by transmission of learned symbols in cultural behaviour. Biological inheritance is non-Lamarckian, cultural inheritance is Lamarckian, in the sense of the inheritance of acquired characteristics.

Similarly, Steven Jay Gould has remarked (1980: 71):

> Cultural evolution has progressed at rates that Darwinian evolution cannot begin to approach. Darwinian evolution continues in *Homo sapiens* but at rates so slow that it no longer has much impact on our history. Human cultural evolution, in contrast to our biological history, is Lamarckian in character. What we learn in one generation we transmit directly to the next by teaching and writing. Acquired characteristics are inherited in culture and technology. Lamarckian evolution is rapid and accumulative. It explains the cardinal difference between our past, purely biological mode of change, and our current, maddening acceleration toward something new and liberating – or toward the abyss.

The reader might consider the above quotes to be mere speculation, but parallel assertions occur in the words of those who specialise in applying Darwinian theory to human affairs. Richard Alexander, for example, advocates a selective framework for human genetic evolution, while reserving a Lamarckian element in the process of human invention, as the generator of variation in culture (mutation and invention are equivalent in function for Alexander, but not isomorphic in nature) (Alexander 1979: 74):

> Immediately, differences are apparent between the processes of change in genetic and cultural evolution. Perhaps the most profoundly, causes of mutation and selection in cultural evolution are not independent. Most of the sources of cultural "mutations" are at least potentially related to the reasons for their survival or failure. A new kind of plow or computer is built for its expected usefulness: it is adopted if it works.

Another unambiguous example of the juxtaposition of the notion of the applicability of biological theory to cultural entities, with the notion that biological theory does not provide an analogy for cultural process itself, is that of Daly (1982: 402): 'Innovation (in culture) is not random in its effect like genetic mutation, but can be Lamarckian'. This assertion is in the midst of a paper which takes up the view that biological theory is nonetheless applicable to culture due to the fact 'that all evolved traits of all organisms serve a single goal: the replication of the focal individual's genes'.

Boyd & Richerson are also careful not to exclude the possibility for Lamarckian evolution in the midst of the application of Darwinian principles to human society (although their theoretical approach has been classified as cultural selectionist for the purposes of the study, the category of theory given attention in chapters 4 and 5). Reiterating similar earlier statements (1982: 329), they write (Boyd & Richerson 1985: 8):

> The cultural information acquired by an individual may be affected by the events of his or her life, and, if so, the changes will be transmitted to an individual's cultural offspring. This property of cultural transmission makes for a kind of "Lamarckian" evolution, in the sense that acquired variation is inherited.

Obviously not all of the above writers could be considered to be sociobiologists; my assertion is that in juxtaposing a Darwinian genetics with a Lamarckian cultural system they are *expressing an essentially sociobiological sentiment*. The point is that Darwinian and Lamarckian processes are commonly seen as acting in concert in human affairs, moreover it would seem that the two positions are implicitly linked (i.e. that a Lamarckian model of culture is logically emergent in any selectionist model of human evolution which ignores selective processes occurring outside the human genome). In such a framework, the order in culture can only be seen to be ordered from without. The explanatory framework implied must, almost by definition, conform to the typical external direction model of causality upon which (environmental) Lamarckism is based.

Concluding remarks

The idea that Sociobiology as a whole has an essentially Lamarckian approach to cultural process may seem counter-intuitive to some readers. But it is certainly the case that cultural process cannot serve the adaptive imperatives of an independent inheritance system without somehow being 'freed' from the Darwinian constraints of its own inheritance patterns. One cannot argue that systems of cultural inheritance exist only to promote organismic survival without also asserting that cultural process is basically non-Darwinian in its intrinsic logistics. To put it another way, in order to be able to exist for the sole purpose of serving the Darwinian requirements of other phenomena, a phenomenon must first be liberated from the Darwinian imperative of serving itself.

In any case, proving the Lamarckian nature of Cultural Sociobiology beyond all doubt would presumably require a more comprehensive analysis of the sociobiological literature than that attempted in this chapter. Yet this extreme position has been employed only in so far as to show that an allegiance to neo-Darwinian theory is no guarantee of a selectionist theory of cultural process (although it is for genetic process), and indeed it appears that for many it implies just the opposite. Certainly, many modern Darwinians explicitly reject any notion of the wholesale applicability of their theories to cultural fields of enquiry, and, as has been shown, some explicitly advocate Lamarckism for these fields of enquiry.

What has been demonstrated is that the tendency of sociobiologists to explain cultural adaptation in terms of human adaptation violates one of the most important principles of neo-Darwinian theory, that of 'adaptive selfishness'. Despite the fact that artefacts, ideas, and socially acquired behaviour patterns undoubtedly display genealogical independence, an explanatory framework is used in which such cultural phenomena are exploited comprehensively by human individuals. Cultural structures are formed exclusively for the benefit of humans, and their fitness is thus measured not in terms of their own likelihood of cultural reproduction, but in terms of human reproduction. Culture is literally viewed as 'man's (and woman's) means of extrasomatic adaptation'.

Had Sociobiology succeeded in fulfilling this agenda (in finding even one example of a culturally reproduced structure which existed solely for the purpose of facilitating human reproduction, without also facilitating its own reproduction), they would have simultaneously refuted their own approach, and any possibility of applying selective principles to cultural phenomena. They would have inadvertently pulled off an ironic oedipal conquest, and 'killed off' the great father of their own approach. In other words, Sociobiology's self-proclaimed agenda (for culture) is a program of self-annihilation (in cultural contexts).

Sociobiology provides a remarkable selective framework for disentangling the convoluted interaction of different human reproductive strategies within a society, and their ultimate effect on human genetic process. But the approach does not represent a neo-Darwinian approach to cultural process itself, as this is precluded by their focus upon the survival and reproduction of individual organisms, and their relative disregard for the implications of social transmission and genealogical independence. By virtue of this curious double bind, we must therefore reject Cultural Sociobiology as a candidate for the 'untried theory', and once again turn our attention elsewhere. Could it be that a third evolutionary approach, Cultural Selectionism, *does* provide a selectionist framework for culture, and could it therefore qualify to fill the gap of the 'untried theory'? This is the basic question addressed in the next chapter.

4
Cultural Selectionism

Overview
In the preceding chapters I have argued that an implicit Lamarckian orthodoxy pervades explanations of cultural process. However, it appears that this orthodoxy is now under threat, due to the rapid development of a new perspective known as Cultural Selectionism. This chapter provides a general overview of Cultural Selectionism and a precise definition of the essential differences between this perspective and other approaches with which it has the potential to be confused; approaches such as the Cultural Sociobiology of the last chapter, and Diffusionism.

A brief definition of Cultural Selectionism
'Cultural Selectionism' may be defined as a neo-Darwinian approach to human behaviour which focuses on the 'survival and reproduction of cultures', in direct contrast with the sociobiological focus on the 'survival and reproduction of organisms'. In other words, a true cultural selectionist is at least as interested in tracing the effects of a particular culture upon its own reproduction, as in tracing the effect that a culture might have upon the reproduction of the organisms which maintain it. Cultural variation is seen to be a product not of genetic selection, but of an intrinsic or purely cultural selective process. It is this basic element – the extension of selective principles into purely non-genetic contexts – which identifies the cultural selectionist, and differentiates his or her position from the sociobiologist.

It was Sociobiology's failure to realise this tenet which caused them to view cultural process as a servant of human genetic process – 'man's extrasomatic adaptation' – and thereby break the fundamental neo-Darwinian principle of reproductive selfishness (the reader is reminded here that the neo-Darwinian use of the word 'selfish' denotes 'that which increases the likelihood of self-reproduction' or reproduction of other 'selves' such as kin, not the more personified 'conscious self-aggrandisement'). History was reduced to natural history rather than explained via an appeal to the intrinsic processes of history itself. Cultural Selectionism, a different approach developed in reaction to Sociobiology, attempts to escape this problem by viewing historical process as another selective process in human affairs, operating separately from and in addition to genetic process.

However, it is worth noting that not all anthropologists and archaeologists examined in this chapter identify consciously with the label 'Cultural Selectionism'. Some, in fact, such as Leonard & Jones (1987: 211) even prefer not to use the term 'Cultural Selectionism' at all. Yet there is a definite similarity in the explanatory frameworks dealt with in this chapter. My use of the term basically encompasses any statements to the effect that selective concepts can be applied to extra-genetic and particularly cultural processes. The essential element in the work which I have classed as 'cultural selectionist' is an interest in transposing principles of the neo-Darwinian synthesis specifically into the context of cultural transmission and evolution. Unlike Cultural Sociobiology, the theoretical approaches of this chapter are not trying to explain cultural variation and invariation in terms of neo-Darwinian models of human genes, individuals, and genomes, but in terms of cultural equivalents of these entities. The identifying characteristic of Cultural Selectionism is thus an attempt to explain cultural change with models which allow invention and cultural transmission to operate separately from each other, but nonetheless explicitly to incorporate both processes into a selectionist explanatory framework.

When we expand the brief definition of Cultural Selectionism above, the distinctive philosophical identity of the approach becomes more and more apparent. The cultural selectionist can be distinguished from the sociobiologist by the fact that he or she sees human evolution as the result of the interaction of two logistically independent neo-Darwinian processes (one in human culture, and one in human genetics), rather than one general (and ultimately genetic) neo-Darwinian process. This is why they may be reliably identified by the notion that neo-Darwinian process can operate in substrates other than DNA.

Leonard & Jones express the position by coining the phrase 'replicative success', which allows them to avoid the genetic connotations they feel are inevitably associated with the phrase 'reproductive success' (1987: 214):

> Replicative success is a pragmatic construct. It implies neither mode of trait transmission, as reproductive success does, nor that some degree of selective advantage is conferred as a result of the transmission of a trait. Success is gauged as changes in the representation of traits through time.

Many other cultural selectionists make parallel assertions, all with the goal of communicating the fact the Darwinian processual framework is not tied to any particular field of enquiry, providing reproduction of some sort occurs in that field of enquiry. Rindos puts the position as follows (1985: 65):

> ... that the mode of transmission of cultural characteristics ('the inheritance of acquired traits') is irrelevant to the applicability of a selectionist model for evolutionary change. . . . Darwinian selectionism requires undirected, heritable variation. . . . The symbolic aspects of culture are not in any sense analogous to the genotype but rather functionally equivalent; because the capacity for symbolling is not directly adaptive, it provides the undirected variation required for a theory of selection-mediated cultural evolution.

Boyd & Richerson put it like this (1985: 173):

> there is no necessary logical connection between Darwin's idea of evolution by natural selection and the particular features of genetic inheritance. There are two necessary conditions in order for natural selection to operate: (1) There must be heritable variation in the phenotype. (2) Phenotypic variation must be associated with variation in individual survival and reproduction.

Most recently, Durham has presented this background assumption of Cultural Selectionism very clearly (1990: 188):

> The word "evolution" has meant many things to many people (e.g. see reviews in 27, 28, 42, 44, 129, 155, 188, 205). Swayed by Darwin's simple yet simple rendering, "descent with modification" (63), I consider evolution to have occurred in any set X whose elements (X1, X2, X3, etc.) are all related by descent – that is, by hereditary derivation from a common ancestor. Using this definition, together with a suitable conception of heredity, one can argue that many things evolve: for example, designs (191), technologies (57), texts (34, 156), languages (90, 91, 197), knowledge (35, 37; but see debates in 97, 163), ideas and theories (111, 158, 201), whole disciplines (80, 202), even Darwinism itself.

Bateson, for final example, has also succinctly articulated the general applicability of models of selection to both genetic and learning processes, and by implication from the latter, cultural process. Bateson prefers to use the word 'stochastic' to describe the dialogue between random variation from the *status quo ante*, and differential persistence, which occurs in selective processes (Bateson 1980: 160):

> ... both genetic change and the process called learning (including the somatic changes induced by habit and environment) are stochastic processes. In each case there is, I believe, a stream of events that is random in certain aspects and in each case there is a non-random selective process which causes certain of the random components to "survive" longer than others. Without the

random, there can be no new thing.

There are other similar assertions (see Dunnell 1980: 53, and Chen *et al.* 1982: 366). Each position expresses that the fundamental premise upon which Cultural Selectionism applies neo-Darwinian theory to culture is one of analogy. This is in stark contrast to Sociobiology (as pointed out throughout the last chapter) which is based on the explanation of human behaviour in terms of genetic process itself. To my knowledge, this fundamental distinction is generally accepted by all anthropologists who have carried out research into neo-Darwinian theory, and the distinction is neatly articulated by Blute (1979: 57–8), Dunnell (1980: 52), Durham (1990: 193), and Rindos (1986b: 315).

Thus the most basic premise of Cultural Selectionism is an extension of neo-Darwinian theory into non-genetic contexts, particularly that of cultural change. Sociobiology, on the other hand, maintains an ultimately organismic context for its neo-Darwinian principles – other processes are not seen to be independent neo-Darwinian processes in their own right, but rather as non-Darwinian influences on the underlying neo-Darwinian processes which take place in organismic populations.

A note on regional differentiation within Cultural Selectionism

Although it has not been customary to make use of regional distinctions in the discussion of archaeological and anthropological theory, some use of them will be made in this part of the study. This is a *selectionist* view of the origin of Cultural Selectionism; it therefore takes the view that independent inventions rarely duplicate each other, and that degrees of regional isolation produce corresponding degrees of regional differentiation (in proportion to the degree to which that isolation impedes the movement of ideas from one population to the other). As a result of these sorts of processes, American Cultural Selectionism (e.g. Boyd & Richerson 1985) is different from those positions which originated in British academia (e.g. Clarke 1978). The American form arose principally as a critique within American Sociobiology which gradually came to terms with human behaviour and cultural transmission as it developed. Its 'human evolution' heritage is most evident in the fact that although cultures are one focus of attention, individual organisms and populations thereof are still the basic units of analysis.

As will become clear, the different versions of Cultural Selectionism which exist bear the signatures of their different heritage, independent origins, and subsequent regional and behavioural isolation; in fact, just the sort of differences one would expect if cultural process were basically selective.

It is worth noting that there is a fourth 'cultural selectionist' position, also with a quite independent heritage, and that is the 'Meme' concept of Dawkins (1976; 1982; 1989). Its origin is essentially British, and more particularly Oxonian, ethology. Memetic approaches are given more attention in chapters 7 and 8, and are only briefly listed here as part of a general overview of Cultural Selectionism. As Maschner (1996) and Mithen (1993a) have remarked, the number of new Darwinian approaches to culture is bewildering. In recent years it would seem that they have undergone an 'adaptive radiation' all of their own.

Distinguishing Selectionism from Diffusionism

There is a certain superficial resemblance between neo-Darwinian selectionist perspectives and the diffusionist theories of the first half of the twentieth century, since both schools treat invention (mutation, innovation), and spatial or temporal expansion via adoption (differential reproduction, selection) as separate, independently operating processes in culture. It is this similarity between diffusion and Selectionism (if properly worked out in selectionist terms, diffusion can simply be a special case of cultural adaptation) which has lead Shennan (1989) to suggest that current renewed interest in the social processes associated with diffusion and the renewed interest in selectionist models of historical process are centred upon similar aspects of cultural fields of enquiry (Shennan 1989: 331). Shennan suggests that the renewed interest in the process of emulation can be, and for that matter would benefit if it were, incorporated into a broader framework of cultural transmission and evolution, using Boyd & Richerson's framework as an example.

Both Diffusionism and Selectionism use two-stage models of transformation (two basic kinds of processual event, involving first an invention or mutation, followed by propagation), in contrast with the one-stage models which prevailed in pre-Darwinian philosophy. The 'double-barrelled' complexity of selectionist perspectives is one of their distinguishing elements (Rindos 1986b: 70):

> Without a method for the non-directional generation of variation and, indeed, some evidence that observable variation is in fact undirected, Darwinian selectionism is far less elegant and parsimonious than Lamarckian evolutionism. Why should we theorise that evolution is a two-stage process when a simple one-stage model for the generation of directed variation will

produce the same results, at least in so far as adaptation and directional change are concerned?

A similar discussion of the two-stage complexity of selective process may be found in the work of the geneticist Wright (1967: 117). The irony of this situation is that the similarity makes Diffusionism more like Selectionism than the Cultural Evolutionism of chapter 2. Because of this, and very ironically, not only were anthropological translations of selective process *mis*translations (in the form of Social Darwinism and Cultural Evolutionism), but Diffusionism, the approach developed by anthropologists as a critique of Cultural Evolutionism (Hugill & Dickson 1989: xii) can be considered a far more similar (although still pre-Darwinian in its basic conformation) explanatory framework. To be fair, however, the second misconception springs out of the first. Once the strange phenomenon of a 'Social Darwinism' which corresponds more to Lamarckism than neo-Darwinism has emerged, it is understandable that a reaction to that position might deliberately *or even inadvertently* lead back towards Selectionism, while simultaneously believing itself to be 'inventing' a completely new position.

Like Cultural Selectionism, Diffusionism developed as part of a reaction to pre-Darwinian Cultural Evolutionism. But important differences between Cultural Selectionism and Diffusionism make it nonsensical to view the latter as an early variety of the former, purely on the basis of its two-stage structure. However, Shennan (1989: 331) is correct when he states that Cultural Selectionism must ultimately present some account of the process of diffusion given that the process itself is clearly a special case of cultural transmission. I only wish to remind the reader that such an account (Shennan uses the term 'neo-diffusionist) would look quite different from early-twentieth-century Diffusionism.

It is not my intention to provide more than a brief summary of the 'two-stage' similarity of the approaches. However, it is important to distinguish the apparently similar language and expression of (early-twentieth-century) diffusion and Cultural Selectionism, and thereby dismiss the superficial similarities in terminology. If this is not done, it is very easy for a reader to attribute (consciously or otherwise), the well-known conceptual problems of Diffusionism to those aspects of cultural selectionist language which bear a false resemblance to the *Kulturkreis* school. My objective for the moment, therefore, before examining some cultural selectionist perspectives in detail, will be to briefly emphasise the differences between the two schools in their areas of greatest apparent similarity. This preliminary contrast is also necessary because many of the familiar terms of the neo-Darwinian synthesis are used in diffusionist explanations of cultural patterning in non-equivalent contexts, and these terms have been discredited within cultural anthropology and archaeology in the process. This is a parallel situation to that suggested in chapter 2, where other familiar terms from neo-Darwinian perspectives had been misappropriated in the language of Cultural Evolutionism and 'Social Darwinism', and similarly discredited. While Cultural Evolutionism misappropriates concepts such as adaptation, progression, survival and species, diffusionist perspectives misappropriate concepts such as traits, homology or actual historical connection, and analogy or functional convergence.

Yet the most basic difference is a general one; while Diffusionism was essentially a descriptive school of thought (in spite of its explanatory aspirations), Cultural Selectionism is genuinely explanatory in that it seeks to model mechanisms and processes of cultural evolution rather than the specific course of history. Other differences can be identified in the analysis of the diffusionist school provided by Hugill & Dickson's *The transfer and transformation of ideas and material culture* (1989).

A more specific difference between Diffusionism and Selectionism involves the source of invention and new variation in the two theories. As mentioned above, both have separate mechanisms for the origin of a new variant and its subsequent persistence. In both approaches there are one or very few places of origin for an innovation or mutation, from which it may or may not subsequently spread. However, while each original invention in a (expanded synthesis) cultural selectionist framework is a random event which can occur in any community in the world (although not with equal likelihood), and anywhere in that community, in Diffusionism all original inventions occur in one of a small number of 'original cultures' or *Urkulturen*. While random inventions can occur anywhere, the location of inventions in the diffusionist paradigm all occurred in a small number of 'superior' cultures, and then 'diffused' down the cultural gradient to 'less enlightened' cultures, in a series of concentric circles (Hugill & Dickson 1989: xii):

> (1) the *Urkulturen* were few in number, (2) the historical configurations of human culture in the world resulted from the diffusion of single traits together with the migration of peoples bearing whole complexes of traits from these *Urkulturen* centres, and (3) diffusion and migration tended to radiate outward from the centres in roughly concentric circles or *kreise* and could thus be traced back to them by means of the careful description and comparison of culture traits.

This situation implies some special propensity for invention in a tiny sample of the world's cultures, a position which would be untenable in an cultural selectionist perspective, which relies on the random and unpredictable generation of new varieties in the inventive process. Cultural equivalents of the concept of mutation would therefore necessarily take up the position that invention was a ubiquitous process occurring in all cultures, while at the same time arguing that very few inventions were absolutely homologous or identical, due to the tendency of random events not to duplicate each other. Cultural selectionist notions of invention and the origin of variation will be covered in greater detail below; at this point the reader need only keep in mind the nature of the fundamental difference outlined above.

Another major element distinguishing Diffusionism from Cultural Selectionism is the simplistic use of structural similarity as evidence for common origin. An expanded selectionist perspective would rely on a similar notion, but in conjunction with awareness of certain limitations. The heritage constraint of common origin is an important aspect of neo-Darwinian process, but it is not the sole cause of similarity. Hugill & Dickson unambiguously point out the irrefutability of the diffusionist linkage between form and origin as follows (1989: xii):

> Despite the systematic nature of their method, the *Urkulturen* "reconstructed" by members of this school were marred by their excessive reliance on formal similarity between culture traits as proof of historical connection. This lead them to the fallacious premise that distance or distributional discontinuity between occurrences of a trait or trait complex were essentially irrelevant to the reconstructions of the historical patterns of diffusion.

Mutation in the expanded selectionist perspective is not 'perfectly' random in the sense of equally likely in all directions, but historically constrained (Foley 1985: 225, after Dawkins 1982; and Rindos 1985: 70 after Gould 1980; see also Fletcher's (1977) discussion of coherent and incoherent change). The range of mutations produced by a population of marsupials in Australia, for example, would be very different to those produced by a population of antelopes in Africa, despite the fact that populations of both can be found in very similar 'savannah' environments. This is because the *status quo* is different in each case, and as mutations are derivatives of the *status quo* they generally bear some fundamental resemblance to it. Thus we can find very different dominant herbivores – kangaroos versus gazelles – in broadly similar environments on different continents. Mutation is, however, random in the sense that it is impossible to predict which of a vast array of possible mutations will appear at any point in time from a given historically or phylogenetically constrained state. Such constraints impose a certain amount of concurrence between form and origin via the mechanism of 'phylogenetic inertia'.

An answer to Daly's charge of non-equivalence

Martin Daly (1982) has published one of the strongest pieces of 'devil's advocacy' against Cultural Selectionism, and it is interesting to observe that cultural selectionists have, on the whole, ignored rather than addressed the elegantly structured arguments he has advanced. Some readers will, perhaps, dismiss Daly as a naïve sociobiologist; yet Daly has in fact pinpointed the weakest premise of Cultural Selectionism, and that he has thereby brought to our attention the important *desiderata* for future development of the approach.

Daly has argued that the conceptual approach used by Boyd & Richerson (1982), Chen *et al.* (1982), Dawkins (1976), Lumsden & Wilson (1981), and Pulliam (1982) is based on a weak and problematic analogy between cultural information and population genetics. These two mediums of transmission have certain fundamental differences which lead Daly to the conclusion that the analogy is without practical or heuristic value. If the analogy between the two mediums is valid, and by inference the cultural selectionist perspective also, then it should be possible to offer a coherent refutation for each of Daly's caveats. There are three basic arguments in the Daly point of view, all focusing on basic differences between cultural and genetic transmission. He adds these differences to two others laid out by Boyd & Richerson, Lamarckian innovation and biased transmission, which he also accepts (see chapter 5). However, due to the general space constraints of this study, I intend to concentrate on what I consider to be the central point of his challenge, the assertion that there are no discrete particles of cultural inheritance. The argument is based on a false conception of both neo-Darwinian genetics and the logistics of cultural transmission. Put simply, Daly both over-estimates the amount of discrete inheritance in genetics, and under-estimates the amount of discrete inheritance in cultural transmission.

The basis of Daly's challenge is that there are no segregating particles underlying any given cultural entity. As Daly writes (1982: 402):

> Memes and culturgens are clearly explicit analogs of the gene; Cavalli-Sforza & Feldman (1981) appear sometimes to follow a similar model (e.g., pp. 70–71). Yet, surely it is more appropriate that the traits in the classes of models correspond; they really seem to refer to the same attributes. Durham recognises this in referring to genetic and cultural "instructions" as

codeterminants of traits. What, then, is to be the gene's analog? What transmission "particle" can we envisage, distinct from the traits, with "polygenic" (polymemic?) effects on a variety of traits? The model of Mendelian genetics remained successful because there really was such a particle. The cultural model has none.

While Daly makes a convincing case for the lack of segregating particles in culture, to suppose that this poses any threat for analogies between cultural and genetic evolution is based on a specious premise. Daly's mistake is not that culture is not perfectly segregated, but that genetics is. While it is generally accepted that the Mendelian concept of segregation was indeed important in the discovery of genes, cases of pure segregation are now recognised to be quite rare in most species. Daly is in fact indicating that he upholds the now-obsolete 'classical' model of genetics (Rindos 1986b: 324, after Lewontin 1974), where segregation is the rule, and not the modern, more systemic 'balance' genetics, where the form in which a gene is expressed is dependent upon a range of contingencies in both the environment of the gene and the genotype of which it is part (for a very lucid example, see also the Dawkins metaphor of individual rowers rowing in different teams: 1989: 38–9; 84–6; 271–2).

Under the 'classical' model of genetics (Rindos 1986b: 324), which Rindos has shown to underlie the Darwinian explanatory frameworks of structuralism and Sociobiology, along with cultural selectionists such as Cavalli-Sforza & Feldman (1981) and Boyd & Richerson (1985), the genetic background for the human capacity for culture is particulate, with individuals being genetically predisposed to realising different cultural states through the possession of different combinations of the particulate capacities. As Rindos writes, in the work of these authors (1986b: 324):

> cultural performance is the result of the fixation of specific genes for specific traits. Here, language acquisition is governed by a process that not only accommodates learning but also dictates the deep structure common to all human languages. General cultural differentiation over time and space must therefore be the result of point substitutions in genes governing traits such as those controlling the ability to learn language.

In this approach, general subcategories of 'culture' are seen to be genetic dispositions towards certain themes, such as temperament, altruism, intelligence, and sexual orientation. The human cultural phenotype is then made up of various 'traits', which while requiring enculturation and learning to be expressed, nonetheless correspond to actual genotypic configurations which convey that particular potential. This one-gene, one-trait model of genotype/phenotype correspondence is now viewed as overly simplistic; genetics is no longer seen as offering discrete 'particles of inheritance' for which, as Daly asserts, cultural equivalents cannot be found. Depew & Weber, in their assessment of the consequences of non-equilibrium Chaos theory for the Darwinian tradition in biology, remark (1988: 320):

> Further, structural and molecular genetic studies have shown in recent years that the genome is not just a string of independently assorting genes. Genes have a complex internal structure. They are, for example, often arranged in "multigene families" that give rise to a variety of non-Mendelian phenomena (Campbell 1982; 1985). For instance, genes can exhibit "molecular drive" (Dover 1982), ramifying copies of themselves throughout the genome in defiance of Mendel's Laws, resulting in the spread and persistence of traits for which there has been no selection.

Rindos has advanced a more sophisticated model of the human capacity for culture to deal with these kinds of genetic phenomena, thus providing both a translation of new biological theory into the particular area of human genetics, and a theoretical prototype (i.e. non-particulate inheritance) by means of which Daly's initial argument against Cultural Selectionism becomes superfluous. Rindos refers to this alternative to 'classical' genetics as the 'balance' model, and the model has been used for many kinds of complex phenotypic phenomena besides the human capacity for culture. The most notable characteristic of these models is their avoidance of notions of particulate inheritance.

In the 'balance' model, culture is viewed not as a trait, but as a range of behaviours (Rindos 1986b: 324). The 'classical' model implies the existence of an optimal genotype which corresponds to the human capacity for culture, a 'particular set of alleles at specific genetic loci'. In contrast, under certain circumstances, the 'balance' model would view any notion of the optimal genotype as misguided. Immense numbers of alleles exist for each relevant locus, with each combination conveying both the general capacity for culture, and a certain amount of individual variance in the nature of that capacity. But the variation persists in the population, since there is no way for the environment to select for one particular combination and 'fix' it in the population at the expense of the others. The full range of behaviours represented by the human cultural capacity is thus selected indiscriminately, due to the general advantages conveyed by the vast set of genes responsible for the capacity.

Not only has discrete inheritance been attacked along this front, but also from the point of the definition of individual genes themselves. Dawkins (1989: 33) has explicitly rejected perfect segregation from his definition of the gene, remarking that the word 'gene' should be defined as a kind of 'fading-out' definition, like the words 'big' or 'old'. Dawkins also points out that even a cistron (piece of DNA which codes for one protein) is occasionally divisible, and any two genes on the same chromosome are not completely independent of each other (see chapter 5 for the full treatment of these remarks).

Lastly, Ho & Saunders (1982) have asserted the obsolete nature of the 'classical' Mendelian model of particulate inheritance, in line with the two papers quoted above. Discussing their 'epigenetic' approach to organismic evolution, they criticise the simplistic Mendelian notions of orthodox, neo-Darwinian adaptationism. They are evidently not aware that 'selfish-gene' theory (again see chapter 5) explicitly includes organisms, and explicitly deconstructs discrete inheritance; Ho & Saunders prefer to deconstruct Mendelian inheritance in their own words (1982: 343):

> There are no organisms, only genes which mutate and compete in a changing environment. The "selfish-gene" concept – widely criticised and condemned, sometimes even by neo-Darwinians themselves – is nonetheless the inevitable, logical conclusion to neo-Darwinism. . . . [But] [a]n organism is not just a collection of accidental mutations, nor is its development an incidental and inconsequential unfolding of a pre-formed genetic programme. On the contrary, it can be understood only in terms of systemic principles and relationships which transcend the properties of individual genes. Moreover, organisms develop and evolve because they are open to the environment. The environment enters into development not as mere disturbances to be overcome, but as necessary formative influences.

Thus Daly's objection becomes a red herring; the requirement of particulate inheritance would be necessary to build a cultural equivalent of Mendelian Darwinism, but not to a Cultural Selectionism based on the expanded neo-Darwinian synthesis of modern evolutionary biology. Cultural analogies with genetic inheritance are under no obligation to demonstrate discrete particles of cultural evolution, since the gene concept involves no necessary 'perfect segregation' in the first place.

Concluding remarks

It can be seen that in the last two decades there has been a gradual renewal of interest in the use of selectionist principles in archaeology and anthropology. This is part of a wider trend within the humanities as a whole (as well documented by Degler 1990; and Durham 1991). Concurrently, there has been a steady growth in the use of post-processualist principles (Hodder 1982b; 1985; 1989a; and Shanks & Tilley 1987a; 1987b), which is also part of a wider post-modernist and post-structuralist trend, such that post-Modernism and Selectionism are now, perhaps, two of the most rapidly growing bodies of theory in cultural fields of enquiry. A general overview of the neo-Darwinian resurgence was provided in this chapter, and it was shown how a number of different sub-traditions have already begun to develop within the perspective, such that it can no longer be viewed as a coherent movement in any but the broadest terms.

However, it may well be that this hypothetical Cultural Selectionism of the future may be substantially different to that of the eighties and early nineties. There are a number of serious problems with current selectionist notions of cultural process, and it is possible that some of these problems will need resolution before the perspective can continue to expand. In the next chapter, these problems are brought out in the Cultural Virus critique, where the Virus position is used as an heuristic alternative to the more established 'organismic or 'phenotypic' form of Cultural Selectionism. A more comprehensive exposition of the Cultural Virus position is not undertaken until chapters 7 and 8.

5
The Darwinian resurgence and the Cultural Virus critique

Overview
While the greater part of recent theoretical discourse within archaeology and anthropology has revolved around the post-modernist manifesto, selectionist metaphysics have been enjoying a milder and less vociferous resurgence. This is reflected in the increasing number and diversity of neo-Darwinian approaches which are now available within cultural fields of enquiry. Two basic approaches may be identified, Sociobiology and Cultural Selectionism, and the latter of these can be further sub-divided into the 'American' or 'Inclusive Phenotype' position and the 'Cultural Virus' position. This chapter presents a critique of the more established 'Inclusive Phenotype' position from the point of view of the 'Virus' position, and as the critique unfolds a number of logical problems are elucidated. It is stressed that this paper is not so much a presentation of the Cultural Virus Theory, as a critique of its nearest philosophical relatives.

Post-modernism and archaeology
Recent years have seen a rapid and vociferous rise in the use of post-processualist principles in archaeology and prehistory (e.g. Hodder 1982b; 1985; 1989a; 1992b; Shanks & Tilley 1987a; 1987b). This is part of a wider trend in cultural fields of enquiry towards increasing involvement in post-modernist discourse, and the increasing use of neo-Marxist, hermeneutic, critical theory and post-structuralist principles. Over the same time period, however, there has also been a somewhat more gradual resurgence in the use of neo-Darwinian principles in archaeological discourse (Clegg 1978a; Cullen 1990; 1991; 1992; 1993a; Dunnell 1980; Fletcher 1977; 1988; Foley 1987b; Lee 1991; Leonard & Jones 1987; Mithen 1989; 1990; O'Brien & Holland 1992; Rindos 1985; 1989; Shennan 1989; 1991). This also is part of a wider trend within anthropology and sociology, and in psychology, psychobiology, philosophy and ethology.

To the reader with little interest in or awareness of the use of neo-

Darwinian principles in purely cultural contexts, the comparison with the rise of post-Modernism might seem irrelevant. Despite its success in genetic contexts, the use of neo-Darwinian principles to explain cultural process is still in its infancy. But I am not arguing that the extent of the neo-Darwinian resurgence is, as yet, anywhere near as great as that of the post-modernist manifesto. The intention is rather to point out that neo-Darwinian approaches to purely cultural and purely psychological processes do exist, and that they have recently begun to sustain wide-ranging, if not comprehensive, interdisciplinary support.

Several significantly different sub-traditions have already begun to develop within the neo-Darwinian perspective, such that it no longer constitutes a coherent movement in any but the broadest of terms. Two well-established lines of thought are those usually referred to as Sociobiology and Cultural Selectionism (e.g. Rindos 1986b; Cullen 1990; Durham 1990; all of whom use this distinction). Summarised very crudely, the sociobiologist is most interested in how human behaviour patterns and social structures affect the survival and genetic reproduction of *individual human organisms* (e.g. Betzig 1986; Betzig *et al.* 1988; Irons 1988), while the cultural selectionist is at least as interested in how the said phenomena affect the survival and cultural transmission of *the cultural phenomena themselves* (e.g. Durham 1991), although such phenomena are still viewed as traits of human individuals rather than individuals in and of themselves (e.g. Rindos 1989). Recently I have tried to show that there is some potential for a third approach, which can also be classified under the cultural selectionist umbrella; the Cultural Virus position (Cullen 1990; 1991; 1992; 1993a). This position focuses attention on the survival and reproduction of particular *ideas, artefacts, and behaviour patterns* in and of themselves, rather than as traits of human individuals.

The present paper seeks to demonstrate that there are logical problems in certain analytical categories employed in mainstream Cultural Selectionism of the kind which uses the Inclusive Phenotype perspective. (The term 'inclusive phenotype' is derived from Leonard & Jones (1987).) The aim of the critique is to show that the 'Inclusive Phenotype' and 'Virus' positions imply surprisingly different cultural interpretations of most of the key neo-Darwinian concepts. It is important to note that the 'Inclusive Phenotype' perspective is not unique to Cultural Selectionism, but also endemic in Sociobiology. The Cultural Virus critique applies equally well to both, showing, in its broadest sense, how the fact of cultural transmission, and the genealogical independence it implies, deconstructs familiar notions of the organism.

Throughout the critique it is maintained that there is great potential for the discovery of more analytically convenient units of cultural selection and evolution through the exploration of the old much-maligned route of 'artefacts as organisms', and populations thereof. But this time the old route should be explored on a very different set of premises; that artefacts, ideas, and behaviour patterns are not 'organisms' as such, but rather 'quasi-organismic' or 'viral' parasitic phenomena, competing for survival in a rich cognitive environment. As parasites, they may then prove to be benevolent, or malevolent; those which best promote their own replicative success through their transmission from person to person undergo differential reproductive success. The phrase 'from person to person' is particularly important, as it encapsulates the fact that human individuals remain significant in the equation – not as the units which are *selected* (as in genetic evolution), but as the units which select. People and their various fears and aspirations, along with their general repository of cultural phenomena, thus form the environment to which particular groups of ideas and artefacts adapt. This environment must therefore be given careful attention if the origin and reproductive success of any given behavioural and cultural phenomena are to be predicted or understood. Cultural Virus Theory is thus quite different from those 'traditional' culture historical, antiquarian, or diffusionist explanations (Renfrew & Bahn 1991: 407–9) usually indicated by the 'artefacts as organisms' phrase, in that the psychological and cultural conditions under which a particular cultural phenomenon undergoes differential reproduction are at least as important as the phenomenon itself. Moreover, unlike the above 'traditional' approaches, it is explicitly committed to the assertion that cultural process is fundamentally neo-Darwinian in every particular, and that all the apparently 'Lamarckian' aspects of cultural change are illusions which can be deconstructed into typical neo-Darwinian processes. This short description not withstanding, it is stressed that Cultural Virus principles are presented in this paper only in so far as they illuminate the critique of its primary alternative, the 'Inclusive Phenotype' perspective. Possible directions for a Cultural Virus Theory are presented in greater detail elsewhere (Cullen 1990; 1991; 1992; 1993a).

An overview of the neo-Darwinian resurgence

'Cultural Selectionism' may be defined as a neo-Darwinian approach to human behaviour which focuses on the extra-genetic survival and replication of culturally transmissible phenomena. This contrasts directly with the sociobiological focus on the survival and genetic replication of organisms. In other words, a true cultural selectionist is at least as interested in tracing the effects of a particular culture upon its own survival, as in tracing the effect that a culture might have upon the survival of the organisms which maintain it. Cultural variation is seen to be a product not of genetic selection, but of an intrinsic or purely cultural selective process. It is this basic element – the extension of neo-Darwinian principles into purely cultural contexts – which identifies the cultural selectionist, and differentiates his or her position from that of the sociobiologist.

Rindos makes the point in the following words (1985: 65):

> ... the mode of transmission of cultural characteristics ('the inheritance of acquired traits') is irrelevant to the applicability of a selectionist model for evolutionary change ... Darwinian selectionism requires undirected, heritable variation . . . The symbolic aspects of culture are not in any sense analogous to the genotype but rather functionally equivalent; because the capacity for symbolling is not directly adaptive, it provides the undirected variation required for a theory of selection-mediated cultural evolution.

Leonard & Jones express the position by coining the phrase 'replicative success', which allows them to avoid the genetic connotations they feel are inevitably associated with the phrase 'reproductive success' (1987: 214):

> Replicative success is a pragmatic construct. It implies neither mode of trait transmission, as reproductive success does, nor that some degree of selective advantage is conferred as a result of the transmission of a trait. Success is gauged as changes in the representation of traits through time.

There are other similar assertions (Bateson 1980: 160; Boyd & Richerson 1985: 173; Chen *et al.* 1982: 366; Dunnell 1980: 53; and Durham 1990: 188). Each position expresses the idea that the fundamental premise upon which Cultural Selectionism applies neo-Darwinian theory to culture is one of an analogy between two similar but independent processes. This is in dramatic contrast to Sociobiology's extension of neo-Darwinian principles to culture, which is based essentially on homology – on the explanation of human behaviour in terms of *genetic process itself*. To my knowledge, this fundamental distinction between Cultural Selectionism and Sociobiology is generally accepted by most anthropologists who have carried out research into neo-Darwinian theory, and the distinction is neatly articulated by Blute (1979: 57–8), Dunnell (1980: 52), Durham (1990: 193), and Rindos (1986b: 315).

Since Cultural Selectionism is by definition a theory of cultural change, selectionist cultural anthropology has the potential to be applied to any instance of cultural change in the archaeological record, just as any theory of genetic process is by default a potential explanatory framework for instances of change in the palaeontological record. In this way any example taken from the cultural selectionist literature, whether explicitly archaeological or not, could be considered as a potential explanatory framework for a temporal or spatial sequence of archaeological phenomena. Among the earliest explicitly cultural selectionist publications are the two papers of Campbell (1960; 1965), which Rindos brought to the attention of archaeologists in his book on the origins of agriculture (Rindos 1984). Other more recent examples are quite numerous, and are indeed not so rare as some anthropologists might think.

Against this general background, let us now proceed to consider the main purpose of this chapter: the Cultural Virus critique.

An introduction to the Cultural Virus critique

The Cultural Virus critique is directed at the general tendency of neo-Darwinian theory to consider the human body as a single phenotype, and the concomitant tendency to interpret all aspects of human endeavour as traits thereof. The problems created by the single phenotype perspective all relate to the implications of the genealogical independence of 'cultural traits', and the problems of defining categories such as 'the organism' and 'the phenotype' when confronted with a 'body' which is composed of independently inherited parts.

American Cultural Selectionism uses a set of interlinked assumptions which is referred to here as the 'Inclusive Phenotype' perspective, a set of assumptions which also pervade Sociobiology. Well-known authors of this tradition include Boyd & Richerson (1985), Cavalli-Sforza & Feldman (1981), Durham (1982; 1990), and Rindos (1980; 1984; 1985; 1986a; 1986b; 1989). A similar, but not identical, perspective is offered by Dunnell (1980), and by Leonard & Jones (1987). In grouping them together I am not trying to suppress or ignore the differences which may exist within American Cultural Selectionism, though it is not the intention here to consider these disputes in detail.

The persistence of the Inclusive Phenotype in any cultural selectionist perspective involves a kind of theoretical paradox. This presents itself most frequently in a tendency to explain cultural change or diversity in terms of a whole range of organism-based word categories. While Cultural Selectionism's distinguishing banner is the shifting of neo-Darwinian theory to a new context, in the American perspective it is a shift to a new mode of organismic inheritance, not a shift to a new class of genealogically independent phenomena. Human individuals remain the only 'organisms', 'individuals', or 'units of selection', although the evolution of 'cultures' (of the 'ethnic group' variety) now also attracts attention. Cultural phenomena are still treated as 'traits' of organisms, and together they make up the 'cultural phenotype' which differs from other traits and other parts of the phenotype only by 'mode' of inheritance. Cultural 'traits' and genetically reproduced 'traits' are thus treated as though they share a coherent, uniform genealogy, jointly comprising an individual organism in just the same way that genetically transmitted traits normally do. In its most extreme form, the evolution of this 'inclusive phenotype' is then explained and understood in terms of DNA-based modes of reproduction.

Even such fundamental words as 'evolution' and 'biology' reflect, at times, the persistence of an Inclusive Phenotype perspective formed around DNA-based modes of reproduction. This is still more common in Sociobiology. Lee (1991), for example, asserts that cultural phenomena can only 'evolve' and are only 'biological' to the extent to which they affect organismic fitness. They are not considered biological phenomena in their own right, evolving in a manner that affects their own cultural fitness. Lee defines the word 'biological' in the following words (1991: 207):

> The term "biological" can be limited to the genetical basis. Since, as we know, genes code for proteins and not behaviour, any genetic link with the evolution of human behaviour would be difficult to substantiate. But a more productive line of reasoning would be to define as "biological" those changes in the genetics, morphology and behaviour that increase the likelihood of an organism surviving and reproducing. Behaviour is thus not placed as some outlier or separate process, but rather integrated into the biology of the organism as a whole.

In Lee's view, then, behaviour is biological, not because of what it *is*, but because of what it *affects*. Behaviour is included in the discipline of biology because of its effect on organismic reproduction, rather than its effect upon its own reproduction along social conduits, or its material reality as a class of actions generated by learned neuronal structures.

Not only are cultural phenomena only biological to the extent that they affect organismic reproduction; only to this extent can they evolve. Thus Lee defines the word 'evolve' in a similar manner to her definition of the word 'biology' (1991: 208):

> We can ask if behaviour itself "evolves"? If, by evolve, we mean that behaviour which increases the relative success of an organism will itself increase in frequency over time, then the answer is yes. If we mean is it under single gene (or even gene complex) control, then the answer is

probably no in terms of complex behaviour. However, behaviour can be shown to play a role in genetic evolution (Boyd & Richerson 1985; Bateson 1988) despite the misgivings of some anthropologists (Ingold 1990). Thus behaviour itself provides the conditions for propagation of adaptive traits, as in mechanisms of female choice, mate selection or learning paradigms.

So while cultural selectionists clearly retreat from the sociobiological premise that genes have any primary effect on behaviour, they do not always retreat from the reverse position; behaviour can very definitely affect genetic fitness. Lee implies that this is the *primary* means through which it affects its *own* survival; thus we read 'behaviour which increases the relative success of an organism will itself increase in frequency over time'. Particular behaviour patterns or artefacts are seen to evolve like any other organismic trait; by affecting the survival of the organism which produces them. There is no discussion of the necessity for a behaviour pattern to somehow facilitate its own replication through the media of cultural transmission. Also implied is the idea that behaviour which does not affect organismic survival or reproduction cannot evolve. Thus learned behaviour patterns which have no effect on organismic survival neither exist as 'biological realities', nor evolve, if Lee's position is to be followed through (see Ingold 1991: 220 for a similar conclusion).

Such 'genetic survival-focused' definitions of the words 'biology' and 'evolution' are dramatic indicators of the persistence of the 'organism's point of view' in Cultural Selectionism. Cultural process is allowed to be a separate neo-Darwinian process to that which operates in genetics, so avoiding Sociobiology. Yet, ironically, organismic survival remains the most prominent and important survival process.

But the Inclusive Phenotype approach not only pervades the use of general words like 'biology' and 'evolution'; it also pervades the use of other key neo-Darwinian concepts. As already suggested in passing, humans remain the only 'individuals' in the approach. In fact, where the word is used it is normally a human individual which is being referred to, although this is generally taken for granted rather than explicitly discussed. Because of this, there is no possibility of defining a 'cultural individual' as a particular idea, or as a particular assemblage of artefacts, or as one copy of a religious text such as the Christian Bible. Instead, a cultural individual becomes all the culturally transmissible phenomena one person holds in their head.

Thus the only 'cultural individuals' in the American approach are those bodies of culture associated with particular human individuals; the only 'cultural phenotypes' are the bodies of culture associated with single human phenotypes; and the only cultural 'populations' are the bodies of culture associated with human populations. In other words, these categories are not the *logistical cultural equivalents* of the old organismic categories; they are merely the *physical cultural correspondents*. Cultural phenomena remain a class of human 'traits', in spite of the fact that they now have – by virtue of cultural transmission – genealogical independence. In other words, although cultural phenomena and human behaviour are not seen as under any sort of genetic control, discussion still concentrates on the effect of behaviour on organismic survival and reproduction; the social transmission of behaviour occurs, but is not the focus of attention. In the American cultural selectionist framework the fitness of the organism remains of fundamental relevance to the interpretation of cultural change, and this is reflected in the way that the words 'organism', 'individual' and 'population' are manipulated in the approach.

The goal of the present critique is to demonstrate that there are inherent inconsistencies in cultural selectionist concepts of *cultural* 'individuals' and *cultural* 'populations', and by inference all other selectionist principles which follow on from these concepts. The elucidation of these inconsistencies, however, will first require an examination of the way in which the concept of the 'individual' is normally used.

'Individuals' and 'populations' in Cultural Selectionism

The 'individual organism' is often said to be the cornerstone of neo-Darwinian theory, and so it is perhaps the most logical point at which to begin in the analysis of any variety of neo-Darwinian theory. Even major critiques of the idea of the 'individual organism' as the 'unit of selection', such as that by Dawkins (1976; 1982; 1986; 1989), can be thought of as *redefining* the concept of the 'individual' at a different level (i.e. that of the gene or 'piece of chromosome'), rather than rejecting it altogether. Drawing directly from neo-Darwinian orthodoxy on this issue (three of the sources most frequently referenced are Darwin 1859; and Mayr 1976; 1982), American Cultural Selectionism uses the human individual as its basic unit of selection, as does Sociobiology (e.g. Betzig 1986).

Integral to the concept of the 'individual' as the 'unit of selection' is the idea of the 'population' of individuals which 'evolves'. Individuals are selected, and, as a direct result, populations evolve. Speaking very broadly, it can also be said that the concept of a population of genes is, structurally speaking, not too different from a population of organisms. In other words, then, anything that is more or less indivisible, or that tends to remain undivided, may be considered to be an individual; a group of such phenomena might then qualify as a population. In each case the population evolves as a result of the differential reproductive success of its more or less undivided units. The question is, at what level does one choose to see 'indivisible units' being selected, and at what level do we see 'populations' of these units evolving?

Even at the level of the gene, where the concept of the 'individual unit of selection' is considered to be most applicable, the size and indivisibility of these units can vary from a single cistron (a piece of DNA which codes for a single protein), to the entire genome of an asexually reproducing organism. Thus Dawkins in different cases defines a 'gene' as 'a unit which survives through a large number of successive individual bodies' (1989: 25); as 'any portion of chromosomal material that potentially lasts for enough generations to serve as a unit of natural selection' (1989: 28); as 'not just one single physical bit of DNA . . . it is *all replicas* of a particular bit of DNA, distributed throughout the world' (1989: 88); and 'in the case of an asexual stick-insect, the entire genome (the set of all its genes) is a replicator' (Dawkins 1989: 273). Where there is no crossing-over between the chromosomes of a population, 'a whole chromosome would have to be regarded as one "gene"' (Dawkins 1989: 43). At times, the gene is even defined by Dawkins (1989: 182) as a virus – 'we might just as well regard ourselves as colonies of viruses! Some of them co-operate symbiotically, and travel from body to body in sperms and eggs. These are conventional "genes". Others live parasitically, and travel by whatever means they can.'

Dawkins's most elegant definition synthesises all of the above (1989: 33):

> I am using the word gene to mean a generic unit that is small enough to last for a large number of generations and to be distributed around in the form of many copies. This is not a rigid all-or-nothing definition, but a kind of fading out definition, like the definition of "big" or "old". The more likely a length of chromosome is to be split by crossing-over, or altered by mutations of various kinds, the less it qualifies to be called a gene in the sense in which I am using the term. A cistron presumably qualifies, but so also do larger units. . . . To be strict, this book should be called not The Selfish Cistron nor The Selfish Chromosome, but The slightly selfish big bit of chromosome and the even more selfish little bit of chromosome. . . .

Dawkins is even careful to exclude Mendelian 'discrete inheritance' from his units of selection (Dawkins 1989: 33–4):

> It was the great achievement of Gregor Mendel to show that hereditary units can be treated in practice as indivisible and independent particles. Nowadays we know that this is a little too simple. Even a cistron is occasionally divisible

and any two genes on the same chromosome are not wholly independent. What I have done is to define a gene as a unit which, to a high degree, approaches the ideal of indivisible particulateness. A gene is not indivisible, but seldom divided.

Despite well-constructed arguments to the effect that all units larger than the gene are 'like clouds in the sky or dust-storms in the desert . . . temporary aggregations or federations' (Dawkins 1989: 34), there is no doubt that Dawkins places great importance on the individual as a unit of analysis precisely because of, rather than in spite of, his understanding of the significance of genes. An 'organism's worth' of genes is a very significant higher category for the Dawkins model, since the genes in an organism 'leave the body in the same vehicle', namely in the haploid sex cells in the case of meiosis, or in whole diploid cells in the case of mitosis. Dawkins discusses the importance of the individual organism with reference to parasites and hosts (1989: 253–4); to wolves and wolf packs (1989: 255–66); and to the extended metaphor of teams of rowers (1989: 38–9, 84–6, 271–2). Far from being unimportant to Dawkins's selfish gene theory, the individual is a crucial unit of selection, since unlike higher ecological categories, it exhibits a degree of reproductive synchronicity, a measure of indivisibility. The gene is the basic 'replicator', while the organism is the basic 'vehicle'.

In contrast to Dawkins's position, American Cultural Selectionism focuses on the 'individual organism' or 'phenotype' as the unit of selection, whether in genetic or cultural evolution. In other words, neo-Darwinian theory is transferred from genetic process to cultural process, without any new definition of the 'individuals' involved. Human individuals remain the basic units which are selected, and populations of human individuals the basic entities which evolve, *even when the phenomena in question are entirely culturally transmitted*. Thus Rindos writes (1989: 7):

> Again following Boyd & Richerson (1985: 33), we may define culture (note, not necessarily human culture) as "information capable of affecting individuals' phenotypes which they acquire from other con-specifics by teaching or imitation". This definition implies that cultural transmission involves populations rather than individuals. Of course, it is the individual that learns culturally transmitted information, and individuals are selected in any evolutionary process, but it is the population that evolves (Ghiselin 1974; 1987; Hull 1976). Cultural traits, like genetic traits, evolve solely at the populational level. Since the culturally transmitted information that modifies phenotypes is heritable, the information possessed by the individuals in a population is capable of evolutionary change over time.

In other publications, Rindos makes it equally clear that he believes the individual phenotype is just as useful an analytical category for cultural process as it has always been in genetic process (consider Rindos 1985: 71–2; Rindos 1986b: 331). Boyd & Richerson share this view, and state the position succinctly in their 1985 comment on Rindos's paper (1985: 83):

> Natural Selection operates whenever (1) heritable variation exists and (2) the variation affects the life chances of individuals.

The individuals implied here are human organisms. But the real question is whether the cultural phenotypes of individual organisms are also the 'seldom divided' units of cultural selection. Clearly, they are not. If anything, the human cultural phenotype is even more often divided than the non-cultural phenotype. The latter are divided into halves during sexual reproduction, which may then be further divided when crossing over occurs between different chromosomes. But a typical human psyche is made up of countless thousands of separately transmissible ideas, concepts, and techniques. Any idea which can be taught or imitated in a single moment of comprehension, or in a series of interdependent moments of comprehension, must surely qualify as a 'cultural individual' far more rigorously than an entire human psyche (which in turn must correspond more closely to a cultural equivalent of a 'local faunal assemblage').

Of course, human individuals are the units which learn, but in doing so they are actually playing a completely different role to the one they play in genetic process. Human individuals are undoubtedly important in both processes, but while they are the *units of selection* in genetic process, they are the *units which select* in cultural process. Humans are thus the selectees in one process and the selectors in the other, playing utterly non-equivalent roles in each. Yet in American Cultural Selectionism, these non-equivalent roles are made equivalent, and human individuals become the basic units of selection in both processes, with culturally transmitted phenomena being viewed as 'traits' of the individual phenotype.

The possibility of treating artefacts as individual organisms in their own right is often discussed, as we shall see below. The problem is that in all the haste to prove the obvious – that artefacts are not organisms – the more modest possibility that they may be some sort of simple viral phenomenon is forgotten. This more subtle claim is never given any attention, as American cultural selectionists are under the impression that artefacts and learned behaviour patterns cannot be granted the status of neo-Darwinian individuals unless we attribute *all the qualities of fully-fledged self-reproducing organisms* to them. Viral status, as far as they are aware, is not enough. Leonard & Jones discuss the issue (with reference to Brew 1946) in the following words (1987: 215):

we still are faced with the fact that, with the exception of skeletal material, the objects and concepts of archaeology are not living organisms or parts of living organisms. Consequently, their development is not properly represented by a classificatory technique based on the genetic relationships of living organisms. But just the same, we ask if the skeletal material Brew refers to, or even the parts of living organisms, reproduces in a manner identical to that of an individual. It does not.

Here we see Leonard & Jones forced to espouse the idea of cultural phenomena being equivalent to other parts of the phenotype; and ignoring the fact that cultural phenomena are genealogically independent while all skeletal material is reproduced as a single blueprint during meiosis. This assumption of equivalence is the basis of the Inclusive Phenotype approach.

Once the possibility of treating artefacts as individual organisms is dismissed (see also Foley 1987a: 280), and the 'artefact's eye view' of adaptation is perceived as a blind alley, cultural phenomena have to be forced back into the human phenotype, or be excluded from the neo-Darwinian scheme. Since, according to Leonard & Jones, we know that artefacts are not organisms, we have to make them parts of others. How else could we fit them into a discourse which mentions the word 'organism' on virtually every page? Yet the 'genealogical independence' or 'reproductive asynchronicity' of culturally and genetically transmitted phenomena is undeniable; surely no one would seriously argue that cultural transmission cannot occur between genetically unrelated organisms. And reproductive synchronicity is perhaps the only tenable way to define a unit of selection (Dawkins 1989: 254–6). How can something that is not a unit of reproduction possibly be a unit of *differential* reproduction (selection)? The 'artefacts as traits or organisms' issue is thus a serious dilemma for the American cultural selectionist tradition.

On a closer examination, however, it can be seen that the very phrase 'artefacts as organisms' is really a *reductio ad absurdum*. The very idea that an artefact might be equivalent to a cow or a human being is inherently ridiculous, and does no justice to the very real theoretical potential of the position to which the words refer. Yet this reduction of the artefactual viewpoint to the absurd has been very successful, and few people are aware that a status as simple viral phenomena is quite sufficient to grant artefacts (or perhaps more properly assemblages) full standing as 'individuals' within neo-Darwinian theory. If we remain unaware of this, the only route left is to classify artefacts as some kind of human trait.

Cultural selectionists have often, therefore, agonised over the 'complexity' of cultural inheritance, trying to show how it is really just another dimension of organismic inheritance, and ignoring the implications of genealogical independence. Rindos (1985: 72) has discussed this issue with reference to an oft-quoted passage from Levi-Strauss (1963):

> ... what makes [evolutionary genetics] valid for the historian is the fact that a horse indeed begets a horse and that, in the course of a sufficient number of generations, *Equus caballus* is the true descendant of Hipparion. The historical validity of the naturalist's reconstruction is granted . . . by the biological fact of reproduction. An axe, on the contrary, does not generate another axe. There will always be a basic difference between the two [tools] . . . because each of them is the product of a system of representation" (Levi-Strauss 1963: 4). Yet neither does an axe generate itself. It is made by a human under the instruction of other humans by means of a culturally transmitted symbolic system. This system, with its products, is passed from generation to generation and from person to person.

Levi-Strauss thus offers a similar challenge to that which Brew offered Leonard & Jones above, and Rindos counters in the same way as Leonard & Jones. Predictably, the genealogical conflicts of genetic and cultural inheritance are down-played, while equivalence is emphasised. The peculiarities of cultural inheritance are dismissed as being merely more complicated than other traits, rather than qualitatively different owing to their unique quality of genealogical independence. A third example of this need to assert the equivalence of cultural phenomena and true organismic traits makes use of a comparison of axes and fingers – thus Dunnell has written, when commenting on Rindos's words (Dunnell 1985: 79):

> ... in noting, as others have done before, that axes don't make axes he seems to be contrasting cultural and genetic evolution. Yet just as clearly as axes don't make axes, neither do fingers make fingers. To get another finger, one has to go through the genome and then translation into a new phenotypic finger. Getting an axe from another axe does not seem so terribly different. More generally, I am led by these kinds of non-contrasts to suspect Rindos's CS2 selection [of cultural phenomena by cultural phenomena] is not nearly as contrastive as his expository form suggests. What differs between cultural and genetic systems is that the selection Rindos identifies as CS2 takes place in the poorly understood and observationally obscure translation from genotype to phenotype in the genetic case. These same processes are much more readily observed in the cultural transmission case because the process of phenotypic development is more obvious.

Dunnell implies that the passage from axe to axe can actually be traced via the human genome – in a complicated manner, but ultimately in a manner no different to that of fingers, and this is where he is patently wrong. Fingers do go through the genome, but axes don't; knowledge of axe-making, like any other parasite, can pass directly between unrelated people, presumably from master to apprentice in the blacksmith's forge, through the media of language, demonstration and imitation. No cellular division or genetic replication takes place, and so it is indeed 'terribly different' to the reproduction of fingers. But Dunnell manages to assert equivalence all the same.

According to American Cultural Selectionism, therefore, cultural phenomena must assume the status of traits of the human phenotype, and cannot be granted the status of 'individuals' in their own right, since they lack the capacity to self-reproduce. What fails to be noted is that like cultural phenomena, microbial viruses also lack this capacity – being unable to reproduce themselves within their own cellular structures, which are at best only simple envelopes, they must instead inject their genetic material into another more complex cell. Yet they are still treated as 'individuals' and as units of selection, and classified on the basis of their phylogenetic relationships, although this is fraught with difficulty (Fenner *et al.* 1974: 1–33; Postgate 1989: 40–44; see also Dawkins's comparison of genes and viral entities 1989: 182; and e.g. Sonea 1988: 38–56). As far as the neo-Darwinian individuality of ideas and artefacts is concerned, neither inanimacy nor reproductive dependence are grounds for disqualification. Artefacts can be considered as individuals (and therefore 'quasi-organisms', or 'viral phenomena'), without attributing anything more to them than the genealogical independence they undoubtedly display.

The 'human-megalith' and 'squirrel-oak' fallacy

Aspects of Cultural Virus Theory are discussed more fully elsewhere (Cullen 1990; 1991; 1992; 1993a), but I should like here to present a brief summary of the Virus Theory, and an illustration of its analytical advantages over an Inclusive Phenotype approach. This illustration makes reference to one of the commonest stamping grounds of new theories – the explanation of megaliths. European megaliths have frequently been used as archaeological archetypes for the comparison of different theoretical perspectives (Renfrew & Bahn 1991: 428–9; Hodder 1992b: 45–80). However, it will quickly become clear that neither the Inclusive Phenotype nor the Virus varieties of Cultural Selectionism compete directly with recent accounts of such phenomena. Rather, they compete with each other, and with other stated or unstated general theories of culture, at a more general level of culture theory. They are the fundamental explanatory frameworks within which relatively specific explanatory packages such as post-processualism or cognitive-processualism may choose, or choose not, to align themselves. Neo-Darwinian theories are not concerned to determine *which* factors cause a particular outcome, but with the more general problem of the *very means by which* any and all such factors take effect. For this reason, megaliths are used here only as hypothetical archetypes, and the issues discussed are entirely different to those normally presented in megalith discourse.

The aim is to show that the widely held Inclusive Phenotype view, conflating culturally and genetically reproduced phenomena into a single human phenotype, is analytically awkward; but that this awkwardness escapes our notice owing to the complicated nature of cultural inheritance. Yet as soon as we transfer the essential problems of the Inclusive Phenotype into a more familiar biological context, the awkwardness becomes readily apparent. For the purpose of simplicity and familiarity, this point will be pursued with reference to two of the most ubiquitous organisms of Northern Hemisphere universities: squirrels and oaks. Yet the example would apply equally well to other mammal/tree relationships, such as that between koalas and gum trees in Australia. The general objective is to show that the inclusion of megaliths in the human phenotype is every bit as confusing and counterproductive as the hypothetical inclusion of oaks in the squirrel phenotype.

First, a short description of the squirrel/oak relationship. Let us imagine that there are two neighbouring forests, one composed of white oaks (*Quercus alba*), the other composed of red oaks (*Quercus rubra*). Let us imagine, again for simplicity, that the red oak forest is inhabited by red squirrels (*Sciurus vulgaris*), and the white oak forest is inhabited by grey squirrels (*Sciurus carolinensis*). Let us imagine that both squirrels eat the acorns of their respective oaks, and also engage in the practice of storing for the winter by burying some of the acorns they find, many of them beyond the borders of the shaded area below the tree. Some acorns are forgotten, and are left behind to germinate in the spring, conveniently buried in positions favourable for successful growth. On the other hand, the squirrels rely on the oaks as places in which to shelter from predators, places in which to build their nests and reproduce, and as a ready supply of nutritious food. Thus in each forest, a particular species of squirrel and a particular species of oak have a close co-evolutionary relationship.

Second, a short description of the human/megalith relationship. Let us imagine that there are two neighbouring groups of people, one of which builds Neolithic chambered tombs, while the other buries their dead using ritualised cremation. Obviously, tombs and cremation rituals are reproduced via human activity, and so are every bit as dependent upon humans for their successful reproduction as the oaks are dependent upon squirrels. On the other hand, the tombs have great significance in their respective cultural contexts. On the one hand they might well provide a range of functional benefits, such as legitimating land ownership of the society as a whole, or legitimating the special rights of a social élite; the kinds of factors which might be emphasised in a processual or neo-Marxist explanation (Renfrew & Bahn 1991: 429). The megaliths might also sustain appeal due to their symbolic significance within the local cultural traditions of western Europe, by 'objectifying and giving meaning to social strategies' in the way that Hodder has remarked (1992b: 75).

As far as the competing neo-Darwinian accounts of culture are concerned, however, the question is not which of these factors are most important, but whether the megaliths can reasonably be included in the human phenotype. A Cultural Virus model of the megalith-building tradition would say that it cannot. A Virus account would consider the megaliths to be phenotypes in and of themselves, extrasomatic expressions of a lineage of socially transmitted learned neuronal structures (similar to a Dawkins 'Meme complex': 1989: 197–9), which have 'actual physical existence' in the nervous systems of people (Dawkins 1989: 323; Delius 1989: 46; 1991: 83; Edelman 1989; 1992) and which display genealogical independence from the human phenotypes in which they reside. These neuronal structures are a set of inter-related ideas which jointly convey to their bearers the capacity to build megaliths. In other words, they constitute a body of knowledge of the various techniques of megalith construction which must be socially transmitted in order to survive. Whether there ever actually were specialised megalith artisans, or whether megalithic techniques were distributed more indiscriminately amongst the community, will probably never be known. The real problem for the Inclusive Phenotype position is the genealogical independence of the tombs; which means that megalith-building does not need to increase the reproductive success of megalith artisans in order to reproduce itself. It could even survive if the artisans were a celibate caste with zero genetic fitness. If the demand for the building of new megaliths is sufficient, megalith-building could continue to pass to new apprentices from genetically successful non-artisan families for an indefinite period of time. Moreover, the demand for the megaliths is governed not by actual benefit, but by perceived benefit; the social context of the megaliths may well lead to a situation where their value for controlling reproductive and productive resources is vastly overvalued. But megalith cultural fitness can only be defined in relation to what is perceived, and not in relation to what is.

A neo-Darwinian account would have to reject any notion of the megaliths being generated in a Lamarckian manner through a rational response to the needs of human societies, or to those of powerful factions within the society, as some processual explanations would seem to imply. The first architectural blueprint which could truly be called a megalith would have had to occur as a result of a spontaneous divergence from a pre-existing body of constructional concepts, most of which would presumably remain unchanged. A good candidate for the immediate cultural ancestor of the megalith could well be the central European long house, given the similarities discussed by Hodder (1990: 141–77) and others. Once invented, the megaliths could then prove to be symbolically adapted to the perceived needs of local and neighbouring communities, and undergo differential cultural reproduction at the expense of other burial practices for these reasons. This would not be a symmetrical and unstructured process of random diffusion, but a highly structured displacement of one burial practice by another, caused by the greater symbolic fitness of the megalith form under local conditions of increasingly restricted resources.

There are many ways in which an Inclusive Phenotype model could be contrasted with a Virus one through these two examples. Let us suppose that a postgraduate student in a biology department decided to devote his or her thesis to the study of the ecology of squirrels and oaks and their symbiotic relationships, and that the researcher discovered a remarkable fact; that only acorns which had been briefly nibbled or handled by squirrels were capable of germination. Imagine that the researcher is so excited by the close evolutionary relationship, that he or she proposes a new model for interpreting the evolution of squirrels and oaks. The whole idea of separating squirrels and oaks is seen to be misguided; the researcher believes that an exciting new example of an 'evolutionary merger' has been found, and from now on insists on speaking of a single organism, the 'squirreloak', whose phenotype includes both the mobile squirrels and the oaks amongst which they live. No longer are squirrels adapting to oaks (amongst other forest conditions), and oaks to squirrels; the researcher feels that it is more accurate to think of squirreloaks adapting in unison to the rest of the forest.

It is intuitively easy to see that it would be unlikely that the thesis would be favourably received. But why? There are many issues, and a specialist in evolutionary biology could no doubt elucidate them more effectively. But I think the key issue is the fact that different parts of the squirreloak display genealogical independence. It is obvious that an oak could never be considered to be a true squirrel organ since the two structures, despite their symbiotic dependence, are genealogically independent of each other. Squirrels and oaks reproduce independently of each other, and indeed exist independently of each other. One may find squirrels without oaks and oaks without squirrels. But even in forests well populated with both squirrels and oaks, there is no guarantee that the offspring of a given pair of squirrels will build their drey in the oak trees that their parents helped to germinate. The grey squirrels in the white oak forest may well, indeed, become so successful as to displace the red squirrels in the neighbouring red oak forest, in which case none of the red oaks would be inhabited by the offspring of the squirrels which buried the relevant acorns.

Dawkins (1982; 1989: 240–42) has analysed the essential difference between parasites inhabiting the body and other structures we interpret as organs, and identified the essential difference between the two. The key characteristic of a parasitic structure is that it is not passed on in the germ cells of its host, but is passed on by other means. Such circumstances do not guarantee that the parasite will exploit its host, but they make exploitation possible, as the parasite can escape its host and go on to infect new unrelated hosts. Conversely, the host's offspring may be infected by other parasites, unrelated to those which inhabit the host itself. What is adaptive for a parasite may not be adaptive for its host, and *vice versa*.

Organs and traits, on the other hand, are structures which are reproduced together; the information which allows their synthesis travels between generations in the germ cells. Since they are reproduced together, such structures cannot escape the lineages in which they currently reside; an organ or trait which inhibits the reproductive success of the body in which it resides also inhibits its own survival. What is adaptive for a trait is adaptive for its host, and *vice versa*. Parasites which are transmitted from generation to generation in the germ cells of their hosts, on the basis of this argument (Dawkins 1989: 243), are virtually indistinguishable from traits, organs, or organelles, and indeed they may become just that. Such an argument has been advanced, for example, for the origin of cellular organelles such as mitochondria (Margulis 1981). In fact, the definition of the organism as a group of structures which are collectively reproduced would appear to be not only a necessary condition, but a sufficient one. It is very hard to define an organism as anything other than a symbiotic assemblage of structures which are reproduced via the same means and at the same time (Dawkins 1989: 182).

We are now equipped with a convenient set of concepts with which to elucidate the problems of viewing cultural phenomena as a class of human traits or organs. True individuals are structural combinations which reproduce together; host/parasite or host/guest structural combinations are those which consist of parts which reproduce at different times and via different means. An Inclusive Phenotype view of culture would classify megaliths as part of the human phenotype, and therefore view Neolithic prehistory in terms of individual humanmegaliths with combined phenotypes of bone and stone, jointly adapting to prevailing ecological and social conditions. The cultural transmission of megalith construction may not always be to the genetic advantage of the people involved, but when this occurs megaliths are viewed as maladaptive traits, rather than as adaptive parasites. This is as misleading as viewing an oak which inhibits squirrel reproduction, but promotes its own reproduction, as a maladaptive squirreloak trait, rather than as an adapted oak. The illusion of maladaptedness is purely an artefact of the insistence of assessing fitness at the level of the inclusive phenotype of the squirreloak, rather than at the level of individual oaks and squirrels. The humanmegalith, like the squirreloak, is a false individual which consists of separately reproduced parts, and what is adaptive for one part may not be adaptive for the other.

But false individuals do not only cause problems for the assessment of fitness and the manipulation of concepts of selection and adaptation. More insidious problems emerge when attempts are made to define *populations* of false individuals. The populations of megaliths and humans do not coincide; they are not sympatric. While the gene pools of the megalith builders may well merge with peoples who build central European long houses, and indeed with those of western Asia, the megaliths themselves are confined almost exclusively to western Europe (Hodder 1990). Moreover, the social transmission of megalith techniques could well have involved a degree of specialisation in knowledge acquisition, a class of 'megalith artisans', and so many members of a community might have little or no knowledge of megalith construction. The question is whether individuals who do not possess any of the neuronal structures for megalith-building should be included in the megalith population just because they share a common gene pool with the tomb-builders. In a Cultural Virus approach the megalith population consists of no more, and no less, than the megaliths themselves, and their attendant neuronal structures of megalith techniques. On the other hand, the Inclusive Phenotype approach, which implies a humanmegalith phenotype, becomes awkward when humans are found without megaliths, or when megaliths are found with completely different cultures or people. Are such individuals to be classified as megalithless humanmegaliths? This would be as taxonomically awkward as a biology which classified oaks, squirrels, and squirrel/oak combinations as three different species of squirreloaks: squirrelless-squirreloaks, oakless-squirreloaks, and standard squirreloaks. A squirrel could alter its taxonomy simply by jumping to another sort of tree. The only way to avoid such conceptual nightmares is to restrict taxonomy to individuals which are seldom divided; in other words to allow single phenotypes to include only those elements which are reproduced together.

Cultural Virus Theory and the 'whole culture' concept

One concept which reflects the American cultural selectionist focus on the human individual is the use of the whole 'culture' (in the 'ethnic group' sense) as the basic unit in which cultural evolution occurs. In other words, the 'culture' operates (implicitly) as the nearest cultural equivalent to a neo-Darwinian population, since it so often corresponds to a human population. Durham provides a quintessential example of the explicit use of the 'culture' as the basic kind of evolving cultural phenomenon, in a section of his 1990 overview of Cultural Selectionism entitled 'What evolutionary culture theory is' (1990: 190):

> Evolutionary culture theory (ECT) is a collection of arguments seeking to explain the "descent with modification" of human cultures. It is, in a word, a theory of cultural phylogeny. It seeks answers to questions like the following: What are the predominant mechanisms of cultural change? How does a new culture get started? How and why does an existing culture assimilate or die out? What is the particular historical branching pattern or "cladogram" of human cultures? And why have there emerged so many different cultures in the course of the human career?

Since this 'whole culture' concept, and the related but distinct 'society as an organism' concept, have been integral parts of non-Darwinian philosophies, such as those of Spencer (Rindos 1985: 66–9) and of Durkheim (Betzig 1986: 67–9), its almost monolithic persistence in Cultural Selectionism would seem to be somewhat counterintuitive. It is all the more unexpected when one is reminded of the fact that the validity of any given category of analysis in neo-Darwinian theory essentially depends upon its having some relationship to units of reproduction or transmission. Yet few would argue that the 'culture' is a unit of transmission, since it is far too large to be comprehended and reproduced all at once.

The persistence of the 'whole cultural system' concept in Cultural Selectionism can, however, be explained as a by-product of the use of 'human individual cultural phenotypes' as the units of cultural selection. An approach which uses human individuals as the units of selection will view human populations as the entities which evolve. Correspondingly, any approach to culture which uses the human individual (its cultural phenotype) as its basic unit of selection would use populations of those human cultural phenotypes as their basic evolving entity. A human 'culture', then, seems to be used in Cultural Selectionism as the nearest cultural correspondent to a population. If a 'culture' is a population of human cultural phenotypes, one would expect that selection can occur within it, and this is indeed the case. Rindos expresses this idea when discussing his distinction between 'demic cultural selection' – where the human group associated with a culture undergoes differential reproductive success in relation to other groups, owing to genetic advantages conveyed to them by their cultural tradition; and 'symbolic cultural selection' – where ideas are selected within a culture on the grounds of 'enculturated rules of meaningfulness'. Thus the second process produces selection within a 'culture' (Rindos 1986b: 321):

> Another reason for clearly demarcating cultural and natural selection is that a second kind of selection occurs within the cultural system. This process will be intimately related to any demographic effects arising from variation in cultural behaviour. Cultural selection of the second kind is more concerned with processes governing the generation, interaction, and selection of traits within a given culture. This "internal" or "symbolic" selection has certain formal similarities to the concept of "transmission biases" as used by Cavalli-Sforza & Feldman (1981) or Boyd & Richerson (1985). It differs in that the variant forms that a symbolic system generates will be so numerous and, initially at least, so highly randomised in terms of the selective pressures existing within the society that selection within the system (perceived according to enculturated rules of meaningfulness by the members of that culture) will be more important than the specific nature of a transmission bias in determining the direction cultural evolution will take.

At least at the superficial level, it appears that there might be some connection between the use of the 'whole culture' concept, and the idea that human behaviour must be considered part of the human phenotype. A culture usually corresponds to some kind of human population; logically, then, any framework which employs the human individual 'cultural phenotype' as its unit of selection, would use the 'cultural population' as its evolving entity. These 'cultural populations' are presumably the 'cultures' which form the unit of analysis. The 'culture' is the cultural entity which most closely corresponds to a human population, and is therefore another indirect corollary of the Inclusive Phenotype perspective.

But once the human individual is rejected as the basic unit of cultural selection, and the viral neuronal structure put in its place, a very different 'cultural population' is implied. The cultural population is defined on a much smaller scale; it may even, at times, exist in the head of a single individual. Groups of ideas, defined on the basis of similarity, become the most appropriate level at which to define the cultural 'population'. In other words, a whole 'culture' then consists of hundreds of different populations of different 'species' (used very loosely) of viral neuronal structures (or ideas), each of them distributed throughout some subset of the human individuals of a community. Once it is recognised that a human cultural phenotype is not a unit of cultural reproduction, we can likewise say that a human 'culture' is not a cultural 'population', but a vast ecological assemblage of many different kinds of cultural populations, some of which are best classified into a series of sympatric and allopatric populations distributed to varying extents within the larger 'culture'. At the other extreme, we can remark that at times a single mind might contain a whole 'population' of ideas, consisting of the awareness of, say, a dozen different definitions of the word 'dialectic', in a community where no other individual had any awareness of that concept. We may conclude that the analytical use of 'whole cultures' as the basic cultural population is an awkward and unfaithful 'cultural equivalent' of the neo-Darwinian population.

Conclusion

The nature of the neo-Darwinian resurgence can be better understood through the identification of two paths of 'philosophical divergence' which have occurred in its relatively short history. On the one hand we have the major distinction between Sociobiology and Cultural Selectionism (Blute 1979; Cullen 1990; Rindos 1986b), and on the other hand we have the secondary divergence which exists *within* Cultural Selectionism between the 'Inclusive Phenotype' position which predominates in American Cultural Selectionism, and the Cultural Virus position. It is this secondary divergence which has been the focus of the paper, which has taken the form of a critique of the Inclusive Phenotype position from the point of view of the Cultural Virus position.

　　The basic goal has been to show that there are very significant structural differences between the two cultural selectionist positions, and that these differences cannot be ignored by anyone hoping to use – or understand – modern neo-Darwinian culture theory. Most importantly, the Cultural Virus critique of Cultural Selectionism highlights the fact that neo-Darwinian anthropologists and archaeologists may be employing wholly inappropriate

Part two

Heritage constraint
and the Cultural Virus Theory

6
Heritage constraint in cultural phenomena

Editors' note and overview

In the middle section of his PhD thesis, Ben Cullen illustrates the principles of selection and of heritage constraint in Darwinian systems using three sets of data. The length of this section of the thesis prevents it from being reproduced here in its entirety. Instead, we have only summarised the key points from the first two chapters of this section, since they provide a link between the preceding critique of Darwinian alternatives to the Cultural Virus Theory and the subsequent outline of that theory itself. The final chapter of this section, in which Cullen demonstrates that cultural data show the pattern expected from a neo-Darwinian system, we reproduce at greater length. Readers wishing for a fuller treatment may consult the full text of the thesis itself (Cullen 1993a).

In chapter 6 of his thesis (1993a), Cullen demonstrates the importance of phylogenetic constraint as a signature of neo-Darwinian processes. If the evolution of form proceeds by natural selection acting on heritable variation, then the outcome of a selective process will reflect not only the nature of the selective environment, but also the effects of the founder population's composition, of the length and degree of its subsequent isolation, and of drift. He demonstrates this point using Howells's data-set of cranial measurements from a large series of human skulls from around the world. Cullen uses Principal Components Analysis (Wright 1989) to identify the patterns of covariance among 33 metric variables, taken as indicators of shape variation. He then plots the crania by geographical region in relation to the second and third principal components identified in his statistical analysis (the first principal component is less informative about shape variation, being more a reflection of variation in size). These graphs show clearly that human skulls from populations of distinct regions of the world tend to cluster in specific areas of the overall scatter-plot. For example, Figures 4 (page 121) and 8 (page 125) (from Cullen 1993a) show the distributions of crania respectively of sub-Saharan African and of European individuals in Howells's sample: they are clearly visible as constrained clusters within the overall sample, as plotted in this 'shape space'. Cullen demonstrates that such patterns are non-random, and proposes that they reflect both selection and heritage constraint due to the restricted variation that characterised each such region's founding population. He argues that if analysis of spatial patterning and diversity in cultural data show similar constraints of ancestry, then this would support his argument that cultural change is a fundamentally selective process acting on heritable variation.

Next, however, Cullen demonstrates in chapter 7 of his thesis the properties of a Lamarckian system. In such a system, traits either appear immediately in response to prevailing needs (which are environmentally determined), or they evolve intrinsically to greater complexity. In either case, forms will converge to the same end-product in analogous environments, either because of common determining environmental factors, or because of a common intrinsic tendency to increase in complexity. In neither case will the pattern of evolution of forms be constrained by the extent of heritable, pre-existing variation in a population. As Cullen has already shown in earlier chapters, this is the Lamarckian system which is implicit in Cultural Evolutionism (which is both progressionist and environmentally determinist), and also in Cultural Sociobiology (which involves a form of environmental determinism).

He analyses data on the environments of 157 human societies of the world, from Douglas White's MapTab demonstration diskette (White 1989), and demonstrates that environmental variability is as great within continents or regions as it is on a global scale (when environments are defined by ten variables, including dryness, agricultural potential, population density, vegetation structure, and latitude). Thus, for instance, in his biplot of the fourth and fifth principal components of this environmental data-set (Figure 5) the distribution of African environments spans most of the existing variability in global human environments in these dimensions. Cullen points out the contrast with the biplots of human cranial shape variation, in which individuals from populations in different regions cluster in constrained regions of the overall scatter. The lack of an effect of spatial proximity on environmental variability within, as opposed to between, continents reflects the way in which environments evolve towards similar forms as a result of common external physical constraints – thus at this gross level, environments vary in the manner of a Lamarckian system without heritage constraint. By contrast, the evidence of an effect of spatial proximity on form in the data-set of human skull measurements shows that human skull form has evolved through a neo-Darwinian process of selection acting on a constrained subset of the pre-existing, heritable variation in the species as a whole. Cullen's next step is to analyse global patterns of human cultural variation, to discern the evolutionary system to which they most closely correspond.

Heritage constraint pervades many levels

In Cullen (1993a; and as summarized above) geographical and biogeographical data were examined in order to illustrate the basic signatures left by selective process in living systems, and also the basic signatures which might be expected in the absence of that process. The patterns brought out in the analysis of human crania can be considered to be basically the same as those patterns intuitively described by Darwin during the voyage of *The Beagle*, but on the scale of a single species rather that of whole faunal and floral assemblages. Human crania were shown to display the same basic pattern of 'descent with modification' as that which pervades the biogeography of other organisms. Moreover, since all the human crania were, by definition, members of the same species, the phylogenetic heritage constraint which emerged in the analysis was thereby demonstrated to exist within one species, and indeed one sub-species; and therefore within one of the most specific levels of biological taxonomy. When we couple this fact with the generally accepted notion of intercontinental phylogenetic constraints, at the family level and above (for example: Ceboid monkeys are only found in South America; Cercopithecoids are only found in the Old World; Prosimians are found primarily on Madagascar; there are no primates whatsoever in Australia; etc.), it becomes clear that phylogenetic constraint is a general quality of many levels of selective systems.

The all-pervading nature of heritage constraint is due to the fact that selective pressures have no direct influence on the course of mutation. We find very different crania in similar environments, and very similar crania in different environments, precisely because those environments are not *determining* (as they would be in a Lamarckian process) cranial shape. Rather, various environmental factors exert a selective pressure, which only produces differential reproductive success of some *existing* traits at the expense of other existing traits. Even if a human population was subjected to a set of selective pressures for which a kangaroo was the perfect adaptation, it is doubtful whether a form which even remotely resembled a kangaroo would emerge. Each human population has a unique phylogenetic heritage, and therefore offers a unique suite of diverse forms (and derivative mutations) to those similar selective forces.

This same principle (for an additional example) is embodied in the forms of the dominant herbivores which Darwin encountered during his voyage. Large herbivores such as kangaroos, zebras, donkeys, horses, antelopes, deer, bison, camels and llamas can all be found in very similar grassland or open woodland environments. Moreover, they are often reliant upon similar food resources, and hunted by broadly similar predators such as dogs and cats. So their considerable diversity cannot be purely due to selective pressures. A marsupial gene pool will 'throw up' very different derivative mutations to an antelope gene pool, which would be different again to the mutations 'thrown up' by a camel (llama) gene pool, and so on. Each population has a unique phylogenetic heritage which constrains the forms that animals can take in that population.

Thus it can be established – with reference to Freeman's exhaustive historical analysis of nineteenth-century evolutionary theory (Freeman 1974), and the work of Desmond & Moore (1992) – that the 'descent-based' *empirical* contribution of Darwin's voyage and indeed other 'descent-based' descriptive work was crucial in the ultimate 'switch' from Lamarckian to neo-Darwinian orthodoxy (see Cullen 1993a: chapter 6). Darwin's claim to the establishment of Selectionism in biology lies not so much in some special claim to precedence (although there are elements of this in his work), but in the immense empirical and interpretative contribution made during his voyage and later life. Ultimately, it was Darwin's voyage around the world (and his exhaustive monographs such as those on barnacles) which enabled the wide-ranging demonstration of the pervasive tendency towards 'descent with modification' in biological systems, a pattern which in turn exemplifies the fact that Natural Selection does not wholly erase an organism's ancestry.

In light of this it is curious that no corresponding account of cultural phenomena has really been achieved, or at least not systematically evoked in support of Cultural Selectionism. By this I mean that while a number of programmatic statements about the neo-Darwinian nature of cultural process have been made, there has not, to my knowledge, been any corresponding attempt to demonstrate the pervasive occurrence of heritage constraint in some synthesised, globally distributed set of cultural phenomena, nor to point out the significance of this underlying pattern for suggesting the existence of some selective dynamic which is intrinsic to cultural process. Studies which do synthesise cultural data on a global geographic scale, or over immense chronological time-scales, such as Cavalli-Sforza (1991), Cavalli-Sforza *et al.* (1988) or Foley (1987a), do not draw out the implications of the selective patterns in culture *for the nature of cultural process itself.* Rather, they employ the cultural data concerned to elucidate or embellish certain primary arguments made in the papers about genetic process. Moreover, the above studies seek to inter-relate genetically and culturally inherited data, rather than to focus exclusively upon the intrinsic patterns of the cultural data, as will be attempted below. Other studies, such as Durham (1990), link cultural descent with Cultural Selectionism, but below an explicit attempt is made to advance cultural heritage constraint as a ubiquitous verification for Cultural Selectionism, and as a refutation of competing accounts of cultural change.

The many attempts to advance the cause of a selective model of cultural process (i.e. those of chapters 4 and 5) all lack what could be considered the most vital component; some cultural equivalent of the voyage of *The Beagle* and its resulting globally distributed biogeographic data. The equivalent act for anthropology would have been a similar voyage, probably around the same time or earlier, in which cultural phenomena, not organisms, were the focus of attention. Some cultural observations were, of course, taken down during Darwin's voyage; for an interesting example consider his comparison of the Gauchos of eastern South America and the Guasos of Chile (Darwin 1889: 258–9). Another more famous example would his detailed description of the Tierra del Fuegians (Darwin 1889: 212–16, 218–30). For a variety of reasons which I will not delve into, however, these observations did not lead Darwin to elucidate a 'Theory of Cultural Selection' to lay alongside his Theory of Natural Selection.

Such voyages, whether they be organismic or cultural in focus, would no longer yield simple, geographically defined 'ecounits' of common heritage. Large amounts of colonisation and cross-colonisation have now occurred in faunal, floral and cultural systems, such that geography no longer closely correlates with phylogenetic heritage. Even if a modern Darwin were to march thousands of kilometres into central Australia he would find as many European artefacts and ideas as he would donkeys, horses, camels and pigs. In other words, the Australian faunal assemblage would not appear to be as distinctive in the eyes of an explorer as it did in Darwin's day, given that it now includes so many Old-World placentals. It is not just indigenous *cultural* assemblages which have been invaded, and made to include structures of European origin.

Biogeography no longer directly reflects phylogenetic heritage, or at least not in the simple linear sense that it once did. Colonisation has by no means been symmetrical – different places have had very different colonising inputs – but without some general knowledge of the history of world colonisation, a voyage around the world would yield some very peculiar biogeography, and, for that matter, some very peculiar ethnography.

If anything, this problem would be the cause of even more confusion in the course of a *culturally* focused voyage. What would a modern ethnographer sailing down the coast of the Americas make of the mixed-up sequence of Amerindian, western European, eastern European, Asian and west African cultural phenomena he or she observed, without being privy to a great deal of historical information? Thus it can be said with some certainty that there can now never be an exact equivalent of a 'Darwin of cultural fields of enquiry', in so far as there can never be a re-enactment of a cultural equivalent of the voyage of *The Beagle*.

Heritage constraint in the Standard Cross-Cultural Sample

While in some sense a cultural equivalent of Darwin's voyage would now be too late, in another sense it is no longer necessary. In over a century of ethnographic description and interpretation, anthropologists have amassed far more information about the world's diverse cultural phenomena than one person could ever collect in a single voyage. So a voyage is not what we need – we have instead a plethora of notes, produced by different people for a variety of different reasons; the problem is more akin to a post-voyage compilation and synthesis. The body of notes to be synthesised is so vast and recorded in so many different forms, however, that analysing and co-ordinating the data is perhaps beyond the capacity of any unaided human being. It is important to remember that heritage constraint does not have to be singular to exist; a society may have a number of different influences in its history, but it is still jointly constrained by its joint heritage. It will be important, however, to arrive at a method by means of which the primary origins and/or influences involved in a given society's history may be estimated with reasonable reliability.

The use of computers makes it possible to review large bodies of data with great speed and accuracy. The basic 'descent with modification' or 'phylogenetic heritage constraint' pattern was quickly and economically elucidated from a database of 2500 crania with the aid of the Principal Components variety of multivariate analysis, and this pattern appeared to emerge again and again when the analysis was repeated with smaller and smaller numbers of variables. Such computer analysis would presumably have been an incredible advantage to any nineteenth-century biologist wanting to find latent structure in a vast body of faunal or floral descriptions, as this form of analysis makes it possible to 'see' complex structure in huge bodies of data. A *Beagle* voyage through ethnography is no longer possible, but multivariate analysis should at least allow us to contemplate the patterns in cultural data at a very general level.

The task is not so much to 'prove' that heritage constraint exists in assemblages of cultural phenomena, as assumptions of local heritage constraint in regional archaeological or ethnographic sequences are already implicit in anthropological 'practice' at the descriptive level of the discipline. Many empirically focused studies in both social anthropology and archaeology work on the assumption of some sort of fundamental historical continuity in regional sequences.

Rather, the role of the test in this chapter is to facilitate a more comprehensive and synthetic understanding of the pervasive and global occurrence of this pattern, and then to point out (particularly to the non-Darwinian archaeologist or anthropologist) that this ubiquitous pattern can be evoked in support of Cultural Selectionism, in the same way that biogeography can be evoked in support of neo-Darwinian genetics.

The cultural data

One problem with any attempt to prepare a wide-ranging geographic sample of ethnographic descriptions involves the non-equivalence of ethnographic studies from different parts of the world. This is due to the tendency for theoretical traditions to focus on a particular region or set of regions for their case-studies. In other words, to use a very simplistic but hopefully heuristic turn of phrase, in comparing cultures the analyst is not comparing Bantu with Irish but rather 'the Marxist anthropologist's Bantus' with 'the Freudian anthropologist's Irish' or *vice versa* as the case may be. For this reason the cultural diversity of different regions of the world is not only a function of actual differences (as perceived subjectively by anthropologists) in the cultures being studied, but also a function of considerable diversity amongst anthropologists in terms of methodology, interpretation, and focus of attention.

Fortunately, however, the problem of diversity amongst anthropologists is, for the purposes of this study, a red herring. However great the cultural diversity that might exist amongst anthropologists, it must, presumably, be less than that empirically encountered in the field of enquiry, since anthropologists themselves have a more restricted cultural heritage than the cultures which they study. Thus even a diverse group of anthropologists would in fact *reduce* the scope of the diversity to be found in the field, since the anthropologists bring a broadly similar set of western 'subjectivities' to the 'foreign' cultures which they then attempt to describe. The fundamentally European heritage of anthropology would, therefore (despite the philosophical diversity which exists amongst anthropologists), bias the study *away* from the primary selective hypothesis (that is, away from the actual and historically specific diversity towards simplified European universalities), and so the question of theoretical diversity within anthropology cannot be used to assail the results.

It is also important to bear in mind that the Selectionist hypothesis of pervasive heritage constraint is unlikely to emerge as a result of the two basic kinds of error which presumably occur in large bodies of ethnographic data. Errors in this sort of data presumably fall into two main categories: either (A), where random inaccuracies are created through human error, or (B), where more systematic inaccuracies are created through the cultural or theoretical bias of the original anthropologist who made the observations. Both these general classes of error would be expected to corrupt the heritage constraint pattern, rather than create or exaggerate it. Errors of the first sort would be expected to gradually corrupt the original structure of the data, making it more and more like a random number matrix than it originally was. Errors of the second sort, for the reasons mentioned in the last few pages, could be expected to reduce the distinctive elements of different cultures, and 'Europeanise' them, thereby diluting the heritage constraint pattern, and making its appearance in the data less and less pronounced.

With respect to the methodology of the analysis, and the multivariate algorithms used in the large-scale comparisons of bodies of information, non-equivalence of ethnographies derived from different anthropological traditions also presents practical difficulties. The basic practical difficulty is that it is more difficult to find mathematically commensurate descriptions of cultural systems.

Non-equivalent theory and method in descriptive studies thus cause the main problem with the synthesis of the cultural data which is already available. Even in the largest databases, which may reach as many as 1200 societies coded for as many as 1000 variables, there was a problem in that no one society is represented in all the variables, and no one variable has been recorded for all the societies. At present, the Principal Components Analysis algorithm available for this kind of study requires a completely full matrix of numbers (including zeros, but no blank spaces). It thus requires every society to be represented in terms of every variable and vice versa. A huge database of 2000 by 1000 usually contains many blank spaces where a society's status with respect to that variable is unknown. As a consequence, the largest number of societies which shared complete records for the same variables turned out to be considerably smaller than the 2000 by 1000 data-set source, as a direct result of the missing data problem.

The other basic problem, occurring in both ethnographic and artefact data, is that Principal Components Analysis requires that the data be coded in the form of numerically meaningful ordinal scales. As a result, the data had to be comprehensively translated, and the details of those translations are laid out below.

The two basic sources used were Murdock's *Ethnographic atlas* (from the 1967 issue of the journal *Ethnology*), and the demonstration diskette for White's *Maptab*. This second source is one of three cross-cultural data-sets published as electronic journal software by the *World Cultures Quorum* (vol. 1, no. 1). The demonstration diskette consists of 172 variables coded on a variety of topics for the 186 societies in what is termed the *Standard Cross Cultural Sample*. Topics span areas as diverse as factors of climate, subsistence and economics, sex and reproduction, family and social organisation, demography, politics and religion, child training and personality. Data from some categories was obviously not cultural in nature; only categories like subsistence and economics, family and social organisation, and politics and religion could offer cultural variables. From these sources, coded data for 25 common ethnographic variables was gathered. They are listed below, firstly in their original format on the *Maptab* demonstration diskette, and then in their final translated form. Added to these ethnographic variables are a further 41 artefact variables, derived from information in the *Ethnographic atlas* about house shape and raw material. These are described in some detail a little later, along with the translation procedures to which they were subjected.

After numerous eliminations of societies or variables, due to many examples of missing data, a 'clean' or 'full' data matrix of 157 societies and 66 variables was gathered. Thus the analysis essentially consists of the multivariate comparison of 157 cultural assemblages from all around the world. A brief list of the societies, and a brief explanation of the variables chosen and the manner of their coding will now be offered.

All 157 societies used in the analysis come from a particular well-used 186-society subset of the *Ethnographic atlas* referred to as the Standard Cross Cultural Sample. This sample was created to mitigate a number of problems which occurred with much larger data-sets, outlined in the following words in the *World Cultures Quorum*, volume 1, number 1 (page 5):

> Many social scientists prefer to use large samples such as the *Atlas* to test hypotheses about human behaviour. However, a major problem of sample design effects arises from using multiple cases of each basic cultural type such as the 186 identified by Murdock and White. In any sample, duplicates lead to underestimates of variances. An "autocorrelation" problem exists to the

extent that neighbouring societies tend to be similar. In a recent unpublished paper on "Design effects in standard samples", Malcolm Dow shows that the use of the *Ethnographic atlas* as a sample may lead to underestimates of variance by orders of magnitude of thirty to one hundred. In contrast, standard deviations estimated from the Standard Sample are often estimated at 70% or more of true magnitude compared to estimates from the *Atlas* at only 10% of true value. To test hypotheses it is thus essential to minimise design effects by using such designs as the Standard Sample.

Thus, this sample was specially chosen to minimise the very factor of cultural systems which causes the 'heritage' or 'descent with modification' pattern. An attempt was made to compensate for the fact that 'neighbouring societies tend to be similar'. Thus it can assumed that a whole level of the data in which heritage constraint was in its most dramatic form has been removed. If heritage constraint can still be found in the 157 cultural assemblages, it will be in spite of sampling procedures which were specifically designed to take it out. As will become clear after the presentation of the results, the pattern does indeed remain, and in a very robust form.

Elucidating phylogenetic heritage constraint in any body of data taken from the products of a selective process often requires some kind of prior knowledge of phylogeny itself. In the case of the Howells cranial data, the genealogical origin of each skull was already known within broad parameters. Each skull collection consisted of a group of skulls of known origin. The cultural assemblages of this chapter were classified into 'common and/or restricted heritage' groups on the basis of common linguistic affiliation. Although linguistic affiliation is also highly correlated with geographic origin, it was thought that the language spoken by a group of people would be a reasonably reliable indicator of their cultural heritage. As will be seen in the groups below, however, some subsets are made up of societies of geographic proximity, when the languages spoken by the societies display no obvious relationship. This is because the cultural assemblages have been included in the restricted heritage subgroups on the grounds of either language spoken or geographic origin, and often both. The 157 cultural assemblages are listed in the order in which they occur in the analysis (these are not their usual numbers in the Standard Cross Cultural Sample), and they are derived from the groups of people listed alongside (see Table 1 below). The first 25 variables (which are principally 'non-material') employed in the analysis are coded and described below (see Table 2, after Table 1), much as they are in Douglas White's Maptab demonstration diskette codebook, although some of them were altered from arbitrary numerical codings to 'quantity-related' numerical or ordinal scales, as explained in detail immediately after the list below.

The codebook is not quoted but rather paraphrased in such a way as to exclude any information other than that which concerns the nature of the variables themselves, as any additional information is superfluous here. Some explanatory notes are added for the purpose of this study (usually in parentheses). Where the original coding system was nominal or arbitrary (that is, where the coding symbol system had no representational element, such as when 1=Donkey, and 2=Zebra, given that Zebras are not 'larger' or 'more' than Donkeys, but merely 'different to'), the numbering system could sometimes be rearranged or simplified to produce a meaningful numeric series (for example, variables 14, 15, and 19).

For Principal Components Analysis information has to be expressed in numeric form, and in the form of ordinal scales, where the first state of that variable (whether it be 0 or 1) has to represent the total absence of the variable; the next state (1 or 2) has to represent a small amount of that variable; the next state (2 or 3) had to represent a larger amount; and so on. The numeric scale has to reflect *increasing quantity,* or the results of the Principal Components Analysis would be indeterminate. In most of the variables from the maptab codebook laid out below, the coded format already articulates an ordinal scale. Few changes had to made, since the coding was already meaningful in terms of increasing quantity.

Table 1. The cultural assemblages included in the analysis.
 (From White 1989.)

Cultural assemblages from Khoisan and Mbuti societies (subsets: Khoisan 1–3; Mbuti 23)
1 Nama. 1860. Gei/Khauan Hottentot.
2 Kung. 1950. Nyai Nyae Bushmen.
3 Hadza. 1930. Tribe.
23 Mbuti. 1950. Epulu net-hunters Ituri Forest.

Cultural assemblages from other African societies (subsets: Niger–Kordofanian 4–20, 25; miscellaneous 21–22, 24; Afroasiatic 26–37)
4 Lozi. 1900. Ruling Luyana.
5 Mbundu. 1890. Bailundo subtribe.
6 Bemba. 1897. Zambia branch.
7 Nyakyusa. 1934. Mwaya & Masoko age villages.
8 Thonga. 1865. Ronga subtribe.
9 Luguru. 1925. Morogoro District.
10 Kikuyu. 1920. Fort Hall or Metume district.
11 Ganda. 1875. Kyaddondo district of Kampala.
12 Tiv. 1920. Tar of Benue Province.
13 Nkundo. 1930. Ilanga group.
14 Banen. 1935. Ndiki subtribe.
15 Ashanti. 1895. Kumasi State.
16 Ibo. 1935. East Isu-Ana group.
17 Fon. 1890. Abomey city & environs.

Table 1 (continued).

18 Azande. 1905. Yambio Chiefdom.
19 Mende. 1945. Bo town and vicinity.
20 Wolof. 1950. Upper and lower
Salum, Gambia.
25 Otoro. 1930. Nuba Hills.

21 Songhai. 1940. Bamba division.
22 Masai. 1900. Kisonko S. Masai of
Tanzania.
24 Shilluk. 1910. Kingdom.

26 Fur. 1880. Jebel Marra.
27 Teda. 1950. Nomads of Tibesti.
28 Kaffa. 1905. Kingdom.
29 Konso. 1935. Buso town.
30 Somali. 1900. Dolbahanta clan or
subtribe.
31 Tuareg. 1900. Ahaggaren tribe.
32 Riffians. 1926. Entirety: Moroccan.
33 Amhara. 1953. Gondar district.
34 Egytians. 1950. Silwa town and
environs.
35 Hebrews. 621 BC. Kingdom of
Judea.
36 Babylonians. 1750 BC. Babylon city
and environs.
37 Bedouin. 1913. Rwala: Unspecified.

Cultural assemblages from west Eurasian
societies (subsets: Indo-European 38–46;
Uralic 47–48; Altaic 49–51)
38 Albanians. 1910. Mountain Gheg of
N/Albania.
39 Armenians. 1843. Vicinty of Erevan
city.
40 Romans. 110. Rome city and
environs.
41 Irish. 1932. County Clare.
42 Russians. 1955. Viriatino village.
43 Kurd. 1951. Rowanduz town and
environs.
44 Basseri. 1958. Nomadic branch.
45 Vedda. 1860. Danigala Forest
hunters.
46 Saramacca. 1928. Upper Suriname
River (South America).

47 Lapps. 1950. Konkama District.
48 Samoyed. 1894. Yurak.

49 Turks. 1950. Northern Anatolian
plateau.
50 Kazak. 1885. Great Horde.
51 Khalka. 1920. Narobanchin
Territory.

Cultural assemblages from east Asian
societies (subsets: Japanese/Korean 52–53;
far north Asian 54–57; Dravidian 58–59;
Mon-Khmer/Austroasiatic 60–65; Tibetan
66–70)
52 Koreans. 1947. Kanghwa Island.
53 Japanese. 1950. Southern Okayama.

54 Ainu. 1880. Saru Basin in Hokkaido.
55 Gilyak. 1890. Sakhalin Island.
56 Chukchee. 1900. Reindeer Division.
57 Yukaghir. 1850. Upper Kolyma
River.

58 Gond. 1938. Hill Maria.
59 Toda. 1900. Tribe.

60 Santal. 1940. Bankura and Berghum
Districts.
61 Lamet. 1940. Tribe, northwestern
Laos.
62 Vietnamese. 1930. Red River Delta
in Tonkin.
63 Semang. 1925. Jehai Group or
subtribe.
64 Nicobarese. 1870. Car Nicobar of
north islands.
65 Andamanese. 1860. Aka-Bea of
south Andaman.

66 Lolo. 1910. Liang Shan & Taliang
Shan.
67 Lepcha. 1937. Lingthem and
vicinity.
68 Garo. 1955. Rensanggri village.
69 Lakher. 1930. Tribe.
70 Burmese. 1965. Nondwin village.

Table 1 (continued).

Cultural assemblages from macro-Austronesian societies (subsets: Thai-Kadai 71; Malayo-Polynesian 72–93)

71 Siamese. 1955. Bang Chan village.
72 Rhade. 1962. Ko-Sier village.
73 Tanala. 1925. Menabe subtribe.
74 Javanese. 1954. Pare town and environs.
75 Balinese. 1958. Tihingan village.
76 Iban. 1950. Ulu Ai Group.
77 Badjau. 1963. Tawi-Tawi & adjacent islands.
78 Alorese. 1938. Abui of Atimelang village.
79 Manus. 1937. Peri village.
80 New Ireland. 1930. Lesu village.
81 Trobrianders. 1914. Kiriwina Island.
82 Tikopia. 1930. Ravenga District.
83 Ajie. 1845. Neje Chiefdom.
84 Maori. 1820. Nga Puhi Tribe.
85 Marquesans. 1800. Te-i'i Chiefdom SW NukuHiva.
86 West Samoans. 1829. Aana, Western Upolu Island.
87 Gilbertese. 1890. Makin & Butiritari Isles.
88 Marshallese. 1900. Jaluit Atoll.
89 Trukese. 1947. Romonum Island.
90 Yapese. 1910. Island.
91 Palauans. 1947. Ulimang village.
92 Ifuago. 1910. Kiangan Group.
93 Atayal. 1930. Tribe (but excluding Sedeq).

Cultural assemblages from south-west Pacific societies (Papuan 94–98; Australian 99–100)

94 Orokaiva. 1925. Aiga subtribe.
95 Kimam. 1960. Bamol village.
96 Kapauku. 1955. Botukedo village.
97 Kwoma. 1960. Hongwam subtribe.
98 Siuai. 1939. Northeastern group.
99 Tiwi. 1929. Tribe: Melville Island.
100 Aranda. 1896. Alice Springs and environs.

Cultural assemblages from North American societies (subsets: Nadene 101–106; Eskimo 107–108; Macro-Algonkian 109–113; Salishan, Hokan, and Siouan 114–119; Uto-Aztecan and Zuni 120–125; Macro-Penutian, Kutenai, Caddoan, Iroquoian, Natchez-Muskogean 126–132)

101 Ingalik. 1885. Shageluk village.
102 Slave. 1940. Lynx Point band.
103 Kaska. 1900. Upper Liard River Group.
104 Eyak. 1890. Tribe.
105 Haida. 1875. Masset town.
106 Chiricahua. 1870. Central band.
107 Aleut. 1800. Unalaska Branch.
108 Copper Eskimo. 1915. Coronation Gulf.
109 Montagnais. 1910. Lake St John & Mistassani.
110 Micmac. 1650. Mainland Division.
111 Saulteaux. 1930. Berens River band.
112 Gros Ventre. 1880. Tribe.
113 Yurok. 1850. Tsurai village.
114 Bellacoola. 1880. Central Group, lower BC River.
115 Twana. 1860. Tribe.
116 Havasupai. 1918. Tribe.
117 Eastern Pomo. 1850. Cignon village, Clear Lake.
118 Omaha. 1860. Tribe.
119 Hidatsa. 1836. Village.
120 Northern Paiute. 1870. Wadadika, Harney Valley.
121 Commanche. 1870. Tribe.
122 Papago. 1910. Archie division.
123 Aztec. 1520. Tenochtitlan city and environs.
124 Huichol. 1890. Tribe.
125 Zuni. 1880. Pueblo.
126 Klamath. 1860. Tribe.
127 Lake Yokuts. 1850. Tulare Lake.
128 Kutenai. 1890. Lower or eastern branch.
129 Pawnee. 1867. Skidi Band or subtribe.

Table 1 (continued).

130 Huron. 1634. Bear and Cord subtribes.
131 Natchez. 1718. Kingdom.
132 Creek. 1800. Upper division in Alabama.

Cultural assemblages from South American societies (Subsets: Mayan, Cariban 133–135; Macro-Chibchan 136–139; Equatorial 140–146; Ge-Panoan 147–152; Andean 153–157)
133 Quiche. 1930. Chichicastenango town.
134 Callinago. 1650. Dominica Island.
135 Carib. 1932. Barama River.

136 Miskito. 1921. Cape Gracias a Dios vicinity.
137 Cuna. 1927. San Blas Archipelago.
138 Warrau. 1935. Winikina of Orinoco Delta.
139 Cayapa. 1908. Rio Cayapas Basin.
140 Goajiro. 1947. Tribe.
141 Mundurucu. 1850. Cabrua village.

142 Cubeo. 1939. Village on Caduiari River.
143 Jivaro. 1920. Tribe.
144 Siriono. 1942. Vicinity of the Rio Blanco.
145 Trumai. 1938. Vanivani village.
146 Tupinamba. 1550. Rio de Janeiro hinterland.
147 Amahuaca. 1960. Upper Inuya River.
148 Nambicuara. 1940. Cocozu Group.
149 Timbira. 1915. Ramcocamecra or Canella.
150 Aweikoma. 1932. Duque de Caxias Reservation.
151 Lengua. 1889. Vicinity of mission.
152 Abipon. 1750. Vicinity of mission.
153 Inca. 1530. Cuzco city & environs.
154 Aymara. 1940. Chucuito Clan community.
155 Mapuche. 1950. Vicinity of Temuco.
156 Tehuelche. 1870. Equestrian.
157 Yaghan. 1865. Eastern and central.

Table 2. The 25 ethnographic variables, derived from White's Maptab.

1 Writing and records
1 none
2 mnemonic devices
3 non-written records
4 true writing; no records
5 true writing; records

2 Amount of gathering
0 0–5% dependence
1 6–15% dependence
2 16–25% dependence
3 26–35% dependence
4 36–45% dependence
5 46–55% dependence
6 56–65% dependence
7 66–75% dependence
8 76–85% dependence
9 86–100% dependence

3 Amount of hunting
(coded in the same manner as 2)

4 Amount of fishing
(coded in the same manner as 2)

5 Amount of animal husbandry
(coded in the same manner as 2)

6 Amount of agriculture
(coded in the same manner as 2)

7 Animals and plough cultivation
1 absent (no plough animals)
2 not aboriginal but well-established at period of observation (altered to 0 in this study)
3 prior to contact

Table 2 (continued).

8 *Food surplus via storage*
1 none or very little
2 moderate
3 complex or more than adequate

9 *Fixity of settlement*
1 migratory
2 seminomadic – alternatively fixed
    and migratory
3 rotating among two or more fixed
    points
4 semisedentary – fixed core, some
    migratory
5 impermanent – periodically moved
6 permanent

10 *Compactness of settlement*
1 dispersed
2 spatially separated subsettlements
3 partially dispersed with central core
4 compact

11 *Money (media of exchange) and credit*
1 no media of exchange or money
2 domestically usable articles as media
    of exchange
3 tokens of conventional value as
    media of exchange
4 foreign coinage or paper currency
5 indigenous coinage or paper
    currency

12 *Economic dependence on trade*
0 0–4% dependence
1 5–9% dependence
2 10–14% dependence
3 15–19% dependence
4 20–24% dependence
5 25–29% dependence
6 55–59% dependence
7 65–69% dependence

13 *Female contribution to subsistence*
(average of three scores)
0 0–5%
1 6–15%

2 16–25%
3 26–35%
4 36–45%
5 46–55%
6 56–65%
7 66–75%
8 76–85%
9 86–99%

14 *Technological specialisation*
1 none
2 pottery only
3 loom-weaving only
4 metalwork only
5 smiths, weavers, potters
as this coding was non-ordinal, it was
changed to an ordinal scale based on
'degree of technological specialisation' as
follows:
0 none
1 specialisation in one trade only,
    whether smiths, weavers, or potters
2 multiple numbers of specialist
    artisans

15 *Land transport*
(especially of food)
1 human carriers
2 pack animals
3 draft animals (sleds, travois)
4 animal-drawn wheeled vehicles
5 motorised vehicles
(the apparently non-ordinal or arbitrary
code system of variable 15 was retained,
and judged to have an indirectly ordinal
quality, as an ordinal scale of 'increasing
similarity to motorised vehicles')

16 *Social stratification (degree of 'vertical'*
differentiation)
1 egalitarian
2 hereditary
3 two social classes, no castes/slavery
4 two social classes, castes/slavery
5 three social classes or castes, with or
    without slavery

Table 2 (continued).

17 *Slavery (degree to which it is hereditary)*
1 absence or near-absence
2 incipient or non-hereditary
3 reported but type not identified
4 hereditary and socially significant

18 *Direction of gift exchanges in marriage
(an ordinal scale of increasing cost of
wedding to bride's family)*
1 bride-price or -wealth, to bride's
    family from husband's family
2 bride-service, to bride's family from
    husband's family
3 token bride-price
4 gift exchange, reciprocal
5 sister or female relative exchanged for
    bride
6 absence of consideration (recoded as 4)
7 dowry to bride from her family

19 *Marital residence with kin (an ordinal
scale of increasing patrilocality)*
0 non-establishment of common
    household, or neo-local and located
    independently of kin
1 matrilocal: with wife's unilineal kin
    group
2 uxorilocal: with wife's parents
3 optional avunculocal or uxorilocal
4 bilocal: with either kin group
5 avunculocal: with husband's mother's
    brother
6 optional avunculocal, virilocal, or
    patrilocal
7 virilocal: with husband's parents
8 patrilocal: with husband's unilineal kin
    group

20 *Household form (an ordinal scale of
increasing household segregation)*
1 large communal structures
2 multi-family dwellings
3 single-family dwellings
4 family homestead
5 multi-dwelling households, each with
    married pair
6 multi-dwelling households, husband
    rotates among wives

7 mother-child households, husbands
    separate
8 multi-dwelling households, each
    dwelling occupied

21 *Family type
(an ordinal scale of more and more extended
family structure)*
1 nuclear monogamous
2 nuclear polygynous
3 stem family
4 small extended
5 large extended

22 *Presence or absence of corporate kinship*
0 bilateral – not a corporate kin group
1 matrilineal – through female line
1 double descent – separate groups
    through male and female lines
1 patrilineal – through one parent in
    each generation
1 ambilineal – through one parent in
    each generation

23 *Community leadership (degree of
complexity)*
1 no centralised local leadership
2 higher level only
3 single local leader
4 dual/plural headmen
5 single local leader and council
6 local councils
7 single local leader and subordinates
8 too complex to be coded

24 *Degree of intercommunity marriage*
1 local endogamy 90–100%
2 local endogamy 61–89% (agamous)
3 local endogamy 30–60% (agamous)
4 local endogamy 11–29% (agamous)
5 local endogamy 0–10% (exogamous)

25 *Levels of sovereignty*
1 stateless society
2 sovereignty 1st hierarchical level up
3 sovereignty 2nd hierarchical level up
4 sovereignty 3rd or higher hierarchical
    level

However, as all of the 25 variables above were ethnographic, attention was then turned to some of the more 'ethno-archaeological' variables recorded in the *Ethnographic atlas*. This sort of data, particularly in the *Ethnographic atlas*, was coded alphabetically rather than numerically, and as a result required a large amount of translation. A global sample of any kind of artefact was now all that was required – it was irrelevant whether longbows, stone-tool technologies, or kitchen stoves were used. A cross-cultural sample of houses were chosen, houses being one of the better-represented artefacts in the *Ethnographic atlas*, and the hope of finding house information for a large number of the Standard Cross Cultural Sample societies was likely. Using the same sources as those used for the ethnographic data-set of the last chapter, a database of house shape and building material was compiled. Where possible, the very same sample communities were used; otherwise a random draw was taken from amongst the same language group as the community for which that particular kind of information was missing (this turned out to be necessary in only one case). At first the data was collected from the *Ethnographic atlas* in its original form (see Murdock 1967). The most common dwelling form was represented by five letters, each letter representing the form of that dwelling with respect to each of five general categories of shape, construction, or material. These five letters form columns 80–84 of the atlas, and the information these columns convey are outlined on page 168 of the *Ethnographic Atlas*, and presented in Table 3 opposite).

Before these artefact variables could be added to the analysis, the data had to be translated from the letter codes into a meaningful series of ordinal scales, in a similar manner to the ethnographic data. This also proved to be a long and involved process (however this process was considerably shorter than were the estimates made of the time it might take to create a similar cross-cultural sample of second-hand (leave alone first-hand) archaeological phenomena). Basically, the information had to be expressed in numeric form, where the number allocated to a house type for a particular variable had to be a meaningful expression of the degree, quantity, or amount of the variable in question, possessed by that house. Because of this, the initial variables had to be broken up. It was not possible to take, say, 'Column 80: Ground plan of dwelling' and then code Circular as 1, Elliptical as 2, Polygonal as 3, and Quadrangular as 4, since the computer would interpret this as meaning that circular ground plans were 'small' ground plans, elliptical plans not so small, polygonal plans somewhat larger, quadrangular plans as larger still, and so on. Instead each individual trait and its associated symbol was made into a single variable, with only two states of

Table 3. The artefact variables in their original form, derived from Murdock (1967: 168–9).

Column 80: Ground plan of dwelling. The symbols used are the following:
C circular
E elliptical
P polygonal
Q quadrangular around (or partly around) an interior court
R rectangular or square
S semi-circular

Column 81: Floor level. The symbols used are the following:
E elevated slightly above the ground on a raised platform of earth, stone, or wood
G floor formed by or level with the ground itself
P raised substantially above the ground on piles, posts, or piers
S subterranean or semi-subterranean, ignoring cellars beneath the living quarters

Column 82: Wall material. The symbols used are the following:
A adobe, clay, or dried brick
B bark
F felt, cloth, or other fabric
G grass, leaves, or other thatch
H hides or skins
M mats, latticework, or wattle
O open walls, including cases where they can be temporarily closed by screens
P plaster, mud and dung, or wattle and daub

R walls indistinguishable from roof or merging into the latter. Cf. Column 84
S stone, stucco, concrete, or fired brick
W wood, including logs, planks, poles, bamboo, or shingles

Column 83: Shape of roof (or of walls and roof where not distinct). The symbols used are the following:
B beehive shaped with pointed peak
C conical
D done shaped or hemispherical
E semi-hemispherical
F flat or horizontal
G gabled, i.e., with two slopes
H hipped or pyramidical, i.e., with four slopes
R rounded or semi-cylindrical
S shed, i.e., with one slope

Column 84: Roofing material. The symbols used are the following:
B bark
E earth or turf
F Felt, cloth, or other fabric
G grass, leaves, brush, or other thatch
H hides or skins
I Ice or snow
M mats
P plaster, clay, mud and dung, or wattle and daub
S stone or slate
T tile or fired brick
W wood, including logs, planks, poles, bamboo, or shingles

that variable being possible – either it is present or it is absent. The new database has 41 variables instead of 5 (added to the 25 above for a total of 66). Presence is given the numeric code of one, and absence is given the numeric code of zero. This kind of solution is a happy compromise; all the original information is preserved, and yet it is perfectly meaningful to say that the presence of mud walls in a house implies a greater quantity of 'mud wallness' than the absence of mud walls in another house. In other words, the implicit ordinal values of the codes 1 and 0 do not conflict with the ontological world of the data. This is the final order which the remaining 41 house shape/raw material variables, the main 'artefact' variables were allocated in the analysis, after this re-coding procedure.

The raw data matrix thus consists of 157 societies each coded for a total of 66 variables. Each of the 157 societies could now be compared multivariately with each of the others, in terms of each of the 66 variables, and it remained to be seen whether, or to what degree, the selective pattern of cultural heritage constraint would emerge.

Table 4. The 41 artefact variables in their final form for the analysis, scored as 0 for absent and 1 for present.

Variable 26: Presence of circular ground plan in most frequent house type
Variable 27: Presence of elliptical ground plan in most frequent house type
Variable 28: Presence of polygonal ground plan in most frequent house type
Variable 29: Presence of quadrangular ground plan in most frequent house type
Variable 30: Presence of rectangular ground plan in most frequent house type
Variable 31: Presence of semicircular ground plan in most frequent house type
Variable 32: Presence of elevated floor level in most frequent house type
Variable 33: Presence of ground level floor in most frequent house type
Variable 34: Presence of floor raised on piles, posts, or piers in most frequent house type
Variable 35: Presence of subterranean or semi subterranean floor in most frequent house type
Variable 36: Presence of adobe, clay, or dried brick walls in most frequent house type
Variable 37: Presence of bark walls in most frequent house type
Variable 38: Presence of felt, cloth, or other fabric walls in most frequent house type
Variable 39: Presence of grass, leaves, or thatch walls in most frequent house type
Variable 40: Presence of hides or skin walls in most frequent house type
Variable 41: Presence of mats, latticework, or wattle walls in most frequent house type
Variable 42: Presence of open (or temporarily closed) walls in most frequent house type
Variable 43: Presence of plaster, mud and dung, or wattle and daub walls in most frequent house type
Variable 44: Presence of walls which are indistinguishable from roof in most frequent house type
Variable 45: Presence of stone, stucco, concrete, or fired brick walls in most frequent house type
Variable 46: Presence of wood walls in most frequent house type
Variable 47: Presence of beehive shaped roof in most frequent house type
Variable 48: Presence of conical roof in most frequent house type
Variable 49: Presence of dome shaped or hemispherical roof in most frequent house type
Variable 50: Presence of semi-hemispherical roof in most frequent house type
Variable 51: Presence of flat roof in most frequent house type
Variable 52: Presence of gabled (two slope) roof in most frequent house type

Variable 53: Presence of pyramidal (four slope) roof in most frequent house type

Variable 54: Presence of rounded (semi-cylindrical) roof in most frequent house type

Variable 55: Presence of 'shed' (one slope) roof in most frequent house type

Variable 56: Presence of bark roofing material in most frequent house type

Variable 57: Presence of earth/turf roofing material in most frequent house type

Variable 58: Presence of felt, cloth, or other fabric roofing material in most frequent house type

Variable 59: Presence of grass, leaves, brush or thatch roofing material in most frequent house type

Variable 60: Presence of hide or skin roofing material in most frequent house type

Variable 61: Presence of ice/snow roofing material in most frequent house type

Variable 62: Use of mats as a roofing material in most frequent house type

Variable 63: Presence of plaster, clay, wattle and daub, or mud and dung roofing material in most frequent house type

Variable 64: Presence of stone or slate roofing material in most frequent house type

Variable 65: Presence of tile or fired brick roofing material in most frequent house type

Variable 66: Presence of wooden roofing material in most frequent house type

Analysis and results

The multivariate method used is Principal Components Analysis, and firstly the space in which the cultural assemblages are to be plotted has to be characterised in terms of the original variables. It is customary in a PCA to discuss the plots of the variables and objects together, so that each is characterised and explained in terms of the other. But in this study the variables will be dealt with briefly, as the purpose of this analysis is to illustrate one aspect of the data only: *the phylogenetic heritage constraint implied by the restricted distribution of groups of cultural assemblages with restricted heritage*, when graphed on PCA biplots. Those readers with some specialist interest in Principal Components Analysis may choose to note, however, that in the analysis the data was first transformed into a correlation matrix, not a covariance matrix (Wright 1989: BIGPCA page 10). This option changes variables of different sizes into variables of the same size. Wright offers the following explanatory example (1989: BIGPCA page 10):

> Imagine an analysis of femurs in which femur head diameters are inherently about 1/10 of the size of femur length. We are surely just as interested in relative variation in femur head diameter as we are in variation of femur length. Yet if we choose the covariance matrix femur length will swamp the analysis by a factor of 10.

As the cultural variables listed above were of different magnitudes, the *correlation matrix* option was used here. It was also used in *every other analysis*, in order that the hypotheses derived from these other analyses would be commensurate with the cultural case-study of this chapter.

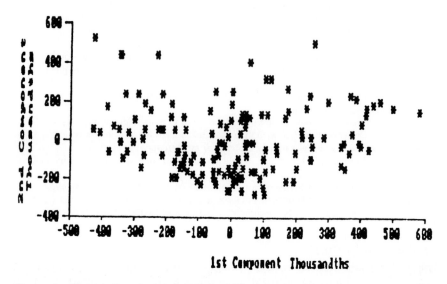

Figure 1. Plot of all cultural assemblages in terms of the 1st and 2nd principal components. (From Cullen 1993a: figure 8.02.)

Figure 2. Plot of Khoisan/Mbuti African cultural assemblages (*) within the plot of all cultural assemblages (–) in terms of the 1st and 2nd principal components. (From Cullen 1993a: figure 8.03.)

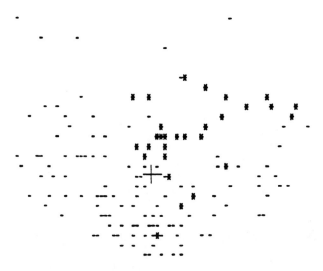

Figure 3. Plot of non-Khoisan/Mbuti African cultural assemblages (*) within the plot of all cultural assemblages (–) in terms of the 1st and 2nd principal components. (From Cullen 1993a: figure 8.04.)

Figure 4. Distribution of sub-Saharan African crania (*) within the plot of all crania (–) in terms of the 2nd and 3rd principal components. (From Cullen 1993a: figure 6.15.)

Figure 5. Distribution of African environments (*) within the plot of all environments (–) in terms of the 4th and 5th principal components. (From Cullen 1993a: figure 7.09.)

The general plot of the entire sample of cultural assemblages (Figure 1) is the first plot in which the results of the 'preliminary' test begin to emerge. As the established procedure of the previous analyses is continued, and limited heritage subsets are plotted, more and more striking correspondence between the neo-Darwinian hypothesis and cultural geography can be observed. Compare, for example, the plot of African cultural assemblages (Figures 2–3 together) with the distributions of African crania (Figure 4), and the 'Lamarckian' or 'environmental determinist' null hypothesis distribution of African environments (Figure 5). Although the African subset – the first 37 cultural assemblages – is centred upon the origin, it will become clear below that it is rare in this regard. Moreover, if the African subset is broken into two smaller subgroups which one might reasonably expect to have somewhat different heritage in terms of cultural origins and influences, two typically non-random distributions are produced. Khoisan and Mbuti societies occupy a tight region in the top-left quadrant of the world distribution (Figure 2), while the other African cultural assemblages are strongly concentrated in the right-hand side of the distribution, occupying

Figure 6. Distribution of Indo-European and Uralic (Lapp, Samoyed) cultural assemblages (*) within the plot of all cultural assemblages (–) in terms of the 1st and 2nd principal components. (From Cullen 1993a: figure 8.05.)

the top of the lower-right quadrant, and the lower area of the top-right quadrant (Figure 3).

The heritage constraint pattern has so far been illustrated purely in terms of ranges and distributions. But as cultural assemblages are the focus of the test, it is interesting to note some additional statistics associated with these groups. The limited range of morphology associated with the cultural assemblages of a particular continent can be represented in terms of other characteristics of the subsets.

The total distribution of the African subset, for example, is non-random with respect to other more restricted distributions in the study, but is in and of itself not obviously non-random. If, however, we compute the mean score of the entire group for each component, we find that the point to which the mean corresponds is not located on the origin, but well into the top-right quadrant (0.07,0.10; the middle of this quadrant, for comparison, being located around 0.20,0.20). Most African cultural assemblages, then, are located more to the right of the origin than the distribution would suggest.

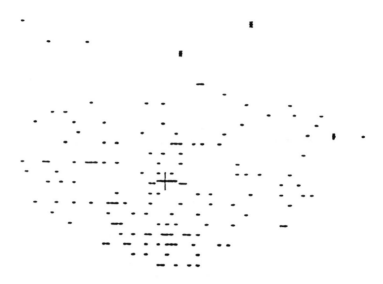

Figure 7. Distribution of Altaic (Turkish, Kazak, Khalka) cultural assemblages (*) within the plot of all cultural assemblages (–) iin terms of the 1st and 2nd principal components. (From Cullen 1993a: figure 8.06.)

Its apparent 'para-random' distribution is a function of a small number of unusual assemblages, not of typical structure.

Moving on from Africa, the distributions of west Eurasian cultural assemblages are graphed in the next illustrations (Figures 6–7 together). The distribution can seen to be concentrated towards the right-hand quadrants, away from the margins of the left side of the world distribution, a somewhat broader distribution on the *y* axis, but narrower on the negative side of the *x* axis, due to its lack of any cultural assemblages resembling those of the click languages in the African distribution. In a similar manner to Africa, a small number of societies, themselves sharing a common heritage which is more limited again, extend the west Eurasian distribution. Thus, Indo-European and Uralic (Lapp and Samoyed) cultural assemblages (Figure 6) tend to congregate in the bottom-right quadrant, but when the three Altaic (Turks, Kazak, and Khalka) cultural assemblages are added (Figure 7), the distribution occupies both right-hand quadrants, extending over the origin.

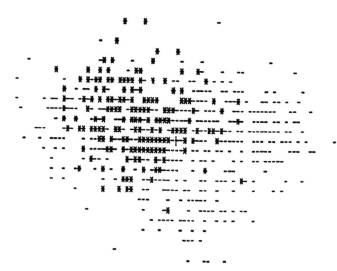

Figure 8. Distribution of European crania (*) within the plot of all crania (–) in terms of the 2nd and 3rd principal components. (From Cullen 1993a: figure 6.16.)

The combined west Eurasian distribution (Figures 6–7 together), can be compared with the corresponding plots of European crania (Figure 8) and the west Eurasian environments (see Cullen 1993a: figure 7.10). Environmental variation in this region is clearly very different to cultural variation. Although the west Eurasian human environments fall into two clearly defined and very different groups (the 'Polar' environments of the Lapp and Samoyed societies, and the moist temperate environments of the others), no such clear distinctions can be detected in the cultural assemblages themselves. Thus the Lamarckian adaptationist hypothesis would seem to be as dramatically refuted at the intracontinental level of the data as it was at the intercontinental or global level, due to the immediate and obvious lack of discrete 'types' of cultural assemblages. This would echo Forde's (1934) conclusions in his book *Habitat, economy, and society,* where he illustrated the general tendency for societies not to be completely determined by their environments, but nonetheless to be broadly influenced by them.

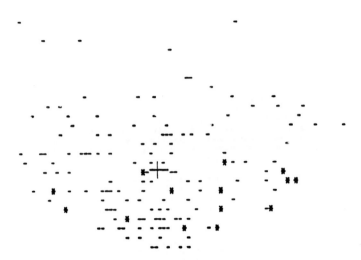

Figure 9. Distribution of east Asian cultural assemblages (*) within the plot of all cultural assemblages (–) in terms of the 1st and 2nd principal components. (From Cullen 1993a: figure 8.07.)

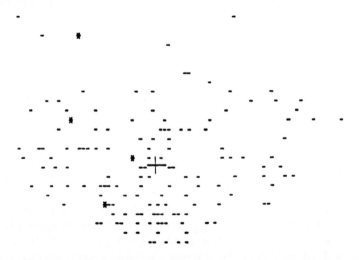

Figure 10. Distribution of north Asian (Ainu and Siberian) cultural assemblages (*) within the plot of all cultural assemblages (–) in terms of the 1st and 2nd principal components. (From Cullen 1993a: figure 8.08.)

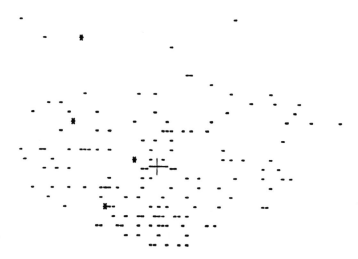

Figure 11. Distribution of Malayo-Polynesian and Thai-Kadai cultural assemblages (*) within the plot of all cultural assemblages (–) in terms of the 1st and 2nd principal components. (From Cullen 1993a: figure 8.09.)

Subset distributions of the remaining assemblages begin to 'migrate' away from the African and west Eurasian areas towards other parts of the global distribution, but each exhibits a visibly restricted distribution. In the next two figures (Figures 9–10 together), Asian cultural assemblages are seen to occupy quadrants other than the top-right quadrant, within which most of the African and European assemblages fell. East Asian assemblages (Figure 9) show a very distinctive and narrow distribution in the two lower quadrants, while the north Asian subset (Ainu, and Siberian isolates Yukaghir, Chukchee, and Gilyak) (Figure 10) occupies the top-left quadrant. Such restricted and distinctive morphology cannot be a function of restricted environmental conditions, as a comparison of the Asian cultural assemblages with the human environments of Asia will reveal (see Cullen 1993a: figure 7.11). All of the basic types of environment are present in this region, and yet, in keeping with the neo-Darwinian hypothesis, the limited heritage of this cultural group prevents certain cultural forms from being present. And like Asian crania, Asian cultural assemblages are far more distinctive than the Asian environments which surround them.

Figure 12. Distribution of Australian and Papuan cultural assemblages (*) within the plot of all cultural assemblages (–) in terms of the 1st and 2nd principal components. (From Cullen 1993a: figure 8.10.)

Pacific cultural assemblages also display dramatically restricted morphology in relation to global diversity. The Thai-Kadai and Malayo-Polynesian assemblages (Figure 11) display a similar range of structures to Asian societies, but with a more narrow distribution.

While Malayo-Polynesian assemblages occupy a restricted area in relation to the Asian range, Papuan and Australian cultural assemblages (Figure 12) occupy a very restricted area to the left of the Asian range. Once again, this is in spite of the fact that Pacific environments fall into two very different and well-defined groups. Common heritage clearly overrides the effects of these different environments, as the Papuan and Australian cultural assemblages display no sign of falling into two well-defined groups, occupying the lower left area of the world distribution.

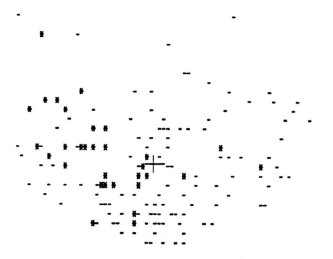

Figure 13. Distribution of North American cultural assemblages (*) within the plot of all cultural assemblages (–) in terms of the 1st and 2nd principal components. (From Cullen 1993a: figure 8.11.)

Figure 14. Distribution of South American cultural assemblages (*) within the plot of all cultural assemblages (–) in terms of the 1st and 2nd principal components. (From Cullen 1993a: figure 8.12.)

North and South America complete the preliminary test, both of them displaying the same limited and distinctive range of cultural phenomena (Figures 13–14 together), in spite of the immense range of American environments, which approximates the world environment range. American cultural assemblages are characterised by broad ranges, which extend into the top-left quadrant to include distinctive morphologies only shared by Ainu and isolated Siberian cultural assemblages; these are forms which are distinctively present in both North and South America. Distinctive absences in the American distributions are certain cultural structures which were so distinctively present on the other side of the Atlantic, in the African and European cultural assemblages. As stated several times already, what forms these distinctive structures take is not the focus of the present study, emphasis is placed only on the fact that distinctive forms of whatever description, or their absence, characterise the faunal and cultural assemblages of particular regions.

The restricted morphology of the American assemblages is all the more remarkable when the wide range of environmental conditions on these two continents is considered. All the basic environmental types of Africa and Europe, where the cultural assemblages were so different, are present, and yet these conditions are quite unable to override the peculiar heritage constraints of Amerindian societies.

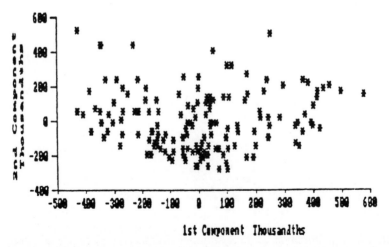

Figure 15. Distribution of all cultural assemblages in terms of the 1st and 2nd principal components. (From Cullen 1993a: figure 8.02.)

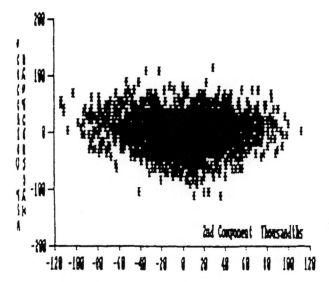

Figure 16. Distribution of all crania in terms of the 2nd and 3rd principal components. (From Cullen 1993a: figure 6.14.)

Further discussion

A global cross-cultural sample has thus been compiled and subjected to the same series of mathematical analyses as the non-cultural data of chapters 6 and 7. The geography of cultural assemblages displayed a remarkably similar general pattern to the cranial data of chapter 6, and this overall result is summarised in terms of idealised 'football'-shaped clusters (Figure 15). Cultural variation clearly conforms to the idealised 'neo-Darwinian' hypothesis defined in Cullen (1993a: chapter 6), with reference to cranial data (Figure 16).

It should be noted that the neo-Darwinian patterns in cultural assemblages simultaneously refute Sociobiology, and leave Cultural Selectionist perspective unrefuted: it refutes one Darwinism, and paves the way for another. Sociobiology is refuted due to the fact that in the approach, as shown in chapter 3 (see sections 3.5, 3.6, and 3.7), cultural assemblages are seen plastically to reflect human adaptive necessities – as 'man's extrasomatic means of adaptation'. In other words, to take up the notion that the only order to be found in history is that imposed upon it by the human genome, or, for that matter, that that order is imposed upon it by anything external to the cultural inheritance system itself, is to take up a Lamarckian position. To propose that culturally reproduced phenomena merely exist for human benefit without serving their own benefit, is to violate the basic Darwinian (Darwin 1859) and neo-Darwinian (Dawkins 1989) principle of selfishness (Cullen 1990). As a consequence, the sociobiological approach to culture does not predict a heritage constraint pattern to appear in cultural data, since human needs, unlike human crania (broadly speaking), are defined by things external to human genes, and are not, therefore, constrained by human phylogenetic heritage. A cultural system which simply reflected human needs would, correspondingly, display a *geography* which simply reflected the *geography* of those needs. General qualities of ecosystems, such as the mere presence of absence of resources for food (of *some* kind) and shelter (of *some* kind), are not a function of phylogenetic heritage.

It may also be noted that cultural diversity (Figure 15) is not 'synchronised' with, or 'codetermined' by, human genetic diversity, as it might be in the obsolete, genetic determinist sociobiological framework for culture, or as the behaviour of an animal without any culture at all would be. Rather, cultural assemblages appear to vary as though they are an independent selective system; as though cultural assemblages consist of a plethora of separate but sympatric species of different socially transmitted phenomena, all of which are genealogically independent from the human genome. Both plots display the general pattern of heritage constraint, and are equally selective, but the pattern is not the same in its specifics. In other words, it is clear that the overall plot of human crania and its internal structure is no means the same pattern as that displayed in the cultural data, either in the overall plot or its internal structure even if we rotate one of the plots about the origin in an attempt to find a position in which it may be perfectly imposed upon the other. There is no such position. The two patterns are equally Darwinian (as shown in other sections), but they are not the same. In other words, it appears as though each set of phenomena are constrained by a pattern of phylogenetic or genealogical constraints, but that the two genealogies are independent of each other. This is entirely consistent with the correlation between human genetic and linguistic groups found by Cavalli-Sforza (1991) and Cavalli-Sforza *et al.* (1988), which is far from perfect due to independent gene or language replacement. It is also consistent with the more generalised correlations between early hominid remains and certain artefacts described by Foley (1987) (and see chapter 8 for further discussion).

We may conclude that while cultural phenomena correlate with human populations, the correlation is very 'temperamental'. It appears that cultural phenomena correlate with human crania only after the manner of domesticate or commensal fauna might be expected to do so (such as dogs or mice), as an independent but equally neo-Darwinian system. Like cultural phenomena, such animals also co-vary with human bone morphology, due to the tendency of their gene pools to share similar corridors of (and barriers to) gene flow, as due to their dependence upon humans they have virtually sympatric distributions. Yet such organisms are, obviously, not reproduced via human genes, but via their own. To summarise this point another way, there may be distinctive 'African dogs' and distinctive 'African humans', and 'European dogs' and 'European humans', which co-occur on their respective continents, but we know that this is not a result of the influence of human genes on dog phenotypes (or, for that matter, the influence of dog genes on human phenotypes). It is rather a corollary of the fact that human interaction takes place in a context of certain cultural and geographic constraints, and that these constraints have parallel effects upon the size and degree of isolation of both human and dog gene pools. Perhaps populations of cultural phenomena, then, are affected by much the same barriers and corridors to information exchange as are humans and their domesticates, and therefore tend to develop as a third class of neo-Darwinian phenomena, but as one which is as disarticulated from the first two as those two are from each other. Moreover, and for similar reasons, one would expect a large number of disarticulated lines of descent to occur within cultural assemblages (for example, pottery and metallurgy), just as multiple lines of descent would occur within a community of domesticates (for example, cows and sheep).

Concluding remarks

The principal objective of this chapter was to provide a general indication of the degree to which cultural diversity displayed the distinctive pattern of heritage constraint, and it appears that this is indeed the case. The implication is that cultural process is primarily selective in nature, and that human innovation tends not to transcend a cultural tradition, or, at least, not on a grand scale. In other words, a cultural tradition would appear to place fundamental constraints either on the nature of innovations, and/or on the uptake of those innovations. It seems that new ideas are derived not from the contemplation of 'necessity', but from old ideas.

It is also interesting to note that if anything the neo-Darwinian pattern is stronger in cultural assemblages than it is in 'known' neo-Darwinian systems. Heritage constraint seems to be an even more dramatic phenomenon in cultural process than it is in genetic process, when the global geography of faunal assemblages is compared with that of cultural assemblages. This is precisely what would be expected to be the case if cultural evolution was every bit as selective as genetic evolution, only very much faster. Comparison of human crania demonstrates the heritage pattern intraspecifically; yet, given the rate of cultural evolution, in comparing cultural assemblages one may be comparing phenomena at the interspecific, intergenus, interfamily or even interphylum level.

One might then pose an interesting question: If cultural process is so perfectly and dramatically neo-Darwinian in its logistics, and yet so much faster and therefore more observable (on the scale of human perception), why was it not the first selective process to be discovered? Perhaps because the patterns in culture could always be explained away as some kind of 'spin-off' from human genetic variation. But as already outlined above, there is no need to evoke genetic constraint; intrinsic neo-Darwinian logistics within cultural process itself are able to explain the general correlation. Moreover, unlike the genetic constraint position, a cultural selectionist position can also explain the few instances of non-correlation (gene or culture replacement) which also occur. Like the 'punctuated equilibrium' explanation in palaeontology (Eldredge & Gould 1972), Cultural Selectionism predicts the 'gaps' in the genes/culture correlation as well as the correlation patterns that *are* there (Cavalli-Sforza 1991: 77):

> Why should genetic and linguistic evolution correspond so closely? The answer lies not in genetic determinism but in history: genes do not control language; rather the circumstances of birth determine the languages to which one is exposed. Linguistic differences may generate or reinforce genetic barriers between populations, but they are unlikely to be the leading cause of the correlation. Human evolution is punctuated by the splitting of populations into parts, some of which settle elsewhere. Each fragment evolves linguistic and genetic patterns that bear the marks of shared branching points. Hence, some correlation is inevitable.

In any case, the pervasive occurrence of cultural heritage constraint makes one thing clear. Building a general theory of cultural change should involve some kind of appeal to notions of selective process. In other words, it would appear that Cultural Selectionism *of some kind* is required if a general theory of cultural change is to be fully developed. The next question to ask is 'What sort of Cultural Selectionism is most appropriate?' The next chapter addresses this question, and (building on the critique of the first five chapters) attempts to argue for a particular form of Cultural Selectionism termed the Cultural Virus Theory.

7

Foundation arguments
of the Virus perspective

Overview

Given the results of the previous chapter, it would appear that the explanation of cultural process will require a selective metaphysic of some kind. The next question addressed is 'Which?'. Here, in the final two chapters of the study, a particular form of Cultural Selectionism, termed the Cultural Virus perspective, is advocated. Firstly, a general outline of the notion of 'viral phenomena' is introduced. Then the academic context which led to the invention of the Cultural Virus position is outlined. It is stressed that while the Cultural Virus position and the Meme position are clearly independent inventions, the two perspectives are basically complementary, although the complementary elements are not fully explored until the first section of the next chapter. Finally, two important foundation arguments for the Virus perspective are discussed; Dawkins's principle of the Extended Phenotype, and Edelman's principles of Psychobiology.

The general notion of viral phenomena

The word virus is frequently used in modern discourse, usually in one of two basic contexts. On one hand, there are a range of diseases caused by microbial viruses which present some of the most frustrating challenges modern medicine has ever faced, from common colds to serious immune system deficiencies. On the other hand, we now have electronically transmitted computer viruses, designed by human programmers, which spread throughout a computer system and then cause the information network to come crashing down.

Yet the concept which the word virus denotes easily encompasses both phenomena. Although the origin of the use of the word 'virus' to describe certain kinds of pernicious computer programs was presumably metaphorical, such electronically transmitted phenomena fit the broader definition of a viral phenomenon remarkably well. Viruses can be broadly defined as phenomena which belong to a grey area in between organic and inorganic fields of enquiry, somewhere between the living and the dead. They are not living in the sense that organisms which breathe, metabolise, and reproduce are living, since, while outside their hosts, they carry out none of these basic processes (although some virologists prefer to view viruses as living when inside their hosts, e.g. Slap 1991: 668). Nor yet are they dead or truly inorganic in the sense of a pebble or a vial of helium, since unlike these phenomena a virus must be reproduced in the body of an organism (or computer) in order to persist in the universe. Viruses are not natural products of the inorganic forces governed by quantum mechanics and relativity, and would therefore cease to exist if there were no organisms to reproduce them.

A viral phenomenon can be alternatively defined as a freelance fragment which needs to 'borrow' other organisms bodies in order to reproduce. Unlike other predators it does not use organisms simply as fuel for its own autonomous metabolic processes (as it has none), but instead causes part of its host to manufacture copies of itself – it diverts an existing process to its own ends. RNA retroviruses, of which HIV is an example, are not capable of direct self-reproduction, as they have to borrow the DNA and the DNA-instructed cellular machinery of other organisms (in an undigested state) in order to reproduce (Delius 1989: 45; 1991: 83). This reliance on the phenotypes of other organisms obviates the need for complex, life-sustaining metabolic processes usually associated with (and often considered definitive of) life. Due to this periodic borrowing of cellular machinery, they have been able to dispense with (or perhaps never had to develop) a range of structures which would be required in order to be more self-sufficient.

Moreover, there is no need to assume that a viral entity will always be parasitic, although most modern usage of the term usually implies some pernicious effect. In fact, under many circumstances one might envisage that a viral entity would be best advised not to hinder, or perhaps even to help its host, and this may be the best way to ensure its own reproductive success. But the 'benefit' conveyed may not be a reproductive one, and therefore not a genuine 'Darwinian' benefit at all. For example, it may be in the interests of a parasite to help host survival rather than host reproduction. Certain parasites of snails (see below) cause their hosts to divert energy normally channelled into producing offspring into thickening and strengthening their shells, thereby prolonging the life of their hosts, but at the expense of their reproductive success (Dawkins 1989: 241). It is important that such parasites keep their hosts alive, but it is not in their interests to let the host waste energy in reproduction.

The great value of the generalised definition of 'viral phenomena' is that it provides an alternative avenue for the 'Darwinisation' of cultural fields of enquiry. Anthropologists and archaeologists who wish to reconcile the humanities with neo-Darwinian evolutionary theory are no longer obliged to incorporate culturally reproduced phenomena into the human phenotype, or to consider them as parts, traits, or organs of human individuals. Nor do we have to go to the other extreme (which Foley 1987a: 280; Levi-Strauss 1963: 4; and Leonard & Jones 1987: 215 have disparaged), and view artefacts as self-reproducing organisms in their own right. The Virus concept provides the archaeologist or, for that matter, any scholar of cultural evolution, with a comfortable seat on the fence between modern evolutionary genetics and the superorganic view of culture. Cultural phenomena may be viewed as both totally biological, and totally extra-genetic; cultural fields of enquiry are thereby grounded in actual biological processes, and yet no disciplinary identity is lost (Cullen 1991: 219). They are a class of psychobiological structures which are reproduced independently from genes. Rather than speaking of microbial viruses with genes and phenotypic products, we are speaking of culturally transmitted viral phenomena, as Memes with phenotypic products. In this sense, the two positions are neatly complementary, where each viral phenomenon consists of a group of Memes and their combined phenotypic product (see chapter 8).

The Cultural Virus Theory is better described as an heuristic simplification of Cultural Selectionism, not as a radical departure from it. The shock value of the word 'virus' forces the reader to envisage populations of artefacts or ideas as evolving in a Darwinian fashion, without the hitherto concomitant fallacy where such phenomena were assumed to be human traits. The term 'Cultural Virus Theory' contains no explicit reference to Darwinism or Selectionism, enabling the concept to 'slip through' the defences of a reader who has a pronounced prejudice against selective concepts as a result of their more frequent contextual association with Sociobiology. At the same time, a selective metaphysic of some kind is implied by the fact that viruses are normally explained in terms of selective frameworks. A term such as 'viral phenomenon', unlike the term 'trait', immediately evokes a mental picture of something that is independent from human genes, yet totally neo-Darwinian in and of itself. Thus the Virus concept has heuristic value for cultural selectionists wishing to defend themselves against the occupational hazard of being lumped with Cultural Sociobiology, despite the fact that Cultural Selectionism has a substantially different research agenda which is focused around cultural reproduced phenomena, rather than genetically reproduced phenomena.

Nonetheless, as will become clear, the concept also has some ontological value. Human behaviour and artefacts can be viewed as the phenotypic products of a class of neuronal structures (sets of strengthened synapses) which are reproduced via the process of cultural transmission (which is defined in the most general sense as socially mediated learning). The word virus simultaneously excludes or attracts attention away from the old Darwinian discourse focused on the adaptation of populations of human individuals, towards a new discourse focused on the adaptation of populations of ideas, while also avoiding any suggestion that ideas are sophisticated organisms in their own right.

Culturally reproduced phenomena do not, therefore, require the complexity or autonomy we normally associate with the word 'organism' in order to have their own unique adaptive history and genealogy, or to demand the status of a Darwinian individual, at least within the framework of Darwin's principles of adaptive selfishness (see also chapter 3 and chapter 5). Any phenomenon which is reproduced independently of the reproduction of its host, in other words which displays 'genealogical independence', qualifies as an 'individual' with regard to the principle of adaptive selfishness, and therefore must demand treatment as an independent lineage with its own idiosyncratic fitness criteria and separate adaptive polarity. By 'adaptive polarity' I mean that what is adaptive to such phenomena may be maladaptive for the body in which it resides, while conversely what is maladaptive for such phenomena may be adaptive for the body in which it resides.

In any case, as a consequence of the genealogical independence of (an otherwise highly dependent) cultural entity, it is quite possible to develop a genuinely Darwinian view of history, one based not on human virility or fecundity, but instead based on cultural virility. Propagation is still the key concept, but the general patterns of history are interpreted in terms of a cultural structure's ability to reproduce itself in new minds before the death of the mind or minds in which it is currently maintained.

The terms 'virus' or 'viral phenomenon' are also intended to capture a sense of the passive reproductive selfishness of artefacts, ideas, and rituals. Like viruses, none of these phenomena are capable of reproducing themselves. Yet the ideas in someone's mind, the recipes of various cookbooks and cuisines, or the technical knowledge of how to make a hand-axe need not be connected to who that person's parents were. An individual can acquire an idea or acquire a recipe from someone with whom they have no genetic relationship, in fact, from almost anyone that seems to be worthy of imitation, or who is willing to demonstrate and explain how to do something. So there is a kind of human behaviour that does not really 'belong' to a particular family of genetically related people in the way that genetic traits such as eye colour or the shape of ears does.

Yet although the influenza virus that someone catches is not inherited from that individual's grandparents via his or her parents, the influenza virus itself has a very solid genealogy of its own. It is a copy of another virus that existed, say, in the body of another individual that shares the same community as another, a virus which in turn was a copy of a virus that this particular individual was exposed to on an international trip, and so on all the way back to the ancestor of all influenza viruses, which may have been, for all we know, a mutant form of another virus which parasitises an altogether different animal species.

And, like any viral phenomenon, ideas also have a genealogy of their own which is usually quite different from the genealogy of the person whose mind they occupy. Consider that behind today's many different Marxist thinkers there is a long chain of other Marxist thinkers leading all the way back to Marx. Yet very few Marxists are genetically related to each other; the process of cultural transmission by means of which Marxism spreads is a result of a learning process which proceeds independently of human reproduction. Marx's ideas left his body via a very different route to his genes, at very different times and places, and consequently ended up, more often than not, in different people. Thus Marx's cultural descendants and his genetic descendants are two very different subsets of modern humanity.

So the generalised definition of a viral phenomenon encompasses not only microbial viruses and computer viruses, but all computer programs, all computers, all artefacts, and all other culturally transmitted phenomena such as scientific or religious concepts, behaviour patterns, rituals and political ideology. All these phenomena display genealogical independence from the human phenotype, and as a result they are not necessarily obedient extrasomatic 'organs'. Unlike true 'organs' and 'traits', their reproduction is not guaranteed by the reproduction of their hosts. At best, if properly controlled, they can be considered as analogous to human domesticates, such as pets or livestock, which have separate genealogies from their human companions, but are entrenched in a mutually beneficial 'symbiotic' relationship (see Delius 1989: 48 for a parallel argument in the Meme position). In fact, all cultural phenomena are domestic in the sense that they are dependent upon humans for reproductive success. Yet neither benevolent nor malevolent viral phenomena need present any difficulty to a selectionist world-view. To survive, no idea or practice need enhance the reproductive fitness of anything but itself. And even the most helpful or reassuring ideas and rituals, such as a belief in life after death or the morning mass, cannot possibly continue to help human communities unless those communities 'reward' them with the ultimate of Darwinian rewards, reproductive success.

As shown in previous chapters, other attempts to reconcile selectionist thought with cultural fields of enquiry have each contained a serious logical flaw which 'deconstructed' their attempts to develop a genuinely selectionist view of cultural process. Social 'Darwinism' was simply shown to be social Lamarckism in disguise; the flaw in this attempt was a misunderstanding of the nature of selective process. Sociobiology's flaw was less obvious. Its grasp of the nature of selective process was not the limiting factor; the fundamental flaw lay in Sociobiology's conception of the cultural phenomenon as an 'organ' rather than as a 'parasite', despite the fact that cultural phenomena undoubtedly display genealogical independence from the human body. Through mistaking a complicated ecological assemblage (i.e. a human individual) for a Darwinian individual, cultural phenomena were viewed as traits of the human phenotype, and viewed as though they were ordered by reproductive events which occurred outside cultural lines of inheritance. The explanatory framework thereby violates the basic Darwinian principle of reproductive selfishness, and thereby degenerates into Lamarckism. Thus the two alternative evolutionary approaches to Cultural Selectionism, Cultural Evolutionism and Cultural Sociobiology, can be dismissed as being explicitly Lamarckian and inadvertently Lamarckian respectively.

As shown in chapter 5, the phenotypic form of Cultural Selectionism retains sociobiological definitions of individual, population, phenotype, environment, and adaptation. But the general notion of viral phenomena opens up the possibility of a fourth attempt to reconcile the modern humanities with modern selectionist notions of process. The parasite or Virus notion of cultural phenomena allows a definition of cultural fields of enquiry as unique, and as lying beyond the boundaries of established biological discourse in certain important ways, but potentially classifiable as a unique branch of biology. The approach thoroughly deconstructs the nature/nurture, biology/culture, and body/mind distinctions. However, one distinction is judged to be very important indeed. This is the distinction between modes of transmission (genetic versus cultural or social). Thus in the Virus account of culture (within humanity) 'all is nature but not all is nurture', 'all is biology, but not all culture', and 'all is body, but not all is mind'. In other words, cultural phenomena are classified as a special case of biological phenomena, but this notion will not be more fully developed until the next chapter.

The origin of the Cultural Virus perspective

In chapter 4, the origins of a number of different cultural selectionist positions were briefly contrasted. It is now pertinent to move on to a more specific discussion of the origin of the Cultural Virus position itself, and its relationship to the various other positions which exist within the larger umbrella of Cultural Selectionism as a whole. The details of the development of this position are quite complicated, and require a general description of the background influences which led me to stumble upon the notion of treating cultural transmitted phenomena as a class of parasite via the use of the Virus concept. The most complicated part of the story is the relationship of the Virus position to the Meme position. The Virus position was most definitely invented independently of the Meme position, despite post-dating the publication of *The selfish gene* by about seven years. This was due to the fact that the Meme position did not have a high profile in mainstream archaeology or cultural anthropology for some time. It is now clear that there are dramatic parallels between the two views, although there are also (presumably as a direct result of their independent origins) *significant differences*. Explaining this in greater detail, however, will require further discussion of the differences which exist within the cultural selectionist literature.

In chapter 4 a classification scheme of *four* basic cultural selectionist positions was outlined. However, there are only *three broad traditions* of cultural selectionist discourse, as one of them encompasses two positions. All three traditions appear to have arisen in the 1970s, each from a different point of origin within academia, and during the early stages of their development each was largely independent of the others. The three different points of origin can be crudely labelled 'American Darwinian Anthropology', 'Cantabrigean Archaeology', and 'Oxonian Ethology'. The fourth position, that of the Cultural Virus, arose in the 1980s within the 'Cantabrigean Archaeology' discourse, but, as we shall see below, made some substantial breaks with that context. It is worth noting also that there has, of course, always been a British Darwinian anthropology throughout this period, but, at least until recently, it did not advocate a view of culture which could be called cultural selectionist.

Without taking up too much space, it is interesting to add a few remarks about the classification system. The first body of discourse mentioned above, 'American Darwinian Anthropology', encompasses the most prominent and established form of Cultural Selectionism, which has been described in this study as the phenotypic or organismic position (for example Boyd & Richerson 1982; Cavalli-Sforza & Feldman 1981; and Durham 1982; Rindos 1985; analysed in chapter 5 from the point of view of the Cultural Virus position). This is the position which arose within American Darwinian Anthropology in the 1970s, inspired by seminal texts such as that of Campbell (1965). This position has, more recently, had some influence over British Darwinian archaeology and anthropology.

The second position mentioned above, the 'Meme' position (1976), of which Dawkins was the architect, arose within the context of general principles of modern evolutionary biology. Originally criticised by Darwinian anthropologists by those such as Alexander (1979), it is clear that Dawkins (1989: 322) originally employed the Meme concept not in order to sculpt a new general theory for culture, but as a more casual illustration of the general applicability of neo-Darwinian principles to non-genetic contexts. Moreover, it appears that the short speculative theoretical statement of the Meme position made by Dawkins was virtually ignored for some time by most exclusively cultural fields of enquiry, and it was only in the 1980s, and particularly the late 1980s, that its influence began to filter through to the cultural selectionist literature to a significant extent. While certain analyses of evolutionary culture theory recognised the existence of the Meme position in the 1980s (Daly 1982; Rindos 1986b), few anthropologists noted the full implications of Dawkins's speculative statements, despite the fact that some academics, such as Ball (1984), showed more interest.

Thirdly, there is a small Australian cultural selectionist discourse (Clegg 1978a; Fletcher 1977; 1981a; 1981b; 1988) the heritage of which is largely Cantabrigean Archaeology, especially the ideas of David Clarke (1978). It is in this context that the various elements of the Cultural Virus position first occurred to me. Although there is no obvious cultural antecedent to be found in the work of either Fletcher or Clegg, it was certainly their interest in the general idea of viewing biological and cultural evolution as independent processes which focused my attention on the use of biocultural analogy in the explanation of cultural change. It is this small Australian discourse, of a primarily Cantabrigean heritage, in which the Virus position originated, and it was developed in dialogue with the alternative positions which were concurrently being explored by Fletcher and Clegg.

The earliest steps in the direction of the Cultural Virus position date to 1983, as I outlined most of the basic elements of the perspective in a second-year undergraduate essay written for Roland Fletcher during that year. The circumstances under which I came to write the essay are somewhat unusual, in that when I approached Roland for the very first time, I already had a specific request in mind. I wanted to write an essay which asserted that cultural process was *fundamentally neo-Darwinian in every particular,* right down to the complete deconstruction of any notion of 'rational' invention, and yet utterly extra-genetic; i.e. that these processes occurred in somatic time. Roland had given a lecture on the use and abuse of evolutionary theory in archaeology, and had seemed to me to be uncertain about the degree to which cultural change could really be considered a genuinely 'evolutionary' process. But having read neo-Darwinian theory as part of a childhood and adolescent passion for biology, I was familiar with the nineteenth-century struggle between the Darwinian and Lamarckian paradigms, and the various conundrums which Darwinism had had to 'explain away' before supplanting the dominant Lamarckian paradigm. It seemed to me that all the 'Lamarckian' aspects of culture could be overcome using the same kinds of argument, and that each of these aspects would prove to be a 'pseudo-Lamarckism' with underlying neo-Darwinian logistics. The thought that what seemed to me to be a perfectly good explanatory framework was virtually absent from cultural fields of enquiry (as Fletcher argued) was a revelation that seemed almost too good to be true. Moreover, Roland made it quite clear in his lectures that at that time even he was not sure whether cultural change was a Darwinian process, expressing this parsimony in his use of the non-committal noun 'development' for cultural change, and his explicit avoidance of the Darwinian noun 'evolution' in such contexts.

At this time, both John Clegg and Roland Fletcher were interested in the general notion that the archaeological variability produced by cultural change was entirely extra-genetic, along with the notion that artefact variability could be explained and analysed without recourse to social reconstruction. Clegg (1977a; 1977b; 1978a; 1978b; but primarily personal communication) had made general statements to the effect that cultural evolution was 'like' biological evolution, in his studies of prehistoric art, and had discussed (Clegg pers. com.) the problem of the most appropriate 'organism' with which to compare artefacts. He used a biological analogy between certain plants which had alternate generations of two completely different structural states (such as cycads and ferns, which have a mobile sperm-like generation, and a sessile plant generation) to address the problem of the mind–artefact–mind–artefact sequence in cultural inheritance.

Roland, however, working in settlement studies, was not so sure about analogies between artefacts and organisms. He explained to me that he felt that there were aspects of cultural evolution which seemed decidedly nonevolutionary, and that this was why he preferred to use the word 'development' rather than evolution. He was not convinced by my point-blank statement that cultural evolution was typically neo-Darwinian in every particular (which was already implicitly a Virus position, as any 'trait' approach must necessarily qualify the neo-Darwinian analogy, see chapter 5), but he agreed to allow me to write an honours essay which set out to prove that this was so. However, his parsimony concerning my cultural selectionist position was reflected in the set of questions he wanted me to address, which implied that in his view the two processes were not equivalent: What is the nature of biological evolution? What is the nature of cultural evolution? What is the difference between biological and cultural evolution? Does cultural evolution exist? Is cultural evolution really just development? I was to begin my research by reading Fletcher (1977), *Settlement studies: micro and semi-micro*; Ghiselin (1969), *The triumph of Darwinian method*; Yoffee (1979), *The decline and rise of Mesopotamian civilisation*; and Dunnell & Wenke's (1980) comments on Yoffee's paper, *Cultural and scientific evolution: some comments on the decline and rise of Mesopotamian civilisation*.

The questions merely exemplified what I had already suspected, but hardly dared believe; that Fletcher felt that cultural evolution was not necessarily a genuine evolutionary process, and that, moreover, that a neo-Darwinian conception of cultural process was still widely doubted. I had always had a dream about being sent back in time to the Lamarckian era to start a Darwinian revolution all over again; now it seemed that this dream, in a strange way, was coming true. The revolution might well have been over in biology, but it was not yet complete, in fact barely begun, in cultural fields of enquiry. I set out to prove to Fletcher that cultural evolution did exist and that there was nothing in cultural systems that presented more of a challenge to neo-Darwinian theory than any of the biological conundrums which it had overcome in the past. The aim was to show that cultural process was perfectly neo-Darwinian in every particular, and that the odd bits and pieces which appeared not to fit had equally problematic equivalents in neo-Darwinian genetics which archaeologists and cultural anthropologists happened not to be aware of.

Despite the fact that the essay had an upper limit of 4000 words, my interest in the issue ultimately produced an essay 13,000 words long. The word Virus was not used in the terminology developed in the paper, as I preferred to use the terms 'metonym' and 'metonymic evolution' to describe my conception of an idea or culturally transmitted phenomenon. 'Metonym' was derived from the literary device of 'metonymy', a kind of metaphor where a concept was represented, not in terms of itself, but in terms of the name of an associated object, such as in the use of 'the Crown' when referring to a monarch, or in the use of the phrase 'the kettle is boiling' where what is actually boiling is the water inside. It seemed to me that all ideas were really metonyms, things we associate with objects, and that they never actually 'were' the reality they were supposed to symbolise. They were composed of brain matter, while the things they symbolised were not; they could therefore never really be 'true' or identical to the things they represented, but different ideas could nonetheless reflect reality to varying degrees. The word 'metonym' was intended to capture the notion that perception was a purely selective process, in which symbols which already existed in our heads were 'matched' with environmental phenomena, so that learning and ultimately cultural evolution never involved the actual formation of psychological phenomena but merely the selection of some at the expense of others. The essay could be summed up as a crude undergraduate re-invention of Edelman's (1978; 1989) Neuronal Group Selection Theory of Psychobiology (no group selection argument is implied, as the 'Group' goes with 'Neuronal', and not with 'Selection'), only at a more 'psychocultural' level. Most particularly, I tried to argue that human creativity was utterly analogous to genetic mutation, in that it was fundamentally random within certain constraints, and that apparent Lamarckisms such as 'rational inventions' could be deconstructed into a series of random moments of insight.

Over the next decade the basic arguments of this undergraduate essay were developed into a perspective which I termed the Cultural Virus position, and it was not until 1986 that Dawkins's Meme concept was brought more forcefully to my attention, and not until 1990 that I analysed the notion in any detail. I was struck by the parallel elements of the two positions, but also intrigued to find out that there were subtly different emphases in each position, presumably as a result of their conceptual isolation. Due to the subtly different emphases, the two terminologies fit quite neatly together, with Memes constituting the 'genetic' level of cultural systems, and the notion of a 'viral phenomenon' incorporating one or more Memes and their combined phenotypic aspects – the 'organismic' level of cultural phenomena. The irony of the similarity was that I had used Dawkins's evolutionary biology as my basic neo-Darwinian authority on which to build viral models of culture during the period of 'isolation', while failing to give Dawkins's Meme discussion any extensive attention. In other words, the Meme and Cultural Virus positions were independent attempts to translate the same body of 'selfish gene' neo-Darwinian principles into cultural contexts. This peculiar situation is reflected in the fact that Dawkins and I appeal to different parts of Dawkins's own selfish gene theories, as starting points for cultural analogies. For example, one of the basic foundation arguments of the Virus position is Dawkins's genetic discussion of host/parasite conflicts; yet Dawkins himself makes no such explicit appeal to microbial parasites in the new edition of *The selfish gene* (or to *The extended phenotype*) when discussing his own Meme position, although it is reasonable to assume that the use of the same principles were implied. Microbial parasite analogies are far more thoroughly explored *vis à vis* the Meme concept by those such as Ball (1984) and Delius (1989; 1991).

The fact of independent emphasis on some kind of parasitic quality in culture, in both the Meme and the Virus position, might appear to be too grand a coincidence. But the notions of the parasitic qualities of cultural phenomena were appearing quite widely in cultural selectionist discourse around the time that the two positions were being developed. I have listed (Cullen 1990: 64) a number of studies which consider the possibility of cultural phenomena having either viral or Meme-like qualities, and in addition to the above-mentioned Dawkins (1976: 207); these include Ball (1984 *passim*); Cloak (1975: 172); and Delius (1989 *passim*). There is also the 'co-evolutionary' concept which implies the potential for some kind of parasitic quality, as in Durham (1990; 1991), and (less explicitly parasitic) Freeman (1983). Secondly, there are references to 'less viral' concepts of parasitism or negativity (again see Cullen 1990: 64) – uses of words like 'disease', 'maladaptive', 'susceptibility', or 'epidemic' with reference to cultural phenomena, such as those notions used by Cavalli-Sforza & Feldman (1981: 342); Fletcher (1977: 46); Richerson & Boyd (1985: 83); and Sperber (1985). Moreover, Delius lists a wide range of popular references to such notions in general discourse in a prologue to a paper (Delius 1989: 26):

> Colleague at Bochum University: "You have set a flea in my ear."
> Disc jockey on German radio: "The song is a proper earwig."
> Report in an English newspaper: "The idea was obviously infectious."
> Passenger on an international flight: "What a contagious, nonsensical habit!"
> American performance artist: "Language is a virus."

The performance artist referred to by Delius, although he does not name her, is Laurie Anderson, and the song, entitled 'Language is a virus', was released in 1986, and which, as it happens, was one of the influences in the beginning of my own shift from the use of the words like 'metonym' to words like 'viral phenomenon' in that year. Given the completely different terminology used in most of the above-mentioned studies, the tendency towards a lack of inter-referencing, and the wide-ranging occurrence of 'viralesque' terminology in non-academic contexts indicated by the Delius epigraph, it would appear that, in fact, independent invention has been more the rule than the exception in the origin of these ideas. It should therefore come as no surprise that the two most extreme cultural parasite positions, the Meme and Virus positions, were invented independently of each other.

Foundation arguments from Dawkins's parasite genetics

The first response of a 'traits' or phenotypic cultural selectionist (or, for that matter, a sociobiologist) to the Virus argument is usually based not on an objection to the basic viability of the analogy, but on doubt as to whether the analogy has any heuristic value which would make it superior to the more established Darwinian positions. David Rindos (pers. comm. 1988), William Irons (pers. comm. 1990), and Robert Boyd (pers. comm. 1992) for example, have all expressed this kind of reservation. Their objection would be expressed something like this: Obviously, we can call anything which is reproduced only through the actions of another organism a virus, but what explanatory advantages does the position offer?

If we already accept that the host/virus analogy for humans and their associated culturally transmitted structures is viable, then the challenge to Cultural Virus Theory becomes that of demonstrating the potential and value of the perspective. Any demonstration of heuristic superiority depends upon finding some fundamental differences between the logistics of evolutionary process in populations of 'individuals' which represent 'single' phenotypes (hosts or parasites), and populations of individuals each of which represents a 'multiple' phenotype (an host/parasite combination, or 'host/guest' relationship in terms used by Delius (1989: 48)).

A population consisting of individual structures constituted from more than one phenotype really consists of two or more populations occupying the same space, unless all those structures of which any given individual is constituted reproduce synchronically. In fact an individual is properly defined as any group of structures which are ultimately reproduced in a single reproductive event. In the argument developed below, definitions of individuality and notions of 'a phenotype' are shown to be crucial to selectionist explanation, and that the Cultural Virus Theory constitutes a more appropriate model of 'individuality' for cultural process than the implicit 'human being' unit of Sociobiology and the implicit or partially declared 'human being' unit of Cultural Selectionism. The key to this argument lies in the special issues of host/parasite evolution.

In response to the concern about demonstrating the heuristic superiority of a Cultural Virus position over a traits discourse, a general discussion of host/parasite ecological relationships will now be used to develop an argument for the necessity of the viral independence approach to cultural process. An appeal will be made to several summaries of host/parasite conflicts of interest presented by Dawkins in the final chapter of the new edition of *The selfish gene* (1989). In this edition, another chapter has been added in which the basic arguments of another book, *The extended phenotype* (1982), are summarised. Dawkins examines the conditions under which host and parasite relationships demand complete co-operation, and conversely, those conditions under which host and parasite relationships are likely to produce a situation of conflict. In indirect opposition to some statements from Durham (1982: 304), but ultimately in partial accordance with other statements of this study (see Durham 1982: 309; and below in this chapter), I will argue that the human/culturally transmitted entity relationship is one where the potential for host/parasite conflict arises. This argument involves the extrapolation of Dawkins's discussion of the extended phenotype from the genetic context to the cultural one.

In his notion of the 'extended phenotype', Dawkins explores how genes can have a variety of effects on bodies other than that in which they reside. Just like ordinary phenotypic effects, such factors can either aid or impede a gene's or group of gene's chances of successful reproduction. In other words, variation in the extended phenotype can provide raw material for natural selection, and a given trajectory in a population of organisms produced by changes in gene frequencies may well be due to effects the favoured genes have on some other group of organisms altogether. Genetic variation for this characteristic may be completely invisible in the phenotypes of the bodies they produce, and manifest only as a 'distortion' of the phenotypes of another species.

The particular interest that host/parasite relations has for the 'human individual versus the Cultural Virus' issue begins with the fact that genes may have extended phenotypic effects in bodies other than the one in which they reside. This is because part of a parasite's extended phenotype includes those effects it has on the phenotype of its host, and part of the host extended phenotype includes all the influences its genes may have upon the phenotypes of its parasites.

Thus the form any particular body takes is not merely the outcome of the information stored in its particular genotype interacting with the inorganic environment, but also influenced by other genes in other genotypes via the structures and molecules that those other genotypes produce. Given that the interests of both parasite and host can involve a body taking a particular form, it might be interesting to pose the question: Do these interests always coincide, and if not, when are they likely to diverge? Quite possibly, the form a body takes may in fact be a convoluted mixture of quite separate genetic influences, each based on somewhat different reproductive interests.

Dawkins, in three examples which will be summarised briefly below, shows how the best interests of parasite and host may often subtly or dramatically diverge, and that this conflict of interest may well be resolved in favour of the parasite rather than the host, or vice versa, rather than always manifesting itself as a symbiotic compromise.

The first example concerns certain kinds of snail which are parasitised by certain flukes (flatworms). One of the effects the parasites have on the snail is to thicken its shell. This thicker shell has the effect of making the snail more resistant to shell damage (presumably), and so we have a situation where (apparently) it is actually advantageous for a snail to be infected with flatworms. Dawkins (1989: 241), however, points out that this begs the question of why (given that shells of greater thickness are obviously possible) do snails not normally grow shells of this thickness? His answer lies in the economic cost of shell production to the owner (Dawkins 1989: 241):

> Making a shell is costly for the snail. It requires energy. It requires calcium and other chemicals that have to be extracted from hard won food. All these resources, if they were not spent on making shell substance, could be spent on something else such as making more offspring. A snail that spends lots of resources on making an extra-thick shell has bought safety for its own body. But at what cost? It may live longer, but it will be less successful at reproducing and may fail to pass on its genes. Among the genes that fail to be passed will be the genes for making extra thick shells. In other words, it is possible for a shell to be too thick as well as too thin.

The fundamental issue is whose physical resources are being used to manufacture the extra shell thickness. If the fluke uses its own metabolic processes and energy resources to add to the thickness of the snail's shell, then all is fair and square. The snail enjoys the added safety of a thicker shell, and is in a position to translate its longer life into increased reproductive success. Each fluke is in a position to do likewise, while enjoying the security of a longer-living host. If, however, each fluke is able to exert subtle chemical influences on the snail, such that the host is forced to use its own valuable energy resources to lengthen its life at the expense of its reproductive success, then the parasites become the sole beneficiaries of the transaction. The chemical which the parasites exude constitutes an aspect of their extended phenotype which allows them to be more reproductively successful than other flukes who cannot influence their hosts in a similar way. Fluke genes with shell-thickening extended phenotypes (i.e. genes with the potential to collaborate with certain fluke genotypes in such a way as to produce an organism which secretes the appropriate chemical) have undergone differential reproduction in the respective fluke population due to their ability to divert host energy away from host reproduction towards their own. Dawkins sums up the situation as follows (Dawkins 1989: 242):

> Both snail genes and fluke genes stand to gain from the snail's bodily survival, all other things being equal. But survival is not the same thing as reproduction and there is likely to be a trade-off. Whereas snail genes stand to gain from the snail's reproduction, fluke genes don't. This is because any given fluke has no particular expectation that its genes will be housed in its present host's offspring. They might be, but so might those of any of its fluke rivals. Given that snail longevity has to be bought at the cost of some loss in the snail's reproductive success, the fluke genes are "happy" to make the snail pay that cost, since they have no interest in the snail's reproducing itself. The snail genes are not happy to pay that cost, since their long terms future depends upon the snail reproducing. So, I suggest that fluke genes exert an influence on the shell-secreting cells of the snail, an influence that benefits themselves but is costly to the snail's genes. This theory is testable, though it hasn't been tested yet.

In the second example of host/parasite reproductive conflict, and two genetic interests competing for influence of one body, parasites exert an influence over the development of their hosts. A species of single-celled animal (protozoan) called Nosema lives in the bodies of flour beetle larvae, and has the capacity to control the timing of the onset of maturity in its host by exuding its own copies of one of the beetle's hormones. This particular hormone, called 'juvenile' hormone, is secreted in the body of a juvenile insect and has the effect of maintaining the organism in its larval state. Pupation, and ultimately adulthood, are later stages brought about by the cessation of 'juvenile' hormone production in the larva's body. The Nosema parasites are able to prevent the onset of adulthood by secreting a close chemical analogue of the 'juvenile' hormone, such that the larva continues to grow way beyond the normal size at which the larval/adult transition occurs. As the larva is not, by definition, sexually mature, it cannot reproduce, and therefore spends all its time eating and growing, supporting its strange assemblage of guests.

The final example which Dawkins uses is that which involves the exploitation of crabs by *Sacculina*. In an extraordinary example of host control, a certain kind of parasite similar to a barnacle is actually able to castrate its crab host, enabling it to continue to thrive but preventing it from translating its stored energy resources into reproductive success. Dawkins describes the situation with vivid imagery (1989: 243):

> *Sacculina* is related to barnacles, though you would think, to look at it, that it was a parasitic plant. It drives an elaborate root system into the tissues of the unfortunate crab, and sucks nourishment from its body. It is probably no accident that among the first organs that it attacks are the crab's testicles or ovaries; it spares the organs the crab needs to survive – as opposed to reproduce – till later. The crab is effectively castrated by the parasite. Like a fattened bullock, the castrated crab diverts energy and resources away from reproduction and into its own body – rich pickings for the parasite at the expense of the crab's reproduction.

These examples lead Dawkins to a definitive statement about the conditions under which the development of host/parasite conflicts in reproductive success become likely (Dawkins 1989: 243):

> I suggest that the most important question to ask about any parasite is this. Are its genes transmitted to future generations via the same vehicles as the host's genes? If they are not, I would expect it to damage the host, in one way or another. But if they are, the parasite will do all it can to help the host, not only to survive but to reproduce. Over evolutionary time it will cease to be a parasite, will co-operate with the host, and may eventually merge into the host's tissues and become unrecognisable as a parasite at all.

To illustrate this dynamic, Dawkins adds a final example in which host and parasite genes do use a common exit, and in which reproductive and therefore adaptive interests essentially coincide. Wood-boring ambrosia beetles harbour bacterial parasites which, unlike the parasites of the previous examples, actually use the beetle eggs as their means of transport to a new host. In other words, their interhost transmission takes place in the body of the current host during the gamete production process, and all new hosts infected by the bacteria must therefore be direct descendants of the old host. As an evolving entity the beetle/bacteria combination becomes practically indistinguishable from the relationship beetles and other organisms sustain with intracellular structures such as ribosomes which possess their own genetic material which reproduces independently of human chromosomes. Providing that parasite and host use the same vehicles for reproduction, what is adaptive for the parasite and what is adaptive for the host should amount to the same thing. As Dawkins puts it (1989: 244):

The two sets of genes can be expected to "pull together" for just the same reasons as all the genes of one individual organism normally pull together. It is irrelevant that some of them happen to be "beetle genes", while others happen to be "bacterial genes". Both sets of genes are "interested" in beetle survival and the propagation of beetle eggs, because both "see" beetle eggs as their passport to the future.

In fact, the two parties do a lot more than just pull together. The beetles are haplodiploid; fertilised eggs develop into females while unfertilised eggs develop into males. However, unfertilised eggs are incapable of developing into male beetles without the intervention of the bacteria. Without the help of their bacterial parasites, these beetles would be incapable of sexual recombination.

We can take Dawkins's rule of parasite ecology and apply it to culturally transmitted phenomena. Clearly cultural reproduction is not synchronised with human reproduction (cultural transmission does not occur exclusively between parents and children), and we can, therefore, expect conflicts of adaptive interest to emerge between artefacts and the people who reproduce them.

I have illustrated this foundation argument of the Cultural Virus position through a brief discussion of the example of the behaviour of a workaholic business employee. Let us say the whole act of working nine to five, having tea breaks and half an hour for lunch, working late, and wining and dining clients and colleagues at dinner is all a daily ritual which the woman or man concerned replicates each day. Let us say that this person has a divorced spouse and two children in their early twenties living on another continent. Finally, let us say that this person is also actively involved in developing the skills of a number of junior partners, and is transferring to them the elements of a disciplined daily regime.

From the point of view of classical Sociobiology, the actions of the workaholic would be interpreted as the maximisation of genetic reproductive success. The workaholic pursues economic, emotional, aesthetic and social rewards, which he or she then cheerfully translates into alimony payments, emotional support, and advice for his or her children, being careful to put a little aside for the possibility of attracting future suitors, having more children, and building up a reasonable inheritance for the family in the event of the person's death. There is an optimum trade-off between the necessity of continuing to live, and the necessity of providing for one's past and future children, just as in snails there is an optimum trade-off between shell quality and numbers of young snails. Strictly speaking, individuals in a business should attempt to manipulate their investment in the workplace in order to increase their chances both of producing genetic offspring, and providing resources, not for only for their children, but for other family members also. In some circumstances, the only way to do this will be through working for the general good of the company, so that all employees and especially the partners benefit from general productivity and increased profits. Under other circumstances, a worker's family may be benefited through more dishonest practices, but the temptation of these must be weighed up against other factors, such as the possibility for self-criticism at a later date via 'morals' or 'one's conscience', an assessment of the physical or emotional attributes required to successfully carry out a particular strategy, the threat of public humiliation, prosecution, and so on.

Human individuals are able to use their intelligence to understand and weigh up the value of these complicated alternatives, although they will almost certainly not think about their lives in these terms. The general information-processing capacities of the brain must be basically adaptive, or such qualities could never have evolved so comprehensively in the first place (Mithen 1989; Rindos 1986b). But as non-reductionists such as Dawkins have so carefully pointed out time and time again (despite unfair accusations of being both determinist and reductionist), genes can only *create* organisms, they cannot *determine or control* them (Dawkins 1989: 20, 271). Once created, the human capacity for culture, like any other organismic structure, may then be 'hijacked' by parasitic structures which colonise it after it has begun to develop. Yet, the end-result of these cultural capacities must still be a net gain, or individuals with no learning capacities would begin to out-reproduce other individuals.

Nonetheless, from the point of view of the Cultural Virus Theory, the whole adaptive equation becomes more complex. The information-processing system, which evolved due to the general advantages it conveyed to its bearers, is by no means perfect. The worhaholic's capacity to translate economic rewards into children can be seriously compromised by his or her fascination with the daily ritual of the work experience, as work rituals of different kinds persist in companies longer than any one employee precisely because of their capacity to sustain appeal amongst their participants. Knowledge of and commitment to this daily ritual constitutes a cultural phenomenon distributed in bits and pieces throughout the minds of the people in the company. Some daily activities tend to be far more appealing than others, due to the degree of satisfaction they offer, the degree of escape from stress, and so on. Every day we spend in the workplace we encounter rituals with a survival pedigree; they are still around precisely because no employee or employer has been able to prevent their cultural transmission from senior employee to junior employee over the decades.

Whether the person concerned views themselves as working because 'they enjoy it', in order to 'gain experience', or 'make money', is not the issue. The main issue is that only two general classes of phenomena have the potential to live on after the individual concerned has died; genes and Memes. The question becomes one of attempting to estimate whether the individual's genes, or perhaps particular Memes, are benefiting from the individual's behaviour. It is possible to imagine a course of behaviour which would lead towards maximum numbers of genetic offspring; conversely, at the other extreme, one can imagine a course of behaviour which would lead to maximum 'teaching' of certain Memes and their corresponding behaviour patterns. Most human behaviour presumably lies somewhere in between these two extremes. Cultural selection will favour work rituals which help the worker to survive, but which have the effect of distracting the attention of this increasingly successful individual away from his or her family, and towards the workplace. In other words, a lethal or highly dangerous yet exciting work practice will tend to have a shortened life-span, unless it can spread very rapidly indeed. Generally, a Meme can be far more successful if it actually *promotes* health, but reduces family interests.

So the work ritual may well tip the workaholic's behaviour in favour of its own cultural reproduction, in the same way as the liver fluke influences the snail to build its shell stronger than it ought. Of course, the workaholic is praised for contributing to company productivity, and may receive financial bonuses and a plump expenses account. In short, the workaholic's life is enhanced and perhaps extended, as was the snails. However, from a Darwinian point of view, the work ritual itself may, under certain circumstances, be deriving a great deal more reproductive benefit from the workaholic's actions than are his or her genes. The energy channelled into the teaching of new employees and helping existing employees, into maintaining and replicating the rituals and activities of the company, may come vastly to outweigh the amount of energy the workaholic channels into children or family. Far from being arranged around genetic reproduction, the workaholic's life is in fact arranged around cultural reproduction. He or she has fallen prey to a viral neuronal structure, and one which has the hypnotic effect of channelling human energies into its replication.

The workaholic example was not included at this early stage as a primary demonstration of the Cultural Virus Theory, as this section is intended only to establish basic foundation arguments from parasite ecology. The workaholic example was included only to outline a basic cultural equivalent of the rule. The basic rule may be summarised as follows: parasite/host combinations = many lines of inheritance = adaptive conflicts. The converse rule would be this: single organism = single (or double, in the case of sexual reproduction) line of inheritance = adaptive co-operation. All the reader need conclude from this is that cultural transmission = many lines of inheritance, and that 'human individuals' are therefore really mini ecological assemblages, and host/parasite or host/guest combinations, with adaptive conflicts.

Brain versus Virus: the psychobiological arms race

A basic implication of this new Darwinian perspective is that the 'environments' or 'niches' which define the fitness of different viral ideas or behaviours are governed by purely symbolic and psychological factors (Cullen 1990: 65). It is thus *exclusively preoccupied* with the very areas of human affairs which neo-Darwinism is normally criticised for ignoring or being unable to cope with (Shanks & Tilley 1987a; 1987b; Ingold 1986; 1990). This is in contrast to fitness definitions which involve both the symbolic and genetic, as fitness is defined in cultural selectionist frameworks. Rindos (1986b: 321), for example, has a category of human benefit ('demic' cultural selection or CS1), where cultural entities can be selected on the grounds of the genetic fitness they convey to their bearers. Other cultural selectionists (Boyd & Richerson 1985; Cavalli-Sforza & Feldman 1981; Durham 1982; Lumsden & Wilson 1981) juggle genetic and cultural fitness in a variety of ways. But fitness must, in the new viral perspective, always be defined purely in terms of the total psychological appeal a viral phenomenon can sustain in a wide range of minds and personalities, with genetic factors only being included to the extent that they affect this appeal. Genetic factors need never be directly discussed, since they cannot affect the psychological fitness of ideas unless they are perceived and valued, i.e. unless they are in fact *other ideas*, and not demographic or reproductive facts. If the idea is viewed to be 'maladaptive yet appealing', then a cultural equivalent of the Wynne-Edwards 'good of the species' group selection fallacy (Dawkins 1989: 7, 69, 282), where a structure persists in a population due to its long-term rather than short-term adaptiveness, is produced. *An appealing idea is an adapted one*, period. An idea or artefact can only be considered 'fit' to the degree to which it has more symbolic appeal than any other at the time. A population of ideas cannot resist short-term infiltration by another idea or artefact with more symbolic appeal, just because the original ideas convey some long-term benefit to the human community that the new idea does not. If a pernicious but appealing new idea appears, it will simply replace the old one before driving that human community and itself to extinction, unless at some critical point in the process it loses that appeal. This may occur, for example, if an individual is aware of the long-term dangers of using a particular artefact, and deliberately avoids using it. However, the artefact is quite free to colonise any minds who are not aware of such consequences.

The overall challenge will be to view the human mind not as a coherent self (although this may often successfully emerge), but as a vast arena for complicated networks of collaborations and conflicts between (and amongst) on the one hand, the phenotypic expressions of genes, and, on the other hand, Memes (Ball 1984: 147; Cullen 1990: 65). Each Meme or gene then persists in a given human community according to its all-round ability to influence a long succession of different people in such a way as to increase its chances of reproduction. More specifically, each Meme competes against other Memes for replicative success on the grounds of its total collaborative potential with hundreds of human phenotypes and many thousands of cultural phenotypes. Evolution in the human capacity for culture could then be expected to favour genes which collaborate with a range of bodies in such a way as to produce highly resistant intellects. In other words, it is in the reproductive interests of human genes to be able indirectly to influence brain ontogeny in such a way as to produce features which help the person to selectively resist pernicious enculturation, and to remain pragmatically sceptical. Symons (1979) has used just such an argument against viral Selectionism, arguing that counter-adaptations in human intelligence will be so complete as to prevent any pernicious concept or behaviour from spreading.

In light of this argument, Cultural Virus Theory ultimately begs the question of how the human cultural capacity could ever evolve, given that the capacity evidently carries with it a general susceptibility to socially transmitted pernicious behaviour. How could something with such a great potential for cultural parasitism be adaptive enough to become comprehensively fixed in the hominid lineage? It is obvious that in some sense the human cultural capacity must be adaptive, or else it could not have spread in the first place. Many, such as Dawkins (1989: 193), Delius (1989: 54), Durham (1982), Freeman (1983), Mithen (1989: 483), Rindos (1986a; 1986b), and, as already implied, Symons (1979), to name a few, have submitted various arguments which relate to this problem of where to fit 'maladaptive' behaviour into a co-evolutionary framework.

Yet the problem of pernicious behaviour itself carries within it the kernel of a solution. It is conceivable that pernicious behaviour, and not beneficial behaviour, has been the primary driving agent in the evolution of the human capacity for culture. To put it another way, it is possible that the Symons challenge does not so much threaten the Virus position as advance it. Perhaps intellectual self-defences did evolve in the human brain, and that *this is precisely what has made the human cultural capacity what it is.*

In the first place, it is possible that the cultural capacity and intelligence evolved as a series of increases which involved a corresponding increase in genetic fitness, which quickly became fixed in each population it spread to. Parasitic viral phenomena of a given complexity require the presence of a correspondingly complex cultural capacity to replicate them. Therefore parasitic exploitation would always have to occur after the fact of an adaptive advance in the cultural capacity. Moreover, since the first pernicious, exploitative cultural phenomena would have to be stumbled upon randomly, via memetic mutation, it is conceivable that there was some time-lag between the appearance of a certain level of the cultural capacity, and the hapless discovery of equally sophisticated neuronal patterns capable of exploiting the new capacity. Time enough, perhaps, for populations of hominids to move on to the new level, and to become completely dependent on the symbiotic and beneficial ideas which the new capacity allowed them to pass amongst themselves. More time could be bought while memetic mutation threw up very pernicious ideas which were rejected not because their dangerous qualities were understood, but because they simply did not fit in with the belief systems prevailing in hominid cultures of the time. Groups of ideas which are co-adapted into mutually assisting complexes, called 'Meme-complexes' by Dawkins (1976; 1989: 197), and 'memomes' by Delius (1989: 65; 1991: 92), and a 'viral assemblage' by the author (as in a eusocial viral complex: Cullen 1990: 66) present barriers to the uptake of mutant Memes which might otherwise be very well adapted. In other words, they might have intrinsic appeal individually, or have great functional potential, but be rejected by certain other concepts in the *status quo* of a given subculture. One example of this kind of problem would be the use of a new technique of swinging a baseball bat which guaranteed a home run; if played in a baseball match, it would presumably be a great success; but if played in a rugby match, it is likely to be frowned upon, and a player with a baseball bat would not be allowed on the field in the first place. Another example would be the Catholic ban on contraception. This Meme presumably conveys genetic fitness to its bearer by preserving the link between the sexual reward system and genetic reproduction. But the 'no-contraception' Meme could well have less intrinsic psychological appeal than contraceptive Memes (the Rhythm Method) and artefacts (pills and condoms). Yet in the appropriate religious and moral context the genetically advantageous Meme also has greater psychological fitness (due to sanction by religious authority), enabling it resist replacement by its intrinsically appealing but genetically pernicious competitors.

Context-dependent factors such as these might prolong the period of time during which hominids with increased cultural capacity were universally more genetically successful than their counterparts. This first adaptive step towards culture would resemble the 'phylogenetically protocultural stage' when 'memes must forcibly have been mutualists' (i.e. beneficial) as the cultural capacity could only spread 'if individuals that had that competence were biologically fitter than those which did not have it' (Delius 1989: 54). Delius goes on to state that each subsequent step in the cultural capacity must depend on the same principle. Mutant genes contributing to improved cultural capacity 'if the memes they enabled resulted in an adaptive advantage for them' (Delius 1989: 54). The brain develops like an 'immune system' (making Edelman's analogy all the more intriguing, see below), but one which is designed to pick out the most advantageous Memes, and avoid all others.

But it is possible that this vast cultural immune system can best convey genetic fitness to its bearer by making the identification of dangerous ideas the top priority. The other half of the 'race' is on the side of viral concepts and behaviours. Selection in the cultural Meme pool will favour cultural phenomena which confuse and confound the individual's struggles to remain sceptical about information, and which confuse the individual's attempts to retain any sense of self that is separate from those ideas. Sooner or later in this scenario, memetic mutation would catch up with each step forward in intelligence and cultural capacity. More sophisticated minds which were able to laugh at the pernicious habits and beliefs of simpler members of their communities would begin to fall prey to new and more sophisticated beliefs, and more complex and addictive amusements or substances.

The general pattern taken by such a scenario would constitute a variety of co-evolutionary process, involving the kinds of factors discussed by Durham (1982; 1990; 1991), Freeman (1983), and Irons (1979), and others mentioned above. But while symbiotic 'mutual benefit' co-evolution occurring between hominids and their cultural phenomena would still occur, it would be a co-evolution primarily driven by conflict. The benefits would not be mutual at all; the viral phenomena would be essentially predating upon their hominid hosts, while hominid gene pools would be principally adapting to minimise suicidal behaviour patterns.

Just as the evolutionary relationship between gazelles and cheetahs can be described as an 'arms race' (Delius 1989: 52), it may be that this phrase also characterises the relationship between hominid genes and their culturally transmitted predators, and more accurately than the mutually beneficial variety of co-evolution. Ironically, the solution to memetic predation would always be more cultural capacity, and more intelligence, rather than less. Due to the time delay in the evolution of new viral phenomena capable of exploiting the new capacity, the immediate effect of improved cultural capacity or intelligence would be resistance to all the current pernicious Memes in a given hominid community. Perhaps the adaptiveness of a more and more intelligent cultural capacity lies in the resistance it conveys to prevailing suicidal behaviours, rather than in its conveyance of a brave new world of cultural symbiotes. The question immediately begged is this: Why not go back? Would not simpler hominid minds, with less cultural capacity, who are immune to the new pernicious cultural phenomena, begin to undergo a reproductive resurgence under such conditions? Without a great deal more research, it is only possible to speculate. Yet there is no reason to suppose that reduced cultural capacity *would* guarantee freedom from pernicious habits. Linden (1974) *inter alia* has shown how hominoid apes may be taught language by a human individual, in other words by individuals who have a greater cultural capacity than themselves. There have also been instances of primates such as those in circuses being taught health-damaging behaviours, such as smoking and drinking. It is unlikely that a chimpanzee could understand the message of an anti-smoking advertisement. So it is quite conceivable that a hominid individual with a reduced cultural capacity would actually be at a *disadvantage* when it came to resisting pernicious cultural phenomena. Perhaps the only way out of the brain/Virus evolutionary spiral is up. Becoming too intelligent for prevailing viral phenomena would at least convey some respite, at least until the next generation of 'superdrugs' came along.

So while pernicious imitation may be the cause of the problem at each stage of the evolution of the human cultural capacity, imitation that is more intelligent still is perhaps the only way out. While all culturally transmitted entities are dependent on human action for their reproduction, the dependence is now mutual. 'We alone on earth are free to rebel against the selfish replicators,' writes Dawkins (1989: 201). But what do we rebel with? Is there such a thing as a 'non-idea'? It seems to me that the only choice available is to choose which viral phenomena we wish to propagate, not whether we use them at all. We need cultural phenomena are much as they need us.

Foundation arguments from Edelman's psychobiology

Recent advances in the study of the psychobiology of the brain indicate that it is valid to speak of culturally transmitted 'structures' in terms of 'material realities' (Dawkins 1989: 323; Delius 1989: 43–7, and in the case of birdsong Edelman 1989: 300–303). In fact, a Meme is no less a material structure than is a gene, and can be described as a group of synapses which have passed from a 'cold' state to a 'hot' state (Delius 1989: 43), a definition which will be expanded upon below. Such patterns form units of highly variable size, and so the word 'Meme', like the words for 'big' or 'old', has no fixed size, much like the word 'gene' in biology (Dawkins 1989: 33). Indeed, there is a whole range of brain structures which can be related to the whole range of corresponding structures in DNA, all the way from 'nucleotide', 'cistron', 'chromosome', 'crossing over', 'sexual recombination', and 'genome', although there is insufficient space to discuss cultural analogues of all of these. As Delius has remarked (1989: 70), and as supported by the early chapters of this study, analogies between biological (I prefer the word 'genetic', as 'biological' implies that 'cultural' is non-biological) and cultural evolution have been explored for a long time. However, the Cultural Virus position is a particularly specific analogy, as the microscopic structure of the brain displays a range of structures and processes which support the notion of indirectly replicating viral neuronal patterns.

Edelman has shown that both brains and immune systems carry out selective processes in somatic time, and indeed the immune system can sometimes be employed as a simplified analogy for the Edelman's models of brain development (Levine 1988). The immune system, like any selective system, is unable to predict the pathogens which an organism will encounter in its lifetime. But it has evolved a system of development where prediction is not always necessary. Although a whole range of common antibodies are always produced during immunodevelopment, an extremely broad range of other antibodies are also produced in small quantities, in the hope that whatever diseases are encountered, some antibody will be found for each. Once any particular antibody turns out to 'match' a new invader, it is thereby 'selected', and the cells of this type undergo differential reproductive success within the immune system, at the expense of other kinds of cells. The key to successful immunity, then, is not prediction, but diversity. The greater the range of antibodies produced, the greater the chance that one or more of them will be able to combat a particular pathogen.

The same rules apply to the ontogeny of neural networks. During the development of the brain, an immense range of neuronal groups are produced, forming what Edelman calls the *Primary Repertoire* (1989: 47):

> We may define a primary repertoire as a diverse collection of neuronal groups whose extrinsic connectivities and potential functions in given brain region are prespecified to some extent during ontogeny and development. Without further qualifications at this point, we shall assume that, if a neuronal group responds with characteristic electrical output and chemical change more or less specifically to an input consisting of a particular spatiotemporal configuration of signals, there is a "match" between that group and the signal configuration.

The range of neuronal groups in this basic repertoire is truly immense, and some estimate of this space can be gained from the possible existence of 10^{15} variable synapses (Delius 1989: 44). This means that the psychocultural equivalent of what Dawkins has termed 'genetic space' (Shennan 1989: 340 after Dawkins 1986; meaning the full range of organismic structures which DNA is capable of coding for), a concept which might be termed the 'neuronal group space', 'memetic space' or 'synaptic space', is, like 'genetic space', unimaginably large. It also appears that at some levels the variation in this primary repertoire is completely random, and that its formation is something like a simulation of the history of life on earth in somatic time, only in the absence of the selective elimination afforded by Natural Selection. In other words, the developing brain simply 'mutates for all it is worth', creating many different neuronal structures of unknown potential. The object of brain development is to yield as much variation as possible, in preparation for a largely unpredictable world. In other words, an immense range of potential Memes and memetic motor products are formed during development, but they are not subjected to selective influences until the organism begins to experience sensory signals of various kinds.

The brain functions in somatic time in a manner which is no less Darwinian than the manner in which the earth's biomass evolves in geological time, except that the processes of mutation and selection are fundamentally separated in time. Brain development is like an hypothetical planetary biomass which is able to go on replicating and mutating for a long period of time without any selective constraints, such that when selective criteria finally do impinge on the variability produced, there will be enough diversity for a large number of forms to 'match' as many niches as possible.

While genetic activity places a range of constraints on brain development, and these constraints vary from species to species, within such parameters the specific structures finally attained are unpredictable and apparently unique to each individual. Moreover, it appears that there is no precise point-to-point wiring within the various localities of neuronal maps (Edelman 1989: 34–9).

One of the basic characteristics of the primary repertoire of neuronal groups, this vast array of pre-formed symbols awaiting sensory experience, is *degeneracy*. This is Edelman's term for the fact that more than one neuronal group is likely to yield a match with a given stimulus, and each symbol is capable of yielding a match with more than one stimulus. The word 'redundant' is avoided, since two symbols or neuronal groups which excite a match with the same sensory phenomenon are usually not the same themselves; indeed, they may be substantially different. Redundancy implies that there is more than one of the same thing, while degeneracy implies that there is more than one kind of thing capable of performing the same function. The difference between the two concepts can be illustrated using the analogy of twin births in animals; Edelman's concept of degeneracy is more consistent with the phenomenon of *fraternal* twins, while redundancy fits the phenomenon of identical twins.

The strange DNA of the Cultural Virus

The degree to which the primary repertoire operates as the starting point for a selective system is surprisingly complete. It seems that for every level of genetic systems, there is a corresponding element in human psychobiology. We can start with the basic building blocks of DNA, nucleotides, and state that the corresponding level of culturally transmitted structure is the synapse. Both of these entities contain little information in and of themselves, as they can only be in one of two states. A given nucleotide may either be present or absent, while a given synapse may be either 'on' (that is, strengthened so as to facilitate the passage of an electrical signal), or 'off'. Nucleotides come in only four basic types (adenine, thymine, cystosine, and guanine). At any locus along a DNA strand, one of the four is present and the rest are absent; genetic diversity is essentially a function of 'what order' this small number of different nucleotides are arranged into. Diversity does not have much to do with the qualitative presence or absence of particular nucleotide bases in a DNA strand, but it has everything to do with the order in which these presences and corresponding absences are arranged. Unlike the computer memory bits, and like nucleotides, synapses also appear to occur in more than one basic type, as there is considerable variation in the structural constituents of neurons, such as in their intracellular structures, axoplasmic flow, transmitter type, and membrane receptors (Edelman 1989: 57). In other words, there is quite a number of different psychobiological 'nucleotides' (synapse types), which can be present or absent in the neuronal equivalent of a nucleotide sequence. However, it would appear that neurons are not arranged in any sort of linear sequence, but in three-dimensional, 'bush'-like patterns. Neurons with different qualities yield different kinds of 'synapses' (points of connection between different neurons within a neuronal group). Synapses then become the basic information elements which are either switched on or off in a particular symbol configuration.

We can then move to the levels above that of the single nucleotide base in DNA, which is the level of a single 'codon' (3 nucleotides) which codes for a single amino acid, while a certain number of codons then constitute a 'cistron', a sequence of nucleotides which codes for a single protein, one enzyme, or one poly-peptide. Cistrons have been called 'genes' in a number of contexts (Poirier 1981: 43), but as shown with reference to Dawkins (1989: 33), this is a rather conservative definition, and it is better to define the 'gene' concept as a much larger and highly variable generic unit of DNA, retaining the word 'cistron' for the smaller, single protein coding units. A gene is best defined as a length of DNA of any size which is seldom divided, as discussed a little later. The relationship between the two categories is one of scale; a gene would normally encompass one or more cistrons.

Logically, then, the psychocultural equivalent of a codon or of a cistron should be the most basic level at which an assemblage of neurons can register what Edelman refers to as a 'match' with some external stimulus (Edelman 1989: 47). We are looking for some level of the brain where there are natural, or 'objective' physical boundaries, actual physical punctuations or limitations in the symbolling capacity, as in the case of codons corresponding to single amino acids, or cistrons corresponding to single protein molecules. At the same time, we should hope, that like cistrons in relation to genes, the physical punctuations of these neuronal units would not necessarily define the physical boundaries of Memes, such that a Meme may include any number of these smaller units. A good candidate for a psychological equivalent of a 'codon' or 'cistron' would therefore appear to be one of Edelman's 'neuronal groups'. (It is very important that the reader reads Neuronal Group Selection as the selection of a neuronal-group, *not* as the 'group selection' of populations of neurons, as if the theory were some kind of psychological equivalent of the Wynne-Edwards 'group selection' conundrum.) It appears that Edelman's 'neuronal group' is 'informationally' or 'logistically' similar to a codon or cistron, in that these, by reversing the comparison, could almost be called 'nucleotide groups' instead of 'neuronal groups'. We might also parsimoniously define the neuronal group, like a cistron which may be referred to as the smallest kind of gene, as the smallest unit capable of functioning as a Meme. Edelman defines a neuronal group as follows (1989: 47):

> For the present, we may consider a neuronal group to be a collection of cells of similar or variant types, ranging in numbers from hundreds to thousands, that are closely connected in their intrinsic circuitry and whose mutual dynamic interaction may be further enhanced by increases in synaptic efficacy. The set of cells constituting a group can vary dynamically as a result of changes in input or output requirements or of competition with other groups. Such variations do not occur anatomically but rather are the result of alterations at either excitatory or inhibitory synapses.

However, it would appear that one neuronal group on its own is capable of registering very little in terms of patterned signals from the outside world. The representation of categories in a certain spatial or temporal order appears to require more than one neuronal group responding in concert to different parts of the same object, separate representations which are then correlated at a higher level of brain function. Parallel signals may arrive at different localities (mapping) in the brain, each selecting a particular neuronal group, but each of these neuronal groups may then respond with characteristic outputs of signals to other localities and each other, a process which Edelman terms 're-entry' (1989: 319):

> The constitution of a procedure or of a representation of categories in a spatiotemporal order occurs by mapping and reentry among parallel channels. While the *minimal* neuronal structure capable of carrying this out is a classification couple, in general, such couples do not act in isolation. Instead, they are embedded in large collections of parallel mapped channels, including re-entry to and from non-mapped regions as well as to motor output systems.

Thus it would appear that there are 'natural' punctuations in the symbolling capacity, such as neuronal groups and classification couples (or classification multiples, as the case may be), which, like codons and cistrons in DNA coding, provide a range of 'building blocks' for incorporation into more complex representations. In DNA, codons and cistrons are parts of genes. Correspondingly, in human psychobiology, the equivalent of a gene, in other words a Meme, should preferably be composed of neuronal equivalents of codons and cistrons. Since the psychological or cultural equivalents of codons and cistrons have been defined as neuronal groups, the cultural equivalent of the gene should presumably be composed of these. In order to be incorporated into more global representations, neuronal groups must first be fixed in the secondary repertoire through selection. Neuronal groups are 'selected' at the expense of other groups through synaptic modification. Edelman uses a population model of synapse modification, where whole sets of synapses are jointly modified, rather than viewing information in terms of single synapse changes (Edelman 1989: 179):

> In general, however, the complexity of the nervous system makes it highly unlikely that there is a simple relationship between changes at any individual synapse and changes in the behaviour of the network. It is much more likely that multiple synaptic modifications occur simultaneously at various sites in the network, reflecting its degeneracy. This prompts the consideration of synapses as populations. The importance of this consideration is obvious: modification of synaptic function serves as the principle means for the selection of neuronal groups and for their competitive interactions that lead to the formation of the secondary repertoire.

Thus it would appear that a neuronal group or groups becomes a Meme when certain synapses are altered in such a way as to make their joint interaction more predictable and more likely. We may then define a Meme as one or more neuronal groups, which, due to their internal structure and structural relationships to each other, bear a sufficient relationship to certain inputs or outputs such that they have been consistently and jointly excited by those inputs, or consistently and jointly involved in exciting those outputs. Another way to relate the appearance of a new Meme to Edelman's psychobiology would be to say that a Meme can only be said to 'exist' in a new brain or mind once it has emerged into the secondary repertoire from the primary repertoire. The primary repertoire is so vast that any number of concepts could be expected to remain at this level, undiscovered by the organism and, therefore, absent from the secondary repertoire.

From this general picture of the psychobiology of the working brain we can build a provisional model of a Meme. Concurrently, it should also be possible to define a general idea of the nature of memetic mutation or innovative learning processes. These two general sketches provide an indication of the psychobiological phenomena which underlie cultural evolution, and which should serve as a starting point for the building of an 'evolutionary memetics' of archaeological and anthropological diversity.

Firstly, let us outline the psychobiological nature of the Meme in greater detail. Edelman's concept of the primary repertoire could be described as a vast universe of latent Memes, each of which requires a particular pattern of signals from the sensory nervous system to be 'awakened', and brought into the secondary repertoire, where it may then be remembered. Presumably, a particular array of strengthened synapses can fade, and be forgotten, passing out of the secondary repertoire, and returning to the primary repertoire. Any given Meme can then be viewed as consisting of one or more neuronal groups in the primary repertoire which display a particular pattern of synaptic interconnection, and which have emerged into the secondary repertoire as a result of the input of a particular pattern of signals which in turn produced synaptic change. The in-coming signals found a match with this particular latent element in the primary repertoire, due to its synaptic structure, and a particular set of synapses were thereby strengthened, and brought into the secondary repertoire.

Cultural reproduction is therefore the means whereby one individual may help another to bring latent Memes from the primary repertoire into the secondary repertoire, and constitutes what Edelman calls 'genuine information processing' (Edelman 1978: 320; 1989: 308–11). In Edelman's selective system, the reproductive dimension of teaching and imitation presumably involves a process by means of which the behaviour of the 'teacher' presents a series of signals to the 'student', while these signals then enter the central nervous system and excite a 'match' with a range of neuronal groups in the student's primary repertoire, thereby initiating first short-term and then long-term synaptic changes in these neuronal groups such that they emerge into the secondary repertoire. The teacher is essentially helping the student to find the nearest memetic equivalent of a given idea in his or her own primary repertoire.

It appears that such cultural reproduction involves a content-dependent rather than address-dependent equivalence (Delius 1989: 44). In other words, the same Meme may be stored in different parts of different brains, as the indeterminacy involved in the finer point-to-point wiring at particular localities in neural maps (Edelman 1978: 34–58; 1989: 318) ensures that the best-adapted neuronal groups for a particular Meme are unlikely to develop at an identical point in any neuronal map. But the overall pattern of altered synapses or 'hotspots' in any two copies of a Meme must be basically equivalent, in order to yield the same behaviour or the same pattern of verbal signals. Delius, discussing Memes under the generic category of psychobiological 'traits', has remarked (1989: 44):

> Any trait (meme) that is taken over by a given individual from another individual must accordingly be thought of as the transfer of a particular pattern of synaptic hotspots within the associative networks of one brain to the associative networks of another brain. Different traits must be thought of

as being coded by topologically different hotspot patterns. That is, a given cultural trait borne by an individual is encoded informationally as a particular pattern of modified synapses in his brain. Naturally the hotspot pattern that a trait has in one brain will not be geometrically arranged in exactly the same way as the pattern that the same trait has in another brain. For that, the brains of different individuals are likely to be too different. But functionally the two hotspot patterns would still be equivalent, at least to the extent that the effective memory contents representing the trait were identical. As an analogy the reader may think of the same text passage stored on two different kinds of floppy-discs by two different computers: spatially not identical but informationally equivalent.

Delius has offered similar arguments for the existence of Memes as actual structures (Delius 1989: 82–4). It is clear that the notion of a Meme does not conflict with modern psychobiology, and that ideas exist as actual structures, and do not exist in some 'twilight' world between fact and fiction.

In light of this general perspective on the nature of Memes, some speculative statements on the nature of cultural mutation are offered; this is the problem of how new Memes are produced. Memetic mutation would presumably involve some mechanism by means of which existing Memes which have already emerged into the secondary repertoire provide some sort of clue or stepping stone to other memetic structures which are lying latent in the primary repertoire. One key concept which may provide a starting point for building a model of memetic mutation is Edelman's notion of *degeneracy* in the primary repertoire.

As described briefly above, a degenerate network is one where a number of different neuronal groups, distributed throughout different points of the primary repertoire, are capable of responding to the same set of signals. It is not accurate to call these different neuronal groups redundant, as they are by no means the same in their structure; in fact, they may be very different. This is a result of the fact that a 'match' between a signal pattern and a neuronal group can, as a rule, never be perfect (Edelman 1989: 47). If some half a dozen neuronal groups are capable of achieving an 80% match, each group may be matching with a different 80% of the signal, and failing to match a different 20% of the signal.

Moreover, while they may all respond to a given set of signals, this is not to say that they all respond equally. As a result of the differences, certain sets of neuronal groups respond under competitive circumstances respond more effectively than others, leading to their selection and their emergence into the secondary repertoire. The strengthened synapses involved in the selection of the particular neuronal group now predispose it towards responding again to a similar set of signals. Yet the degenerate nature of the symbolling system ensures that, particularly in the early stages of learning, a range of neuronal groups all respond to any one group of signals. In other words, memetic reproduction is not so precise that one single Meme is brought out 'cleanly' from primary to secondary repertoire. Rather, a whole population of competing neuronal groups is excited, and this population may be highly variable in structure at the same time as being approximately equal in their ability to respond to a signal pattern. In time, the neuronal groups with the highest level of response activity will be amplified, and become more and more likely to respond exclusively to the pattern, while others with a response level that is not quite so high may recede; yet even the receding groups are now more likely to match with new signals than before. It is possible that such ranges of degenerate groups constitute a population of partially amplified 'mutant' Memes which all bear a thematic relationship to the dominant Meme, and which might compete more successfully with the dominant synaptic pattern for other sensory signals of a similar nature. Further elaboration of this possibility would require a deeper analysis and discussion of the degeneracy concept.

Another source of variation in neuronal repertoires is caused by the *long-term pre-synaptic* changes which take place in the formation of the secondary repertoire (Edelman 1989: 319):

> The proposed epigenetic mechanism for the selection of such secondary repertoires invokes independent pre- and post-synaptic rules for changing synaptic efficacy over greater or lesser times. These rules operate to enable correlation of stimuli in time with receptor sheet space in such a way as to favour the responses of certain groups of neurons. At the same time, the rules also act to bias certain short-term responses by long-term responses; this bias emerges from the recursively connected neurons in groups obeying both rules. While this increases the likelihood that certain groups will respond upon repeated stimulation, the long-term pre-synaptic changes can at the same time enhance the variability of synaptic efficacy within connected domains, generating additional diversity. The degree of variability by the operation of the rules and is constrained by the degree of competition offered by different correlated stimuli affecting other groups in these domains. This process provides not only a basis for both novelty and generalisation but also a continuous source of variation.

Thus long-term synaptic changes establish particular combinations of neuronal groups in the secondary repertoire, thereby increasing the likelihood that the same groups will respond when similar signal patterns are experienced again. In this sense the selection of one neuronal group over another eliminates certain elements from the primary repertoire and favours others, which are established as parts of the secondary repertoire, thereby reducing variation amongst populations of neuronal groups. Yet it appears that this process of reduction simultaneously enhances variability in other neighbouring or connected neuronal groups, thereby preparing parts of the primary repertoire for emergence which might otherwise have lain dormant, and which had no primary 'match' with the original signal pattern. The memetic implications of such mechanisms are not obvious, but it is possible that once a certain Meme is received into a brain, a whole suite of related but hitherto inconceivable Memes or ideas then become conceivable, by virtue of their location in one of the 'connected domains' of which Edelman speaks. It such were the case, is clear that such mechanisms would provide another source of variation, in addition to that of populations of partially amplified degenerate symbols.

It is clear that the above models of psychobiological phenomena require more discussion, analysis and synthesis before they could be incorporated into a series of processual models for an 'evolutionary memetics'. Yet it is equally clear that the emerging picture of the working brain does not present any obvious obstacle to the Cultural Virus or Meme positions, and that Memes and viral phenomena can be viewed as actual neuronal structures capable of influencing human behaviour and being socially transmitted as a direct or indirect result of that behaviour. Moreover, it can be seen that a number of Edelman concepts, such as degeneracy, reentry, and pre- and post-synaptic rules for changing synaptic efficacy, suggest a range of conceptual starting points for building models of memetic mutation.

Concluding remarks

A series of foundation arguments for the Cultural Virus Theory have been outlined in this chapter and they can be summarised in four basic points.

Firstly, the general notion of viral phenomena was introduced, and it was shown how such phenomena could be considered as neo-Darwinian individuals in their own right. This can be done without attributing any organismic qualities to them, other than the genealogical independence they undoubtedly display.

Secondly, the origin of the Virus position was discussed, and it was shown how the Virus and Meme positions were independent but parallel. While the Meme position was invented in the 1970s in a discourse derived from evolutionary biology, the Virus position was developed in the 1980s in a discourse derived from archaeological theory. It was briefly stated that the two positions were largely complementary, in that each viral phenomenon would logically incorporate both memetic structures and a phenotypic or 'quasi-organismic' level of behavioural and artefact products. Memes thereby constitute the memetic or hereditary components of whole viral phenomena. The complementary nature of the two concepts was not elaborated upon, as this task has been left for the first section of the final chapter.

Thirdly, some principles of parasite ecology which highlight the significance of genealogical independence were discussed. If a parasite or guest of another organism reproduces in synchrony with its host there is very little to distinguish it from a trait. Indeed, some structures long thought to be traits of organisms, such as mitochondria, are actually symbiotic parasites (Delius 1989: 48), while these and other organismic structures could well be the result of ancient mergers between parasites and their hosts (Margulis 1981; Dawkins 1989). Not only can synchronised host/parasite combinations be viewed as single organisms; it can even be argued that this is all an 'organism' ever was in the first place (Dawkins 1989: 182, 243). Conversely it can be argued that structures which consist of parts which display genealogical independence from each other are *not* organisms, but rather small ecological assemblages, which unlike single organisms, and like populations, are capable of evolution. Moreover, as ecological assemblages, the potential arises for adaptive conflicts to emerge amongst their constituent structures. Since cultural phenomena display genealogical independence from human genes it can be argued that human individuals are small ecological assemblages rather than single organisms, and this would explain both the fact that cultural evolution can occur in somatic time, and the fact that adaptive conflicts emerge between human genes and human behaviour. A brief example of a human individual caught in the midst of an adaptive conflict between cultural and genetic reproduction was offered in a hypothetical example of a 'workaholic', but in a more rounded discussion of such conflicts it was briefly shown how the genetic underpinnings of the 'human cultural capacity' could undergo differential reproductive success, despite the susceptibility to parasitic cultural phenomena that capacity produced.

Finally, the psychobiology of learning and cultural reproduction was discussed, and it was shown that Memes and cultural phenomena are just a much 'real biological structures' as DNA and genes, yet the manner in which cultural phenomena evolve is utterly extragenetic. It cannot be overemphasised that cultural phenomena actually exist, as socially transmitted learned neuronal structures and their behavioural and artefact products. Memes and their products are both perfectly intrabiological and perfectly extragenetic. Yet many archaeologists and anthropologists seem to view culture as some kind of 'non-existent' phenomenon which transcends 'biology', and freely speak of a distinction between 'biology' and 'culture'. Others disparage the distinction, but then speak of the undeniable distinction between genes and culture as though it is equally invalid (Lee 1991; Ingold 1991). Some even warn of the dangers of 'reifying' (Rindos 1989: 4; Dunnell 1980) culture, as though it is some metaphysical construct which has no real existence, and which we must refrain from treating as if it actually did exist. It seems to me that the arguments of Edelman and Delius make it clear that it does. In particular, Edelman's work constitutes a development for theories of cultural evolution akin to the discovery of DNA in genetic evolution; a basic understanding of psychobiological code structure. These sort of advances may be coupled with the 'Mendelesque' role of assertions from Dawkins (1976), who explicitly suggested the possibility of 'hereditary discreteness' in social transmission (implicit in his invention of the word 'Meme'). The aim of these metaphorical comparisons is not to equate disparate inventions of ideas, but to make it clear that there is nothing in psychobiology which presents any obvious obstacle to future developments of an 'evolutionary memetics' within a Cultural Virus framework. Cultural phenomena really do exist, as wholly extragenetic but thoroughly biological 'things', so there is no danger of 'reification'. Yet while the 'biology versus culture' distinction is easily deconstructed, in some contexts the distinction would appear to function as a metaphor for another and very valid distinction; that between 'genetically reproduced' and 'culturally reproduced' phenomena.

When all of the foundation arguments outlined above are brought together, it becomes clear that the Virus position is no ordinary metaphor. It has the potential to become a coherent perspective supported by qualitative evidence and 'in principle' arguments from a wide range of scientific domains. In the next chapter these general principles will be used as foundation arguments for a provisional outline of the Cultural Virus Theory.

8
An outline of Cultural Virus Theory

Overview

Here the basic propositions of the Cultural Virus Theory (CVT) are introduced. In a very general sense, this new Darwinian perspective could be described as a reversion to a position not dissimilar to the old-fashioned view of artefacts as organisms, only within a neo-Darwinian rather than a Lamarckian framework. Ironically, this is precisely the view which other Darwinian anthropologists such as Foley (1987b: 380) and Leonard & Jones (1987: 215) believe should be avoided at all costs. But the Cultural Virus position can not be simply reduced to the phrase 'artefacts as organisms'. For, far from being autonomous, each 'quasi-organism' or viral phenomenon is simple, passive, and dependent upon human agency for reproductive success in what is essentially a psychological and social environment – a 'jungle of human sentiment'. 'People' are not, therefore, excluded from the Cultural Virus position, but rather redefined at a more complicated super-organismic level of neo-Darwinian categorisation; they are modelled as a dynamic ecological assemblage of one organism and many viral phenomena, evolving in somatic time, and capable of doing all the things that only ecological assemblages are able to do.

Merging with Memes

There are a number of subtle variations between the Meme and Virus perspectives, but these amount more to minor differences in emphasis than major theoretical conflicts. Such differences would be expected as a result of the fact that the two perspectives are parallel but largely independent inventions, which developed in isolation from each other. Yet, at the most general level, the two positions fit together as two complementary aspects of the same basic principles, with Memes corresponding to the level of the Cultural Virus Theory originally occupied by phenomena termed 'metonyms', or more generally, 'ideas', while each viral phenomenon consists of one or more Memes, and their motor products or phenotypes. In

172

fact, the Virus and Meme positions complement each other in much the same way as the 'virus' and 'gene' concepts complement each other in biology. In modern evolutionary biology, the Virus is the 'whole entity', encompassing both its genes and the phenotypic products of those genes. Correspondingly, in Cultural Virus Theory, a Cultural Virus or viral phenomenon is the socially transmitted 'whole entity', encompassing both its memetic information or 'hotspot' synapse patterns, and the behavioural and artefact products of such neuronal structures. Dawkins has incorporated a great deal of variability into his definition of a Meme, in much the same way that variability was also incorporated into his definition of a gene (see also chapter 5) (Dawkins 1989: 195):

> ... I divided the 'gene complex' into large and small genetic units, and units within units. The 'gene' was defined, not in a rigid all-or-none way, but as a unit of convenience, a length of chromosome with just sufficient copying-fidelity to serve as a viable unit of natural selection. If a single phrase of Beethoven's ninth symphony is sufficiently distinctive and memorable to be abstracted from the context of the whole symphony, and used as the call-sign of a maddeningly intrusive European broadcasting station, then to that extent it deserves to be called one meme.

Like a gene, the Meme is not a rigid unit, but a division of analytical convenience imposed on a quasi-continuous medium. Ball (1984: 147) also discusses a series of Dawkins definitions of Memes, but does not highlight the quasi-continuous element to the same degree. Memes then produce the non-memetic aspects of viral phenomena, the behavioural and artefact 'phenotypic aspects', through complex interactions with other Memes and with the 'decision making' apparatus of the brain. Since this memetic interaction to produce the viral phenotype is complicated, a false 'blending' effect can thereby be produced. Just as the particulate inheritance of vast numbers of skin colour genes at many loci can produce an even blending through the 'averaging out' of all the different effects on skin colour, so it ought to be possible to produce the appearance of blending in behaviour when individuals strategically combine the effects of large numbers of their Memes (Dawkins 1989: 195):

> It is possible that this appearance of non-particulateness is illusory, and that the analogy with genes does not break down. After all, if we look at the inheritance of many genetic characters such as human height or skin-colouring, it does not look like the work of indivisible and unblendable genes. ... This does not mean that the genes concerned are not particulate. It is just that there are so many of them concerned with skin colour, each one having such a small effect, that they *seem* to blend.

Beyond this focus at different but complementary levels of cultural systems, the positions are basically similar in a that both the Virus and Meme position essentially casts culturally transmitted structures in the role of parasites (whether harmful or beneficial), or 'symbionts' (Delius 1989: 48; 1991: 85), as distinct from the role of 'traits' or organs. As a result of their genealogical independence from their hosts, they cannot be considered to be parts of their hosts' bodies, and therefore terminology which implies traithood or organhood is abandoned. Interpretation of behaviour in terms of adaptation of 'people' therefore involves the juggling of two lines of reproductive benefit (host reproduction, versus reproduction of the viral phenomenon), and all combinations of those two lines of benefit. These would potentially include cases where only the host benefits, where only the viral phenomenon benefits, where both benefit, and where neither benefit (see also Ball 1984 for an interesting taxonomy of this kind).

Thus at the most general level of comparison, the Virus and Meme positions may be considered to be two parallel conceptions of parasitic potential in socially transmitted behaviour focusing at a different level of inclusiveness in cultural phenomena. As a consequence, I propose to use the Meme concept freely when referring to the 'memetic' level of viral phenomena (as an improved term for what I originally termed either just an 'idea' or 'metonym'), and the more encompassing term 'viral phenomenon' when referring to the 'entire' entity, encompassing both Meme and 'phenotypic aspect'. I use the word 'phenotypic aspect' rather than 'phenotype' or 'traits' to embody the fact that, like any gene in an organism, a Meme's phenotypic aspect will be highly variable and context-dependent. Its expression in the behaviour of the human individual in which it occurs depends upon what other Memes are present, and what other non-memetically reproduced psychological phenomena are present in the mind in which it is found. A Meme does not code for any single 'trait' which will be displayed by all its bearers, any more than does a gene. Rather, it constituted from neuronal structures corresponding to one or more ideas, which can be combined or recombined with other ideas, and suppressed or emphasised by different emotional states, according to the mood of the moment. Nonetheless, the structure of a particular idea should limit the number of contexts in which it can be used, and the number of other ideas with which it may be combined. Each Meme, then, can be expected to have a range of highly contingent phenotypic expressions or aspects.

It is also interesting to note that unlike genes, the phenotypic aspects of Memes are, strictly speaking, 'extended' phenotypes, rather than immediate ones. The term 'Extended Phenotype' comes from Dawkins (1982; 1989), and applies to effects that the genes of one organism may have on the body of another organism altogether. Thus the extended phenotype of the rabies virus is not the body of the virus itself, but its effects on the nervous system of the animal in which it resides, such as salivation, lack of swallowing, and hydrophobia. Similarly, the extended phenotype of the liver flukes of chapter 7, is not the body of the fluke, but certain effects the fluke has on the snail's body, such as the exaggerated hardness of the shell. The interesting thing about the Dawkins Extended Phenotype concept in the case of Memes is that they have no bodies of their own on which to have effect; they have, therefore, an extended phenotype, but no ordinary phenotype. The only way Memes can be transmitted is through their influence upon the nervous system of a body made by genes – or, at least, until very recently with the advent of computers. Their effect on the human nervous system is not chemical, but structural and electrical; unlike the genes of ordinary parasites, they do not have to secrete any manipulative substance into their hosts nervous tissue. Memetic phenotypes directly involve thoughts, behaviour, and artefacts, produced by the body in which they reside. Thus each viral phenomenon consists of one or more Memes and their combined extended phenotypes.

This can be imagined using stone-knapping techniques as an example. The learning of a technique such as pressure-flaking, where flakes are 'popped' off a core via a precise exertion of pressure (pressing rather than striking) at a strategic point and angle along the margin of a core, involves the observation and imitation of someone performing the technique, who by definition already possesses that particular viral phenomenon. There are two sources of information for transmission. Firstly, there is the observation of the phenotype of the viral phenomenon, rather than its Meme; this is the behaviour itself. Secondly, the 'master' knapper may also be able to discuss and direct the student, through verbalising a set of other Memes which he or she has developed in order to explain the experiences or sensations of the technique. These are also part of the extended phenotype of the 'pressure-flaking' Meme, but they are even 'further' away from the neuronal structure of the Meme itself. The point to be made here is that even the most basic level of the phenotype of the Meme, the behaviour, is already 'extended', in that it consists of an affect on a body which the Meme was not involved in creating.

Besides the levels-of-inclusiveness (viral phenomenon equals Memes + phenotype of motor products) difference, there is another subtle difference in emphasis between the two perspectives. This difference can be expressed in terms of a distinction between the words replicatee and replicator . While at a general level the two words can be more or less equated, as in gross neo-Darwinian terms they are not vastly different in their implications, the two words also reflect a tendency in each perspective to focus attention upon different adaptive scenarios within cultural systems. For example, human 'intentions' and 'emotions' are more featured as selective pressures in the Virus discourse, while physical or sensory limitations and other more unconscious psychological factors are the featured selective pressures in the Meme position. The Cultural Virus position emphasises that cultural phenomena are the passive beneficiaries of unconscious *and conscious* attempts by human individuals to control their lives; while Meme discourse places more emphasis on examples where Meme benefit is a little more insidious, replicating without any great self-consciousness on the part of their hosts. It is stressed that the set of cultural examples in the Virus position is perfectly in keeping with those of Meme position, and vice versa, and indeed each is implied by the other. We are speaking of two different but complementary (and indeed overlapping) sets of 'cultural parasite' examples, ranging from the most intentional to the least.

It is important to note that Dawkins concept of a 'replicator' (see also Ball 1984 *passim*) does not involve any notion of intrinsic 'intent' or machiavellian intelligence on behalf of that replicator, either in the case of genes or Memes. However, unlike the word 'replicatee' of the Virus discourse (Cullen 1992), nor does it imply any necessary presence of such factors anywhere else. The replicator concept implies *self*-reproduction, leading the Meme discourse, as we shall see a little later, towards scenarios in which the role of human intentions in forming the Meme's environment, while never dismissed, is rarely explicitly discussed (Dawkins 1989: 193):

> Whenever conditions arise in which a new kind of replicator *can* make copies of itself, the new replicators *will* tend to take over, and start a new kind of evolution of their own. Once this new evolution begins, it will in no necessary sense be subservient to the old. The old gene-selected evolution, by making brains, provided the "soup" in which the first "memes" arose. Once self-copying memes had arisen, their own, much faster, kind of evolution took off.

While Memes have thus been quite specifically defined as the new *'replicators'* by Dawkins, the Cultural Virus Theory has used terminology which implies that each viral phenomenon is a *'replicatee'*, not a *'replicator'* – a concept more akin to an RNA retrovirus, and not a piece of DNA. Ideas and artefacts are not replicators in quite the same way that DNA is, because they cannot reproduce themselves. They require external reproductive agencies, such as human minds, which may include all sorts of conscious and unconscious goal-oriented behaviour, occurring in their 'environment', in order to produce and transmit their offspring for them. They are selected for their capacity to become the passive beneficiaries of strategic decision-making. Because of this humans may well, at times, be aware of the fact that they are reproducing cultural phenomena, and they may even have some idea of why they are doing so. But such 'intentionality' presents no more of an obstacle to selective principles than does 'artificial' (whether conscious or unconscious) selection in domestication, which may be viewed a special case of symbiosis (see Rindos (1980; 1984)). Hence the special emphasis on the use of words like virus, and viral; these words denote that ideas and artefacts, *unlike genes*, are incapable of self-reproduction, and that they are dependent upon human agency (Cullen 1990; 1992; 1993a; 1993b). Because the word virus denotes that ideas and artefacts are replicatees, and therefore, at best, only a 'special case' of the category 'replicator', Cultural Virus Theory (CVT) in no way denies human intentions, purposes, or planning; instead these become fundamental elements of the psychological landscape – the idea's 'environment' – to which populations of ideas adapt.

But as already implied, the influence of human intentions on the 'environment' of any given cultural phenomenon is never *denied* by any aspect of the Meme discourse, and indeed it is sometimes mentioned (Dawkins 1989: 193). However, it is not made such a featured part of primary theoretical statements as it is in the Cultural Virus position, and this could well be a reflection of the use in the Meme discourse of terminology which implies self-replication rather than 'proxy'-replication.

The 'individuals' of cultural process are individual viral phenomena, and they are therefore quite different to the individual organisms of genetic process. In CVT the basic 'individuals' under focus are not human individuals, but ideas or Memes of highly variable size and complexity, along with their highly variable behavioural and artefact products. Any piece of information that can be learned or taught in a 'single event' of comprehension, or a series of interdependent moments of comprehension, along with its extended behavioural phenotype, can be considered an individual. A convenient term for these pieces of information would be 'cultural phrase' or 'symbolic phrase', 'metonym', or even 'idea', and I have used such terms elsewhere (Cullen 1990; 1993a; 1993b); but, as already suggested, there is no reason why the neuronal structures which underlie ideas – which constitute the genetic level of viral phenomena – may not be called Memes. Phrase length, or Meme length, then, in the quasi-continuous neuronal medium, may vary greatly (Cullen 1993a); the comprehensibility of a concept will vary according to who is teaching it, and who is learning it. Sometimes a phrase will be intrinsically meaningful, and might spread independently from other ideas. At other times it may only 'make sense' with reference to a number of other phrases, and its 'symbolic appeal', and therefore its reproductive fitness, may be entirely dependent on the success of other phrases (the parallel of this concept in the Meme discourse is the notion of a 'Meme complex'). Without recourse to certain key definitions, a student may find many otherwise limpid ideas quite incomprehensible. The fitness of an idea or phrase may depend on the existence of half a dozen, a few hundred, or even thousands of other concepts to which it can be 'symbolically connected' to. Thus in CVT an 'individual' is a single phrase or body of phrases which are usually taught or learned together.

The individuals of more traditional Darwinian approaches, individual organisms, are therefore not considered to be appropriate units of analysis in cultural evolution, despite their undeniable relevance in genetic evolution. However, as already implied from another angle, human individuals, and both their conscious and unconscious intentions, remain the important 'agencies' of cultural change. It is just that they are not the individuals being reproduced in the discharge of that agency. They are the selectors, not the selectees – the reverse of what is the case in genetic process. As such, the individual psyche constitutes the most basic unit of any viral phenomenon's environment, but not the most basic unit in the definition of a viral 'self'.

As mentioned in the overview of this chapter, what is being recommended is a reversion to a position not dissimilar to the old-fashioned view of 'artefacts as organisms' – except that here artefacts and behaviour are seen to be the extended phenotypic product of viral neuronal structures. Ironically, this is precisely the view which other cultural selectionists such as Foley (1987b: 380) and Leonard & Jones (1987: 215) believe has brought evolutionary theory into disrepute in archaeology. However, in the Virus form of the view, each cultural 'organism' is so simple, passive, and dependent upon human agency for reproductive success, and its reproductive fitness so dependent upon a particular psychological and social milieu, that the resulting framework is ultimately very different to the antiquarian form of the 'artefacts as organisms' analogy.

Put most simply, then, in CVT the primary 'individuals' of cultural process are ideas (equivalent to Dawkins Memes), and their behavioural and artefact products. However, *human* individuals remain crucial units of analysis, as the most obvious units of the viral idea's psychological and cultural *environment*. Each individual mind consists of a vast ecological assemblage of thousands of different ideas, built upon a genetically reproduced landscape of open-ended instincts and susceptibilities, to which populations or groups of comparable and/or mutually exclusive ideas must adapt. In other words, the fitness of each idea is a function of its fit to a total psychological environment; this psychological environment includes both a fundamental landscape of genetically inherited capacities and propensities (which are probably shared by all humans), and the many thousands of learned concepts, both viral (teachable) and inchoate (unteachable), which then 'populate' this somewhat more immutable landscape. All of the terms of description of this paragraph are, however, highly metaphorical, and this form of discussion will not be elaborated upon just yet.

The aim of this section has been to provide a working definition of a cultural 'gene' and a cultural 'individual'. The cultural equivalent of a gene is the 'Meme', the psychobiology of which was extensively discussed in the previous chapter. Some possible mechanisms for the means by which novel Memes arise, which could be called models of memetic mutation, were also discussed in this part of the previous chapter.

The cultural individual is then defined as a single viral phenomenon, which consists of one or more Memes (one or more of Edelman's 'classification couples' involving pairs of neuronal groups along with their extended phenotype of behavioural, emotional, and artefact products (or its total set of potential effects on the human body). The subtle difference in the cultural 'level' focused upon by the Meme and Virus positions (equivalent to the genome versus whole organism distinction) is thus perfectly complementary.

Another subtle difference has also been discussed above. This is the difference in the replicative terminology currently employed by the two positions. While the Virus employs terms which reflect not only passivity, but pronounced 'environmental agency' in the psychological context of ideas, in terms such as 'replicatee', and indeed the term 'viral phenomenon' itself, the Meme position uses terms such 'replicator' and 'self reproduction'. Once again, it is stressed that in many senses such minor differences in terminology may be purely semantic, we shall see in the next section that these mild differences in terminology have lead to correspondingly different sets of 'hypothetical examples' of what are essentially parallel principles. Meme examples have more commonly explored cases where human individuals are the passive, or at least relatively inactive, recipients of new Memes, rather like the ecological relationships between wild animals and wild parasites, or between humans and microbial parasites (see Ball 1984: 146–153 for an excellent example of this focus). On the other hand the Virus perspective, as we shall see below, more explicitly incorporates situations where individuals plan and manipulate to the best of their abilities, deliberately attempting to control the viral phenomena they receive, and deliberating colonising other individuals with ideas, or withholding them from others, rather like the relationship between humans and their animal and plant domesticates. But the two areas of cultural transmission are really just two ends of the same continuum (as, indeed, are wild and domestic animals, see references to Rindos 1980 and 1984 above), running from the most 'conscious' forms of teaching and learning to the most 'unconscious' and imitative forms. In any case, the two sets of examples have a substantial overlap, as we shall see below; the difference which I aim trying to describe is really just a quantitative difference in the amount of 'conscious' input of human agency emerging in the illustrative examples employed by each approach. Thus the two sets of favoured examples, then, like the two levels of cultural systems considered, are perfectly complementary.

So *both* minor differences between notions of Memes and viral phenomena are complementary facets of the same coin. The difference between the entities themselves (Memes and viral phenomena) is equivalent to the difference between the genetic and phenotypic levels of organismic systems. And the difference between scenarios involving different degrees of intentional human agency merely reflect the fact that cultural transmission itself involves varying degrees of human intentionality. In the next section, a series of Meme explanations of cultural phenomena are discussed, and it is shown how Dawkins has tended to favour explanations which involve reasonably low levels of deliberate human intervention. A series of highly 'intentional' viral alternatives are then discussed, and it is concluded that highly deliberate, goal oriented thinking on the part of a human host provides no guarantee that a viral phenomenon will not continue to exploit the situation. In other words, the tendency towards simple and elegant explanations in the Meme discourse is to be commended; but the aim of the alternative permutations offered from the point of view of the viral discourse is to show that even the most convoluted attempts by people to exert conscious control over memetic replication can be explained in terms of 'cultural symbiont' principles.

Memetic hypotheticals

So it can be seen that theme of the self-propagating Meme, i.e. propagation without any special role for deliberate human agency, occurs again and again. Ball has extended this theme to its logical conclusion, remarking 'that civilisation or culture is only a Meme's way of propagating and perpetuating itself' (Ball 1984: 153). The 'sensory prominence' argument, as a special case of this kind of explanation, is a particularly passive way to pick up a Meme. 'Sensory prominence' arguments are not so pervasive in Dawkins's explanations of the fitness of certain 'Meme complexes' involved in religious systems. Yet the kinds of cultural transmission discussed are still relatively 'unwitting'.

Consider the Meme complex associated with some forms of Christianity. Dawkins focuses on five different elements of this Meme complex, under the nouns 'God', 'immortality', 'hellfire', 'faith' and 'celibacy'. Speculative explanations are offered for the psychological factors which increase the fitness of these various Memes, and each Meme is one of the factors which increases the appeal of each of the others (Dawkins 1989: 193):

> Consider the idea of God. . . . What is it about the idea of a god that gives it its stability and penetrance in the cultural environment? The survival of a god meme in the meme pool results from its great psychological appeal. It provides a superficially plausible answer to deep and troubling questions about existence. It suggests that injustices in this world will be rectified in the next. The "everlasting arms" hold out a cushion against our own inadequacies which, like a doctor's placebo, is none the less effective for being imaginary. These are some of the reasons why the idea of God is copied so readily by successive generations of individual brains. God exists, if only in the form of a meme with high survival value, or infective power, in the environment provided by human culture.

Here we see how two Memes can increase each other's appeal. The idea of God and the idea of immortality are mutually supporting, such that someone who feels convinced of the value of one Meme is more likely to be receptive to the other. Dawkins has not relied upon any 'sensory prominence' arguments, and speculates about the nature of appeal. The theme emphasised is that of the appeal an idea has for a potential recipient; why someone would want to *learn* an idea, and then to hold on to it. Dawkins has not, however, chosen to speculate about the roles that the conscious attempts by priests and other religious people to 'convert' new individuals play in the process, nor the reasons why some people may have a strong desire to do this, possible additional factors which will be discussed in the next section in a which a series of 'viral permutations' of Dawkins's hypotheticals will be presented. The main elements contributing to psychological appeal in Dawkins's Meme examples so far are the intrinsic qualities of the Meme itself, and its phenotypic manifestations, rather than all the emotional, intentional, and aesthetic factors which make up the Meme's psychological niche.

This theme is pursued when Dawkins moves on to other elements in the Christian Meme complex. He discusses another idea which occurs in a variety of contexts within various Christian denominations, the concept of hellfire. Hellfire is preached as a potential punishment for those who do not observe Christian principles in their daily lives, and submitted as a contrast to the reward of eternal life, which is granted to those who do behave as requested. There are thus two reasons for observing the Christian code; the hope of attaining ever-lasting life in Heaven, and avoiding ever-lasting damnation in hell. Some may laugh at such notions, but the idea of hellfire has caused many people a great deal of psychological distress through the ages (Dawkins 1989: 197). It also appears that fear of punishment in hell is a significant factor in the maintenance of belief in some Christian Meme complexes, and that people may actually continue to observe religious concepts precisely for this reason. Dawkins considers the possibility that priests may have actually designed the concept of hellfire to fulfil this role, but once again rejects the role of conscious factors in favour of the theme of intrinsic qualities of the hellfire concept, and its ability to *self*-replicate, almost like genes capable of meiotic drive, where one gene at a particular locus is able to become represented at that locus in more than 50% (the usual number) of the gametes produced during meiosis (Dawkins 1989: 235). The theme of Memes being gene-like *replicators* rather than Virus-like replicatees, spreading without any conscious intervention on the part of the minds they occupy, is quite explicit (Dawkins 1989: 198):

> ... the threat of hellfire. . . is a particularly nasty technique of persuasion. . . . But it is highly effective. It might almost have been planned deliberately by a machiavellian priesthood trained in deep psychological indoctrination techniques. However, I doubt if the priests were that clever. Much more probably, unconscious memes have ensured their own survival by virtue of those same qualities of pseudo-ruthlessness that successful genes display. The idea of hellfire is, quite simply, self-perpetuating, because of its own deep psychological impact. It has become linked with the god meme because the two reinforce each other, and assist each other's survival in the meme pool.

The next part of the religious Meme complex discussed is the idea of 'blind faith', and the significance of the tale of Doubting Thomas. This 'faith' Meme protects both itself and other Memes through limiting the exposure of the religious Meme complex to sensory verification. If the human individual whose mind a Meme occupies were to look for evidence, there would always the danger that certain information would be found which refuted that Meme. Nothing is more lethal to Memes held purely on faith than a willingness seriously to consider the views of others, or to submit the idea to any sort of testing procedure. The 'faith' Meme promotes its social transmission from person to person through 'the simple unconscious expedient of discouraging rational enquiry' (Dawkins 1989: 198), as it even discourages rational enquiry into the phenomenon of 'faith' itself. Once acquired, it is thus able to protect itself and the Memes to which it is attached.

The final Meme of the religious complex discussed involves the phenomenon of celibacy. The psychological appeal of this particular Meme is judged as being concerned with the fact that reproduction tends to distract energy away from the religious Meme complex, towards the needs of the family (rather like the workaholic viral phenomenon of chapter 9). Here Dawkins uses an explanatory structure which comes closest to the themes which are of special interest in the Cultural Virus Theory, as a certain amount of conscious intent on behalf of the priests is definitely implied (Dawkins 1989: 199):

> The meme for celibacy is transmitted by priests to young boys who have not yet decided what they want to do with their lives. The medium of transmission is human influence of various kinds, the spoken and written word, personal example and so on. Suppose, for the sake of argument, it happened to be the case that marriage weakened the power of the priest to influence his flock, say because it occupied a large proportion of his time and attention. This has, indeed, been advanced as an official reason for the enforcement of celibacy among priests.

Dawkins proposes that such Meme complexes evolve in much the same way that co-adapted gene complexes evolve in gene pools. Evolution in Meme pools over a period of time comes to favour certain Memes which are adapted to the environment of the Memes. Part of the environment of each Meme is all the other Memes in the Meme pool, and so the Memes are selected on the grounds of their 'fit' to other Memes which have already been selected, Memes which in turn are now more fit than before because of the presence of the new Memes.

In sum, it can be seen that there is a tendency in the variety of illustrative examples employed by Dawkins for a focus upon situations where Memes spread as a result of unconscious factors of human thought or action. In the next section, it is shown how the possibilities for memetic transmission can also encompass an immense range of deliberate and intentional acts of cultural transmission, and a wide range of other 'intentional' aspects, within a Virus framework, without violating any basic neo-Darwinian principles.

Virus hypotheticals, people, and the jungle of human sentiment
While the Meme discourse has focused on examples of the kind outlined above, the Virus discourse has contemplated the possibility of applying

cultural parasite principles to the most 'conscious' and 'intentional' aspects of individual psychology; in short, the aspects of human affairs which are normally considered to be most problematic for a parasitic interpretation. In order to illustrate this difference between the foci of interest in the two perspectives, I will now propose some possible alternative explanations of Dawkins's hypotheticals in which human intent is brought into greater prominence, not only in order to illustrate that it is possible to do so, but rather to indicate that such 'motive-driven' alternatives can be constructed in such a way as to be every bit as neo-Darwinian as the more unconscious examples which occur in the Meme discourse. This exercise will highlight the significance of the Virus position's preference for the term 'replicatee' and 'viral phenomenon' over the Meme position's term 'replicator'. Memes are not capable of physically assembling copies of themselves; and they are therefore actually better considered as resembling viral phenomena, and not true self-replicators. To put it another way, it appears that in some sense memetic material occurs only in a form analogous to RNA, and not DNA. Despite an interesting and sophisticated discussion by Ball (1984: 155–8) of the critique of the Meme concept by Midgeley, Bonner, and Lumsden & Wilson, which points out that Memes, unlike genes, are not independent replicators, he ultimately asserts equivalence on the grounds that genes are not wholly independent either. Despite the fact that he even mentions RNA viruses in this very section, he does not focus upon the fact that retroviruses are somewhat less of a true 'replicator' and more of a 'replicatee'. I prefer to defend culture from this direction; I accept that genes are independent replicators, and that cultural phenomena are not. However, as already argued extensively in the last chapter, there are special kinds of parasites (i.e. retroviruses) *which have no independent replicating material either*. The key to silencing the Meme critics is, therefore, not to argue that *genes* are not independent replicators (as they are capable of replication outside the organism, such as in a test tube, without any other genetic material being present), but rather, to argue that *retroviruses* are not independent replicators, as these require the presence of host DNA in their environment.

This is where the terminology of the Virus perspective has advantages on the 'independent replicator' terminology of the Meme discourse. The analogy with actual viruses fits with remarkable precision. When microbial retroviruses parasitise cells, they hijack cellular machinery which has successfully survived due to its capacity to produce a range of 'desirable' products, which generally serve the 'purpose' of promoting organismic survival and reproduction. Let us then 'personify' the cell for the purposes of the discussion. The cell can be imagined as 'trying to achieve' something, which we could define as something not too dissimilar to its part in the overall purpose of the organ in which it resides (of course it is only blindly performing these tasks, but it is not stretching the metaphor too far to speak of many of these tasks as functions or goals). Liver cells are trying to achieve a set of goals which could be crudely referred to as 'liverness', kidney cells are struggling to achieve 'kidneyness', brain cells 'brainness', and so on. Presumably, continuing the metaphor, a normal cell is still 'trying' to achieve this task even when it has come to contain a virus, and is either failing or partially failing in its attempts to do so. It is logical to suppose that viruses have evolved to 'cash in' on the various task-related chemical assembly lines of the cell, diverting existing processes away from their intended objectives towards making viruses. Each adaptation could be expected to be highly specific to certain 'goal structures' in the cell. This would be far more economical than trying to establish their own assembly lines from scratch. In other words, it is fair to suppose that a virus is actually adapting, first and foremost, to a chemical environment criss-crossed with all sorts of 'intentional' and 'teleological' processes, and that the presence of such ordered, intentional and even, in the case of cultural phenomena, emotional environmental features, are actually crucial to its survival.

Thus the words 'virus', 'viral', and 'replicatee' not only suggest a lack of intrinsic agencies in the phenomena concerned (qualities which DNA also lacks in any case, apart from its self-replicating capacity), but also suggest the possibility of, and even the necessity for, *considerable* agency in the *environment* of the said phenomena. The word virus thus implies a relatively inactive phenomenon selected for its capacity passively to benefit from a highly 'active' environment full of all sorts of agencies. Rather than adapting in such a way as to develop its own structures of agency, it has adapted directly to the agency structures of other phenomena. A viral phenomenon is not a conscious, purposeful agent; but a viral phenomenon which possess qualities which incite the agency of other phenomena or organisms is more likely to be replicated than one which cannot.

Such 'replicatee' premises lead to scenarios where human intention is featured, rather than merely implied or even ignored as tends to be the case in the Meme discourse. This can best be illustrated by exploring a number of Cultural Virus Theory permutations of Dawkins's Meme examples, and showing the potential for all sorts of highly 'intentional' alternatives to the basically unconscious scenarios he employs.

The interesting implication which emerges from the exploration of a range of more 'viral' alternatives to the Dawkins hypotheticals is that *no amount of human interference* can really violate the selective principles of cultural transmission. No matter how much 'intent' we attribute to our hypothetical actors, the same principles ultimately remain. Far from denying the existence of people and their intentions, such phenomena become absolutely crucial, as some of the most important features of the psychological environments to which populations of viral phenomena adapt.

So if we follow the lead of the words 'replicatee' or 'viral phenomenon', the task is not to find the few cases of cultural transmission where deliberate human agency is either negligible or absent; the real problem is to attack the vast majority of deliberate transmissions, and to show that such cases actually exemplify, rather than threaten, a parasitic or symbiont perspective.

Let us begin with the phenomenon of the erroneous version of Burns's 'Auld Land Syne'. As described in greater detail above, the correct line of the refrain, 'For auld lang syne', becomes the longer 'For (the sake of) auld lang syne' in the mutant version of the song. The English phrase of 'the sake of' has been added to the original idiomatic Scots expression 'auld lang syne' which translates literally as 'old long since', and means something like 'days long ago'. Under the Dawkins approach to explanation, the theme emphasised is that of the acoustic prominence of certain consonants such as 's' and 'k', which render the erroneous version more audible than the original. The mutant Meme is spread without any necessary knowledge of the participants, and the possibilities for any deliberate or manipulative forms of cultural transmission are not explored.

Yet when more 'intentional' scenarios are explored within a viral perspective, any perceived threat to a neo-Darwinian interpretation can be quickly deconstructed. No amount of deliberate intervention on the part of the hosts of the 'Auld Lang Syne' phenomenon – the people who are singing it – ever corrupts the fundamentally Darwinian nature of the underlying processes involved. For instance, it is conceivable that if an adult was trying to teach a child how to sing the song, they might deliberately teach the mutant version instead of the original, thinking that the addition of the English phrase 'the sake of' would make the words more meaningful to the child. To most people, whether they be adults or children, the meaning of the words 'auld lang syne' (old long since) would presumably be rather obscure. The 'the sake of' addition makes 'auld lang syne' appear to be the mysterious subject of an otherwise perfectly comprehensible sentence. But such deliberate intervention in the cultural transmission process on the part of the adult does not challenge any aspect of the Virus framework. The adult is actually surmising about the relative fitness of the two versions in the 'local environment' represented by the mind of the child, and then deliberately choosing to replicate one instead of the other. The model that the adult has of the particular child's aesthetics constitute a set of local psychological 'conditions' which temporarily raise the fitness of the erroneous version in that part of the adult's mind. The desire of the adult to choose a version which the child will understand need not be viewed as an intentional subversion of memetic fitness; rather, the presence or absence of such desires in a given mind define and thereby change the local parameters of memetic fitness in the first place.

Alternatively, let us suppose, that during an evening speech at an annual club dinner held near the time of New Year's Eve, an influential personality who was an expert on Burns's songs decided to speak about the two versions of Auld Lang Syne, and to explain which was the right version, and which was the wrong. Suppose that the speaker concerned considers that the 'correct' version can only be defined in terms of the original score; and that he or she follows the somewhat conservative ethic that the original version is always the best. Despite the fact that the 'majority' now consider the mutant form to be correct, our imaginary speaker has no qualms in informing anyone of their error. He or she is a self-confident moral crusader for 'accuracy' and 'truth', and considers the mutant version of the song to be an insult to Burns. The audience might well be comprehensively convinced by such a person, and at the next New Year's Eve everyone might then sing the correct version in confident synchrony. The speaker feels a sense of satisfaction in being able to 'rectify' what he or she felt to be a sad state of affairs, restoring the correct version to its rightful place, and condemning the erroneous version to the scrap heap. The two song versions are merely passive replicatees in this sequence of events, and, moreover, it is clear that the speaker is deliberately and intentionally manipulating the circumstances of cultural transmission so as to favour one version over the other.

But no reversal of the 'Darwinian order' has occurred. The influential after dinner speaker has not forced the 'less fit' version to prevail at the expense of the 'fitter' mutant. Rather, the relative fitness of the two phenomena has been altered by the sudden appearance and propagation of other Memes in their local psychological environment. The speaker has achieved this through increasing the knowledge of the audience with respect to the two phenomena, and the mutant phenomenon begins to find it more and more difficult to compete with the 'original' 'Auld Lang Syne' in the enriched and more knowledgeable milieu in which it now finds itself. The speaker is in a position to alter the psychological environment of the ideas through the cultural transmission which occurs during the after-dinner speech. Whether the speaker has a conscious intention to alter the knowledge of the listeners or not is irrelevant to the fact that the basic means of doing this is to alter the 'environment' of the two phenomena in question, rather than the phenomena themselves.

Let us envisage a final permutation of the 'Auld Land Syne' phenomenon where an attempt is made deliberately to influence the course of cultural transmission, only in the opposite direction. Suppose that in the audience of the above speaker, there is someone else who is also called upon for the odd after-dinner speech themselves, and that this person views the political persuasion of the current speaker to be too far to the 'right'. In fact, let us imagine that this listener finds the whole idea that the original version is the 'best' and the most 'correct' to be arrogant and offensive, and an insult to his or her egalitarian principles. He or she is a linguistics graduate, and an editor of a respectable dictionary, and feels that it is not antiquity but usage which defines what is 'correct'. If the mutant version now holds sway, then that is the way that 'Auld Lang Syne' is now sung, and as far as our second speaker is concerned, that is that. In order to redress this injustice, the second speaker resolves to expound the principle of 'majority rules' and the virtues of what really ought to be called the 'new' rather than the 'erroneous' Auld Lang Syne, at their next guest-speaking appointment.

But once again the Virus principles would not be subverted, even if our second speaker was able to fulfil his or her aim. Even though the mutant 'Auld Lang Syne' has only spread as a result of the intentional and highly directed 'agency' of the leftist guest speaker, it has spread none the less. The fact that it has been a wholly passive 'replicatee' does not present any major barrier to an explanation which employs a neo-Darwinian perspective. The mutant version appeals to its host precisely because it is different to the original, and these differences make it seem more appealing to someone whose morality resembles that of the second speaker. It has been spread as a direct result of such differences. That the successful spreading of the mutant version required, in this case, the presence of a highly motivated person with leftist political leanings, does not present a challenge to neo-Darwinian principles. A given viral phenomenon's requirement for the presence of particular kinds of people with a social or political agenda in its milieu is no different to a cow's need for grass, or a lion's need for wildebeest.

Thus the viral replicatee concept frees the cultural parasite perspective from any dependence on or preference for 'unconscious', 'insidious' or 'Meme driven' scenarios. Human intentions and individual identities of all sorts can be explicitly incorporated into the perspective as crucial environmental phenomena, without which few instances of cultural transmission could be understood or satisfactorily explained. When 'people' are relegated to the environment in this way, they are not being dismissed or discarded, but quite the opposite. In fact, the (very human, and very cultural) environment and the individual phenomenon are of equal importance in Cultural Virus Theory, as indeed they are, for that matter, in neo-Darwinian theory in general.

But the Virus concept also suggests a starting point for a comprehensive explanation of another area of cultural systems which appear to challenge the parasitic perspective. This is the pervasive occurrence of ideas, behaviours, and artefacts which are not apparently used for cultural transmission. I believe that large numbers of this kind of phenomenon can be explained through evoking cultural equivalents of the general neo-Darwinian concept of genetically selfish (which would become 'memetically selfish') altruism. Complex altruism and their attendant social structures would presumably not be possible in microbial viruses. Yet, as will be discussed in the next section, the viral phenomena of culture are able to 'borrow' the complicated social structures of human communities in such a way as to achieve 'societies' based on memetically selfish altruism.

The eusocial Cultural Virus

While the main explanatory theme of Dawkins's Meme examples involved the unconscious effect of certain Memes on their hosts, the above section showed how the 'Auld Lang Syne' Meme hypothetical could form the basis of a whole range of more 'viral' permutations where deliberate strategies of cultural transmission on the part of individual people were involved. The aim of the section was to show how the notion of the passive 'replicatee' status of cultural phenomena, explored within the Virus perspective, can supply a whole range of scenarios of deliberate human intervention which are no less neo-Darwinian than the more unconscious factors emphasised in the Meme examples.

Dawkins's religious Meme complex of God, immortality, celibacy, hellfire and faith was also discussed a little earlier, and once again it was seen that explanatory factors which involved deliberate machiavellian or benevolent factors were avoided wherever possible. For example, Dawkins emphasised that the idea of hellfire 'ensured its own survival', and that it was 'self-perpetuating, because of its own deep psychological impact' (Dawkins 1989: 198). Dawkins's discussion of the unconscious factors involved in the cultural fitness of Memes was interesting, but it is important to note again that a Virus perspective does not require 'unconscious self-perpetuation' in order to work as an explanatory framework. Rather, as already discussed with reference to 'Auld Lang Syne', a framework based on the Virus concept often implies and at times even requires the presence of individual people who are struggling to carry out all sorts of conscious and unconscious goals, regardless of whether these goals are perceived as 'rational' or 'irrational' by an observer.

The theme of personal intentions and goal-oriented behaviour, made explicit in the Virus perspective, will now be explored with reference to Dawkins's religious Meme complex, in the hope of illustrating once again how these factors can be integrated under the neo-Darwinian umbrella using a Virus perspective.

Let us suppose, for example, that Dawkins's 'self-perpetuation' explanation of the hellfire concept proved at some later date not to be true, and that a general policy of machiavellian intervention on the part of the priests who spread the hellfire concept began to look more and more likely. The real strength of the Virus 'replicatee' concept is that if such were the case, the perspective could expand to accommodate the new facts, with the 'machiavellian intentions' of the priests being classified as a suite of local psychological phenomena acting as selective criteria for the hellfire phenomenon, which the priests then spread.

Advancing a fully fledged and more obviously 'viral' alternative to the Dawkins's Meme complex hypothetical will require, however, the introduction of the concept of 'cultural eusociality' (Cullen 1990: 65). This is where the complicated interplay of both intentional and unintentional human behaviour with assemblages of viral phenomena produces a cultural equivalent of the phenomenon of eusociality in organisms (Dawkins 1989: 174). Most biological examples of this phenomenon occur in social insects such as the hymenoptera (ants and bees), although quite recently (see Brett 1986, in Dawkins 1989) a case of this kind of social structure was found amongst *Hydrocephalus glaber*, the naked mole rat of Kenya. Such societies are usually founded by a single male/female couple, or by a fertilised female, which then begins to produce offspring. But the offspring produced do not develop into replicas of their parents; instead, they grow into sterile individuals (such as 'workers', 'soldiers' and 'nurses') which work exclusively towards the general well-being of the close kin community. Such individuals increase the resources and facilities available to their parent (the queen) who only then begins to produce a percentage of fertile offspring (young queens and drones) which go off to found other hives. This is perfectly in keeping with neo-Darwinian principles, as in helping their mother to produce sisters and brothers the non-reproductive workers reproduce their genes as effectively, or even more effectively than the queen herself (Dawkins 1989: 175). The behaviour of workers is thus perfectly altruistic as far as each individual is concerned, but perfectly selfish in terms of genetic survival.

When I first began to develop the Virus perspective in the early 1980s (see chapter 7.2) other academics would often point out a range of challenging examples where ideas, artefacts or behaviour patterns were being used to human benefit, without any apparent cultural transmission of the phenomenon occurring as a result, apparently refuting the Virus hypothesis. Such phenomena are extremely numerous; examples would include cassette tapes or records which are played and played without ever being reproduced in the process, the horse-shoe which is used until worn out, and then discarded, the exploitation of secret knowledge by an individual who never tells anyone else, and many others.

It was quite possible that many such phenomena were simply in the process of becoming extinct. But it occurred to me that these phenomena, while not functioning as reproductives in their own right, might actually be increasing the fitness of their 'cultural relatives' through their existence. This would explain why, for example, a stables might discard every horse-shoe they ever used for centuries, and never make any of their own, while at the very same time horse-shoes in general could be surviving very well. There might be a whole range of non-reproductive 'worker' cultural phenomena, distributed throughout human communities, which through their functional or aesthetic appeal increase the reproductive success of the 'master' copy from which they were originally made, while in the meantime these 'worker artefacts' convey a general impression of perfect 'altruism' (in the Darwinian sense).

Complicated networks of social interaction and stated and unstated goals set up a rich and complicated psychological environment, a 'jungle of human sentiment', in which equally complicated patterns of viral exploitation can emerge. If single structures can survive through their capacity to exploit this environment, then there is no reason why a whole complex of phenomena – which generates not one phenotypic expression, but a range of different expressions – cannot also be successful.

This is one particular set of biocultural analogies in Cultural Virus Theory which appear to have no equivalent in the Meme discourse so far. A related element which also seems to be absent in the Meme discourse is the development of Cultural Virus equivalents of the general notion of genetically 'selfish' altruism, and kin selection, of which the eusocial phenomenon is a special case. As Dawkins points out in his principal research area, genetic process, all parental investments in offspring represent a ubiquitous kind of *genetic* kin selection (Dawkins 1989: 108). Perhaps 'selfish' altruism is equally ubiquitous in *cultural* systems. But to what existing psychological factors could populations of cultural phenomena adapt in this way? The beginnings of the answer could lie in the capacity of viral phenomena to hijack systems of vague, inchoate human instincts which originally evolved due to their capacity to produce genetically selfish altruistic behaviour. Say, for example, there was a human tendency to invest more energy in helping those which they perceived to be similar to themselves. It is easy to imagine the genetic advantages which might result from such behaviour; this tendency might produce behaviour which, while detracting from the reproductive opportunities of the actor, might in fact increase the number of reproductive opportunities available to the individual's genetic kin. This would only be effective under social conditions where a similar person would tend *to be* a relative. When the individual is removed from the close kin community, the possibility for cultural exploitation of these tendencies emerges. If an idea can entwine itself with an individual's sense of self to the point at which that person considers that idea to be a fundamental part of their identity, it might also lead that person to define similar others (potential kin) on the basis of their acceptance of that idea.

However at this point care must be taken coherently to translate concepts of altruism into purely cultural analogues, and to avoid becoming bogged down in some form of biocultural confusion. *Culturally* selfish altruism must involve the sacrifice by a cultural phenomenon of the opportunity to culturally reproduce, not the sacrifice by a human individual of an opportunity genetically to reproduce. We are not looking for human martyrs who sacrifice life or reproduction for cultural advancement, but for cultural structures which remain silent or untransmitted in order that other copies of that structure are transmitted.

So, for example, one might envisage a teaching establishment such as a school or university as a vast hive of culturally transmitted viral behaviours and beliefs. The vast majority of copies of a department's concepts reside in alumni who leave the institution and never become directly involved with teaching. Their copies remain as silent or 'sterile' phenomena which 'work', or aid a given individual and his or her family to live off the proceeds of a particular profession, rather than acting as a template for cultural transmission. The principal way in which they can affect the next generation of copies of their particular enculturated state is by demonstrating its value to other people who are then attracted to the master copy back at the original institution, the 'queen' neuronal structure, which is exclusively 'taught from' rather than used. The existence of a 'queen' viral phenomenon is made possible through the attraction of people who identify closely with the idea, who then 'tend' or 'farm' the concept in the workplace. Music recordings constitute another example; millions of recordings, most of which will never become primary reproducing templates themselves, are produced by a recording company. These constitute a vast assemblage of sterile 'worker' viral phenomena which indirectly affect the likelihood of continued preservation of a master copy back at the company, and ultimately divert energy back to the 'queen of queens' residing in the mind of the original musician. Some recordings have actual sterility features, such as the anti-recording devices built into cassettes (or, for that matter, computer software). If record sales are really successful, they will enable the survival of an elite lineage of 'queen' recordings, each reproduced from the one before, and not from the damaged copies which have been continually played. The more successful the worker recordings, the more resources available to the original musician to produce recordings of new songs. Furthermore, if all master copies are lost, then a new master copy may emerge from the rank and file, competing with other copies *vis à vis* prevailing enculturated definitions of 'authenticity'. Alternatively, the recordings might well have reproduced themselves quite successfully into the minds of the people who played them. This does not change the fact that the cassette or record itself is not employed in the making of new cassettes or records, and is therefore a genuinely 'sterile' cultural phenomenon.

But the 'eusocial virus' idea might also provide an alternative scenario to Dawkins's religious Meme complex hypothetical. I stress that it is not my intention to carry out any sort of in-depth scholarly analysis of the history of patterns of cultural transmission in the Christian church. The discussion which now follows is purely hypothetical, intuitive, and it is employed for heuristic purposes only. All of the following assertions would have to be verified with sociological or ethnographic research before they could be considered reliable representations of actual cultural systems.

Yet it is conceivable that the viral complex of God, hellfire, immortality, celibacy and faith might not manifest itself as a series of identical phenomena which function in the same way in every mind they occupy. Instead, like bees, ants, and mole rats, religious concepts may occur in a whole range of reproductive and non-reproductive forms, which persist in history due to their tendency to facilitate the cultural transmission of the reproductive forms. Their existence might work altruistically towards the good of the Church, and towards the general well-being of the people who maintain them, increasing the wealth and resources available to the reproductive viral phenomena residing in the minds of priests.

So one of the main distinctions in the eusocial order of the viral phenomena of religions would presumably be that between the ideas in the minds of priests and the ideas in the minds of the congregation. There is the central line of cultural descent from priest to acolyte, and the knowledge transmitted down this line consists of a vast viral assemblage of inter-related ideas which takes years to successfully reproduce to a satisfactory extent. Replication of this sort would consist of the kind of learning normally involved in obtaining a theology degree. This main line of descent could be called the 'queen' viral assemblage, and if this were all that existed, and priests never preached to anyone but future priests, then its strategy of survival would not be fundamentally different to that of smaller ideas such as 'Auld Lang Syne'. As in the case of 'Auld Lang Syne', the cultural fitness of concepts such as 'hellfire' and various ideas about the nature of 'God' could well involve more than the various unconscious and unintentional aspects of psychological appeal explored by Dawkins. The theologians in any teaching body might be involved in all sorts of personal conflicts and collaborations, and these social struggles would affect which ideas they spend the most time teaching and how. One theologian might advocate one idea purely because an arch-rival advocates another, and *vice versa*. Moreover, some theologians may even be aware of the subjective nature of their teaching focus. In any case, factors such as these will only affect which ideas establish themselves in the main line of cultural descent from priest to priest.

But there is also the cultural transmission from priest to congregation to consider. This occurs during church services, particularly during sermons, and the more intense one-to-one interaction which occurs during situations such as confession, or a priest's 'rounds' of personal visits to administer pastoral care of various sorts. It is in these situations that the cultural reproduction involved becomes less than straightforward. The priest is teaching concepts to people who are unlikely to become involved in teaching novices themselves. There is also likely to be a significant gap between the theological knowledge of the priest and that of the listeners. Nor are the listeners likely to be able to preach to each other with confident authority, as, generally speaking, someone is more likely to believe what a priest says about aspects of the religion than they would a layman (other things being equal, of course). Moreover, it is not just a matter of a layman finding someone to listen to them; many of the doctrines of the church are so complicated that it is almost impossible to expound them effectively without some form of intensive training. Such ideas could never be spread beyond the cloisters, and copies of these ideas that exist outside the theological milieu are therefore effectively sterile.

Yet members of the congregation may listen very carefully to a priest expounding these ideas, and come to feel that they have a reasonable understanding of a whole range of concepts which are integral to the religion they follow. Nonetheless, their understanding may be highly individualised and not easily expressible in words. Some regular church-goers may not be as articulate as the highly educated theologian they listen to on a Sunday. The average layman can speak for hours about all sorts of religious concepts, but a well-trained theologian who listens to these expressions can generally recognise a range of concepts which have been substantially individualised, altered, simplified or left out altogether. The contrast in depth of understanding must have been particularly pronounced during the early periods of missionary activity in the British colonies in America, Africa, and Australia, when large numbers of indigenous people became 'Christians' virtually overnight. In most cases these rapid conversions must have produced individuals whose basic psychological make up consisted of the indigenous religion with a superficial overlay of Christian notions. The personalities of these 'Christians', and their religious ideas, must have remained substantially different to that of their cultural conquerors. Moreover, it is quite possible that some indigenous individuals simply continued to worship their old religion in a new terminology, and that the few truly English religious concepts that they did identify with were not easily communicable, and therefore culturally or memetically sterile.

Indeed, while both priest and different members of a congregation use common words such as 'God', 'faith' and 'hellfire', the concepts behind the words which denote religious concepts can be quite varied, even in a congregation which speaks English as a first language. One example of this is afforded by an article of Catholic faith known as the 'Immaculate Conception'. Almost any person who considers themselves to be Catholic, whether priest or layman, will adamantly insist that they know whose conception this doctrine refers to. However, most Catholic laymen, and even some priests, mistakenly believe that the Immaculate Conception is all about how Christ was conceived in the womb of the Virgin Mary. Yet this is not the case. As almost any priest well versed in the doctrines of the Catholic church will testify, the Immaculate Conception is actually an account of how Mary herself was conceived in the womb of her own mother in a manner which rendered her free of original sin, *preparing* her for the later events associated with the conception of Christ, but in no way *part of* this second and later conception. But could the inaccurate, and even nonsensical derivatives of this complicated doctrine, which are unlikely to make it to the next generation of priests, and which exist in the congregation, possibly work towards the replicative success of the correct doctrines in the mainline of theological descent? Could some of the replicative success of the 'Immaculate Conception' doctrine, as part of the general complex of the Catholic faith, derive in part from the personal appeal of its erroneous versions? Misappropriations of the words 'immaculate conception', so that they are thought to apply to the conception of Christ in Mary's womb, might, for example, enhance the general metaphorical power of the personality of Christ in the general congregation. Exploring the possibility further, however, would presumably require actual sociological or ethnographic fieldwork.

Other elements of a religious cultural complex might also occur in a range of forms, some more suited to cultural reproduction, and others more suited to the indirect facilitation of that reproduction. A priest might have a thorough knowledge of the many different meanings that words like 'faith', 'celibacy', 'hellfire', 'immortality' and 'God' may take. But he or she may not preach these concepts in precisely the same form that they were laid out in theological lectures. Having faith in an idea, for example, in the opinion of the priest, may not represent a complete absence of doubt, or even any absence of the ability to challenge that idea. But the more extreme ideal of absolute faith may nonetheless be preached as something for a congregation to aspire to.

Conversely, other concepts may occur in their most extreme form in the minds of priests. When celibacy occurs in a religion, it is normally only advocated for a small minority such as the priesthood itself, although it may also be advocated for other groups, such as unmarried women. But related and less comprehensive notions of various kinds of sexual repression, such as rules against sex in certain positions, with someone of the same sex, or with someone other than one's primary partner, commonly occur in religions with celibate priests.

Similarly, if a number of people who consider themselves to be Christians are asked to define who or what they consider the word 'God' to signify, a wide range of responses is often received. Many would say that their particular idea of 'God' was influenced by or inspired by the teachings of some priest or theologian, so there is no doubt that each version is usually learnt from some source. But one of the most common complaints is the idea itself is intensely personal, and cannot be adequately communicated to anyone. Ideas which cannot be communicated have, by definition, zero cultural fitness, and so notions of 'God' which are too personal to be expressed must have some other means of survival other than direct transmission. This is in contrast to theological notions of 'God' being transmitted from priest to acolyte within an academic institution. Like the complicated and counterintuitively named concept of the Immaculate Conception, a complex definition of the nature of God can be learnt far more coherently by an acolyte, who is privy to many hours of religious instruction and supervised study, than it can by a member of the congregation. Yet, whether they can express it or not, most congregationists believe they 'know' what 'God' is, that they 'know' what the 'Immaculate Conception' is, and so on. In any case, members of a congregation may only be required to say that they 'believe in God', and not to give a personal description of Him (or Her). Such non-specific commitments allow much scope for the aesthetic 'customisation' of non-reproductive (i.e. non-priest) forms of a given idea.

Obviously, then, it would appear that ideas occur in religious communities in both reproductive and non-reproductive forms. The question is how to interpret the non-reproductive forms, and I have been implying that the fragmented, simplified or distorted nature of the congregation's versions of certain religious concepts may actually work to the reproductive advantage of the 'master' or 'queen' copies in the minds of priests. There is space enough to consider the possibility of eusocial cultural altruism with reference to one of the above ideas, that of celibacy, in a little more detail. Firstly let us define the notion of total celibacy, or at least total repression of both heterosexual and homosexual yearnings, to be the 'queen' or 'master' phenomenon. It is easy to imagine, as already discussed with reference to Dawkins, where this viral phenomenon derives most of its cultural fitness from: the prevention of the normal outlet of one of the basic appetitive drives. It is able to use this drive as a vast supply of surplus energy which is diverted into the cultural transmission of both the idea itself, and that of other elements in a religious ideology. The ideal of celibacy is the basic line of descent, as it is what is taught in our hypothetical institution to each new acolyte.

Let us imagine, then, that our acolyte, once ordained, goes out and is able to rigidly adhere to a celibate lifestyle. Imagine also that our young priest gives sermons which advocate celibacy, in no uncertain terms, for all unmarried members of his or her congregation. It is unlikely that all of the congregation will be able to live up to the ideal of the sermon, but it is equally likely that most of them will try to hide the fact. Some young people may try to restrict their activity to 'heavy petting'. Others may come to other private solutions. In hiding their personal solutions, each person creates a culturally sterile derivative of the priest's ideal; a distorted, compromised, or corrupted version of the original which is excluded from primary 'reproductive' location of the priest's consciousness by the original idea itself.

In this way each of the descendant ideas is restricted to a worker role in the genealogy of the religion. Being derived from the 'celibacy' model, repression is likely to remain the theme of the ideas about sexual activity in the congregation. Each digression from the ideal is likely to create emotional energy in two forms. Firstly, there would presumably be a measure of guilt involved in not measuring up to the ideal of complete celibacy. Secondly, this guilt is likely to redouble the individual's efforts to repress other aspects of their sexuality which remain unexpressed, presumably on the implicit grounds that 'partial' celibacy is better than none at all. The two forms of energy are thus guilt for those desires which are illicitly satisfied, and the sublimated desire of those which remain repressed. The viral assemblage wins both ways: energy lost in the satisfaction of desire is regained in guilt, while successful repressions of aspects of sexual desire produce energy which may then be harvested by the church in the same way that the repressed desire of the celibate priest may be. As long as the resulting guilt and repressed desire is discharged back in the direction of the church, whether on the Sunday collection plate or in more extreme forms such as missionary activity, the master phenomenon of celibacy is able to harvest the 'work' of its silent cultural offspring in the congregation.

The possibilities for the viral perspective on culture are so vast that the full implications could not be discussed in a study twice as long as this one. As in the case of single viral phenomena such as Auld Lang Syne, intention need not be excluded from eusocial viral assemblages either. No amount of deliberate intervention in the cultural transmission process need pose any threat to a neo-Darwinian interpretation. The desire to intervene, and the presence of one or more goals which lead to such desire in an individual's mind, can merely be counted as additional (and very interesting) elements of the psychocultural milieu which affects the fitness of a viral assemblage. Indeed, the strategic introduction of a cultural phenomenon into another culture could even be considered a kind of cultural 'biological warfare', where a pernicious idea or artefact (such as alcohol, or nicotine) is introduced in the hope of hindering the functioning of a community. Even more 'benevolent' introductions, such as those involved in missionary activity, could sometimes be included under the this general umbrella. There are other genetic processes which could yield useful cultural analogies. Delius (1989: 69; 1991: 95), for example, has even discussed cultural equivalents of sexual recombination, although there is insufficient space to go into this interesting direction here. A particularly interesting biocultural analogy is the one developing between viral spores and various forms of stored cultural information (Ball 1984: 153; Delius 1989: 54). Moreover, there are many other sub-directions which have been left unexplored.

The importance of being pernicious

Most of the hypothetical examples considered above do not specifically involve artefacts or the archaeological record. In order partially to redress this shortfall, let us think in terms of attempting to explain an idealised transition from one artefact type to another in the archaeological record. The artefact hypothetical will involve six different structures, each competing with the rest for continued existence in a band of *Homo erectus*. Let us imagine that a band of some fifty *Homo erectus* individuals inhabits a particular area, and that variation exists within the band with respect to a number of factors.

Firstly, let us imagine that two basic kinds of thumbs are present in the *erectus* population, and that one of these thumb types is a little more mobile than the other. Relatively speaking, then, within the population, we have a beneficial thumb type and a pernicious thumb type.

Secondly, let us imagine that two basic kinds of flea can be found on the bodies of our *erectus* individuals: one which spreads a serious but not deadly disease, and can jump a long way; and one which if eaten by the bearer or the bearer's grooming companion, provides a valuable source of B-group vitamins, but can only jump a short way. In other words, we have a pernicious but contagious parasite, and a beneficial but non-contagious parasite.

Thirdly, let us imagine, for the sake of argument, that there are two basic kinds of scraper in use in our *erectus* community: a Mousterian side-scraper, and an Acheulian hand-axe (the hand-axe being cast in the functional role as a 'scraper' by definition for the sake of simplicity) along with the neuronal structures associated with the knowledge of how to manufacture them. Let us also imagine that in the peer group of our imaginary hominid, side-scrapers are in, and Acheulian hand-axes are out. Most *erectus* individuals find that side-scrapers much more aesthetically appealing than the old-fashioned hand-axes. However, hand-axes still perform the scraping tasks involved in *erectus* leatherwork a little more effectively than the new scrapers (nonetheless, the scrapers function quite adequately). So if the side-scraper is a pernicious but popular cultural phenomenon, the hand-axe is beneficial but banal. There are therefore two traits, two parasites, and two artefacts; one of each pair is relatively pernicious, while the other is relatively beneficial.

The Cultural Virus Theory is based on the general proposition that cultural process is neo-Darwinian in every particular. A corollary of this premise is that memetic mutation is logistically or mathematically homologous to genetic mutation in every conceivable sense. Each new viral phenomenon, therefore, must be derived from some previous set of Memes or concepts, some previous viral phenomenon. For the purpose of simplicity, then, let us imagine that the side-scrapers in this hypothetical were derived via a quasi-random memetic mutation from an Acheulian industry of some sort. The word 'quasi-random' is used to denote the fact that although memetic mutation is locally random, in a broader sense it is subject to profound heritage constraint. This is due to the fact that the first conception of the new technique which in turn lead to the manufacture of the first side-scraper occurred *as a derivative of some old technique* that the particular *erectus* individual concerned had previously learnt. Heritage constraint is embodied by the fact that the side-scraper displays a whole range of similarities to the hand-axe, when compared to the full range of possibilities of artefacts. It is made of the same raw material, using some of the same techniques, it is of similar complexity, and the two artefacts are much the same size when compared to the largest and smallest possible artefacts – such as large buildings, or artificial molecules.

Moreover, while the side-scraper may be marginally more appealing, and the hand-axe (as defined) marginally more functional as a scraper, neither is likely to be perfectly functional or perfectly appealing. The knapper who makes these tools is not able to transcend the constraints of his or her own manufacturing notions (except by the relatively small conceptual leaps of memetic mutation) to produce the perfect solution to prevailing *erectus* concepts of either efficacy or aesthetic appeal. This principle can be crudely illustrated with a little thought experiment; by imagining the artificial introduction of a Swiss army knife into the *erectus* band. It is easy to imagine that such an artefact (especially with an appropriate demonstration of its scraping and butchering possibilities) could beat the old scrapers on both functional *and* aesthetic grounds. Yet it is highly unlikely that the principles of metallurgy and forgery involved in replicating the army knife could be stumbled upon via memetic mutation from the Acheulian tradition. Like the Coca Cola bottle in the Kalahari Bushmen band of the film *The Gods Must be Crazy*, a Swiss army knife in an *erectus* band is a 'charismatic survival success' but a reproductive *cul de sac*. Thus the side-scraper may be an aesthetic improvement (as defined *ipso facto*) on the hand-axe, but the cultural heritage constraint implicit in the Acheulian industry ensures that it is also thematically similar to other artefacts in the assemblage from which it was derived.

Now let us attempt to develop some kind of general picture of the different survival challenges which face the six different structures in the *erectus* community. Firstly, the thumbs. Hominid thumbs share their genealogy with all the other traits of *Homo erectus*. There is only ever one place that the traits of a particular *erectus* body can hope to escape the death of their host, and that is in the bodies of his or her descendants. Thus thumb genealogy is, strictly speaking, *erectus* genealogy. Thumbs are part of a single organism, and there can be no question that what is good for either of the thumbs is synonymous with what is good or adaptive for the rest of the hominid.

Conversely, what is pernicious for the thumbs is likely to be pernicious to *Homo erectus*. The only way a thumb can enhance its chances of reproductive success is by contributing to the reproductive success of the body of which it is part (or at the very least through a nepotistic relationship with other bodies related to that body). An immobile thumb cannot adopt an exploitative or parasitic relationship to its hominid host, as it cannot 'leap across' the genealogy of the *erectus* population and infect new or unrelated lineages. The only recourse open to the immobile sector of the thumb population is to 'hope' that mobile thumbs prove to be as much of a disadvantage as an advantage. The pernicious immobile thumb may therefore be legitimately referred to as a 'maladaptive trait', while the beneficial mobile thumb may be legitimately referred to as an 'adaptive trait'.

So much for the thumbs: now, I would like to turn attention to the fleas. The fleas, unlike our hypothetical thumbs, do not have synonymous genealogies with the *Homo erectus* individual, and they, therefore, need not necessarily throw in their lot with their host. Fleas are not automatically reproduced at human conception, and can only hope to colonise infant *Homo erectus* individuals after birth. But fleas are able to colonise unrelated *Homo erectus* individuals, and so those fleas which carry disease, thereby being pernicious to their hosts, are not necessarily at a disadvantage. Being a pernicious thumb is definitely maladaptive; but being a pernicious parasite may, under certain circumstances, be highly adaptive, particularly if you can jump much further than your beneficial competitors.

Finally we come to the Acheulian hand-axe, which has been defined as beneficial but boring, and the Mousterian side-scraper, which has been defined as pernicious but pretty. Are they tied traits, like *erectus* thumbs? Or are they genealogically independent, like *erectus* fleas? It is really not difficult to see that the side-scraper, along with the knowledge of its manufacture, is much more like the freewheeling flea than it is like a thumb. Like fleas, knowledge of the manufacture of hand-axes and scrapers is not passed on during human meiosis. *Homo erectus* embryos don't know much about making stone tools. There is no 'hand-axeness' in hominid genes, in any but the most general of senses. The capacity for hand-axes is genetically reproduced, but this capacity can be put to so many diverse ends that the reappearance of hand-axes in the next generation could never be guaranteed by the genetic reproduction of hand-axe-making potential. There is always the chance that this capacity could be channelled into the manufacture of another tool, such as the side-scraper. While it is thus more difficult for scrapers to gain access to their host's offspring than it is for a thumb, they can do something which no *Homo erectus* trait could ever do. They can spread directly to their host's brothers and sisters, aunts and uncles, cousins and nieces, mothers and fathers-in-law, even to the strangers just across the gorge. In this way, pernicious artefacts, like pernicious parasites, have a special escape route which maladaptive traits do not.

Now let us imagine that our hypothetical *erectus* band attends a long and arduous 'central-place' gathering. We can then continue the thought experiment, by imagining which structures are most likely to be able to take advantage of several weeks of sustained interaction between large numbers of people. When the gathering has dispersed it is quite possible that side-scrapers have been a great success, and that every *erectus* body who is any *erectus* body appears to be using them. In fact, as long as at least one member in each band now knows how to make them, and thereby cater for the eager and fashion conscious market of *erectus* communities, it is quite possible that they will take over from hand-axes as the most common scraping tool. This is, of course, provided that its functional disadvantages are not too obvious, and that the penny doesn't drop in too many *erectus* minds. If its inefficacy is perceived, the scraper is effectively polluting its own psychological environment with the depressing *erectus* experiences it causes. Provided, however, that its rate of social transmission exceeds the spread of *erectus* disillusion, i.e. that the rate at which it finds new pastures exceeds the rate at which it destroys the old, it will successfully displace the hand-axe. Because it has the potential for this strategy, the scraper cannot be called a maladaptive trait. It is instead an adapted parasite. Like the scrapers, the pernicious fleas could well have been quite successful, each band now having its new population of resident parasites. Although each new host that the fleas have found will be recovering from the disease they carry, the negative affect of this could potentially be offset by the huge number of new hosts infected.

Thus both pernicious parasites, both fleas and scrapers, would probably do very well at a central-place gathering. But the distribution of immobile thumbs will always remain precisely where it was before the central-place gathering was held; along strict lines of *erectus* descent. Immobile thumbs will always be restricted to the family of the original immobile thumb individual, and the future of the thumbs will always be clouded with the difficulties which they convey to their bearers.

So the pernicious scraper, by virtue of cultural transmission, has the opportunity for a whole new strategy of adaptation which would not be possible if it were merely a maladaptive trait, like the thumb. As long as it can continue to sustain a reasonable rate of social transmission, it can continue to survive. For the immobile thumb, on the other hand, there is little hope.

Some general archaeological implications: memetic mutation and cultural heritage constraint

There is not enough space here to expand on any of the other elements of CVT, or to provide an in-depth Virus account of a particular archaeological or historical sequence. That will have to be left for a later study. But a few general statements about the empirical implications of CVT's account of cultural process can now be summarised. CVT implies a particular view of the archaeological record, and two points are prominent in this view. The first of these is the concept of heritage constraint, discussed in chapter 6 with respect to Cultural Selectionism as a whole. Here heritage constraint is discussed with respect to the developing notion of memetic mutation within Cultural Virus Theory, where all new ideas are derived from thematically related ideas elsewhere in the primary repertoire (see also the 'Swiss army knife' discussion in the section above).

Most of the above discussion focuses on one half of the cultural evolution story; selection, to the exclusion of the other basic neo-Darwinian process, mutation. 'Cultures' have been presented as ecological assemblages of viral neuronal structures, distributed asymmetrically throughout the minds of a human community. Selection favours those ideas which, through their symbolic connection to other ideas, and/or through their 'fit' to open-ended human dispositions, appeal to human minds in that community. Many ideas enhance their fitness and reproductive success through their extended phenotype of behaviour or artefacts which, through association with the original idea, add to its appeal.

Another element which is not be developed in this chapter is of course mutation or invention; those processes which produce the variation in populations for selection to then act upon. Selection cannot create variation, only delineate it; therefore it must be supplied with variation by mutation. What psychological processes produce mutations in culturally transmitted viral phenomena? As discussed in the penultimate section of the previous chapter, the complete answer to this question will eventually be found as archaeologists and anthropologists acquire a more and more detailed knowledge of human psychobiology. For the time being, the simple answer must go something like; the imperfect process of 'remembering' constantly causes viral neuronal patterns to be partially forgotten, accidentally extended, and mistakenly confused or recombined with other neuronal patterns. All new ideas, then, are derived from other ideas; sometimes from the reassociation of two or more well-understood other ideas, but they are probably more often derived from spontaneous reassociation within a miscellaneous 'scrap heap' of nonsense, fragments of old ideas, long since forgotten, lying around in our unconscious. Either way, new ideas do not spring spontaneously out of nothing.

So an important empirical implication for archaeologists to note about CVT is that ultimately nothing *determines* the structure of cultural phenomena except perhaps previous cultural phenomena. Since all mutations or inventions are derived from existing forms, all new forms share the same heritage or historical constraints of their parents. The primary constraint, then, in a Darwinian system is cultural heritage. No invention, however different it may appear to be, ever completely transcends the structural limitations imposed upon it by its history. There will always be particular discoveries which can only be 'accessed' via mutation from a particular cultural *status quo*; and conversely there will always be a range of structural forms which can never be 'accessed' via random mutation from that point. CVT's conception of archaeological variability is one of a ubiquitous pattern of indefinitely increasing local specificity, with periodic cultural 'whitewashing' occurring when a particularly successful structure spreads throughout a region and displaces all the rest. Generally, in a CVT system form reflects phylogeny; cultural history is the fundamental cause of the cultural present. If anything *does determine cultural phenomena, it is previous cultural phenomena; all other influences are selective.*

The second implication to note is that the environment to which populations of artefacts adapt is not the one to which hominid bones adapt. Artefacts, and their corresponding viral neuronal patterns, do not adapt to the large-scale environment of, say, the savannah, the steppe, or the metropolis. Their world exists inside human brains; their palpable existence as objects is largely irrelevant to their survival except, of course, to the extent that as objects they can re-enter the psychic world of the human mind via the peripheral nervous system. Their world is a place where human fantasy and desire, likes and dislikes, plans and suspicions, fears and hopes, hates and loves are all as influential and concrete as the droughts and carnivores which affect hominid survival in the world at large. The 'survival of the fittest' (or, as is more specifically neo-Darwinian in many cases, yet often forgotten: the 'survival of the altruist') battles in cultural phenomena take place not in the rainforest or savannah, but in a jungle of human sentiment. But as these forces only select from within the variation supplied by psychological mutations, they can only favour forms which the population is capable of producing in the first place. Selective pressure does not enable a population of concepts to transcend its own cultural heritage, no matter how desperate the bearers of those concepts may have become.

The viral domesticate: a brief reinterpretation of Foley's hominid/artefact correlation

As stated in chapter 6, the pervasive pattern of cultural heritage constraint is no new idea. As a result, the 'preliminary test' half of this study involves as much ostension (pointing in order to draw attention to a pattern which already exists) as it does research (the creation of new patterns). By this I mean that often the easiest way to illustrate the ubiquity of heritage constraint in cultural data is simply to 'point' to any and all of the data produced already by archaeological research. The pattern is implicit in practically any archaeological report in existence. There is no special methodology required to make the cultural heritage constraints of regional archaeological sequences apparent, and as a consequence the pattern appears throughout archaeology. The function of the analyses of chapter 6 was not to introduce the 'cultural heritage constraint' pattern for the first time, but to show how pervasively this pattern occurs on a global scale, and also to show its equally pervasive occurrence in a 'known' selective system governed by human genetic inheritance. Moreover, to say that anthropologists have known of the existence of cultural descent is not to say that it has been frequently used (Durham 1990: 190). Although some readers may ask whether genealogical heritage constraint could not be explained equally well by a non-selective theoretical framework, so far those who have made such suggestions have been unable to name a theory which predicts heritage constraint without evoking a selective metaphysic of some description.

But while archaeologists have always been aware of cultural heritage constraint at the empirical and methodological levels of the discipline, the pattern has not been interpreted as having any particular implications for the general evolutionary frameworks used at more general levels. On the other hand, biologically oriented anthropologists, and sociobiologists in particular, have made quite extensive use of the Darwinian patterns in artefacts and ethnography for heuristic demonstrations of the validity of their own approach. But the 'artefacts as viral phenomena' approach advocated here makes possible a vastly different interpretation of the very same patterns. The distinctive selective patterns to be found in artefacts, and their corresponding tendency to co-vary with similar selective patterns in human bones, cannot be evoked in support of Sociobiology. The bones of domesticates and commensal animals also co-vary with human bones; yet it would be preposterous to claim that the morphology of dogs and mice was determined by human genes (except in a Dawkins's 'extended phenotype' sense, which is presumably a relatively insignificant factor). Domesticates and commensals are better considered to be adjacent hereditary systems, with their own intrinsic selective logistics. While genes do not determine language, they may have an indirect influence on which language an individual is exposed to in early childhood, by virtue of the simple fact that language is normally learnt from parents (Cavalli-Sforza 1991: 77). Similarly, genetic make-up may also come to correlate with which artefacts an individual is exposed to, and which domesticates they come to be responsible for. This is a correlation of an altogether different kind, yet one which deceptively similar at first glance.

Cultural Selectionism is in a position to 'slay the dragon' and 'get the treasure' all at once; to win both fame and fortune in the same moment. It should now be possible to refute Sociobiology, alienating it from its 'riches' or amassed data of neo-Darwinian patterns, and appropriate that very same data in support of Cultural Selectionism. Rather than attempting to refute the empirical support for the perspective, the aim is to appropriate that empirical support for itself. Performing comprehensive tests of its own into the nature of cultural data may not be necessary; if Sociobiology has established beyond reasonable doubt that there are Darwinian signatures to be found in the archaeological record, Cultural Selectionism need only make a more robust claim for those same patterns to advance its cause. The critique of culturally oriented Sociobiology offered in light of basic selectionist principles in chapter 3 attempted to show that Sociobiology's conception of the nature of cultural process itself cannot be considered properly Darwinian. Logically, therefore, they cannot validly continue to claim 'explanatory rights' to the Darwinian patterns they have nonetheless proved to exist.

This ironic situation, where culturally oriented Sociobiology has refuted itself, and left Cultural Selectionism unrefuted, with the very patterns it intended to find, is well illustrated in Foley's synthetic study of hominid remains. The paper (Foley 1987b) focused on the tendency of artefacts and hominid remains to co-vary in the early archaeological record. Clearly, in order to co-vary with the Darwinian patterns in human remains, artefacts have to exhibit Darwinian patterns themselves. The assumption I would like to challenge here is that such patterns are imposed upon the archaeological record by the selective logistics involved in human genetic evolution. In other words, no notion of genetic determinism or even genetic constraint is required to make sense of these patterns. Cultural Virus Theory can make a direct claim to these patterns through its claim that artefact systems are in fact ordered by intrinsic Darwinian logistics of their own, which take place in fully developed human brains, and that they are not ordered by the other Darwinian processes which occur in hominid gene pools. Most importantly, a viral explanation of these patterns would not depend upon tenuous claims for a series of highly specific genetic constraints on hominid behaviour.

It is quite clear that Foley rejects any notion of cultural phenomena having genealogical independence, as a class of viral phenomena analogous to very simple organisms. In fact, he blames the 'artefacts as organisms' approach for bringing evolutionary theory a bad name. But as already discussed in the early part of chapter 7, there is very little to prevent archaeologists treating artefacts precisely in this way. The only mistake would be to treat artefacts as self-reproducing organisms, and this can be avoided by using the concept of a viral phenomenon, as this concept implies a dependency of the said phenomena on human action for their replicative success. Foley goes far beyond this criticism however. Any notion of artefact production systems which grants some independence to cultural process is seen to be guilty of separating culture from biology altogether (as distinct from merely separating culture from genetic inheritance). The possibility that culturally transmitted behaviour *is* properly distinguished from the biological process of genetic evolution, but only as another 'nested' subset of the general category 'biology' (i.e. as a special case encompassed by a larger category, like the category 'square' is encompassed by the category 'rectangle') is not given consideration. As far as being 'biological' is concerned, in this fallacious view, it would appear to be a case of 'genes or nothing'. Culture is not allowed to have a material and thoroughly biological reality all of its own, independently of the aspects of the organism which are organised around genetic reproduction. Thus Foley writes (1987b: 380):

> Perhaps the central problem in the unification of palaeoanthropology as a single discipline lies in the way "biology" and "culture" have been dichotomised. On the one hand the evolution of human anatomical form is seen as the product of natural selection, much as that of any other species: archaeology, however, dealing as it does with behaviour, has been considered to be beyond the scope of natural selection, and change has been accounted for through other, usually cultural, mechanisms.

But while post-Modernism (which I would assume to be Foley's most recent implicit target) may indeed claim some fundamental separation of culture from biology, the newly defined account of culture in terms of viral phenomena only claims separation of cultural process from genetic process. Separating culture from biology, thereby transforming it into some sort of 'supernatural phenomenon', becomes completely unnecessary. Cultural Virus Theory can thus provide a unique third alternative to conventional Darwinian Anthropology and post-Modernism; one that is simultaneously as Darwinian as the first and as purely cultural as the latter. Foley is absolutely correct about the existence of these patterns; but there is no need to appeal to the neo-Darwinian processes of hominid gene pools to explain them; a neo-Darwinian conception of the intrinsic logistics of cultural process will suffice.

In other words, Cultural Virus Theory offers a completely different explanation for the 'stone/bone' correlations of the archaeological record. Sociobiologists may predict a virtually complete correlation of the two, and then, when finding a somewhat imperfect yet positive correlation, consider their view to be verified. For Sociobiology, the temperamental nature of the stone/bone correlations is something to be explained away. For Cultural Selectionism, however, a temperamental correlation is predicted in the first place, as any total correlation is prevented by the cultural or genetic substitutions (Cavalli-Sforza 1991), which are themselves a function of the genealogical independence of genes and culture.

Armed with a cultural selectionist or viral perspective, archaeologists wishing to avoid any notions of genetic constraint on behaviour no longer need to fear the ubiquitous heritage constraint patterns found in archaeology, as such patterns can now be viewed as a result of the intrinsic neo-Darwinian logistics of human thought, and not as the result of neo-Darwinian process in human gene pools. At the risk of confounding the issue with another metaphor, Cultural Virus Theory could perhaps be considered the 'anti-Sociobiology vaccine' that modern anthropology – post-modernists included – have inadvertently been 'waiting for'. It is a safe 'dose of biology' which 'immunises' the cultural anthropologist against the more serious condition involving the discussion of cultural diversity in terms of genetic constraint, on the grounds of the stone/bone correlations which Foley has elucidated. Cultural Virus concepts allow Foley's correlations to be explained via an alternative scenario, as a result of the fact that cultural and genetic evolution are equally Darwinian, but not as a result of the causal influence of hominid genomes on cultural systems. The theory conveys to cultural anthropology recourse to a perfectly Darwinian biology all of its own: it grounds cultural studies in the extra-genetic biology of the human nervous system, while simultaneously securing the independence of cultural phenomena from human genetic process.

Concluding remarks

The Cultural Virus Theory is thus first and foremost a conception of socially transmittable psychological phenomena as human parasites, and not as human traits. Correspondingly, the individuals of cultural process are not individual animals, but 'seldom divided' socially reproduced viral phenomena, each consisting of one or more Memes (or ideas) and their thought, behavioural and artefact products. A 'population' in CVT is therefore a population of individual viral phenomena, not a population of enculturated animals. A viral population can therefore exist within a single brain, several brains, or any subgroup of the brains of a human population – it need not be sympatric with the genetic population. New viral phenomena emerge from spontaneous reassociation amongst fragments of old ideas. All inventions, then, are derivative, and never completely transcend the cultural heritage from which they come. And since the fitness or sustainable appeal of an idea depends upon the prevailing cultural milieu, further heritage constraint is imposed upon the viral population by culturally specific selection.

Although it may be difficult to accept that cultural phenomena are parasites, not traits, their undeniable genealogical independence can lead to no other conclusion. We should not retreat from a strange idea purely because of that strangeness. Nor should the difficulty (or even impossibility) of reconstructing the psychological environment which any given artefact technology inhabited in the past deter us from recognising that that environment *was* an essentially psychological environment. The specifics of grand-scale ecological environments of animals from the palaeontological record are almost as difficult to reconstruct, yet Palaeontology has nonetheless wholeheartedly accepted a range of neo-Darwinian principles, despite the fact that selective forces are so difficult to reconstruct. That the archaeological record may be a transcript of artefacts selected on the basis of partially unrecoverable 'psychocultural' selective criteria may seem unsatisfactory to some, yet, in this regard, archaeology would be, at the very worst, no worse off than Palaeontology.

Part three

Applications
of the Cultural Virus Theory

9
The eusocial pottery assemblage

Overview

CVT, like any selective theory, is all about explaining the results of archaeological excavations after they have been described and published as archaeological reports. Where cultural selectionist explanatory structures are more established in the discipline, they would be expected to have more influence on decisions about excavation and post-excavational analysis. Where they are not so established, an archaeologist is more likely to require an understanding of Cultural Selectionism only after questions of what, where, and when have been at least provisionally answered, and attention is being turned to how and why. CVT is designed to act as a provocative set of answers to the question of 'what?' in archaeology, one which is intended to suggest a framework to questions of 'how?' and 'why?'

Defining the artefact in eusocial terms

The archaeological implications of CVT may be understood in terms of a fundamental consideration of the question: 'What is an artefact?' and the related question: 'What is an artefact assemblage?' Below, this question is considered with reference to the generically more specific questions: 'What is a pot?' and: 'What is a pottery assemblage?' A range of archaeological and anthropological implications of CVT have been discussed elsewhere (Cullen 1993a; 1994), but the main theme outlined here is the idea that most artefacts, when conceived as viral phenomena, would seem to exhibit an extraordinary reproductive structure which is considered to be rare and challenging in modern evolutionary biology, and which is quite unknown in almost all of the world's DNA- or RNA-based species, including microbial viruses. If this remarkable phenomenon was ever discovered in the biology of viruses, it would probably make an incredible impact, not only on virology, but on evolutionary biology as a whole. Yet, disguised as this phenomenon is in the familiar patterns of everyday archaeological practice and domestic life, it escapes the notice of archaeologists. This is the phenomenon known as 'eusociality', of which the most well-known

212

examples are those of social insects such as bees and termites. where a range of sterile, functional 'worker' individuals are produced in order to serve the survival of a minority of reproductive individuals which act as 'breeders'. Such concepts have even been exploited by the cinema in box-office hits such as the *Alien* series, and *Arachnophobia*, whose fantasy life-forms have eusocial colony structures, although the average cinema-goer would not be familiar enough with modern evolutionary biology to notice. And if this particular CVT-generated hypothesis is correct, the archaeological record is littered with artefact assemblages, the hereditary structure of which is every bit as complicated as a beehive or termite nest. Cultural fields of inquiry could well be sitting inadvertently on a discovery of huge significance to the life sciences, a virtual kingdom of cultural phenomena where eusociality is as common as it is rare in DNA-based phenomena. This could also explain the long delay in the Darwinisation of cultural fields of inquiry, since the remarkable altruism of sterile bees, ants, and termites was also a major conundrum for neo-Darwinism, and one which took many years to solve.

First, it is pertinent to communicate some of the fascination that eusocial structures such as beehives hold for many biologists. Here is a short description (Dawkins 1989: 172):

> A social insect colony is a huge family. usually all descended from the same mother. The workers, who seldom or never reproduce themselves, are divided into a number of distinct castes. including small workers. large workers, soldiers and highly specialised castes like honey pots [individuals with swollen abdomens which act as food storage vessels]. Reproductive females are called queens. Reproductive males are sometimes called drones or kings. In the more advanced societies, the reproductives never work at anything except procreation, but at this one task they are extremely good. They rely on the workers for their food and protection, and the workers are also responsible for looking after the brood. In some ant and termite species the queen has swollen into a gigantic egg factory. . . .

For a long time this kind of social structure was thought to occur only in social insects, but recently it was discovered in a hairless and virtually blind rodent, the naked mole rat, which is found in arid areas of Kenya, Somalia, and Ethiopia (Dawkins 1989: 173, 313). This mammal has a main lineage of 'queen' and 'drone' reproductive forms, and a continuum of sterile forms which spend their lives eating, sleeping and carrying out the various activities required to maintain the colony.

Naked mole rats inspired so much interest among biologists that captive colonies made of many metres of labyrinthine transparent tubing were set up in at least two universities and at the London Zoo (Dawkins 1989: 314) within a relatively short time, attracting the attention of such notables as Jennifer Jarvis, Richard Alexander, and Paul Sherman, in addition to that of Dawkins, while Robert Brett undertook field observations of mole-rat colonies in Kenya. In some sense, these insect and mole-rat colonies are multi-organismic equivalents of single organisms, with each non-reproductive caste fulfilling a role similar to that of organs such as the liver or the skin; these structures cannot reproduce themselves, and can only work towards the general reproductive success of testes and ovaries, organs which specialise in producing the next generation. But in social insects and naked mole rats the principle of altruistic sterility has been shifted to the level of whole bodies, where the modular unit of adaptive differentiation and specialisation becomes the organism rather than the cell. The benefit for the social insect colony is that now there are a multiplicity of structures, a multiplicity of animated organs if you like, each capable of moving, living, and dying independently of each other, which can serve the reproductive interests of the main lineage in a very sophisticated manner. Individual cells are far more limited in their movements than are individual organisms.

I would like to submit the proposal that this kind of 'multi-object' reproductive strategy, where sterile non-reproductive structures are produced in order to facilitate the reproductive success of a central lineage of reproductive forms, is also present in cultural fields of inquiry. Indeed, I would like to go further than this, and tentatively submit the possibility that such complicated reproductive structures are not only present in cultural phenomena, but are in fact the *norm*. For instance, imagine the various artefacts present in the modern home environment, such as computers, furniture, crockery, cutlery, books, stereos, and so on. How many of such objects are actually produced in the home? And how many of such objects will ever be *reproduced* where they are found? Human individuals surround themselves with a plethora of sterile objects which can neither reproduce themselves, nor will they *be reproduced* by their owners. Surely the key to the explanation of such phenomena lies in the way they divert resources back to the industries which reproduce them. Like worker bees, their role is to obtain energy from their environments, through the symbolic resonance they excite in the minds of the people who bought them and might buy again. or in the minds of visitors to the household. This symbolic resonance is not so much divided into distinct categories of functional and aesthetic, but is rather a cocktail of perceived beauty, perceived functional efficacy, and any number of additional symbolic dimensions. The stronger the psychological profile a worker artefact excites, the greater the desire to buy or trade for such phenomena, and the more energy is diverted back into the industry. This energy is then used both to replicate the manufacturing industry and to produce more non-reproductive worker objects to go out and forage in new human communities.

Relationship of the pot and the potter

There is only enough space to consider the form that this kind of replicative strategy might take in one kind of artefact in even a cursory manner, and ceramic artefacts have been chosen. First, let us imagine what the hereditary material of pottery assemblages is made of. This material consists of the knowledge of everything to do with making ceramic artefacts: knowledge of where to look for raw materials, of extraction, preparation, and mixing of such materials, and of the manufacture of the pots themselves, of hand techniques such as coiling and the manufacture and use of pottery wheels and kilns, and lastly of the drying, firing, and marketing of the finished pots. This is the hereditary material of the pottery assemblage, and it is housed in the minds of one or more potters, just as the genome of a beehive or mole-rat colony is housed in the bodies of reproductives like queens and drones. Except, of course, for the fact that the body that the pottery hereditary material inhabits is not a body of its own making, nor wholly of its own using. In this sense it is like a hive which is built into a living structure, such as a tree in a rain forest, which is inhabited and used by many other phenomena all seeking their own reproductive success, not least the reproductive organs of the tree.

All of the behaviour patterns and manufacturing techniques performed by the potters, along with the pots themselves, constitute the phenotype of the above-mentioned hereditary material, as the second and third tiers of the pottery industry. Together they constitute the body of the viral phenomenon we call a pottery assemblage; which is best envisaged as a whole colony of viral phenomena, a multi-object assemblage in which different kinds of structure specialise at different tasks, many of which are not directly concerned with reproduction. As far as the potter is concerned, the pottery-making knowledge is gradually acquired over a period of apprenticeship. In some sense, from time to time in his or her life, the potter may be thought of in sociobiological terms, as an individual attempting to accumulate and control the flow of resources in his or her community, in such a way as to provide for a family of genetic relatives, despite increasing interference from a personal assemblage of acquired ideas.

As already discussed in more general terms, the relationship between potter and pot may be viewed as ecologically equivalent to the relationship between shepherd and sheep. We have a potentially symbiotic relationship, which is maintained through the discharge of various forms of human agency and initiative. Yet once the pottery knowledge has been acquired it can now influence the thought processes to various degrees, depending on how important being a 'potter' becomes to the identity of a pot-maker. This is of course thematically similar to the degree to which the role of being a shepherd colonises the consciousness (and unconsciousness) of someone who becomes involved with herding sheep. While parasitic relationships may emerge, where potters become completely celibate and spend their entire lives making pots and contributing nothing to their family, more often the Darwinian stakes involve *relative* amounts of benefit in an ongoing symbiotic relationship. It is not a question of the pottery industry getting all of the potter's energy for nothing, but of getting *more* benefit than the potter's family, in a situation where both will usually benefit to some degree.

For example, we have the structures which inhabit the minds of the potters, the manufacturing knowledge itself. These are the 'queen' structures, as it were, and consist of a series of neuronal groups distributed throughout the potter's brain, which display a particular pattern of connectivity which allowed them to represent pottery-making techniques better than any others, according to the mechanisms of neuronal group selection developed by Edelman (1989; 1992). While the potter was an apprentice, these particular patterns of neuronal connectivity were 'selected' and amplified during the process of instruction of the apprentice by another tradesman. The ultimate 'goal' of this assemblage of pottery-making knowledge (although, of course, it has no intrinsic consciousness) is to replicate itself, and to draw new apprentices into the pottery trade.

The role of the pots is then ecologically analogous to that of worker bees, termites, or naked mole rats. Obviously, pots cannot physically collect energy and bring it back to the potter's workshop. Their service to the pottery industry is far more subtle than that, and does not involve active behaviour but rather an emerging involvement in the activities of the various human agencies and intentions which surround them, and which they sometimes embody. Some worker pots will be put to use in the workshop, facilitating the daily practice of the production of more worker pots, or even acting as archetypes for imitation by apprentices. These are equivalent to the nurses in a beehive. Other pots will be manufactured for local markets, diverting local products and currencies back to the potter's workshop. Their success in this task will depend on how well they are *perceived* to hold food or drink, act as storage or vessels, how good they look, what social information they can convey and so on; that is, they are successful to the extent that they fit the culturally and individually specific notions of efficacy and beauty which exist in the minds of the people of the local community. Such pots fulfil an equivalent role to foraging workers in the hive, except that they make only one journey, and all movements of resources occur as a result of human agency. And finally, in a community which is visited by traders, a remarkable dimension of the pottery phenotype may emerge. Ceramic artefacts which are traded can extend the catchment area of the pottery assemblage for many thousands of miles, as in the case of the trading of fine porcelain. Such large-scale movements can only serve the survival of the pottery trade if a significant percentage of the traded price eventually makes it back to the original workshop, either in the form of disposable goods or currency which can be channelled into the workshop, or in the form of eager foreign apprentices wanting to learn to make fine porcelain themselves.

While there is no space to expand on this purely hypothetical model of pottery assemblages in the archaeological record, it is hoped that the brief sketch has helped the reader to envisage one of the possible implications of CVT. An actual case-study would be impossible in a paper of this size, particularly in the case of a new theoretical framework, which has to be at least summarised before any of the archaeological implications can be explored.

Conclusion

Attention in the last section of the chapter has been focused on just one of the basic implications of CVT. The aspect of CVT outlined here has been the remarkable potential of artefacts to form extremely complicated eusocial object assemblages which are selected in history according to their ability to arouse the attention of people in such a way that a central core of technological knowledge is reproduced. Presumably, such artefact eusociality reaches its crescendo in the form of widely traded items, but the principle could be applied just as easily to less organised manufacturing industries.

How does the eusocial hereditary structure of pottery assemblages fit in with the general CVT notion that cultural reproduced phenomena are ecologically equivalent to domesticates? Does this mean that artefacts are only analogous to domesticated eusocial insects. such as bees? The answer is most definitely no. Once the vision of a eusocial pottery or stone-artefact assemblage is firmly grasped, it quickly becomes apparent that not only are we surrounded by other eusocial artefact assemblages, such as computers, sheets of paper. household crockery and cutlery, stoves, automobiles, garden tools, and packaged foods, but almost as many eusocial animal and plant structures too. These would include cut flowers, de-sexed family pets, meat-producing animal populations which supply human communities with non-reproductive individuals such as suckling pigs and fat lambs, castrated draught animals such as oxen, sterile hybrid varieties of animals and plants; and the list could be extended indefinitely. Each one of these organisms has little chance of reproducing themselves, and must presumably function as sterile workers for other copies of their genes. Thus, it can be seen that by exploring only one angle of CVT, we are offered not only a new vision of the nature of the archaeological record, but new visions of the nature of genetic process as well. Human agents seem to be able to impose an artificial eusocial structure on domesticated populations such that the vast majority of a particular variety of animal or plant are sacrificed in various ways which nonetheless allow the dramatic reproductive success of a selected few.

If even a few of the above cases of eusocial artefact assemblages are correct, archaeology has the potential to turn the tables on modern evolutionary biology for the first time, and actually submit extraordinary cases of neo-Darwinian dynamics which biologists have never encountered. It is important to note that this is not to say that culture is any less *neo-Darwinian* in its logistics, as some have remarked; the uniqueness of cultural phenomena does not consist of Lamarckian processes. It is rather that we find unique but perfectly neo-Darwinian inheritance structures in artefacts, a plethora of eusocial artefact assemblages which could well be responsible for much of the distinctive ontology of the archaeological record.

10
Megalithic predator, Neolithic prey: symbiosis, parasitism and monumentality in prehistoric north-west Europe

Overview
Megaliths were not only tools fashioned to aid human adaptation or embody active social strategies; they were also the scattered organs of a culturally reproduced organism which unconsciously sought its own reproductive success. Wholly and intimately dependent upon networks of human agency, megalithic religions evolved into a range of symbiotic and predatory forms, adapting to the rich and unique biocultural ecosystems of Neolithic north-west Europe.

Megalithic tools
European megaliths are often viewed as lifeless, passive objects, as tools which embodied the objectives of the people who built and used them. Megalithic masonry benefited either the whole community, or a smaller group of people therein, often at the expense of other groups. One common theme involves the role of megaliths as social centres (Case 1969; Fleming 1972; 1973; Jarman *et al.* 1982; Sherratt 1984). Pursuing this theme, Renfrew (1973a; 1973b; 1979; 1983) proposed that monuments functioned as the territorial markers of segmentary societies, jointly benefiting the whole community. Chapman (1981) has discussed related ideas, and argued that funerary structures containing ancestral remains can substantiate claims of inherited rights over land when it becomes a scarce resource, while Boujot & Cassen (1993: 487) have emphasised the role that megaliths played in social reproduction. Whittle (1988: 180–83) has also pursued the group-benefit theme, writing of the intimidating effect of monuments on other groups, along with their power to assert the identity of a group during periods of inter-group competition, and to guard the secrecy and privacy of the rituals performed within.

219

In addition to the above scenarios, European megaliths have been explained as instruments of conversion to an agricultural way of life (Sherratt 1990; 1992), thereby indirectly benefiting those who were best positioned to take advantage of the switch to food production. Doubtful of the role of any monument as an aid to a precise astronomy, Chippindale (1994: 230) nonetheless accepts that there is evidence in monuments for solar alignment, and does not completely dismiss the role that megalithic structures could have played in Neolithic cosmology. This possibility suggests yet another beneficial function – as a kind of seasonal clock which allowed precise synchronisation of group activities such as ritual gatherings and harvests.

Since the early 1980s, some archaeologists have increasingly highlighted the active role that European megaliths and other items of material culture have played in prehistoric societies (Hodder 1982b; 1986; Shanks 1992; Thomas 1994; Tilley 1990; 1991). Approaches pursuing this theme have discussed how megaliths were involved in active social strategies in the existing historical context of late Mesolithic and early Neolithic Europe (Hodder 1984), and how they help to reproduce or change societies, rather than simply reflecting them. Monuments enabled powerful individuals or groups to justify and maintain social inequality and to legitimate ideology (Shanks & Tilley 1982; Shennan 1982; Tilley 1984), sometimes achieving this end via the orchestration of the movements of people in or near the monument, or by concealing art, artefacts and the rituals associated with them inside the tomb (Thomas 1990; 1991a; Tilley & Thomas 1994). Active restructuring of social realities is also embodied in the placement of artefacts within monuments, such as in the spatial ordering of ceramic designs (Shanks & Tilley 1987: 155–71). Relating social strategy to changes in burial practices during the British Neolithic and Bronze Age, Barrett (1990) suggests that the sequence of monuments and increasingly elaborate funeral practices reflect a search for more effective media for competitive displays of rank. More recently, Hodder (1994) has focused on the way in which tombs help people deal with emotions such as grief, loss and anger, a concern shared by others (Scarre 1998).

Approaches which emphasise the principle of active material culture might seem to be moving away from conceptions of the lifeless, passive megalith, and to some extent this may be the case. However, such studies do not go so far as to grant megalithic masonry a living organism-hood, nor do they abandon the principle of human benefit. Active megalith scenarios are more concerned with benefit at another level, that of particular interest groups *within* communities. As in the megalithic religions portrayed by

Childe (1957) within a Marxist framework, such approaches view megaliths as symbolic tools which one social group can use to seek power, not as something which is able to exploit both the powerful and the disempowered alike. Masonry is more often seen as active in terms of what people can do *with it*, than in terms of what it can *get* people to do *for it*.

Similar themes also emerge in explanations for megaliths elsewhere in the world, despite the fact that the category 'megalith' – rather like the category 'megafauna' in Palaeolithic studies – embraces a bewildering diversity of phenomena with very little in common other than size (Hodder 1994). Explanations of Polynesian monuments, for example, often focus on the theme of benefits to chiefly personalities (Bahn & Flenley 1992; Kirch 1990; Kolb 1994; Trigger 1990). Human-benefit explanations can be considered instances of a general attitude which places artefacts and technology either in the role of extrasomatic adaptations or in the realm of the inorganic. Approaches which attribute organism-like qualities to cultural phenomena have even attracted scorn from some scholars (Brew 1946; Dunnell 1985; Foley 1987a; Leonard & Jones 1987; Levi-Strauss 1963: 4). Yet megalithic religions display a host of qualities which suggest that they have much in common with the organic world.

Megalithic anatomy

If organised megalithic masonry is to be understood as an organism a precise definition of a megalithic body and its constituent structures is needed. However, while echoes can be found in some genetically reproduced species on the planet, megalithic anatomy, like that of other cultural reproduced phenomena, is quite different to familiar organismic forms. Yet one quality characterises all organisms, and hints at a definition: genealogical dependence, or reproductive association. Genetic information for the various organs of an organism is reproduced as a unit and passed on to the same body, in sexually reproducing species as sperm and eggs. Even though a single egg cell, like any gamete, contains only half the full genetic complement of a normal individual, each gamete contains enough information to produce a complete organism by itself, as shown by the capacity for unfertilised eggs to develop via parthenogenesis, as in asexual lizards (Crews 1994) and in the haploid drones of bees (Brian 1983: 220). Thus, although sex splits the organism, it is only split in two; it does not explode the internal logic which systematically co-ordinates the many different organs to produce a viable whole. Structures within the body that are *not* passed on in sperm or egg cells are likely to be parasitic guests

(Dawkins 1982; 1989: 245) and are therefore not part of the host organism. Conversely, parasites which *do* manage to be passed on in the sperm or eggs of their hosts *can* thereafter be considered as part of the host organism; they become genuine organs or organelles of their host, a theme developed by Margulis (1981) in her study of the role of bacterial symbiosis in the evolution of cells.

An organism can therefore be defined as a set of structures which are *reproduced together*, passed on to the same individuals, and which, as a consequence, share a *common genealogy*. Such structures share a common future and each is therefore obliged to propagate the other structures if it is to propagate itself – they all share the same 'vehicle' into the next generation. Following this generic definition, a megalithic organism would consist of all the knowledge required to make a repertoire of monuments, together with any other aspect of Neolithic identity that was culturally reproduced along with it, and the rituals and material products enabled by such knowledge. In reality this may or may not have included the religious and ritual knowledge associated with the use of Neolithic monuments. Individuals may have specialised in one or the other, or both. As there is insufficient space to give full attention to all possibilities, however, it will be assumed that the two bodies of knowledge were taught together, and were therefore part of the same culturally reproduced organism. 'Masonry', in this sense, includes the ritual practices associated with the use of the monuments.

Thus defined, the complicated anatomy of megalithic masonry could be schematically represented. Spanning the brains and central nervous systems of a number of fully initiated individuals (making four inner circles) would be a core of shared primary hereditary material or culturally reproduced knowledge (where those inner circles intersected), stored in the form of unique neuronal structures which can only be inculcated in a novice's brain through contact with full initiates. Once imparted through the teaching/learning process, the new information actually exists in the new initiate's brain as physical structures (Cullen 1993a). The materiality of learned information is supported by a wide range of recent brain studies (Crick 1994; Dawkins 1993b; Dennett 1993; Delius 1989; 1991; Edelman 1989; 1992; Horgan 1994; Sacks 1993). The size of the inner group of initiates or 'adepts' could have varied greatly in size, from a single individual to all individuals in a community above a certain age or rite of passage. Such unique neuronal structures convey to their bearers knowledge of the nature and extent of organised masonry, techniques of transport, erection, carving, spatial organisation, and religious ideology, associated rituals, and artistic iconography – the kinds of actions corresponding to and enabled by such knowledge are listed after the next paragraph.

Other versions of such megalithic hereditary material or knowledge are located in the brains of partially initiated novices (they would be four outer circles in a diagram of megalithic anatomy), fragments of knowledge which are either incomplete or imperfectly understood (they would be shaded sections of those outer circles). Masonry has a limited claim on the time, labour and identity of each novice just as it does on each adept. As in the case of the adept group, the number of novices could vary all the way from one individual, to all the children, adolescents and un- or partially initiated adults of a Neolithic community. A novice's brain, by definition, contains less of the masonic religion than that of an adept. The masonic religion therefore makes up less of the novice's identity. However, novices may be disempowered and obliged to obey adepts in some circumstances, particularly if they want to become adepts themselves. In this way, masonry does have a limited hold over the rest of the novice's body. That megalithic knowledge was unevenly distributed finds support in other recent studies which discuss the exclusiveness of ritual knowledge (Lewis-Williams & Dowson 1993; Stoddart *et al.* 1993; Tilley 1990; 1991).

The second level of masonic anatomy consists of the rituals and actions associated with the building and use of monuments . Just as the first level of anatomy is only a small part of the mind of any one person, so the second level is only a fraction of the total active potential of each person . Such actions play the same role for masonry that metabolism plays for DNA-based organisms – they are the practices by means of which human energy is directed into the masonic organisation, and converted into monuments, rituals, and new masonic adepts.

Techniques of transport of large blocks of stone, including the use of large wooden levers (Thom 1967), and the use of ropes for rocking, rolling and swivelling (Bahn & Flenley 1992), would belong to this category, although the stones of European megaliths may only have been moved 1–2 km (Thorpe & Williams-Thorpe 1991). Other building techniques, such as those involved in the raising of capstones (Atkinson 1956; Renfrew 1973a; Chippindale 1994: 269), and in the patterned subdivision of space (Chippindale 1992), also belong here. Since the religion associated with megalithic monuments is also part of the organism as defined above, rituals in and around the monument are also included (Tilley & Thomas 1994), along with less conspicuous aspects of monument construction such as the actions/rituals which lead to the construction of deliberate pit deposits (Thomas 1991a) and art (Lewis-Williams & Dowson 1993; Tilley & Thomas

1994). Meetings arranged to organise future constructions or rituals would be another crucial aspect. An additional element of the action-based part of masonic anatomy would include the labour of people who were neither adepts nor novices of the masonic organisation, whenever this labour was successfully directed into megalith-making, although this has not been schematically represented in the diagram.

Artefacts constitute the third level of masonic anatomy: the megalithic monuments themselves. While the third level consists of the entire material-culture assemblage produced by the culturally reproduced knowledge of the first level, this is only achieved through a process of complicated interaction with many other bodily structures. Every physical transformation which is imparted to megalithic structures by the practices associated with their use is also part of megalith anatomy. The mounds and ditches which surround or overlie the monuments, the dry-stone walling, the ritual assemblages deposited in the ditch infills, and the art on the interior surfaces of the tomb are all part of the third level. Pots and polished stone axes are clearly products of other technological systems, and therefore belong to other culturally reproduced organisms in the logic of this paper.

The megalithic organism is obviously very different to any known genetically reproduced organism. For one thing, its body or vehicle is distributed throughout a multitude of other bodies; it cannot be located within the perimeters of any one individual or object. Like other organisms, many of its constituent structures are dead (like hooves and claws in mammals, megalithic tombs and other monuments in the case of organised masonry). Yet, like hooves and claws, even megaliths are organic in the sense that they can only be produced by a living technological system, and their long-term survival ultimately depends upon the reproductive success of that system. Another dramatic difference lies in the fact that megalithic masonry stores its hereditary material in the brains of other organisms, in this case *Homo sapiens*.

Coupled with dramatic differences such as these (and many others), are striking similarities, echoes of more familiar organismic forms. In so far as the morphology of an artefact production system is embodied in a range of objects or bodies, and not just one, they evolve like the genetic kin-based societies of eusocial insects such as ants, bees and termites, where many non-reproductive bodies work to promote the reproductive success of a primary lineage of reproductive forms such as queens and drones (Cullen 1990). In so far as they are inanimate and dependent upon external agencies to get things done, artefact assemblages and other cultural phenomena resemble viruses in many respects, as elaborated upon elsewhere. And like any organisms which are dependent upon others, viral entities can opt for a parasitic or symbiotic relationships with other organisms (Cullen 1994), although symbiotic viruses are all but impossible to trace, given their tendency to vanish without a trace into the DNA of their hosts (Mitchison 1993).

Megalithic heredity

Early explanations for the origins of European megaliths focused on the process of diffusion, and the spread of new religious ideas associated with their use (Childe 1957; Piggott 1965), such as the funerary goddess cult (Fleming 1969). While diffusionist scenarios have attracted adverse comment (Renfrew 1973a; Chapman 1981), critics have been careful to qualify their remarks, pointing out that 'all this is not to say that diffusion – the transmission of innovation from one group to another – does not take place' (Renfrew 1973a: 122), and that 'innovations are frequently made in one place and adopted in neighbouring areas' (Renfrew & Bahn 1991: 409). Such comments reveal that processual critiques of traditional megalith explanations were directed more at the migrationist variety of Diffusionism (Renfrew & Bahn 1991: 407–10), where whole 'cultures' or 'peoples' were often seen as moving *en masse*. The alternative explanations advanced by processualists subsequently emphasised local ahistorical factors. However, it would now appear that there is a strong element of historical descent in Neolithic burial practices, in terms of varying amounts of both diffusion (history from without) *and* local heritage (history from within), as discussed in a variety of works (Boujot & Cassen 1993; Hodder 1984; 1990; 1998; Scarre 1998; Sherratt 1984; 1990). Such renewed interest in historical explanation has even led some archaeologists explicitly to recommend a 'genealogical' approach to cultural phenomena (Thomas 1991a: 5, 57, 85, 178; 1991b: 15; Tilley 1990: 305–7), after Foucault and Nietzsche.

Writing about diffusion on a more general level, archaeologists and anthropologists have discussed the significance of information exchange between different cultures from time to time (e.g. Clarke 1978: 164; Kroeber 1952). Diffusion 'is what distinguishes human culture and differentiates human existence from that of all other animals' (Renfrew 1973a: 122). Such discussions contrast the reticulate or network pattern of cultural descent with the inviolable phylogenetic tree which they attribute to organic evolution. Yet this contrast is based on a conception of genetic evolution which has since been radically amended. We now know that genes can be conferred laterally between unrelated lineages by means of viruses (Deleuze

& Guattari 1987 [1992]: 10; Gould 1991: 38; Jacob 1974). According to some biologists 'many mammal species . . . carry a significant complement of . . . benign and even useful viral genes' (Mitchison 1993: 105), while Dawkins has pronounced 'we might just as well regard ourselves as colonies of viruses' (1989: 182).

Some organisms have taken genetic exchange of Virus-like entities to extremes, leading one microbiologist to proclaim the entire bacterial kingdom as 'the global organism' (Sonea 1988). Bacteria regularly emit segments of DNA in the form of single virions, and these entities are able to enter other bacterial cells which may have no connection with the parent bacterium in time or space. A bacterial cell may even rupture and die under difficult circumstances, releasing a significant proportion of its DNA as virions (Sonea 1988), which then go on to enter new bacterial cells. The model allows us to envisage a new kind of 'organism', one which is capable of collapsing into an assemblage of viral entities under certain circumstances. Bacteria have a system of heredity which periodically explodes, scattering genetic debris into other lineages. Moreover, this kind of genetic recombination is obviously much less structured than sexual recombination in complex organisms.

Because of processes like this, viral entities can sometimes come together and interact to produce a larger whole. Indeed, the latter can be composed of the former, and the megalithic organism as defined in this paper would be no exception. Megalithic masonry has a loose organismhood. Like some bacterial organisms, it is composed a quasi-autonomous parts which may have spent some of their evolutionary history in different contexts. The megalithic religion is a loose confederation of parts which retain the potential for genealogical independence, even during periods in which they are being reproduced together. As long as they are reproduced together, and constitute part of the same organisation, the different parts will tend to evolve towards a mutualistic or symbiotic set of internal relationships. As an integrated entity of this kind, the megalithic organisation may then evolve towards an equally symbiotic relationship with the rest of Neolithic society, or a parasitic relationship, depending on various circumstances discussed in later sections. The heredity of the megalithic organism therefore involves loosely integrated bits and pieces – an uneasy confederation of potentially autonomous viral phenomena. It becomes possible to see the various megalithic traditions of western Europe as the hybrid descendants of a number of cultural ancestors, by means of a pattern of heredity that is far more fluid than sexual reproduction and recombination in animals and plants.

Megalithic genealogy

One primary cultural ancestor of Atlantic Neolithic masonry appears to be the *Linearbandkeramik* (LBK) and *Stichbandkeramik* (SBK) long houses of central Europe and the associated domestic ideology of the *domus*, a link which has been explored by Ashbee (1982), Whittle (1988); Hodder (1984; 1990), Sherratt (1984; 1990) and others. There are a number of morphological similarities between houses and tombs, which, when taken together, make 'the "null hypothesis" of no diffusion . . . appear unreasonable' (Hodder 1992b: 51). Hodder has summarised them as follows (1992b: 59):

1. Construction of houses and earthen long barrows includes use of continuous bedding trenches, lines of simple posts and some combination of the two techniques.
2. Trapezoidal and rectangular shapes with similar length/maximum breadth ratios for trapezoidal forms.
3. The entrance of the trapezoidal mounds and houses are at the broader end.
4. The entrances of the rectangular and trapezoidal houses and barrows frequently face towards the south-east.
5. The entrances are elaborated, specifically with façades, antechambers, 'horns', or activity concentrations.
6. There is a tripartite division of the long house or mound, although frequently only one division is found one-third of the way along the length from the entrance.
7. Tombs and houses frequently have internal decoration.
8. Ditches flank the long sides of houses and barrows.

Another more implicit element can be added to this list of similarities, and that is tomb-hood itself: like tombs, houses or near-by pits were occasionally used for burials, indicating that the conceptual association between house and death was not inconceivable. For example, scattered burials sometimes occur in central Europe in graves or rubbish pits near houses (Whittle 1985: 89), while three LBK houses are associated with child burials (Hodder 1990: 107).

Sherratt (1990; 1997) sees this line of descent from central European long houses as occurring in two stages. In the first stage, primarily in central Europe and in loess regions, whole communities spread along with the food production economy, remaining relatively intact culturally. In the second stage, along the Atlantic margins of western Europe, this cultural order broke down. An interesting genealogical implication of the second stage is the increased likelihood of rupture of old genealogical associations and the fusion of hitherto unrelated architectural and religious traditions. The two genealogical elements discussed so far, long-mound structure and central European *domus* ideology, could now be combined with elements of western Mesolithic traditions. Where fusion of this kind occurred, we would expect to find monumental forms which combined characteristics of long mounds with earlier Mesolithic burial practices or religious ideology. One possible element of this kind would be the persistence of house shapes other than the *Bandkeramik* long house in Breton passage-graves, a hypothetical 'round-house' chamber under a long mound (Scarre 1998). However, as Scarre has noted, there is no strong evidence that there was a Breton round-house tradition which could have given rise to the round chambers of passage-graves.

A more promising candidate for a burial practice which could have an Atlantic Mesolithic origin is that of collective burial, an element which seems to be all but absent from the *Bandkeramik* tradition. Collective burial is present in the local Breton Mesolithic on the offshore islands of Teviec and Hoedic, and subsequently in the early Breton Neolithic (Scarre 1998), suggesting continuity in the face of in-coming traditions which emphasised single inhumations. Scarre points out that local continuity is further supported by the fact that the earliest passage-graves at Bougon are firmly dated to 3800 BC, while the earliest classic long mounds date only to 3200 BC. Here Scarre develops arguments explored by Case (1969), Hodder (1984; 1990), and Tilley & Thomas (1994), who also recognise a possibly endemic tradition in collective burial in Brittany. A similar Atlantic continuity has been suggested for the religious ideology associated with such burial practices, which may stretch back into Palaeolithic cave traditions (Hodder 1992b: 75; Lewis-Williams & Dowson 1993: 63), given the fact that Palaeolithic cave art is concentrated in western Europe. Yet elements such as these were almost certainly fusing with, rather than displacing, the religious ideology of the in-coming *domus* tradition. In the words of Boujot & Cassen (1993: 485), 'megalithism in western France cannot . . . be viewed only as the local product of the inventive genius of local peoples, in contrast with the farming settlers of the Paris Basin further east'.

While the megalithic tombs of the Breton tradition are perhaps the most dramatic example of the coming-together of multiple lines of cultural descent, mixing is likely to have occurred in many parts of Atlantic Europe. Renfrew (1973a: 142), for example, has argued for four independent origins for the practice of collective burial – Denmark, south Britain, Brittany and Iberia – while not excluding outside influences altogether. As Whittle has remarked (1988: 165): 'there is no good reason to abandon the long-considered long-house connection altogether, but all the evidence for variation in regional sequences and chronological development suggests that it can only be considered one element in a very complex picture'.

So it would seem that at least four general traditions are involved in the cultural ancestry of the megalithic religions of the Neolithic – both western European and central European architectural structures, and both western and central European religious ideology. It is also likely that the ideas within these four traditions were juggled and rearranged on a smaller scale. Presumably there were many cutting and pasting episodes, where bits and pieces of masonry and religious practices sometimes even 'leap-frogged' over others in time and space, for example when menhirs were incorporated into the later religious discourse of tombs in western France (Thomas & Tilley 1994), possibly without direct contact with the original discourse. Additional processes such as 'stimulus diffusion' (Kroeber 1952; Renfrew 1973a: 122), where megalithic structures or rituals are imitated in the absence of direct cultural contact, could well have added further diversity to an already complicated genealogical pattern. Finally, it should not be forgotten that some early Neolithic burials (Bradley 1984) involved no monument whatsoever, megalithic or otherwise, suggesting occasional Mesolithic continuity in non-monumentality itself, in addition to that of collective burial.

Megalithic mutation and diversity

Genealogical recombination cannot, by definition, give rise to qualitatively new components; cognitive invention and innovation play this role for culture. Modelling megalithic religions as organisms would imply that technological and religious innovation is ultimately the outcome of random mutation in megalithic hereditary material. Yet we are accustomed to thinking of human invention as rational. Can a random mutation model of technological innovation account for megalithic diversity? Can it be reconciled with notions of rational human invention?

Random mutation produces a number of easily identifiable effects. The first of these is diversity itself – the absence of mutation would produce a population of perfect duplicates. A second effect is phylogenetic constraint (Foley 1985: 225; Dawkins 1982) – random mutation is loaded with history. Mutations are derived from previous forms, and are therefore not completely random in the sense of equally likely in all directions (Gould 1980; Rindos 1985: 70). Mass extinctions of whole classes of animals can, therefore, permanently influence future anatomical diversity by exerting phylogenetic constraint on the range of future mutations (Gould 1994). The third effect is that, being random, mutations tend to produce different results each time, leading different populations in different directions, even in closely related populations under similar selective constraints. Random mutation produces unique trajectories, and we would expect the evolution of life on earth to produce a different result if it were run all over again (Gould 1994). The last two effects differentiate random mutation from rational or directed mutations, which would be identical under different circumstances, regardless of history or isolation. Fourthly, once coupled with selection, random mutation is quite capable of producing very effective and apparently 'rational' forms, as shown by, for example, the range of similar yet phylogenetically distinctive adaptations to flight found in birds, bats and reptilian pterodactyls.

Each of these four qualities appears to be present in the megalithic structures of western Europe. Firstly, the diversity of European megaliths is well documented, and not only at the level of genealogy explored in the last section. Sherratt (1994: 167) emphasises regional differentiation in monument forms, while Whittle has emphasised that the European transition to farming is 'complicated, and varies from area to area' (Whittle 1994: 136), remarking that for tombs 'the variety and individuality is endless' (Whittle 1988: 181). Boujot & Cassen (1993: 477) write of the 'astonishing architectural diversity' of megalithic tombs in one area alone, in the Gulf of Morbihan in western France. Such specific observations of diversity at the level of megalithic morphology can be backed up by general models of the nature of culture. Emerging studies of the psychobiology of learning in the brain show that diversity is far more than merely possible in the learning process; it is actually unavoidable. Psychobiologists such as Edelman (1989; 1992) have shown that no two neural networks or neurons are the same, even when comparing individual nerve cells in the relatively simple nervous systems of insects (Edelman 1989: 35). One consequence of this is that cultural reproduction must, at best, be an approximation; perfect copying is impossible. The second feature of random mutation listed above is underlying continuity; mutation is subject to phylogenetic constraint. Clearly, there is some fidelity in cultural reproduction, despite the great potential for confusion, and Delius has called this 'informational' equivalence (1989: 44; 1991: 82). Like copies, mutants too are derived from parent forms, and this produces an underlying continuity in the range of mutant morphology. If human invention produces mutant derivatives, then continuity ought to be implicit in any cultural tradition. Some of the most dramatic examples of continuity can be found in Lower and Middle Palaeolithic lithic assemblages, such as the Mousterian assemblages of western Europe. Such assemblages contain the same tool types for thousands of years (Jelinek 1994: 72), changing only in relative frequencies of types and in the presence or absence of biface production.

European megaliths show evidence of a similar cultural tradition. Despite their diversity, Sherratt (1994: 167) has noted that there are broad similarities in Atlantic megaliths. For example, the masonry of both houses and tombs embraces the three raw materials of wood, earth and stone. There is no dramatic discontinuity in raw materials, no sudden jump to exclusively megalithic tombs. The first long barrows of south Britain contained wooden burial chambers (Case 1969), yet were replaced by barrows of similar plan but with stone chambers such as West Kennet (Renfrew 1973a: 141). Other long barrows had wooden structures which were as massive as many megalithic chambers, as in the 'megaxylic' structures at Haddenham (Hodder 1990; Thomas 1991a), thereby combining the megalithic 'style' with the raw material of wood. Some structures were even composed of both megalithic and wooden components, such as the horseshoe-shaped building at the site of Tustrup in Denmark (Joussaume 1988: 41). In fact, wood remains in the repertoire of megalithic masonry throughout the Neolithic and into the Bronze Age. The continued use of wood is reflected both in timber circles (Gibson 1992), and in stone circles which show evidence of building techniques associated with timber work, such as the mortise-and-tenon and tongue-and-groove techniques (Atkinson 1956), the former being used to good effect (Chippindale 1994: 271) at Stonehenge. Going back in time the use of stone is equally pervasive, being used not only in monuments, but also in houses (Sherratt 1994: 169), although such use is rare. Further underlying continuity is embodied in megalithic shape, in so far as a large number of monuments are composed of various combinations of dolmen-like squares (Kinnes 1975; Chippindale 1986; 1992).

The third feature of random mutation listed above is the production of unique trajectories; strings of random occurrences tend to have idiosyncratic outcomes, even when mediated by selective processes. A random mutation model of cognitive innovation would predict that the European megaliths are likely to be a unique phenomenon. Rational invention, on the other hand, as implied by functional processual models of culture, should be capable of producing similar solutions wherever there are similar problems. While there is obviously insufficient space to compare megaliths on a global scale in order to demonstrate the uniqueness of each tradition, others have already commented on the non-equivalence of so-called 'megaliths' in different regions of the world, and the need to consider them as independent phenomena (e.g. Hodder 1994; Joussaume 1988: 297). Apparent resemblances soon turn out to be superficial on closer examination. Easter Island *ahus* and their famous statues, for example, have a wealth of characteristics which are rare or absent from their European counterparts, and *vice versa*, including: the lack of capstone lintels between statues; the placement of large stone structures high on one other which then acts as its sole support; the use of individual platform supports rather than post-holes; the figurative nature of the whole statue; totally different spatial patterning of monuments; and many other unique elements (Bahn & Flenley 1992: 150). Even the much more recent historical divergence between western and central Europe was enough to produce a completely different trajectory in the latter, which proceeded towards increasing funerary elaboration but *not* monumentality (Sherratt 1997). Nonetheless, under rare circumstances where only one shape is feasible, even random insights in different traditions could lead to the same form, as in the case of Egyptian and Mesoamerican pyramids (Chippindale 1992: 263).

The fourth and final characteristic of random mutation, that of highly effective forms which nonetheless show evidence of their ancestry, is also displayed in European megaliths and needs little elaboration. It is clear that Neolithic people were ingenious in putting the results of their random insights to very good use. The wide range of human benefit scenarios which have been advanced for European Neolithic monuments was summarised earlier, and there can be no doubt that there is some truth in many of these functional scenarios.

It may well be impossible to 'prove' that human invention is based on random cognitive mutations of some sort; physical models which mimic the mechanisms for creativity in thought processes still present a fundamental challenge to the field of artificial intelligence. What is demonstrated by the brief analysis of this section is that there is nothing in the European megalithic tradition which is obviously beyond the scope of random derivative inventions, coupled with strategic exploitation of some new ideas once randomly conceived. Just as the interplay of random mutation with selection was able to produce superb but unique adaptations to flight in birds, bats and pterodactyls, the interplay of random cognitive insights with very deliberate cognitive selection would have the potential, on occasion, to produce tools which embodied human needs and social strategies very effectively. In this way, the 'rational' dimension of human innovation emerges not in the exclusive conception of 'rational' ideas, but in attempts to assess the relative merits of a range of ideas of varying potential, *after* conception.

Megalithic symbiosis and predation

One of the most persuasive arguments for the organismic status of megalithic religions or other cultural phenomena is their capacity to play the role of 'parasites' or 'predators' – organisms which live at the expense of other organisms, from which they gain organic nutrition (Hale & Margham 1988: 403, 435). Such phenomena have a broader spectrum of adaptive strategies available to them than do traits or organs, whose interests coincide with the body they are associated with. The biologist Richard Dawkins has recently popularised the notion of religion as a 'virus of the mind' (Dawkins 1992; 1993a; 1993b), advancing a scenario in which religions are described as a 'disease', along with artefacts such as baseball caps and the 'St Jude' chain letter. Such concepts have been discussed in the literature from time to time over the last two decades (Ball 1984; Dawkins 1976; 1982; Delius 1989; 1991; Cloak 1975; Cullen 1990; Heylighen 1992; Sperber 1985). Apart from the recent relatively detailed discussion of religion by Dawkins (1993a), few in-depth case studies of the Meme idea have been attempted, although case studies may be found in other bodies of Darwinian culture theory (Boyd & Richerson 1985; Durham 1991; Soltis *et al.* 1995).

The purely pejorative use of the word 'virus' *always* to imply 'disease' is entirely inconsistent with the nature of both parasitic organisms in general, and viruses in particular. Organisms which depend on others for their survival display a wide spectrum of adaptive strategies, ranging from symbiosis to predation. Symbiotic viruses, however, unlike more complex symbionts, are difficult to find, not because they do not exist, but because they are able to become incorporated into the DNA of their hosts (see section 3), as a result of their capacity to reverse-transcribe (Greene 1993). There can be no doubt that there are many 'good' parasites – the intestinal bacterium *E. coli* being a well-known example (Delius 1989: 48) – and viruses are no exception, leading some biologists to suggest that many mammals may contain a significant complement of benign or useful viral genes (Mitchison 1993). Even harmful viruses, such as the human AIDS virus, evolve towards decreasing virulence if the rate of transmission is low (Ewald 1991; 1993: 60) and viral populations are forced to spend longer and longer periods inside the host before the opportunity to invade a new host comes along.

Thus the reason that symbiotic or benign parasites exist is because it is often in their best reproductive interests to be so – collaborators are sometimes more reproductively successful than predators. Dawkins has linked symbiotic adaptive strategies to parasites which tend to be transmitted from parents to their offspring and whose genes are therefore obliged to use the same series of vehicles as the genes of their hosts. Wood-boring ambrosia beetles and their resident bacteria are used by Dawkins as a case in point (Dawkins 1989: 243); both beetle genes and bacteria are passed on to the next generation in sperm and eggs. Such bacteria are completely dependent on their hosts for food and shelter. Yet the beetles are equally dependent upon their bacteria. Male beetles develop from unfertilised eggs; however, this parthenogenetic development can only be initiated by the presence of bacteria in the egg itself. For Dawkins, these are 'just the kind of parasites that . . . should cease to become parasitic and become mutualistic, precisely because they are transmitted in the eggs of the host, together with the host's 'own' genes. Their own bodies are likely to disappear, merging into the 'host' body completely' (Dawkins 1989: 244). The association of vertical transmission with symbiosis or benignness have also been reported in other kinds of parasite (Ewald 1994a: 47).

Conversely, the most virulent parasites, such as the vector-borne organisms which cause typhus and malaria (Ewald 1994a: 41–3), are capable of horizontal transmission, being spread (without discrimination as to host relatedness) by fleas and mosquitoes respectively. Large carnivores, whose survival depends upon the death of their prey, demonstrate an extreme form of the rule. If we think of predation as a 'disease', then it is a horizontally transmitted one, in so far as predators are obviously not obliged to target the offspring of their last victim; and the 'condition' could not be more dramatically lethal. In general, unless most future victims of a parasite or predator are likely to be the offspring of the current victim, it is in the predator's best interest to extract as much energy from its prey, in a manner which maximises its chances of finding the next victim.

Cultural phenomena also display the potential to follow vertical patterns of inheritance, passing from parent to child, as others have discussed (Boyd & Richerson 1985; Cavalli-Sforza & Feldman 1981). It is obvious that religions are no exception in this regard, as children are often brought up in the same faith as their parents. Nor was the vertical transmission of religion overlooked in the case-study undertaken by Dawkins, as he writes: 'If you have a faith, it is statistically overwhelmingly likely that it is the same faith as your parents and grandparents had. . . . The convictions that you so passionately believe would have been completely different, . . . if only you had happened to be born in a different place' (Dawkins 1993b: 25). However, the implications of such vertical transmission are not taken up at any stage in Dawkins's arguments, and the resulting thesis – that religion is a vertically transmitted disease – is therefore in complete conflict with neo-Darwinian theory. Vertically transmitted religions, far from being 'diseases', should evolve towards benign or symbiotic configurations.

Consequently, we would expect megalithic religions which were vertically transmitted to evolve in a similar direction. However, beneficial cultural information can never be 'captured' once and for all by a human genetic lineage in the way that genetic material from a symbiotic virus can. Symbiotic megalithic traditions could not 'disappear' into the DNA of their host, since at no stage of its life-cycle was the megalithic 'text' ever written in nucleotide form. Thus, no matter how vertical its recent history of transmission, a megalithic religion would always retain the potential to become horizontally transmitted and predatory at a later date. Relationships between megalithic religions and their human hosts must therefore have been deeply ambiguous. Distinguishing between symbiotic, benign and parasitic cultural phenomena in the prehistoric past will surely prove to be a very challenging task.

While it is not possible ever to be certain about whether a particular megalithic tradition was vertically or horizontally transmitted, there are circumstances in which a given mode of transmission might be more likely than in others. Vertical or quasi-vertical transmission would seem to be most likely during the first of Sherratt's two stages of the spread of agriculture (Sherratt 1990; 1997), for example. The first stage, down to *c.* 4000 BC, involved the spread of timber and earth long mounds by a variety of groups of *Bandkeramik* origin, as part of a discrete cultural assemblage that included other elements such as pottery, religious ideology and food production. In south-east and central Europe, where farming was introduced by population expansion, this assemblage maintained its coherence.

Such communities 'probably formed a relatively closed breeding network' (Sherratt 1994: 176), and the 'cultural network and the mating network were largely congruent' (Sherratt 1997: 8). If such communities were typical of kinship-based segmentary societies, they would have been constituted of a high proportion of people who had some genetic relationship to each other. Moreover, within the community, house-building and its associated *domus* ideology (Hodder 1990) could easily have been passed on from generation to generation within specific families, being so closely related to the process of establishing new domestic units through the marriage of children of residents of established households. Religious and architectural traditions of this kind would be expected to evolve towards benign or symbiotic configurations, and this could explain the relatively modest investment of labour in early Neolithic houses in comparison to later monuments. Moreover, once built, the structure could have retained the primary everyday purpose of shelter – in this sense a religion which made use of domestic space had 'ready-made' structures at its disposal.

In the second stage of the spread of agriculture, which occurred between 4500 and 4000 BC, in western France, southern Britain and Kujavia, this coherence began to break down (Sherratt 1997: 6). Settlement patterns became more flexible as a result of the relative increase in economic significance of livestock-rearing, hunting and foraging, and increasing contact with indigenous Mesolithic populations. However, the social relations formerly embodied in village settlements remained important, and some substitute was required to replace the village and its long houses. Tombs, in the form of earthen long barrows, provided the new focal points that these groups required. Neolithic societies needed to recruit labour, and this created the social will required to convert Mesolithic populations to a farming way of life. One implication of this model is that Mesolithic populations survived alongside the first farming groups in outer Europe for much longer than is often supposed (Sherratt 1997: 8), exchanging both genetic and cultural material.

Under circumstances such as these, particularly the will to recruit labour and perhaps intermarry with Mesolithic communities, the quasi-vertical pattern of transmission could easily have begun to break down, as individuals outside the kinship system were recruited into the community. The tie between religious ideology and actual domestic structures would have been loosened still further as the ideology moved into new contexts beyond the edges of the primary horticultural community, where the old domestic structures were no longer practical. As Sherratt writes (1997: 5), 'rituals, including burial, which had formerly taken place within the context of the settlement, now came to be associated with special places that were not necessarily places of habitation'. For the first time, megalithic religions were no longer solely dependent upon the fecundity of particular families or single kinship-based communities for new hosts, as these could now come from other communities also. Distributions of genetic features within some tombs (Scarre 1984; 1994), such as Chaussée-Tirancourt, seem to support the notion that more than one family or kin-group was interred within, which would imply that the megalithic religion itself was transcending the boundaries of particular communities.

Megalithic religions which demanded stronger commitments and greater investments from adepts, novices and congregations could now prove more successful than practices which only required a more 'reasonable' commitment. From this point onward some traditions could be expected to evolve towards greater and greater investments of labour, as the grip of the religion on its initiates and their associated labour forces became tighter and tighter. Moreover, by spreading itself over a wider and wider area, the megalithic discourse would increase the chances of encountering new victims before particular individuals or groups collapsed under its weight. While the labour of construction would have been only a fraction of the total amount of energy employed in the various forms of religious activity associated with the monuments, it is easiest to assess. Moreover, if control over physical labour is a general indication of the social power wielded by religious adepts, then it might also indirectly reflect the amount of ritual labour available to the organisation. Estimates of the amount of labour involved in the building of long barrows from 4000 to 3500 BC in southern Britain suggest that 1000 to 10,000 person-hours were involved (Renfrew 1983: 131), which could have been achieved by 20 people working for 50 to 500 days. A barrow such as West Kennet, at 3500 BC (Scarre 1988: 106) required as much as 15,700 hours, and was 100 metres in length. Some structures were already well beyond the scale of long houses, which ranged from 6 to 45 metres in length, and were usually 6 to 7 metres wide (Whittle 1994: 157). Causewayed camps represent further increases in labour investment. According to Renfrew, the labour required for causewayed camps in southern Britain was an order of magnitude higher than that required for long barrows, some 40,000 to 100,000 person-hours (Renfrew 1983: 131), which could have been achieved by 200 people working for 200 to 500 days.

Later, from 3000 BC onwards, the labour directed into the megalithic religion continued to rise, indeed accelerate, in the form of the great henges of the late Neolithic. Wainwright's estimation for Durrington Walls, for example (Wainwright 1969), is another order of magnitude higher again at 900,000 hours. If organising labour on such a scale required a centralised administration or chiefdom, as Renfrew has argued (1973a: 170), then bureaucracy may have been an outcome, as well as the cause, of the process – a new bureaucratic dimension to the megalithic religion itself. Once it was set in place, bureaucracy may have consumed even more energy than the labour it was supposed to organise. It may have helped labour investment to continue to grow, and grown even faster itself.

Administration networks for organising the labour of many communities would also have provided a new and more efficient information network for spreading religious ideas further and further afield. Perhaps most diagnostic of all, the energy investment in these monuments increases all the way up to the sudden cessation of their building at around 1500 BC (Scarre 1988: 107), with the great monuments of Silbury Hill and Stonehenge at 18,000,000 and 30,000,000 hours respectively (Renfrew 1983: 131). While this last estimate for Stonehenge is to some extent undermined by the new suite of radiocarbon dates which make it clear that the monument was constructed over a period of some 1400–1500 years (Allen & Bayliss 1995), the new dates do not refute the notion of a general trajectory towards larger monuments, given that the stone settings are all considered to belong to one conceptual as well as chronological phase. The stone settings (phase 3) were erected over a period of 850–1090 years (*ibid.*) and, even taken alone, would represent a labour investment comparable with Silbury Hill.

The principal individual stone settings at Stonehenge have now been dated, and mathematical modelling of the radiocarbon dates indicates a period of construction for each setting (each 'event' as opposed to 'phase' in Allen & Bayliss's terms) of between *c.* 250 and 370 years. To a certain extent arguments about the reduced labour required per unit (or event) at Stonehenge can also be applied to smaller or earlier monuments, thereby preserving the incremental pattern. Barrett (1993: 26) argues that the building programmes of Avebury and other monuments were long-term projects rather than single planned events, as is clearly demonstrable at Stonehenge, while Startin & Bradley (1981) have argued for smaller labour forces, arguments which imply less labour per unit time and longer building periods. Reduced labour per unit time at Durrington Walls and Avebury is further implied by the lower overall estimates of labour made by Startin & Bradley. They have suggested that some of the Renfrew estimates may be too high, estimating 11,000 hours for the timber structures at Durrington Walls and 500,000 hours each for the ditches of Avebury and Durrington, a point recently reiterated by Barrett (1993). These reductions in labour can be carried even further down the line if we consider that many British chambered tombs – including Wayland's Smithy, Oxfordshire; Pen-y-Wyrlod I, Powys; both Tulloch of Assery and Balvraid, Highland; Mid Gleniron I and II, Dumfries and Galloway; Notgrove, Gloucestershire; and Dyffryn Ardudwy, Gwynedd – show evidence for multi-period construction (Darvill 1987: 66). Thus, if protracted building periods were implicit in a wide range of the original labour estimates employed by Renfrew, and not just in estimates for late Neolithic Wessex, the observation of increasing monumentality would stand. Recent remarks by Barrett support this conclusion: 'The labour requirements . . . are clearly greater than those demanded by the earthen long barrows and by most of the so-called causewayed enclosures of the late fifth and fourth millennia' (Barrett 1993: 26).

Similar trajectories towards monumentality occur in western France (Boujot & Cassen 1993; Scarre 1998), and these systems also appear to come to a halt, depending on the locality, between 2000 and 1500 BC. It seems the megalithic religion became so massive it could no longer support its own weight, and like other organisms composed of quasi-autonomous viral entities under prolonged stress (Sonea 1988), the megalithic organism shattered once more into its constituent viral phenomena, scattering genetic debris into other cultural lineages. One such surviving missive could have been the new ritual discourse focused around the deposition of artefact hoards in rivers, lakes and bogs.

Conclusion and future research

Evidence for accelerating labour investment and the breakdown of kin-based community structure have been the focus of attention in the final section of this paper. However, there are many other categories of information on the 'cultural symbiosis versus predation' question which offer promising avenues for future research. The complex interpretative schemes of some authors (e.g. Hodder 1990; Thomas & Tilley 1994) could be used to explore the adaptive strategies employed by megalithic religions on a more intimate level. The elaboration of ritual discourse (as distinct from building) could be examined with reference to trajectories in grave goods, art and increasing regional diversification in monument form. Trends towards increasing numbers of single burials – suggestive of more building and ritual discourse per buried person – and towards increasing bureaucracy, could also shed light on the internal ecology of Neolithic societies. Use of narcotics in rituals (Sherratt 1990; 1997; Lewis-Williams & Dowson 1993; Scarre 1998), and the role of addiction in commitment to religious discourse offers another promising lead to follow. Yet another direction would involve correlation of signs of high stress or disease in skeletal remains with periods of heavy monumentality. As far as agricultural societies in general are concerned, it has already been established that the shift to food production involved some negative effects, such as reduced life-span and stature, and increased stress (Rindos 1984).

One particularly interesting area for future research could be studies of predator/prey demography. For instance, computer programs capable of simulating evolution in a virtual reality of artificial life-forms are now available. They confirm that parasites are a ubiquitous and inevitable part of any ecosystem, and also that anything that is successful tends to attract parasites (Rennie 1992: 112); without any special help in the programming, artificial parasites make an appearance, often within five minutes of simulation time. Later European prehistory is characterised by a decline in carnivores in the 20–10,000-year period (Gamble 1986: 319), a process which was subsequently accelerated by the advent of agriculture. Against the backdrop of this decline we see a dramatic rise in human population (Renfrew & Bahn 1991: 148), a population which is largely free of the fear of predation, unlike earlier groups such as *Homo erectus* (Dean & Delson 1995: 473). Although agricultural populations may have suffered increased exposure to microbial parasites, in contrast to some parasite-free hunter-gatherer populations (Patrucco *et al.* 1983), it is clear that parasite infestations did not begin with food production or sedentary lifestyles. Those who wish to dispute the organismic status of cultural phenomena, and to refute the cultural predation hypothesis, are presented with the question: 'Where are the large predators of recent human ecosystems?' Such questions are particularly challenging in light of the experience of some computer simulators (Rennie 1992: 112), who found that even when parasites were exterminated by particularly successful hosts, new types of parasites eventually evolved out of the host population. If the view of megaliths presented in this paper is correct, then something of the sort would appear to have happened in Neolithic north-west Europe. After the conquering of the wild *agrios* by the *domus* (Hodder 1990), predation by large carnivores must have become an infrequent event. Yet, having vanquished the predator without, they became prey to the predator within.

Acknowledgements. I would like to thank Bill Durham, Roland Fletcher, Ian Hodder, Tim Ingold, Martin Jones, Chris Knight, Herbert Maschner, Steven Mithen, Colin Renfrew, Michael Shanks, Stephen Shennan, James Steele, Greg Wyncoll and Ezra Zubrow, all of whom have commented extensively on some aspect of the material presented in this paper.

11
Parasite ecology
and the evolution of religion

Overview
The blanket view of religion as a disease, advocated by Dawkins, is inconsistent with the principles of parasite ecology. These principles state that vertically transmitted parasites evolve towards benign, symbiotic states, while horizontally transmitted parasites increase their virulence. Most of the world's established religions are transmitted vertically, from parents to children, and are therefore expected to be benign towards their hosts. Yet, certain horizontally transmitted cults, such as the Aum Shinrikyo, seem to effectively exploit their hosts in a way similar to an infectious disease.

Note by Francis Heylighen, editor of the conference volume in which this chapter first appeared: On 29 December 1995, while preparing this paper for publication, Ben Cullen unexpectedly died. This paper was one of two wonderful presentations which he had given at the conference 'Einstein meets Magritte' the previous summer. The unfinished manuscript consisted basically of the text he had read aloud during his presentation, which means that it lacked the structure typical of texts meant for publication. Therefore, I have edited the manuscript by dividing it into paragraphs and sections, eliminating references to photographs projected during the presentation, adding an overview and references, and correcting various small errors.

Let me elaborate why I find it important for Ben's work to be brought to the attention of the public. An Australian born in 1964, Ben Cullen graduated from the University of Sydney in 1987, with a degree in Prehistoric Archaeology. After a stay as Research Fellow at the University of Wales, Lampeter, he moved to the Queen's University of Belfast a few months before his death. He had just defended his PhD thesis in archaeology, in which he developed his 'Cultural Virus Theory', a stimulating new model of the evolution of culture, reminiscent of, but distinct from, the memetics view proposed by Dawkins (1989).

I met him in 1992 in London at a conference, where we were both presenting models of cultural evolution. We were obviously on the same wave length and had several long discussions after the lectures. I was impressed by his sharp intellect and the depth of his knowledge and understanding. Afterwards, we kept in touch by exchanging papers. Just a few weeks before his death, he sent me a pre-print (Cullen 1995) which he asked me to 'really read, not like some others', which I interpreted to mean that many people misinterpret his ideas. There does not seem to be much danger of misinterpretation with the following paper, which is a jewel of clarity and simplicity.

Introduction

There has been much recent publicity of the idea of religion and chain letters being diseases of the mind, or human information parasites as they are sometimes termed. Prominent amongst these have been pieces by the biologist Richard Dawkins in the London press, and also a piece about the St Jude chain letter in a letter published recently in the leading scientific journal *Nature* (Goodenough & Dawkins 1994). Headlines such as the one about the 'St Jude' mind virus, have not excited a great deal of controversy, presumably because few people publicly identify with chain letters.

However, other headlines, such as 'Is religion just a disease?' in the *Daily Telegraph* (Dawkins 1993a), have excited a great deal of vociferous debate, and pricked many egos. Richard Dawkins' view of religion (1993a; 1993b) as a disease not surprisingly offended members of the Church of England, and various bishops wrote pieces condemning both Dawkins and his view. But most objections to the 'religion as a disease' idea have come from the Church acting in self-defence, guarding its cultural capital so to speak. Most defences have come from theologians who submit the general idea that Dawkins is discussing spiritual matters beyond his understanding, a predictable theologian response. Very few objections have come from the sciences, human or otherwise. Few articles have explicitly disputed the scientific credentials of the Dawkins view, or the neo-Darwinian logic behind it.

In this paper I intend to go against this trend, and argue against the 'religion as a disease' position, on the grounds that Dawkins has not manipulated neo-Darwinian logic consistently. In other words, I will argue that Dawkins has erected a highly personal view of religion which is in complete conflict with both his own selfish gene theories (Dawkins 1989), and a growing body of parasite research.

Principles of parasite ecology

Let me enumerate the basic principles emerging in recent parasite ecology, the rules which the Dawkins view of religion are in direct conflict with, yet also the rules which Dawkins himself helped to articulate.

The first rule is that *vertically transmitted* parasites, namely, those that tend to pass from parent to child, evolve towards decreasing virulence, ultimately approaching benign or symbiotic configurations. Vertically transmitted parasites find themselves in the same sequence of bodies as the genes of their hosts, generation after generation, and the two therefore share a common future. They are in the same evolutionary boat, so to speak, and if the boat sinks, both parties drown.

One classic example of this type of relationship is that between wood-boring ambrosia beetles and bacteria, an example which Dawkins has featured in discussions of this nature. The bacteria are entirely dependent upon the beetles for food and shelter, and live their entire lives inside beetle tissue, being carried into the next generation inside the eggs which the females lay. This route to the future, however, ensures that they pass from each parent beetle to the beetle's offspring, and they are, therefore, vertically transmitted. Thus the rule would predict that these bacteria should be symbiotic, and indeed they are, as without them the beetles would be unable to reproduce. This is because male beetles can only develop from eggs in which the bacteria are present. Without the bacteria, the beetles would be a race of female individuals who could only reproduce through sexual reproduction, a difficult situation at the best of times.

This general rule linking symbiosis with long-term host/parasite cohabitation and vertical transmission also finds support elsewhere, particularly in the field of 'Darwinian medicine' (Nesse & Williams 1995), and in the work of researchers such as Paul Ewald (1990; 1995). For instance, it has been shown that new and less virulent strains of the AIDS virus are proving more successful in human populations where condoms are frequently used, and where viruses therefore have to spend longer periods of time in each host (Ewald 1994b).

Rule number 2 is simply the reverse of Rule number 1. Disease is often connected to *horizontal modes of transmission*, where parasites are transmitted indiscriminately with respect to host relationships. Horizontally transmitted parasites are as likely to be passed on between families as within families. Parasites of this kind tend to evolve towards a typical 'disease' configuration. The presence of the parasite significantly alters the host body or behaviour in such a way as to improve the parasite's chances of reproduction, and decrease that of the host. Curiously, this may involve enhancing the host's chances of survival, while preventing its reproduction, in an attempt to produce a thriving parasite factory. Some barnacles, for example, parasitise crabs by targeting the crab's sex organs first, and the vital organs last, so maintaining a living resource for the parasite for as long as possible.

One of the most spectacular parasites of all is not an animal, but a plant which hunts other plants. It too is horizontally transmitted, and conforms to the rule. The corpse flower, or *Rafflesia*, is a family of plants so called because many of them exude a smell of rotting meat, mimicking the smell, colour and texture of a corpse. At 30 to 40 inches or about 1 metre across, it is the largest known single flower, and one of the most extraordinary predators of the plant world. It is an inhabitant of the rainforests of Borneo and Sumatra. The corpse flower has no leaves, no stem, no roots or trunk. It actually lives inside the tissues of another plant, one of the many vines which grow so abundantly in the rainforest canopy, as a net of tiny threads. How it actually gets inside these vines is not known. Thus the stem from which this truly monstrous flower grows does not belong to the flower, but to *Rafflesia*'s victim. Once the parasitic flower grows to its full size, the host vine has usually collapsed into the leaf litter of the forest, and is hidden from view.

The *corpse flower* is an excellent example of a predator which stalks its prey from within, biding its time in the body of the host vine, before leaping to new victims by means of its extraordinary flowers. To move through the forest, it enlists the help of tree shrews (small arboreal mammals) and insects. Viewed from the inside, the corpse flower is even more remarkable. Exuding a powerful aroma similar to a pile of fish after three days in the hot sun, it not surprisingly attracts flies. The flies crawl down to the sex organs, and there they are daubed with pollen which may then be carried to female flowers. The female flowers produce seeds which are then transported by small tree shrews to new vine hosts, elsewhere in the rainforest.

Religions as parasites

Rafflesia is particularly relevant to the 'religion as a disease' debate because it represents a rare example of a large predator that inhabits the bodies of its prey. It allows us to begin to imagine how an organisation such as a religion could be seen as a life-form which inhabits the bodies of people, in the same way that *Rafflesia* inhabits the bodies of rainforest vines. Anatomically, the corpse flower and cultural life-forms have much more in common than one might expect.

This is a representation of the anatomy of a religion and its material products, in this case the megalithic tombs of Neolithic western Europe (Cullen 1994). The outer ring of structures represent megaliths, but they could just as well be churches, or mosques or cathedrals. The central structures of the religion are composed of people, which are represented by the figure in the bottom corner, a circle for a head and a monk's robe for the body. There is an outer ring of acolytes or novices, whose heads are represented by circles A, B, C, and D their bodies by a robe, and the actions they perform in service of the religion by arrows. Finally there is an inner circle of priests or clergy, whose heads are represented by circles 1, 2, 3, and 4, their bodies by robes, and their actions by arrows. The religion or cultural organism consists solely of the shaded black areas and their material products – the people involved in the organisation may perform many other roles in society, some of these roles might work against the religion. So this schematic diagram gives us some idea of what a cultural life-form looks like.

Now, using the rules of parasite ecology discussed a little earlier, we can begin to predict which religions will evolve towards disease-like states, and which religions should evolve towards benign or symbiotic states. Vertically transmitted religions, like vertically transmitted viruses and other parasites, should evolve towards symbiotic or benign states. This immediately disqualifies most of the world's established religions from the 'disease' scenario, because they are generally passed on from generation to generation within the family. Family-dependent religious affiliation should therefore evolve towards benign or symbiotic configurations. Dawkins actually points out the vertically transmitted nature of religions, although he does not connect it to any prediction of symbiosis.

For the same reasons, we would expect the religions of small-scale, kinship-based societies, such as those of indigenous Australian cultures and their associated artistic traditions, to evolve towards symbiotic configurations. When a religion occupies a small community in which members of subsequent generations are of close genetic relationship to previous generations, a pathological religion would tend to plunge itself and its community into oblivion.

But this is not to say that there can be no such thing as a parasitic religion. However, if we are to find a truly pathological religion, we will have to look for examples where the pattern of transmission is horizontal, or essentially indiscriminate with respect to genetic relatedness of new recruits. Established world religions cannot be totally excluded from the picture, as while congregational membership may be essentially vertically transmitted, membership of the priesthood is not so rigid. Nor can the religions of kinship-based communities be totally excluded, as kinship is often employed as a means of social categorisation for both strangers or newcomers and family alike. So-called 'fictive' kinship of this kind can and often does follow a line of descent which does not conform to strict lines of genetic inheritance. So we might expect occasional parasitic forms of religion to arise in the established traditions.

But are there any more dramatic examples around? I think that we may not have to look too far. Religious cults would appear to be a good candidate. Chizuo Matsumoto, better known as Shoko Asahara, is the leader of the doomsday cult of Aum Shinrikyo or Way of the Divine Truth. The Way of the Divine Truth organisation was apparently responsible for the recent nerve-gas attack on the Tokyo subway system.

The Aum Shinrikyo doomsday cult undoubtedly follows a horizontal pattern of transmission, selecting its recruits more for what they can do for the cult than for their relatedness to existing members. The rate at which it acquired members, many of them outside Japan, is testimony to the non-vertical nature of its reproduction. In the space of a decade or so, the cult acquired some 30,000 members in Russia, presumably none of them related to Asahara himself. Within Japan the cult boasted a surprising number of members from all walks of life. Asahara carefully chose the most talented individuals for his priests, recruiting lawyers, scientists, chemists and engineers. With so many thousands of members in such a short time, it is clear that the cult did not rely on the fecundity of its members for its expansion. Clearly, then, the Aum Shinrikyo doomsday cult was a horizontally transmitted phenomenon.

Parasite ecology, then, would predict that it would exploit some or all of its members. Is there any evidence of this? It would appear that there was. One recruit had to provide a list of her assets and promise that they would be passed over to the cult on her death. The most privileged were allowed to drink Asahara's blood or semen, but actually had to pay an incredible 74,000 pounds for the pleasure. Cult members received very little in return for these immense financial contributions to the cult. Apart from the lucky few allowed to drink a little blood or semen, they received dormitory or boarding school style accommodation, and two meagre vegetarian meals per day. The 53 children moved from the cult's commune proved to be suffering from severe malnutrition, while Asahara himself lived in luxury. An older recruit related how he was told to drink several gallons of water and vomit them as part of his training. So it would seem that the Aum Shinrikyo doomsday cult of Shoko Asahara does indeed conform to principles of parasite ecology.

Conclusion

In conclusion, then, it would appear that the blanket view of religion as a disease, as advocated by Dawkins (1993a; 1993b), is not consistent with recent research into the nature of parasite evolution. Many religions are vertically transmitted or family-dependent, and we would therefore expect them to evolve towards symbiosis or at least benignness. As Dawkins has remarked, it is an extraordinary fact that if we adhere to a faith at all, it is overwhelmingly likely to be the same as that of our parents. This simple fact ought to ensure that if a religion which followed this pattern of transmission ruthlessly exploited its congregation, it would eventually plunge both itself and its people into extinction.

12
Art academies,
cultural copying fidelity and society:
later European visual representation
as a predatory phenomenon

Overview

An attempt is made to understand art academies and other cultural or social phenomena as living things, evolving towards forms which seek their own survival, and the social reproduction of their constituent parts. In pursuing their goals, institutions may often exploit the hopes, intentions and energy of people, maintaining a predatory relationship with the human bodies upon which they depend for survival. Approaches of this sort cross-cut 'common sense' and sociobiological models of institutions, which generally assume that the role of an organisation is either to serve 'society' in a general way, to serve the 'powers that be', or even to serve as a tool to increase the genetic fitness of the people which construct or run the institution. While art academies are used to illustrate most of the arguments presented here, scientific institutions, universities or other kinds of religious societies would fit the model equally well. Toward the end of the paper, it is suggested that, in a similar manner to the AIDS virus, the low copying fidelity of modern art enhances its diversity, enabling it to fool the cognitive immune system of the modern viewer.

The case of the missing predators

Humans are generally recognised as one of the most successful large mammals of all time, at least in numerical terms. However, we are not the only species to have reached such high densities. Early European colonists of North America were amazed at the vast herds of bison, a species which could then be found as a sea of beasts which stretched as far as the eye could see. Numbers of individual bison numbered as many as 30 million in the year 1800 (Hodgson 1994: 71). Similarly, vast single-species herds of other kinds, such as wildebeest migrating across the plains of sub-Saharan Africa, provide a consistently fascinating subject for the wildlife documentary industry.

Yet, while such herds often reached sizes in excess of several million, their statistics do not compare with the statistics of modern human communities. Firstly, even when their numbers are at their highest, both bison and wildebeest display very restricted distributions on a global scale, in North America and southern Africa respectively. Secondly, the numbers themselves never approached the huge figures attained by the exploding human population of the planet, which of course numbers billions rather than millions. Lastly, while herd sizes of wild herbivores are shadows of their former glory in centuries past, the human population continues to climb, showing no sign of decline or even stabilisation. This phenomenal growth is embodied in the fact that we now swarm in vast cities, packed at densities few could have imagined even half a century ago, although visionaries such as Fritz Lang, in his film *Metropolis*, attempted to do so. Human consumption now accounts for a whopping 40% of the world's combined plant productivity (Flannery 1994: 100), a figure which must surely be far in excess of any herbivore in the Earth's history. It seems obvious that human bodies are very likely to become the 'bison' of the twenty-first century, the body on which all other bodies depend, and the nexus of many future ecosystems.

Which leaves an intriguing problem: Where are the predators of these great herds of hominids which now roam the planet, these herds of which we are all a part? Our combined biomass, even calculated on a conservative 50 kilograms per person, and an equally conservative 5 billion individuals, already exceeds 250 billion kilograms. In any other known ecosystem, such a quantity of meat on the hoof would attract an enormous number and range of predators, and provide them with a stable and reliable livelihood. The wildlife documentary archetype of sub-Saharan Africa is a typical example of this. The list of predators would include lions, hyenas, leopards, cheetahs, hunting dogs, jackals, vultures, maribou storks and, of course, for much of the last 5 million years, humans themselves. Overall, East Africa has a total of 20 mammalian predators which exceed 5 kilograms in weight, while Thailand has 24, and North America 27 (Flannery 1991: 725). In other ecosystems, such those of Australia and New Guinea, the list does not include so many mammalian predators (Flannery 1991: 724; 1994: 108–17), but the shortfall is made up by the relative success of reptilian meat-eaters such as large snakes, monitor lizards and crocodiles.

In fact, until quite recently on an archaeological time-scale, large carnivores were common in all ecosystems, including areas such as Europe, where they are now in such dramatic decline. In collections of bone remains found in European caves from 118,000 to 35,000 years ago (Gamble 1986: 312), the presence of carnivores remains steady, despite fluctuations in the relative proportions of different kinds of herbivores. A wide range of large carnivores remain present throughout succeeding periods, and bear, wolf, leopard, lynx, wolverine, badger, and lion are all still present between 20,000 and 10,000 years ago (Gamble 1986: 314).

Broadly speaking, predators are merely large parasites, and parasites are merely small predators – ecologically they are both dependent upon the prey or host species for the energy which they need to survive and reproduce (Hale & Margham 1988: 403, 435). Could it be that large parasites have simply been replaced by smaller ones? To make an argument of this nature one would have to show that there has been a significant rise in numbers of microbial parasites per person. Although a more detailed study might lead to a different conclusion, it would seem to be a safe assumption that disease has been a part of life at regular intervals throughout the evolutionary history of the human species. It is not uncommon for hunter-gatherer populations in temperate climates and open country to be parasite free, but, equally, there are many examples of prehistoric parasite infestations (Renfrew & Bahn 1991: 387; Frankel 1991: 30;). Moreover, most if not all populations which are preyed upon by large carnivores have a wealth of microbial parasites as well. Large carnivores have never targeted disease-free herds (if such were ever to exist), nor have they ever displayed a preference for disease-free individuals. In fact, the reverse is probably more true – lions and other predators are notorious for deliberately targeting sick or injured animals. Recent reviews of parasite ecology (Rennie 1992: 112) clearly show that parasites are present in all known ecosystems, and there is no reason to believe that this would not have been true in the past.

So we cannot view the disease caused by microbial parasites as a new human phenomenon, which takes the place of large carnivores in the new agricultural ecosystems dominated by humans and their domesticates. It would appear that the whole 'predator' dimension of these new ecosystems is missing, and in a most dramatic and peculiar manner.

The question of cultural predators
But perhaps we are not looking carefully enough for the predators whose

absence seems so notable. Could it be that we are defining the category too narrowly, and that the predator concept needs to be used more creatively? Perhaps we are surrounded by predators so new and strange that we do not even recognise them as such. More specifically, it is perhaps worth pointing out that the presence of a predator is usually betrayed by a movement of some kind. Could it be that today's predators do not rely on movement? There is also a natural assumption that a predator is something quite separate from our 'self' or body. The idea that a predator may actually live within our bodies, or may even be a part of ourselves, part of our identity in the most fundamental sense, is essentially alien. In the rest of the paper the aim will be to question such assumptions, and show that the human body is an ecosystem in which (and of which) predators play a very real part.

A more general objective is to develop the idea that predators are as endemic to modern ecosystems and human herds as they are to other kinds of ecosystems. In the view proposed here, the new predators are everywhere. Modern day predators are not only inside us, but an integral part of who and what we are. The ubiquitous prey species is *Homo sapiens*, and all its adaptations, which could potentially include the various psychological 'algorithms' and 'modalities' outlined by the 'evolutionary psychology' school (Brodie 1996; Buss 1994; Cosmides 1989; Steele 1996), regardless of how 'weak' one imagines these modularities to be (Mithen 1993b), or even if they exist at all (Whitehouse 1996). The predators (or symbiotes, as the case may be) are cultural phenomena in their many and diverse forms, all of them dependent upon *Homo sapiens* for their survival.

Each person is therefore an ecosystem, not a single organism, and like any ecosystem, our ancestry combines many genealogies; multiple lines of descent rather than just one. In other words, it is obvious that zebras, lions and wildebeest embody totally different phylogenetic histories within the ecosystem of the African savannah. Similarly, for example, Marxist ideas, archaeological methodologies, English-language constructs and human bones embody completely different phylogenetic histories within the body of an English Marxist archaeologist.

Thus, in the model advocated throughout the paper, we are neither just predator nor just prey, but both together, intertwined as one, like nothingness entwined in the heart of being in Jean Paul Sartre's famous metaphor. Age-old struggles between predator and prey have shifted from savannah, desert and rainforest, to the dark and secret landscape of the human body. Art, science, religion and technology are all good examples of cultural predation; and art, science, religion and technology are all part of us. But the bodies of cultural predators themselves are totally alien to familiar carnivores such as large cats and the like, such that it is best to abandon these archetypes completely, at least when understanding cultural *anatomy* is the goal at hand. Cultural life-forms may be 'life', but they are certainly not life as we know it. On the other hand, analogies with familiar predators have great value in understanding cultural *ecology*, as will be discussed a little later below.

Cultural anatomy: the biology of academies

What is meant by the notion of a 'cultural life-form'? One way of putting the idea across would take the form of a diagram. Institutions are obviously living things in so far as they consist of bits of living people (and see also Callon & Law (1995) on 'hybrid collectifs', and Law (1991; 1994) on the 'sociology of monsters', for some interesting parallel alternatives). One could draw, greatly simplified, a schematic representation of an art tradition or art academy. The general point being made is that such traditions are made up of parts of people, parts of actions, and material culture, all intimately related and all influencing each other. Firstly, parts of any art tradition are embodied in actual physical structures in people's bodies, so these would be shown by the shaded heads of human figures, some of which would of course be 'artists'. One obvious example of art's structures in the body would be the artist's knowledge of painting techniques, remembered in the form of patterns of strengthened and weakened synaptic connections between neurons, in his or her nervous system, patterns of strengthened and weakened muscles, and so on. Needless to say, there is no boundary between these structures and other bodily structures, and this would be symbolised by the dotted line at the border of the shaded areas.

Secondly, in addition to the part of the art academy composed of restructured human flesh, there is also a dimension of human action, the metabolism of the cultural organism, if you like: any aspect of the human metabolism or individual action which is likely to have consequences for the life of the art academy or tradition itself. Actions would be symbolised with arrows, integrally bound up with bodies; hence, once again, there would be no boundary between the two in the figure.

Thirdly, we have the material culture of the art academy/tradition, paintings, easels, paint-brushes, wood-carving equipment, potter's wheels, etc. In the figure, material culture would be symbolised by stacked canvases awaiting the attention of the artists. The material culture of the institution, in so far as it is produced by the people who participate in it, is a direct product of the living parts, in the same sense that dead structures such as finger nails or fur are integral parts of the living tissues of organisms. In some cases, the material culture of an institution may involve the re-appropriation of ready-made artefacts from other technological systems, such as in the case of purchasing supplies, or in recycling rubbish (Gidlow in press). One obvious example of the latter in the case of art traditions would be Marcel Duchamp's 'Ready-made' (1913), made from a wooden stool with a bicycle wheel mounted upon it. This was the first of series of works based around the theme of recontextualising unaltered artefacts (Piper 1994: 417), including constructions of glass, metal and wood (Read 1974: 114). Picasso's 'Bull's head' (Berger 1989: 101) is another famous example.

So we have a model of an art academy as a life-form, as at least partly composed of the living flesh of artists. Elsewhere, I have discussed some arguments of this section in greater detail. Here, the focus of attention will be the implications of these arguments: a discussion of some general aspects of the technology and reproduction of art traditions. Such systems of visual depiction can very effective at getting reproduced through the actions of artists, and, of course, through the actions of other people working in close social proximity, such as art dealers.

Art academies, naturalism and reproduction

People are capable of reproducing cultural phenomena with very high copying fidelity, and this is reflected in the persistence of some art styles in a state of little or no change over long periods of time. Many aspects of oil painting in Europe, for example, changed slowly or very little for much of the last millennium, when compared with the dramatic changes which have taken place in the last century or so. Giorgio Vasari, in his 'Lives of the most excellent Italian architects, painters and sculptors from Cimabue to our times' (Rubin 1995: 1–2), saw art as united by a single goal, the imitation of nature, for over three hundred years. The new naturalism started in the thirteenth century, in which the earliest examples of easel-painting also appeared in the form of altar-pieces (Piper 1994: 78). For Vasari, there were three periods, corresponding roughly to the fourteenth, fifteenth and sixteenth centuries, and embodied in the work of Giotto, Donatello and Raphael respectively, and culminating in the work of Michelangelo. Synonymous with this project was the restoration of the lost techniques and knowledge of antiquity, 'the mastery of the principles and models offered by ancient art' (Rubin 1995: 1), which in turn suggests an even greater time-depth for the naturistic tradition.

Somewhat later paintings, of which 'The artist's studio' (*c.* 1665–70) by the Dutch painter and art dealer, Jan Vermeer (Piper 1994: 230), is just one of hundreds of examples of a naturalistic tradition reproduced with almost perfect fidelity. Nor was this copying fidelity manifest only at the general level of naturalism itself. In 'The artist's studio', the single source of silvery light, coupled with the vanishing perspective of the flat, geometrically precise plane defined by the black and white tiles of the floor, create a consistently readable space for the tiny details of figures, clothing and drapery. Concern with such details of anatomy, foreshortening and linear perspective were also of primary concern to Vasari (Rubin 1995: 265–6), although some Renaissance artists, such as Michelangelo, may have despised the everyday subject-matter of Dutch traditions (Piper 1994: 213). Some seventy years later, the paintings of Jean Baptiste-Simeon Chardin, such as 'The house of cards' (Piper 1994: 246), show how faithfully the western European tradition of naturalism, perspective, light and detail had been reproduced, despite the fact that Chardin himself did not pass through the Academy. So limited was the scope for creativity available to artists of these periods, that Piper lists the major distinguishing themes of Chardin's style as a shift not in manner of depiction, not in light, or *chiaroscuro*, or brushwork but in the fact that he preferred to paint his still-lives in the kitchen, rather than the dining room, and in that his genre subjects were of 'below-stairs' subjects (Piper 1994: 246) – servants in the midst of daily chores, or children playing. From the point of view of twentieth-century art, these are small differences indeed.

Thus, quite rigid formulae may be reproduced with high copying fidelity over many centuries, although there are many subtle variations and explorations which seem small to the twentieth-century eye, so accustomed as it is to large-scale breaks with tradition. Not only are the works similar, but there are also actual connections linking one artist to another, each the student or teacher of others. Other links can be traced through the sale of artworks which are then bought by other artists, many of whom doubled as dealers (Piper 1994: 213). While there is no direct academic or 'apprentice' link between Vermeer and Rembrandt, for example, Vermeer owned three paintings of little-known Fabritius, who happened to be a student of Rembrandt's (Piper 1994: 226). Rembrandt in turn owned six paintings of the early genre painter Adriaen Brouwer, while another seventeen paintings of Brouwer's belonged to Rubens (Piper 1994: 227). Both Rubens and Rembrandt were influenced by Titian, who was heavily influenced by Giorgione, whose soft painting style was judged by Vasari to link him with

Leonardo (Rubin 1995: 136), and so on. Today, at the other end of the tradition, links with academic art can still be traced. For example, even the most explicit anti-academic art movement of the early twentieth century, Futurism, which held all forms of imitation in contempt, still appealed to the names of great painters of the past in its rhetoric (Read 1974: 110).

Such networks of informal and formal contact criss-cross the western European art tradition throughout its history, and the education of artists through a variety of means is a revealing topic in the history and interpretation of western European art (Black 1987; Dempsey 1980). But copying fidelity probably reaches a crescendo in the form of art academies, and the systematic apprenticeships they imply. From the early to mid nineteenth century (Piper 1994: 334), European art became a booming technology, as the numbers of potential patrons were swelled by the prosperous middle classes. Mass-produced prints were available for the first time, as a result of the invention of the printing press (Eisenstein 1979). Demand was met, for the most part, by artists trained in the official academies, such as the French academy (Piper 1994: 334):

> The principles of the academic tradition were rooted in the *disegno* of early Renaissance Florence – stressing the importance of drawing, the defining contour of line; the detailed preliminary study; the subordinate role of colour; and the necessity both of classical balance and of "finish". These principles had long been upheld in the French Academy by a long line of painters from Lebrun to David. The highest themes were classical or Christian, and the noblest subject was the human form, to which a certain decorum of "nobly' expressive pose and gesture were appropriate. These principles persisted throughout the nineteenth century, but interiors, sentimental scenes of peasant life, views of exotic lands and customs, portraits, genre scenes in the Dutch mode – these were all also in great demand, painted again in a closely detailed manner.

As the words of Piper show so clearly, the torch of classical and Renaissance naturalism was still burning bright as it was passed into the hands of the academy's students, many centuries after it was first lit. Nor was the torch to be extinguished with the advent of modern art. Academic naturalism is reflected in the twentieth-century works of artists such as Edward Hopper, Balthus, Christian Berard and Stanley Spencer, and to a lesser extent Maurice Utrillo (Read 1974: 8). Naturalism even remained in the repertoire of the quintessential modern artist, as in the early (and occasional later) works of artists such as Picasso (Berger 1989: 41–5), who was so instrumental in the rise and continued development of modern art itself.

The artful predator

So artistic academies are life-forms, and able to reproduce themselves, but how are they predatory? Are not such traditions symbiotic, or at least benign? Do not painters do pretty well for themselves? The answer is, of course, yes they do, or at least some of the time. But that is not the point. From the point of view of a predator the question is how much energy can be diverted away from the genetic kin of its prey into the body of the predator, the cultural life-form itself? Yet how can this be achieved, given that both the identity as an 'artist' – the academy's representative in the body, and the rest of the artist, inhabit the same bodies? The answer to these questions lies in the subtle inter-relationships which exist between the individual success of the artist, through career success and social advancement, and the causes towards which the proceeds of that career are diverted. Various primary 'receptacles' present themselves to those that enjoy economic prosperity. Conflict of interest can emerge between genetic kin and family, further career enhancement and the art profession more generally, and any number of 'good causes' that may be unconnected to either of these.

If western European art is to be thought of as a predator, then clearly, along the course of its long naturalistic tradition, it had found a very successful formula. Put succinctly, naturalism 'worked' in western European society for a very long time. In the early Renaissance, patronage was the crucial energy source upon which the art production systems depended. It was to this context that they were uniquely adapted. In addition to patronage, humanism (Black 1987) was also a vital element contributing to the aesthetics to which art catered. Made up of prosperous merchant guilds and wealthy merchant princes, and under the influence of the 'rapidly expanding humanist rediscovery of the pagan classics . . . its ideals to be expressed in changed conceptions of the human figure' (Piper 1994: 100), art became a medium of competitive displays of rank. Humanism fuelled the focus on anatomy and proportion, as distinct from naturalism in the simplest sense of the word. Not only were elites anxious to display their wealth and sophistication, churches were equally keen to do so. Once established as the appropriate medium, the art academy was now in a win/win situation. The more social conflict, the more need for competitive displays, and as Piper points out 'the Renaissance flourished – perhaps strangely – in small, newly rich, independent cities torn more or less continuously by internecine struggles' (Piper 1994: 100). Most patrons, all of whom with a few exceptions from the elite strata of Italian society, had already had their perceptions shaped by the *status quo* embodied in prevailing 'masterpieces' by the time they were in a position to commission painters and paintings themselves. Thus the academy was in a position to shape both market and product, with the artist's body being the primary agent of production.

The biography of the painter Vasari reveals a few of the parameters at work. Vasari was initially motivated by altruistic motives towards kin, for example to provide for the dowries of his three orphaned sisters (Rubin 1995: 21). Such drives are championed by sociobiologists and Darwinian psychologists as genetically emergent orientations, which promote the success of genetic kin at the expense of the genes of the bearer (Badcock 1994: 48, 57, 114–18; Brodie 1996: 127–8; Dawkins 1989: 88–107; Ridley 1993: 74). It is not my intention to discuss the degree to which Vasari's own concerns for his sisters fit the 'Darwinian Psychology' template. What is clear is that this orientation, whether genetic or constructed, can easily be exploited by the art academy, which can offer itself as a 'solution' to the artist's anxieties at every turn. What is equally clear from Rubin's exhaustive study of Vasari is that his identity was far more deeply bound up with his profession as an artist than with any notion which could be interpreted as genetic reproduction (Rubin 1995: 21):

> His was a pragmatic idealism. He believed in what he did and what it could do for him. He counted himself among those "who had their spirit turned to becoming famous" and was prepared to exert every effort to become a celebrated son of his native Arezzo. Moved by love for his work and indefatigable, Vasari more than fulfilled his ambition, succeeding as an architect, court artist, and writer as well as a painter.

Vasari's success as an individual cannot be called into question. But it is also clear that he chose to direct the greater part of his energies into the life, reproduction and propagation of Renaissance art, than into the replication of his own genes. Another way to put it might be to say that art inspired him to become a 'Trojan Horse' to his genes. Art contributed to his survival, health, quality of life and social status, but ultimately prevented these resources from being implemented in the business of genetic reproduction. Despite his remarkable professional success indicated by Rubin in the quote above, he married relatively late at the age of 38 (Rubin 1995: 14), apparently had only one illegitimate son (*ibid.*: 53), although nephews are also mentioned (*ibid.*: 37). Nor was this 'sociobiological shortfall' regained in later generations, at least as far as patrilineal descent was concerned. The direct line of the Vasari family died out in 1687 (Rubin 1995: 40), only a little over 100 years from the death of Giorgio in 1574. Other Renaissance artists, such as Michelangelo and Leonardo da Vinci, were similarly consumed by their professional lives to the extent that all other commitments became secondary if not non-existent. Moreover, the general lack, in the history of western European art, of father-son artist 'dynasties' spanning more than two generations, illustrate the same point at a more general level. Even where artists do have children, the academy seems to have no special interest in reproducing the father's identity to those children. In summary, then, the 'artist' structures of Vasari's body successfully predated upon the *Homo sapiens* genetic dimension, inspiring him to choose to employ the bulk of his energy and agency in the maintenance and social reproduction of renaissance art.

Despite the many changes in European society over subsequent centuries, the 'wealthy patron' niche did not change dramatically enough to allow a totally different system of representation the chance to compete with the naturalistic academic tradition. The success of academic naturalism, then, was peculiar to a particular, time, place and social context. In another society, or at a different time, naturalistic visual images on two-dimensional pieces of canvas could not have served this purpose. Competitive displays of rank would have found, in all likelihood, a completely different medium.

Another way to demonstrate the contingent nature of western European art traditions is to contrast them with the image production systems of other cultures. Much of the naturalistic tradition is so ingrained in our personal definitions of the word 'art' that even today many people view 'naturalism' as 'natural' for art. We have busied ourselves with tiny nuances within naturalism, becoming attuned to subtle differences. We identify various movements and sub-traditions. Yet the formulaic dimension of the western European art tradition can quickly be brought into stark relief by a comparison with the art and visual representation systems of a completely different cultural tradition, such as that embodied in the material culture of Australian Aboriginal societies.

While Maynard has argued that Aboriginal art evolves towards naturalism (Maynard 1979), as have others (McCarthy 1967), it can be argued that these statements are applying Eurocentric criteria to an entirely non-equivalent cultural phenomenon. Some rock art is definitely representational, in the sense of enabling recognition of subject-matter in the form of animal species (Murray & Chaloupka 1984; Chaloupka 1986; Lewis 1986; Mcdonald 1983), and modes of warfare (Taçon & Chippindale 1994), but there are many fundamental differences in the medium and mode of depiction, and in the social roles of painters. As far as naturalism is concerned, Layton (1992: 14) has remarked that there is no simple, functional reason why an artistic tradition should evolve in this direction.

Moreover, the complex figurative style as defined by Maynard (1979), which she sees as the culmination of the trend towards naturalism, in fact includes an 'x-ray' element where a variety of internal organs are depicted, just one of many elements which make these images completely different to those of the European Academy. Two other unique elements would include systematic repainting and the lack of an art 'profession'. In the first case, rock-art is maintained over long periods by being painted over again and again to 'keep the drawings fresh' (Layton 1992: 27). In the second case, there is the fact that there was no specialist 'artist' profession in traditional Aboriginal society. In the western Kimberleys, retouching of Wandjina paintings was done once a year, at the start of the wet season, by people who were otherwise involved in normal economic activities all year round (*ibid.*: 38). There were, therefore, neither 'masters' nor untouchable 'masterpieces' in the Australian traditions, at least in the sense that such are usually understood in a European context.

Concluding remarks:
niche diversity and the modern art 'quasispecies'

The comparison with Australian rock art demonstrates the historically and geographically contingent nature of the Academic art of western Europe. If naturalism is not to be viewed as the result of some inexorable drive towards 'perfection' or some 'higher ideal', that is, not to be viewed as the result of 'natural' progression, then we would expect a change of direction to occur in the event of any major change to the patronage system. The most obvious change against which to test such an assertion are the social changes associated with the role of art in the nineteenth and twentieth centuries, and the rise of 'modern' art. Such changes began slowly in the nineteenth century, but gathered momentum in the twentieth, involving both social and geographic changes (Piper 1994: 411):

> But the post-1914 avant-garde was distinguished above all to go beyond stylistic innovation, to work for change in life and society as a whole. . . . Such far reaching ambitions did not survive the further shock of World War II, and the concerns of the most influential post-War artists have tended to be more personal. The persecution which accompanied Nazism drove many of Europe's best artist's to America. Their interaction with a generation of talented and energetic American artists, and with a society not only wealthy but receptive to novelty, brought about, for the first time in history, artistic leadership in the New World rather than the old.

Expressing the same sentiments in a metaphorical style, Marcel Duchamp, describing his inspiration for the Modern art classic 'Nude descending the staircase', writes 'When the vision of the *Nude* flashed upon me, I knew that it would break forever the enslaving chains of naturalism' (Read 1974: 114). Art's niche in society, then, would seem to be fundamentally changed, changed away from the narrow, relatively predictable market of the gentrified patron, towards a veritable *smorgasbord* of possibilities. So many possibilities that an art teacher or mentor could not possibly know which one to prepare a pupil for. Such diverse and unpredictable niches may sometimes require extraordinary adaptations on the part of the life-forms which inhabit them. One of the most diverse environments a parasite can possibly inhabit is the immune system, since diversity is the very basis of immune system effectiveness. Obviously, a system of antibodies and white blood cells cannot 'know' or 'predict' what diseases or invaders will challenge a body in its lifetime. Thus the AIDS virus inhabits a almost unimaginably diverse niche. Recent research into the biology of HIV (Human Immunodeficiency Virus) has revealed that it solves this problem in a most peculiar and disturbing manner. Put bluntly, the virus constantly mutates, averaging a staggering 5–10 mutations for every reproductive event (Kuby 1992: 467). No two AIDS viruses are the same, and they therefore differ both in every person infected, and in the same person through time. The AIDS virus is so diverse that some scientists prefer to call it a quasi-species rather than a species (Eigen 1993). Moreover, diversity is the very basis of the strategy employed by the virus.

In some circumstances, this diversity becomes so great, and the range of viral forms so wide, that the host immune system can no longer find enough antibodies to neutralise each form, and finally collapses. That collapse facilitates the spread of the virus, as hosts become more and more infectious as their immune systems begin to break down. The key factor triggering immune-system collapse is therefore not the number of viruses present, but their diversity. Thus low-copying fidelity is used by the AIDS virus as a weapon, and a switch from high-fidelity copying to low-fidelity copying could well be part of its success.

A cultural equivalent of a switch of this kind may be involved in the switch from the precise, naturalistic art traditions of Vermeer, Chardin, Rembrandt, Corbet and others to early modern art, in the work of the Impressionists. Modern art becomes not so much a species, but a quasispecies, adopting a form where one generation underdetermines another. Such low copying fidelity produces a quasitradition, rather than a tradition. Within a few decades a totally different pattern of evolution becomes manifest, with a rapid succession of styles and techniques. Works such as 'Women I' by Willem De Kooning, painted between 1950 and 1952 (Piper 1994: 464), are dramatically different from the naturalistic frames of reference of the seventeenth and eighteenth centuries, but also from dozens of other twentieth-century styles. Starting with Impressionism, we see the rapid proliferation of subjects and modes of depiction, including Postimpressionism, Expressionism, Cubism, Futurism and Fauvism, Surrealism and Photographic Realism, Pop Art and Dada, Optical and Conceptual, De Stilg, and so on (Piper 1994; Read 1974). Moreover, artists have not stopped painting in more traditional ways – it is just that they are painting in many other ways as well – we are not seeing successive replacement, but adaptive radiation. And many of these styles can themselves be further subdivided. The tradition of Expressionism, can be further divided into abstract and figurative forms, such as abstract and figurative Expressionism, and abstract and figurative Surrealism. And yet the diversity within just one of these sub-traditions, such as Abstract Expressionism, is far greater than the differences we can see in centuries of earlier art traditions. If Vermeer or Chardin would have had problems conceiving of De Kooning's 'Woman' as a work of art, they would probably be even more confused by the work of someone such as Josef Albers, as in his painting 'homage to the square – confirming' (Piper 1994: 469), consisting of concentric yellow squares on a grey background. Yet this work from Josef Albers is not only classified in the same tradition as the previous De Kooning, namely Expressionism, but in the same sub-tradition of Abstract Expressionism.

Such runaway diversity in modern art is reflected in the remarks of commentators such as Piper, who has remarked that 'the years since 1915 have seen more changes than in any early period, in art no less than in science' (Piper 1994: 411). Yet, in conclusion, while there is no space left to pursue the issue in any depth, it would seem that some of the same predatory factors are still at work. Artists are still captured by the practice of image production, sometimes even to the exclusion of all other parts of their life. As John Berger has remarked (1989: 12), discussing the period from 1880 to the present, 'From Stendhal onwards, every major artist, however Romantic he may have been in other respects, believed that his works – the only things which could survive in the future – were the justification of his life.' The diverse, shape-changing quasitradition of modern art is as effective today as Naturalism was in the past. Picasso, for example, may not intended to seek immortality through his works, but his life was virtually governed by the act of painting 'Painting is stronger than I am. It makes me do what it wants.' (Picasso, in Berger 1989: 29). As Berger himself puts it, 'He is single-minded; he works like a man possessed; and all his relationships are more or less subservient to the needs of his art' (Berger 1989: 9). Yet, unlike Renaissance painters such as Vasari, Picasso is not possessed by a style – 'Picasso is fascinated by and devoted to his own creativity . . . . the creative spirit, genius as a state of being, was celebrated as an end in itself' (*ibid.*: 9–10). Yet, in keeping with the quasispecies concept, the diversity of styles which constitute Picasso's own style (quasistyle?), are not random structureless wanderings. They represent quite accurately a fleeting but very real state of mind in the artist, each of which returned at different stages of his career: 'The several manners I have used in my art must not be considered as an evolution or as steps to an unknown ideal of painting. All I have ever made was for the present, and with the hope of that it will always remain in the present. . . . Everything interesting in art happens right at start. Once past the beginning you're already at the end' (Picasso, in Berger 1989: 30, 35). The underlying continuity does not escape the attention of Berger, who writes (1989: 35): 'Picasso's paintings, however much they appear to change, remain essentially what they were at their beginning. . .', and goes on to remark, 'sudden inexplicable transformations: a life's work which, despite appearances, has left unchanged and intact its first vision – that is to say the vision of the young Picasso in Spain.'

In conclusion, it seems that the predatory niche occupied by the modern art traditions today is almost unbelievably unpredictable, and it is perhaps through diversity itself that it manages to maintain appeal, sometimes through admiration, sometimes through notoriety. Art may be horrifying, soothing, exciting, upsetting, disturbing, erotic – the range of emotions and responses it can evoke are as unlimited as the works of art themselves, and the diversity of people who come to see them in the gallery, or studio. Yet the many millions of pounds or dollars which works of famous artists command rarely find their way into the pockets of artists (Picasso being a notable exception), who are nonetheless encouraged by rumours of status, fame and astronomical prices. Artists, then, are the real victims of the art bug, but it is important to remember that they are willing and intentional victims in most cases, for art becomes a part of who and what they are. They, like everyone else, are part predator, part prey, joint products of both genes and culture. Thus, in a sense, it may not be 'the artist' who is the victim, but the genes of the *Homo sapiens* individual in which 'the artist' resides.

Acknowledgements. I would like to thank Jeffrey Tyssens for organising what proved to be a very interesting session, and the Einstein meets Magritte committee for organising a memorable conference.

References

ACTON, J. E. E. D. 1948. *Essays on freedom and power*. Boston (MA): Beascon Press.

AIELLO, L. C. & R. I. M. DUNBAR. 1993. Neocortex size, group size, and the evolution of language, *Current Anthropology* 34: 184–93.

ALEXANDER, R. D. 1979. *Darwinism and human affairs*. Seattle (WA): University of Washington Press.

ALEXANDER, R. D. 1988. Evolutionary approaches to human behaviour: what does the future hold?, in L. L. Betzig, M. Borgerhoff Mulder & P. Turke (ed.), *Human reproductive behaviour: a Darwinian perspective*: 317–25. Cambridge: Cambridge University Press.

ALLAND, A., JR. 1975. Adaptation, *Annual Reviw of Anthropology* 4: 59–73.

ALLEN, P. M. 1981. The evolutionary paradigm of dissipative structures, in E. Jantsch (ed.), *The evolutionary vision: towards a unifying paradigm of physical, biological, and sociocultural evolution*: 25–72. Boulder (CO): American Association for the Advancement of Science, Westview Press.

ALLEN, P. M. 1989. Modelling innovation and change, in S. E. van der Leeuw & R. Torrence (ed.), *What's new?: a closer look at the process of innovation*: 32–43. London : Unwin Hyman.

ALLEN, M. J. & A. BAYLISS. 1995. Appendix 2: the radiocarbon dating programme, in R. M. J. Cleal, K. E. Walker & R. Montague, *Stonehenge in its landscape: twentieth-century excavations*: 511–35. London: English Heritage. Archaeological report 10.

ASHBEE, P. 1982. A reconsideration of the British Neolithic, *Antiquity* 56: 134–8.

ATKINSON, R. J. C. 1956. *Stonehenge*. London: Hamish Hamilton.

BADCOCK, C. 1994. *Psychodarwinism: the new synthesis of Darwin and Freud*. London: HarperCollins.

BAHN, P. & J. FLENLEY. 1992. *Easter Island, earth island*. London: Thames and Hudson.

BALL, J. A. 1984. Memes as replicators, *Ethology and Sociobiology* 5: 145–61.

BARGATSKY, T. 1984. Culture, environment, and the ills of adaptationism, *Current Anthropology* 25: 399–415.

BARNETT, H. G. 1953. *Innovation: the basis of cultural change*. New York (NY): McGraw Hill.

BARRETT, J. C. 1987. Fields of discourse, *Critique of Anthropology* 7: 5–16.

BARRETT, J. C. 1990. The monumentality of death: the character of early Bronze Age mortuary mounds in southern Britain, *World Archaeology* 22: 179–89.

BARTLETT, F. 1923. *Psychology and primitive culture*. New York (NY): Macmillan.

BARTON, C. M. & G. CLARK (ed.). 1997. *Rediscovering Darwin*. Washington (DC): American Anthropological Association.

BATESON, G. 1980. *Mind and nature*. Glasgow: Fontana/Collins.

BATESON, P. 1988. The active role of behaviour in evolution, in M. W. Ho & S. W. Fox (ed.), *Evolutionary processes and metaphors*: 191–207. New York: Wiley & Sons.

BAXTER, P. T. W. & A. BUTT. 1953. *The Azande, and related peoples of the Anglo-Egyptian Sudan and Belgian Conmgo*. London: International African Institute.

BENDER, B. 1993. Cognitive archaeology and cultural materialism, *Cambridge Archaeological Journal* 3: 257–60.

BERGER, J. 1989. *Success and failure of Picasso*, London: Granta.

BETZIG, L. L. 1986. *Despotism and differential reproduction: a Darwinian view of history*. New York (NY): Aldine.

BETZIG, L. L., M. BORGERHOFF MULDER & P. TURKE (ed.). 1988. *Human reproductive behaviour: a Darwinian perspective*. Cambridge: Cambridge University Press.

BIAGIOLI, M. 1993. *Galileo, courtier: the practice of science in the culture of absolutism*. Chicago (IL): University of Chicago Press.

BINFORD, L. R. 1982. Meaning, inference and the material record, in A. C. Renfrew & S. Shenmnan (ed.), *Ranking, resources and exchange*. Cambridge: Cambridge University Press.

BINFORD, L. R. 1987. Data, relativism and archaeological science, *Man* 22: 391–404.

BLACK, R. 1987. Humanism and education in the Renaissance Arezzo, *I Tatti Studies* 2: 171–237.

BLUTE, M. 1976. Review symposia on Edward O Wilson's *Sociobiology: the new synthesis*, *Contemporary Sociology* 5: 727–31.

BLUTE, M. 1979. Sociocultural evolutionism: an untried theory, *Behavioral Science* 24: 46–60.

BOTTOMORE, T. B. & M. RUBEL (ed.). 1963. *Karl Marx: selected writings in sociology and social philosophy*. Harmondsworth: Penguin.

BOUJOT, C. & S. CASSEN. 1993. A pattern of evolution for the Neolithic funerary structures of the west of France, *Antiquity* 67: 477–91.

BOYD, R. & P. J. RICHERSON. 1982. Cultural transmission and the evolution of co-operative behaviour, *Human Ecology* 10: 325–51.

BOYD, R. & P. J. RICHERSON. 1985. *Culture and the evolutionary process*. Chicago (IL): University of Chicago Press.

BRADLEY, RICHARD. 1984. *The social foundations of prehistoric Britain: themes and variations in the archaeology of power*. London: Longmans.

BRAUN, D. P. 1990. Selection and evolution in nonhierarchical organization, in S. Upham (ed.), *The evolution of political systems*: 63–86. Cambridge: Cambridge UP.

BRAY, W. 1973. The biological basis of culture, in C. Renfrew (ed.), *The explanation of culture change: models in prehistory*: 73–92. London: Duckworth.

BRETT, R. A. 1986. The ecology and behaviour of the naked mole rat (*Hetereocephalus glaber*). Unpublished Ph. D dissertation, University of London.

BREW, J. O. 1946. The use and abuse of taxonomy, in *The archaeology of Alkali Ridge, southern Utah*: 44–6. Cambridge (MA): Papers of the Peabody Museum 24.

BRIAN M. V. 1983. *Social insects: ecology and behavioural biology*. London: Chapman & Hall.

BROCK, R. G. C. 1918. Some notes on the Zande tribe as found in the Meridi district, *Sudan Notes and Records* 1: 249–62.

BRODIE, R. 1996. *Virus of the mind*. Seattle (WA): Integral Press.

BROWN, D. 1991. *Human universals*. New York (NY): McGraw-Hill.

BUSS, D. M. 1994. *The evolution of desire*. New York (NY): Basic Books.

CALLON, M. & J. LAW. 1995. Agency and the hybrid collectif, in B. Herrnstein Smith & A. Plotnitsky (ed.), *Mathematics, science and postclassical theory* (Special issue of the *South Atlantic Quarterly*) 94: 481–509.

CAMPBELL, D. T. 1960. Blind variation and selective retention in creative thought as in other knowledge processes, *Psychological Review* 67: 380–400.

CAMPBELL, D. T. 1965. Variation and selective retention in sociocultural evolution, in H. R. Barringer, G. I. Blanksten & R. W. Mack (ed.), *Sociocultural change in underdeveloped areas: a reinterpretation of evolutionary theory*: 19–48. Cambridge (MA): Schenkman.

CAMPBELL, J. H. 1982. Autonomy in evolution, in R. Milliman (ed.), *Perspectives on evolution*: 190–200. Sunderland (MA): Sinauer.

CAMPBELL, J. H. 1985. An organizational interpretation of evolution, in D. J. Depew & B. H. Weber (ed.), *Evolution at a crossroads: the new biology and the new philosophy of science*: 133–67. Cambridge (MA): MIT Press.

CASATI, G. 1891. The Sandeh, in G. Casati & E. Pasha (ed.), *Ten years in equatoria and return*. London: Frederick Warne.

CASE, H. 1969. Settlement patterns in the North Irish Neolithic, *Ulster Journal of Archaeology* 32: 3–28.

CAVALLI-SFORZA, L. L. 1991. Genes, people and languages, *Scientific American* 265: 72–8.

CAVALLI-SFORZA, L. L. & M. W. FELDMAN. 1981. *Cultural transmission and evolution: a quantitative approach*. Princeton (NJ): Princeton University Press.

CAVALLI-SFORZA, L. L., A. Piazza, P. Menozzi & J. L. Mountain. 1988. Reconstruction of human evolution: bringing together genetic, archaeological and linguistic data, *Proceedings of the National Academy of Sciences* 85: 6002–6.

CHAGNON, N. A. 1982. Sociodemographic attributes of nepotism in tribal populations: man the rule breaker, in King's College Sociobiology Group (ed.), *Current problems in sociobiology*: 291–318. London: Cambridge University Press.

CHALOUPKA, G. 1986. Dreamtime or reality? Reply to Lewis, *Archaeology in Oceania* 21: 145–7.

CHAPMAN. R. 1981. The emergence of formal disposal areas and the 'problem' of megalithic tombs in prehistoric Europe, in R. Chapman, I. Kinnes & K. Randsborg (ed.), *The archaeology of death*: 71–81. Cambridge: Cambridge UP.

CHEN, K. H., L. L. CAVALLI-SFORZA & M. W. FELDMAN. 1982. A study of cultural transmission in Taiwan, *Human Ecology* 10: 365–82.

CHILDE, V. G. 1957. *The dawn of European civilisation*. 6th edition, London: Routledge.

CHIPPINDALE, C. 1986. Archaeology, design-theory, and the reconstruction of prehistoric design systems, *Environment and Planning B: Planning and Design* 13: 445–85.

CHIPPINDALE, C. 1992. Grammars of archaeological design, in J.-C. Gardin & C. S. Peebles (ed.), *Representations in archaeology*: 251–76. Bloomington (IN): Indiana University Press.

CHIPPINDALE, C. 1994. *Stonehenge complete*. Revised edition. London: Thames and Hudson.

CHOMSKY, N. 1980. *Rules and representations*. Oxford: Basil Blackwell.

CLARK, J. G. D. 1952. *Prehistoric Europe: the economic basis*. London: Methuen.

CLARKE, D. L. 1978. *Analytical archaeology*. 2nd edition, edited by B. Chapman. London: Methuen.

CLEGG, J. K. 1977a. The meanings of 'schematisation', in Peter J. Ucko (ed.), *Form in indigenous art: schematisation in the art of Aboriginal Australia and prehistoric Europe*: 21–27. Canberra: Australian Institute of Aboriginal Studies. Prehistory and Material Cultures series 13.

CLEGG, J. K. 1977a. A method of resolving problems which arise from style in art, in Peter J. Ucko (ed.), *Form in indigenous art: schematisation in the art of Aboriginal Australia and prehistoric Europe*: 260–76. Canberra: Australian Institute of Aboriginal Studies. Prehistory and Material Cultures series 13.

CLEGG, J. K. 1978a. Mathesis words, mathesis pictures. Unpublished MA thesis, Department of Anthropology, University of Sydney, Sydney, Australia.

CLEGG, J. K. 1978b. A Saussurian model of prehistoric art, *The Artefact* 2: 151–60.

CLEGG, J. K. 1981. *Notes toward mathesis art*. Sydney: Clegg Calenders.

CLOAK, F. T. 1975. Is a cultural ethology possible?, *Human Ecology*: 3(2): 161–83.

COHEN. R. 1981. Evolutionary epistemology and human values, *Current Anthropology* 22: 201–18.

CORNING, P. A. 1987. Evolution and political control: a synopsis of a general theory of politics, in M. Schmidt & F. M. Wuketits (ed.), *Evolutionary theory in social science*: 127–70. Lancaster: Reidel.

COSMIDES, L. 1989. The logic of social exchange: has natural selection shaped how humans reason? Studies with the Wason selection task, *Cognition* 31: 187–276.

COSMIDES, L. & J. TOOBY. 1987. From evolution to behaviour: evolutionary psychology as the missing link, in J. Dupre (ed.), *The latest on the best: essays on evolution and optimality*: 277–306. Cambridge (MA): MIT Press.

CREWS, D. 1994. Animal sexuality, *Scientific American* 270: 108–14.

CRICK, F. 1994. *The astonishing hypothesis: the scientific search for the soul*. London: Touchstone.

CRONIN, H. 1991. *The ant and the peacock: altruism and sexual selection from Darwin to today*. Cambridge: Cambridge University Press.

CROOK, J. H. & S. J. CROOK. 1988. Tibetan polyandry: problems of adaptation and fitness, in L. L. Betzig, M. Borgerhoff Mulder & P. Turke (ed.), *Human reproductive behaviour: a Darwinian perspective*: 97–114. Cambridge: Cambridge UP.

CULLEN, B. R. S. 1990. Darwinian views of history: Betzig's virile psychopath versus the Cultural Virus, *Crosscurrents* 4: 61–8.

CULLEN, B. R. S. 1991. Comment on 'Biology and behaviour in human evolution', *Cambridge Archaeological Journal* 1(2): 217–19.

CULLEN, B. R. S. 1992. Cultural viruses and Darwin's fools, *The Independent* (9 May): 33.

CULLEN, B. R. S. 1993a. The Cultural Virus. Unpublished Ph. D thesis, University of Sydney. (Published in full as Cullen 1996a.)

CULLEN, B. R. S. 1993b. The Darwinian resurgence and the Cultural Virus critique, *Cambridge Archaeological Journal* 3: 179–202.

CULLEN, B. R. S. 1994. When megaliths behave like a bad cold, *British Archaeological News* (December): 4.

CULLEN, B. R. S. 1995. Living artefact, personal ecosystem, biocultural schizophrenia: a novel synthesis of processual and post-processual thinking, *Proceedings of the Prehistoric Society* 61: 69–90.

CULLEN, B. R. S. 1996a. *The Cultural Virus*. Ann Arbor (MI): University Microfilms International. (The 1993 Ph. D thesis, published in full.)

CULLEN, B. R. S. 1996b. Cultural Virus Theory and the eusocial pottery assemblage, in H. D. G. Maschner (ed.), *Darwinian archaeologies*: 43–60. New York (NY): Plenum.

CULLEN, B. R. S. 1996c. Social interaction and viral phenomena, in J. Steele & S. Shennan (ed.), *The archaeology of human ancestry : power, sex, and tradition*: 1–16. London: Routledge.

CUNLIFFE, B. 1994. *The Oxford illustrated prehistory of Europe*. Oxford: Oxford University Press.

CZEKANOWSKI, J. 1924. *Researches in the region between the Nile and the Congo* 2. Leipzig: Klinkhardt und Biermann. HRAF translation.

DALY, M. 1982. Some caveats about cultural transmission models, *Human Ecology* 10: 401–8.

DARVILL, T. 1987. *Prehistoric Britain*. London: Batsford.

DARWIN, C. R. 1859. *The origin of species by means of natural selection*. London: John Murray.

DARWIN, C. R. 1871. *The descent of man, and selection in relation to sex*. London: John Murray.

DARWIN, C. R. 1889. *A naturalist's voyage: journal of researches into the natural history and geology of the countries visited during the voyage of the HMS 'Beagle' round the world*. London: John Murray.

DARWIN, F. (ed.) 1888. *The life and letters of Charles Darwin* 2. London: John Murray.

DAWKINS, R. 1976. *The selfish gene*. Oxford: Oxford University Press.

DAWKINS, R. 1982. *The extended phenotype: the gene as the unit of selection*. Oxford: W. H. Freeman.

DAWKINS, R. 1986. *The blind watchmaker*. London: Longman.

DAWKINS, R. 1989. *The selfish gene*. New edition. Oxford: Oxford University Press.

DAWKINS, R. 1992. The mind is prey to virus and parasite, *Independent* (2 May): 30.

DAWKINS, R. 1993a. Is religion just a disease?, *Daily Telegraph* (15 December): 18.

DAWKINS, R. 1993b. Viruses of the mind, in B. Dahlboum (ed.), *Dennett and his critics: demystifying mind*: 13–28. Oxford: Blackwell.

DEAN, D. & E. DELSON. 1995. *Homo* at the gates of Europe, Nature 373: 472–3.

DEGLER, C. N. 1990. *In search of huma nature: the decline and revival of Darwinism in American social thought.* New York (NY): Oxford University Press.

DELEUZE, G. & F. GUATTARI. 1987 [1992]. *A thousand plateaus: capitalism and schizophrenia.* Minneapolis (MN): University of Minnesota Press.

DELIUS, J. D. 1989. Of mind memes and brain bugs: a natural history of culture, in W. A. Koch (ed.), *The nature of culture*: 26–79. Bochum: Studienverlag Brockmeyer.

DELIUS, J. D. 1991. The nature of culture, in M. S. Dawkins, T. R. Halliday & R. Dawkins (ed.), *The Tinbergen legacy*: 75–99. London: Chapman & Hall.

DEMPSEY, C. 1980. Some observations on the education of artists in Florence and Bologna during the later sixteenth century, *Art Bulletin* 62: 552–70.

DENNETT, D. 1993. *Consciousness explained.* London: Penguin.

DENNETT, D. 1995. *Darwin's dangerous idea.* New York (NY): Simon & Schuster.

DEPEW, D. J. & B. H. WEBER. 1988. Consequences of non-equilibrium thermodynamics for the Darwinian tradition, in B. H. Weber, D. J. Depew & J. T. Smith (ed.), *Entropy, information and evolution: new perspectives on physical and biological evolution*: 319–34. Cambridge (MA): Bradford Books, MIT Press.

DESMOND, A. & J. MOORE. 1992. *Darwin.* London: Penguin.

DICKEMANN, M. 1981. Paternal confidence and dowry competition: a biocultural analysis of the Purdah, in R. D. Alexander & D. W. Tinkle (ed.), *Natural selection and social behavior: recent research and new theory*: 417–38. New York (NY): Chiron.

DOVER, G. 1982. Molecular drive: a cohesive mode of species evolution, *Nature* 299: 111–17.

DUNBAR, R. 1988. Darwinising man: a commentary, in L. L. Betzig, M. Borgerhoff Mulder & P. Turke (ed.), *Human reproductive behaviour: a Darwinian perspective*: 161–9. Cambridge: Cambridge University Press.

DUNNELL, R. C. 1978. Style and function: a fundamental dichotomy, *American Antiquity* 43: 192–202.

DUNNELL, R. C. 1980. Evolutionary theory and archaeology, *Advances in Archaeological Method and Theory* 3: 38–99.

DUNNELL, R. C. 1985. Comment on 'Darwinian selection and symbolic variation', *Current Anthropology* 26: 78.

DUNNELL, R. C. 1989. Aspects of the application of evolutionary theory in archaeology, in C. C. Lamberg-Karlovsky (ed.) *Archaeological thought in America*: 35–49. Cambridge: Cambridge University Press.

DUNNELL, R. C. & R. J. Wenke. 1980. Some comments on 'The decline and rise of Mesopotamian civilisation', *American Antiquity* 45: 606–9.

DURHAM, W. H. 1982. Interactions of genetic and cultural evolution: models and examples, *Human Ecology* 10: 289–99.

DURHAM, W. H. 1990. Advances in evolutionary culture theory, *Annual Review of Anthropology* 19: 187–210.

DURHAM, W. H. 1991. *Coevolution: genes, culture, and human diversity.* Stanford (CA): Stanford University Press.

DURKHEIM, E. 1893 [1933]. *The division of labor in society.* Glencoe (IL): Free Press.

DURKHEIM, E. 1895 [1966]. *The rules of sociological method.* New York (NY)): Free Press.

DURKHEIM, E. 1915. *The elementary forms of the religious life: a study in religious sociology* (1912), translated by J. W. Swain. London: Allen & Unwin, reprinted 1976.

EDDY, P. & S. WALDEN. 1993. Aids – a special investigation, *Telegraph Magazine* (20 November): 28–36, 57–62.

EDELMAN, G. M. 1978. Group selction and phasic re-entrant signalling: a theory of higher brain function, in G. M. Edelman & V. B. Mountable (ed.), *The mindful brain: organization and the group-selective theory of higher brain function*: 51–100. Cambridge (MA): MIT Press.

EDELMAN, G. M. 1989. *Neural Darwinism: the theory of neuronal group selection*. Oxford: Oxford University Press.

EDELMAN, G. M. 1992. *Bright air, brilliant fire: on the matter of the mind*. London: Allen Lane.

EIGEN, M. 1993. Viral quasispecies, *Scientific American* (July): 42–9.

EISENSTEIN, E. 1979. *The printing press as an agent of change*. Cambridge: Cambridge University Press.

ELDREDGE, N. & S. J. GOULD. 1972. Punctuated equilibrium: an alternative to phyletic gradualism, in T. J. M. Schopf (ed.), *Models in palaeobiology*: 82–115. San Francisco (CA): Cooper.

ENGELS, F. 1884 [1972]. *The origin of the family, private property and the state: in the light of the researches of Lewis H. Morgan*. London Lawrence and Wishart.

EWALD, P. W. 1990. Transmission models and the evolution of virulence: with special reference to cholera, influenza and AIDS, *Human Nature* 2(1): 1–30.

EWALD, P. W. 1991. Transmission modes and evolution of the parasitism-mutualism continuum, *Annals of the New York Academy of Sciences* 503: 295–306.

EWALD, P. W. 1993. The evolution of virulence, *Scientific American* 268: 86ff.

EWALD, P. W. 1994a. *Evolution of infectious disease*. Oxford: Oxford University Press.

EWALD, P. W. 1994b. Evolution of mutation rate and virulence among human retroviruses, *Philosophical Transactions of the Royal Society of London* 346: 333–43.

EWALD, P. W. 1995. The evolution of virulence: a unifying link between parasitology and ecology, *Journal of Parasitology* 81(5): 659–69.

EWALD, P. W. & J. SCHUBERT. 1989. Vertical and vector-borne transmission of insect endocytobionts, and the evolution of benignness, in W. Schwemmler (ed.), *CRC handbook of insect endocytobiosis: morphology, physiology, genetics and evolution*: 21–35. Boca Raton (FL): CRC Press.

FAGAN, B. M. 1980. *People of the earth: an introduction to world prehistory*. 3rd edition. Boston (MA): Little, Brown.

FENNER, F., B. R. MCAUSLAN, C. A. MIMS, J. SAMBROOK & D. O. WHITE. 1974. *The biology of animal viruses*. 2nd edition. London: Academic Press.

FIELDS, B. N. & D. M. KNIPE (ed.). 1991. *Fundamental virology*. 2nd edition. New York (NY): Raven Press.

FLANNERY, K. V. & J. MARCUS. 1993. Cognitive archaeology, *Cambridge Archaeological Journal* 3: 260–267.

FLANNERY, T. F. 1991. The mystery of the Meganesian meat-eaters, *Australian Natural History* 23: 722–9.

FLANNERY, T. F. 1994. *The future eaters: an ecological history of the Australasian lands and people*. Sydney: Reed.

FLEMING, A. 1969. The myth of the mother-goddess, *World Archaeology* 1: 247–61.

FLEMING, A.1972. Vision and design: approaches to ceremonial monument typology, *Man* 7: 57–73.

FLEMING, A. 1973. Tombs for the living, *Man* 8: 177–93.

FLENNIKEN, J. J. & J. P. WHITE. 1985. Australian flaked stone tools: a technological perspective, *Records of the Australian Museum* 36: 131–51.

FLETCHER, R. J. 1977. Settlement studies: micro and semi-micro, in D. L. Clarke (ed.), *Spatial archaeology*: 47–162. London: Academic Press.

FLETCHER, R. J. 1981a. People and space, in I. Hodder, G. Isaac & N. Hammond (ed.), *Patterns of the past*: 97–128. Cambridge: Cambridge University Press.

FLETCHER, R. J. 1981b. Space and coomunity behaviour, in B. Lloyd & J. Gay (ed.), *Universals of human thought*: 71–110. Cambridge: Cambridge University Press.

FLETCHER, R. J. 1988. The evolution of human behaviour, *Australian Natural History* Supplement 2.

FLETCHER, R. J. 1989. The messages of material behaviour: a preliminary discussion of non-verbal meaning, in I. Hodder (ed.), *The meanings of things*: 33–40. London: Unwin Hyman.

FLETCHER, R. J. 1992. Time perspectivism, *Annales*, and the potential of archaeology, in A. B. Knapp (ed.), *Archaeology, Annales, and ethnohistory*: 35–49. Cambridge: Cambridge University Press.

FLINN, M. V. & R. D. ALEXANDER. 1982. Culture theory: the developing synthesis from biology, *Human Ecology* 10(3): 383–97.

FOLEY, R. 1985. Optimality theory in anthropology, *Man* (NS) 20: 222–43.

FOLEY, R. 1987a. *Another unique species: patterns in human evolutionary ecology*. London: Longman.

FOLEY, R. 1987b. Hominid species and stone tool assemblages: how are they related?, *Antiquity* 61: 380–92.

FRANKEL, D. 1991. *Remains to be seen: archaeological insights into Australian prehistory*. Melbourne: Longman Cheshire.

FREEMAN. D. 1974. The evolutionary theories of Charles Darwin and Herbert Spencer, *Current Anthropology* 15: 211–21.

FREEMAN. D. 1983. *Margaret Mead in Samoa: the making and unmaking of an anthropological myth*. Cambridge (MA): Harvard University Press.

FREEMAN, D. 1992. *Paradigms in collision: the far-reaching controversy over the Samoan researches of Margaret Mead and its significance for the human sciences*. Canberra: Research School of Pacific Studies, Australian National University.

FREUD, S. [1962.] *Two short accounts of psychoanalysis*. Harmondsworth: Penguin.

FROST, R. 1968. *A masque of reason: the poetry of Robert Frost*. New York (NY): Holt, Rinehart and Winston.

GAMBLE, C. 1986. *The Palaeolithic settlement of Europe*. Cambridge: Cambridge UP.

GAMBLE, C. 1994. The peopling of Europe 700,000–40,000 years before the present, in B. Cunliffe (ed.), *The Oxford illustrated prehistory of Europe*: 5–41. Oxford UP.

GARDIN, J.-C. 1992. Semiotic trends in archaeology, in J.-C. Gardin & C. S. Peebles (ed.), *Representations in archaeology*: 87–104. Bloomington (IN): Indiana University Press.

GARDIN, J.-C. & C. S. PEEBLES (ed.). 1992. *Representations in archaeology*. Bloomington (IN): Indiana University Press.

GELLNER, E. 1992. *Reason and culture: the historic role of rationality and rationalism*. Oxford: Blackwell.

GHISELIN, M. T. 1969. *The triumph of Darwinian method*. Berkeley (CA): University of California Press.

GHISELIN, M. T. 1974. A radical solution to the species problem, *Systematic Zoology* 23: 536–44.

GHISELIN, M. T. 1987. Species concepts, individuality, and objectivity, *Biology and Philosophy* 2: 127–44.

GIBSON, A. 1992. The timber circle at Sarn-y-Bryn-Caled, Welshpool, Powys: ritual and sacrifice in Bronze Age mid-Wales, *Antiquity* 66: 84–92.

GIDLOW, J. In press. *Arguing the case for rubbish*, in H. Dalwood (ed.), *Interpreting stratigraphy* 6: 1–12. Worcester: Hereford and Worcester County Council.

GOLDSCHMIDT, W. 1993. On the relationship between biology and anthropology, *Man* 28: 341–59.

GOLINSKI, J. 1993. Shining star who courted controversy, *Times Higher Education Supplement* (17 December): 22–3.

GOODENOUGH, O. R. & R. DAWKINS. 1994. The 'St Jude' mind virus, *Nature* 371: 23–4.

GOULD, S. J. 1980. *The panda's thumb: more reflections in natural history*. Harmondsworth: Penguin.

GOULD, S. J. 1983. The hardening of the modern synthesis, in M. Greene (ed.), *Dimensions of Darwinism*: 71–93. Cambridge: Cambridge University Press.

GOULD, S. J. 1991. *Wonderful life: the Burgess Shale and the nature of history*. London: Penguin.

GOULD, S. J. 1994. The evolution of life on earth, *Scientific American* 271: 85-91.

GRANT, S. C. B. 1992. Detection and partitioning of bacteriophage in fluid-solid systems: application to the ecology and mobility of viruses in the environment. Unpublished Ph. D dissertation, California Institute of Technology, Berkeley (CA).

GREENE, W. C. 1993. Aids and the immune system, *Scientific American* 269: 66–73.

HALDANE, J. B. S. 1956. The argument from animals to man: an examination of its validity for anthropology, *Journal of the Royal Anthropological Institute* 86: 1–14.

HALE, W. G. & J. P. MARGHAM. 1988. *Dictionary of biology*. London: Collins.

HARRIS, M. 1968. *The rise of anthropological theory: a history of theories of culture*. New York (NY): HarperCollins.

HARRIS, M. 1974. Comment on 'The evolutionary theories of Charles Darwin and Herbert Spencer', *Current Anthropology* 15: 222–4.

HEYLIGHEN, F. 1992. 'Selfish' memes and the evolution of co-operation, *Journal of Ideas* 2: 77–84.

HINDE, R. A. 1991. A biologist looks at anthropology, *Man* (NS) 26: 583–608.

HO, M. & P. T. SAUNDERS. 1982. The epigenetic approach to the evolution of organisms with notes on its relevance to social and cultural evolution, in H. C. Plotkin (ed.), *Learning, development and culture*: 24–35. Chichester: John Wiley.

HODDER, I. (ed.). 1982a. *Symbolic and structural archaeology*. Cambridge UP.

HODDER, I. 1982b. *Symbols in action*. Cambridge: Cambridge University Press.

HODDER, I. 1984. Burials, houses, women and men in the European Neolithic, in D. Miller & C. Tilley (ed.), *Ideology, power and prehistory*: 51–68. Cambridge: Cambridge University Press.

HODDER, I. 1985. Post-processual archaeology, *Advances in Archaeological Method and Theory* 8: 1–25.

HODDER, I. (ed.). 1989a. *The meanings of things*. London: Unwin Hyman.

HODDER, I. 1989b. Post-structuralism, post-modernism, and post-processual archaeology, in I. Hodder (ed.), *The meanings of things*: 67–79. London: Unwin Hyman.

HODDER, I. 1990. *The domestication of Europe: structure and contingency in Neolithic societies*. Oxford: Basil Blackwell.

HODDER, I. 1991. Interpretive archaeology and its role, *American Antiquity* 56: 7–18.

HODDER, I. 1992a. Symbolism, meaning and context, in I. Hodder, *Theory and practice in archaeology*: 11–23. London: Routledge.

HODDER, I. 1992b. *Theory and practice in archaeology*. London: Routledge.

HODDER, I. 1993. Social cognition, *Cambridge Archaeological Journal* 3: 253–7.

HODDER, I. 1998 . The domus: some problems reconsidered in M. Edmonds & C. Richards (ed.), *Understanding the Neolithic of north-western Europe*: 84–101. Glasgow: Cruithne Press.

HODDER, I. & M. SHANKS. 1994. Interpreting archaeologies: a glossary of terms, in I. Hodder *et al.* (ed.), *Interpretive archaeologies*. London: Routledge.

HODGSON, B. 1994. Buffalo: back home on the range, *National Geographic* 186: 64–90.

HOLE, F. 1973. Questions of theory in the explanation of culture change in prehistory, in C. Renfrew (ed.), *The explanation of culture change: models in prehistory*: 19–31. London: Duckworth.

HORGAN, J. 1994. Can science explain consciousness?, *Scientific American* 271: 88–94.

HUGILL, P. J. & D. B. DICKSON (ed.). 1989. *The transfer and transformation of ideas and material culture*. College Station (TX): Texas A&M University Press.

HULL, D. 1976. Are species really individuals?, *Systematic Zoology* 25: 174–91.

INGOLD, T. 1986. *Evolution and social life*. Cambridge: Cambridge University Press.

INGOLD, T. 1990. An anthropologist looks at biology, *Man* (NS) 25: 208–28.

INGOLD, T. 1991. Comment on 'Biology and behaviour in human evolution', *Cambridge Archaeological Journal* 1: 219–21.

INGOLD, T. 1993. Comment: on 'The Darwinian resurgence and the Cultural Virus critique', *Cambridge Archaeological Journal* 3: 194–5.

IRONS, W. 1979. Cultural and biological success, in N. A. Chagnon & W. Irons (ed.), *Evolutionary biology and human social behavior: an anthropological perspective*: 257–72. North Scituate (MA): Duxbury Press.

IRONS, W. 88. Parental behaviour in humans, in L. L. Betzig, M. Borgerhoff Mulder

& P. Turke (ed.), *Human reproductive behaviour: a Darwinian perspective*: 307–14. Cambridge: Cambridge University Press.

JACOB, F. 1974. *The logic of living systems*. London: Allen Lane.

JAMES, W. 1896. *The principles of psychology* 1. London: Macmillan.

JARMAN, M. R., G. N. BAILEY & H. N. JARMAN (ed.). 1982. *Early European agriculture: its foundations and development*. Cambridge: Cambridge University Press.

JELINEK, J. 1994. In M. H. Nitecki & D. V. Nitecki (ed.), *Origins of anatomically modern humans*. New York (NY): Plenum.

JONES, M. 1993. Comment: on 'The Darwinian resurgence and the Cultural Virus critique', *Cambridge Archaeological Journal* 3: 197–8.

JOUSSAUME, R. 1988. *Dolmens for the dead: megalith-building throughout the world*. Syracuse (NY): Cornell University Press.

KIMURA, M. 1983. *The neutral theory of molecular evolution*. Cambridge: Cambridge University Press.

KIMURA, M. 1985. The neutral theory of molecular evolution, *New Scientist* 11: 41–6.

KINNES, I. 1975. Monumental function in British Neolithic burial practices, *World Archaeology* 7: 16–29.

KIRCH, P. V. 1980. The archaeological study of adaptation: theoretical and methodological issues, *Advances in Archaeological Method and Theory* 3: 101–56.

KNIGHT, C. 1991. *Blood relations: menstruation and the origins of culture*. New Haven (CT): Yale University Press.

KNIGHT, C. 1993. Comment: on 'The Darwinian resurgence and the Cultural Virus critique', *Cambridge Archaeological Journal* 3: 1–3.

KOLB, M. J 1994. Monumentality and the rise of religious authority in precontact Hawaii, *Current Anthropology* 35: 521–47.

KROEBER, A. L. 1952. *The nature of culture*. Chicago (IL): University of Chicago Press.

KUBY, J. 1992. *Immunology*. New York (NY): W. H. Freeman.

KUHN, T. S. 1970. *The structure of scientific revolutions*. 2nd edition. Chicago (IL): University of Chicago Press.

LAGAE, C. R. 1926. *The Azande of Niam-Niam*. Brussels: Veromant. HRAF translation.

LAMARCK, J. B. MONET DE. 1809 [1914]. *Zoological philosophy: an exposition with regard to the natural history of animals*. London: MacMillan.

LAW, J. 1991. Introduction: monsters, machines and sociotechnical relations, in J. Law (ed.), *A sociology of monsters? Essays on power, technology and domination*: 1–23. London: Routledge. Sociological Review Monograph 38.

LAW, J. 1994. *Organizing modernity*. Oxford: Blackwell.

LAYTON, R. 1992. *Australian rock art: a new synthesis*. Cambridge University Press.

LEE, P. C. 1991. Biology and behaviour in human evolution, *Cambridge Archaeological Journal* 1: 207–26.

LEONARD, R. D. & G. T. JONES. 1987. Elements of an inclusive evolutionary model for archaeology, *Journal of Anthropological Archaeology* 6: 199–219.

LEONE, M. 1982. Some opinions about recovering mind, *American Antiquity* 47: 742–59.

LEVI-STRAUSS, C. 1963. *Structural anthropology*. New York (NY): Basic Books.

LEVI-STRAUSS, C. 1970/81. *Introduction to a science of mythology*. London: Cape.

LEVINE, D. S. 1988. Survival of the synapses, *The Sciences* 28: 46–52.

LEWIS, D. 1977. More striped designs in Arnhem Land rock paintings, *Archaeology and Physical Anthropology in Oceania* 12: 98–111.

LEWIS-WILLIAMS, J. D. & T. A. DOWSON. 1993. On vision and power in the Neolithic: evidence from the decorated monuments, *Current Anthropology* 34: 55–65.

LEWONTIN , R., S. ROSE & L. J. KAMIN. 1984. *Not in our genes: biology, ideology, and human nature*. New York (NY): Pantheon.

LINDEN, E. 1974. *Apes, men, and language*. New York (NY): Saturday Review Press.

LORENZ, K. 1963. *On aggression*. London: Methuen.

LOURANDOS, HARRY. 1983. Intensification: a late Pleistocene–Holocene archaeological sequence from southwestern Victoria, *Archaeology in Oceania* 18: 81–94.

LUMSDEN, C. J. & E. O. WILSON. 1981. *Genes, mind and culture: the coevolutionary process*. Cambridge (MA): Harvard University Press.

LYMAN, R., M. O'BRIEN & R. DUNNELL. 1997. *The rise and fall of culture history*. New York (NY): Plenum Press.

MCCARTHY, F. 1967. *Australian Aboriginal rock art*. 3rd edition. Sydney: Australian Museum.

MCDONALD, J. 1983. The identification of species in a Panaramittee style engraving site, in M. Smith (ed.), *Archaeology at ANZAAS 1983*: 236–72. Perth: Western Australian Museum.

MARGULIS, L. 1981. *Symbiosis in cell evolution*. San Francisco (CA): W. H. Freeman.

MARX, K. 1867. *Capital*. New York (NY): International Publishers.

MASCHNER, H. D. G. (ed.). 1996. *Darwinian archaeologies*. New York (NY): Plenum.

MAYNARD, L. 1979. The archaeology of Australian Aboriginal art, in S. Mead (ed.), *Exploring the visual art of Oceania: Australia, Melanesia, Micronesia, and Polynesia*: 83–111. Honolulu (HI): University of Hawaii Press.

MAYR, E. 1976. Typological versus population thinking, in E. Mayr (ed.), *Evolution and the diversity of life: selected essays*. Cambridge (MA): Harvard University Press..

MAYR, E. 1982. *The growth of biological thought*. Cambridge (MA): Harvard University Press.

MELLARS, P. & C. STRINGER (ed.). 1989. *The human revolution: biological and behavioural perspectives in the origins of modern humans*. Edinburgh: Edinburgh University Press.

MILLER, D. & C. TILLEY (ed.). 1984. *Ideology, power and prehistory*. Cambridge UP.

MILLER, J. 1993. *The passion of Michel Foucault*. London: Harper/Collins.

MITCHISON, A. 1993. Will we survive?, *Scientific American* 269: 102–8.

MITHEN, S. 1989. Evolutionary theory and post-processual archaeology, *Antiquity* 63: 483–94.

MITHEN, S. 1990. *Thoughtful foragers: a study of prehistoric decision-making*. Cambridge: Cambridge University Press.

MITHEN, S. 1991. 'A cybernetic wasteland'? Rationality, emotion and Mesolithic foraging, *Proceedings of the Prehistoric Society* 57: 9–14.

MITHEN, S. 1993a. Comment: on 'The Darwinian resurgence and the Cultural Virus critique', *Cambridge Archaeological Journal* 3: 194–5.

MITHEN, S. 1993b. Pictures in the mind, *Times Higher Education Supplement* (9 July): 17.

MONOD, J. L. 1974. On the molecular theory of evolution, in R. Harre (ed.), *Problems of scientific revolution*: 11–24. Oxford: Clarendon.

MORGAN, L. H. 1877. *Ancient society: or, researches in the line of human progress from savagery through barbarism to civilization*. Chicago (IL): Charles H. Kerr.

MORITZ, E. 1990. Memetic science 1: general introduction, *Journal of Ideas* 1: 1–23.

MOSER, S. 1992a. The visual language of archaeology: a case study of the Neanderthals, *Antiquity* 66: 831–44.

MOSER, S. 1992b. Visions of the Australian Pleistocene: prehistoric life at Lake Mungo and Kutikina, *Australian Archaeology* 35: 1–10.

MURDOCK, G. P. 1967. Ethnographic atlas: a summary, *Ethnology*6: 109–236.

MURRAY, P.& G. CHALOUPKA. 1984. The Dreamtime animals: extinct megafauna in Arnhem Land rock art, *Archaeology in Oceania* 19(3): 105–16.

MURRAY, T. 1993. The childhood of William Lanne: contact archaeology and Aboriginality in Tasmania, *Antiquity* 67: 504–19.

NEFF, H. 1992. Ceramics and evolution, *Archaeological Method and Theory* 4: 48–63.

NEFF, H. 1993. Theory, sampling, and analytical techniques in the archaeological study of prehistoric ceramics, *American Antiquity* 58: 23–44.

NESSE, R. M. & G. C. WILLIAMS. 1995. *Evolution and healing: the new science of Darwinian medicine*. London: Weidenfeld and Nicolson.

O'BRIEN, M. (ed.). 1998. *Evolutionary archaeology: theory and applications*. Salt Lake City (UT): University of Utah Press.

O'BRIEN, M. J. & T. D. HOLLAND. 1990. Variation, selection, and the archaeological record, *Archaeological method and theory* 2: 177–97.

O'BRIEN, M. J. & T. D. HOLLAND. 1992. The role of adaptation in archaeological explanation, *American Antiquity* 57: 36–59.

OYAMA, S. 1985. *The ontogeny of information: developmental systems and evolution.* Cambridge: Cambridge University Press.

PATRUCCO, R., R. TELLO, R. & D. BONAVIA. 1983. Parasitological studies of coprolites of pre-Hispanic Peruvian populations, *Current Anthropology* 24: 393–4.

PAUL, W. E. 1993. Infectious diseases & the immune system, *Scientific American* 269: 56–65.

PETERS, S. 1980. Comments on 'The decline and rise of Mesopotamian civilisation', *American Antiquity* 45: 610–14.

PIGGOTT, S. 1965. *Ancient Europe from the beginnings of agriculture to classical antiquity: a survey.* Edinburgh: Edinburgh University Press.

PIPER, D. 1994. *The illustrated history of art.* London: Hamlyn.

POIRIER, F. E. 1981. *Fossil evidence: the human evolutionary journey.* 3rd edition. Toronto: C. V. Mosby.

POSTGATE, J. 1989. Microbial happy families, *New Scientist* (21 January): 40–44.

PULLIAM, H. R. 1982. A social learning model of conflict and co-operation in human societies, *Human Ecology* 10: 353–63.

RAPPAPORT, R. A. 1971. The sacred in hjuman evolution, *Annual Review of Ecology and Systematics* 2: 23–44.

RAPPAPORT, R. A. 1979. *Ecology, meaning, and religion.* Berkeley (CA): North Atlantic Books.

READ, B. 1974. *A concise history of modern painting.* London: Thames and Hudson.

RENFREW, C. 1973a. *Before civilization: the radiocarbon revolution and prehistoric Europe.* London: Penguin.

RENFREW, C. 1973b. Monumnents, mobilisation and social organisation in Neolithic Wessex, in C. Renfrew (ed.), *The explanation of culture change: models in prehistory*: 539–58. London: Duckworth.

RENFREW, C. 1976. Megaliths, territories and populations, in S. J. De Laet (ed.), *Acculturation and continuity in Atlantic Europe*: 298–320. Brugge: De Tempel. Dissertationes Archaeologicae Gandenses 16.

RENFREW, C. 1979. *Investigations in Orkney.* London: Scoiety of Antiquaries.

RENFREW, C. 1982. *Towards an archaeology of mind.* Cambridge: Cambridge University Press.

RENFREW, C. 1983. The social archaeology of megalithic monuments, *Scientific American* 249: 128–36.

RENFREW, C. 1993a. *The roots of ethnicity. archaeology, genetics and the origins of Europe.* Rome: Unione Internationale Degli Instituti di Archeologia Storia e Storia Dell'arte in Roma.

RENFREW, C. 1993b. Cognitive archaeology: some thoughts on the archaeology of thought, *Cambridge Archaeological Journal* 3: 248–50.

RENFREW, C. 1994a. Explaining world linguistic diversity: towards a new synthesis, *Scientific American* 270 (January): 104–112.

RENFREW, C. 1994b. Towards a cognitive archaeology, in C. Renfrew & E. B. W. Zubrow (ed.), *The ancient mind*: 3–12. Cambridge: Cambridge University Press.

RENFREW, C. & P. BAHN. 1991. *Archaeology: theories, methods and practice.* London: Thames & Hudson.

RENFREW, C. .& E. B. W. ZUBROW (ed.). 1994. *The ancient mind.* Cambridge UP.

RENNIE, J. 1992. Trends in parasitology: living together, *Scientific American* (January): 104–13.

RICHERSON, P. J. & R. BOYD. 1978. A dual inheritance model of the human evolutionary process 1: basic postulates and a simple model, *Journal of Social and Biological Structures* 1: 127–54.

RICHERSON, P. J. & R. BOYD. 1985. Comment on 'Darwinian selection and symbolic variation', *Current Anthropology* 26: 83.

RIDLEY, M. 1993. *The red queen: sex and the evolution of human nature.* London: Penguin.

RINDOS, D. 1980. Symbiosis, instability, and the origin and spread of agricultural systems: a new model, *Current Anthropology* 21: 751–72.

RINDOS, D. 1984. *The origins of agriculture: an evolutionary perspective.* Orlando (FL): Academic Press.

RINDOS, D. 1985. Darwinian selection, symbolic variation, and the evolution of culture, *Current Anthropology* 26: 65–88.

RINDOS, D. 1986a. The genetics of cultural anthropology: toward a genetic model of the origin of the capacity for culture, *Journal of Anthropological Archaeology* 5: 1–38.

RINDOS, D. 1986b. The evolution of the capacity for culture: sociobiology, structuralism and cultural selectionism, *Current Anthropology* 27: 315–31.

RINDOS, D. 1989. Undirected variation and the Darwinian explanation of cultural change, *Archaeological Method and Theory* 1: 1–48.

ROSS, C. 1987. Comment – a misuse of evolutionary models in archaeology: 'The evolution of Polynesian chiefdoms', *Archaeology in Oceania* 22: 37–8.

RUBIN, P. L. 1995. *Giorgio Vasari: art and history*. New Haven (CT): Yale University Press.

RUHLEN, M. 1991. *A guide to the world's languages* 1: *Classification*. London: Hodder and Stoughton (Edward Arnold).

RYMAN, G. 1990. *The child garden: a low comedy*. New York (NY): St Martins Press.

SACKS, O. 1993. Making up the mind, *New York Review of Books* (8 April): 42–9.

SAHLINS, M. D. 1960. Evolution: specific and general, in M. D. Sahlins & E. R. Service (ed.), *Evolution and culture*: 12–44. Ann Arbor (MI): University of Michigan Press.

SAHLINS, M. D. & E. R. SERVICE (ed.). 1960. *Evolution and culture*. Ann Arbor (MI): University of Michigan Press.

SARTRE, J. P. 1957. *Being and nothingness*. London: Methuen.

SCARRE, C. 1984. Kin-groups in megalithic burial, *Nature* 311: 512–23.

SCARRE, C. (ed.). 1988. *Past worlds: the Times atlas of archaeology*. London: Times Books.

SCARRE, C. 1994. The meaning of death: funerary beliefs and the prehistorian in C. Renfrew & E. B. W. Zubrow (ed.), *The ancient mind*: 75–83. Cambridge: Cambridge University Press.

SCARRE, C. 1998. Traditions of death: mounded tombs, megalithic art and funerary ideology in Neolithic western Europe, in M. Edmonds & C. Richards (ed.), *Understanding the Neolithic of north-western Europe*: 161–87. Glasgow: Cruithne Press.

SCHIFFER, M. 1988. The structure of archaeological theory, *American Antiquity* 53: 461–85.

SERVICE, E. R. 1962. *Primitive social organization: an evolutionary perspective*. New York (NY): Random House.

SERVICE, E. R. 1971. *Cultural evolutionism: theory in practice*. New York (NY): Holt, Rinehart & Winston.

SHANKS, M. 1992. *Experiencing the past: on the character of archaeology*. London: Routledge.

SHANKS, M. & C. TILLEY. 1982. Ideology, symbolic power and ritual communication: a reinterpretation of Neolithic mortuary practices, in I. Hodder (ed.), *Symbolic and structural archaeology*: 129–54. Cambridge: Cambridge University Press.

SHANKS, M. & C. TILLEY. 1987a. *Reconstructing archaeology: theory and practice*. Cambridge: Cambridge University Press.

SHANKS, M. & C. TILLEY. 1987b. *Social theory and archaeology*. Cambridge: Polity Press.

SHENNAN, S. 1982. Ideology, change and the European Early Bronze Age, in I. Hodder (ed.), *Symbolic and structural archaeology*: 155–61. Cambridge University Press.

SHENNAN, S. 1989. Cultural transmission and cultural change, in S. E. van der Leeuw & R. Torrence (ed.), *What's new?: a closer look at the process of innovation*: 331–46. London : Unwin Hyman.

SHENNAN, S. 1991. Tradition, rationality and cultural transmission, in R. W. Preucel (ed.), *Processual and postprocessual archaeologies*: 197–208. Carbondale (IL): Southern Illinois University. Center for Archaeological Investigations, Occasional Paper 10.

SHERRATT, A. G. 1984. Social evolution: Europe in the later Neolithic and Copper Ages, in J. Bintliff (ed.), *European social evolution*: 324–43. Bradford: University of Bradford.

SHERRATT, A. G. 1990. The genesis of megaliths: monumentality, ethnicity, and social complexity in Neolithic north west Europe, *World Archaeology* 22: 147–67.

SHERRATT, A. G. 1992. Instruments of conversion? The role of megaliths in the Mesolithic/Neolithic transition in north west Europe, in paper to conference on *Comparative studies of megalithics*, Reiss-Museum. Mannheim. Also published as chapter 14 of Sherratt 1997.

SHERRATT, A. G. 1994. The transformation of early agrarian Europe: the later Neolithic and Copper Ages 4500–2500 BC, in B. Cunliffe (ed.), *The Oxford illustrated prehistory of Europe*: 167–201. Oxford: Oxford University Press.

SHERRATT, A. G. 1997. *Economy and society in prehistoric Europe: changing perspectives*. Edinburgh: Edinburgh University Press.

SKINNER, B. F. 1953. *Science and human behavior*. New York (NY): Macmillan

SLAP, J. K. 1991. Virile viruses, *Australian Natural History* 23: 668.

SOLTIS, J., R. BOYD & P. RICHERSON. 1995. Can group-functional behaviors evolve by cultural group selection – an empirical test, *Current Anthropology* 36: 473–94.

SONEA, S. 1988. The global organism, *The Sciences* 28: 38–56.

SPENCER, H. 1873. The study of sociology XV: conclusion, *Contemporary Review* 22: 663–77.

SPERBER, D. 1985. Anthropology and psychology: towards an epidemiology of representations, *Man* (NS) 20: 73–89.

SPUHLER, J. N. 1984. *The evolution of apes and humans: genes, molecules, chromosomes, anatomy and behaviour: the Douglas Ormonde Butler lecture for 1984*. Brisbane.

STARTIN, W. & R. BRADLEY. 1981. Some notes on work organisation and society in prehistoric Wessex, in C. L. N. Ruggles & A. W. R. Whittle (ed.), *Astronomy and society in Britain during the period 4000–1500 BC*: 289–96. Oxford: British Archaeological Reports. British series 88.

STEELE, J. 1996. Weak modularity and the evolution of human social behaviour, in H. D. G. Maschner (ed.), *Darwinian archaeologies*: 185–96. New York (NY): Plenum.

STEVENSON, L. 1987. *Seven theories of human nature*. Oxford: Oxford University Press.

STEWARD, J. H. 1955. *Theory of culture change*. Urbana (IL): University of Illinois Press.

STODDART, S., A. BONNANO, T. GOUDER, C. MALONE & D. TRUMP. 1993. Cult in an island society: prehistoric Malta in the Tarzien period, *Cambridge Archaeological Journal* 3: 3–19.

SWANTON, J. R. 1911. *Indian tribes of the lower Mississippi Valley and adjacent coast of the Gulf of Mexico*. Washington (DC): Government Printing Office. Bulletin of the Smithsonian Institution, Bureau of American Ethnology 43.

SYMONS, D. 1979. *The evolution of human sexuality*. Oxford: Oxford University Press.

TAÇON, P. S. C. & C. CHIPPINDALE. 1994. Australia's ancient warriors: changing depictions of fighting in the rock art of Arnhem Land, N. T., *Cambridge Archaeological Journal* 4: 211–48.

THOM, A. 1967. *Megalithic sites in Britain*. Oxford: Clarendon Press,.

THOMAS, J. 1990. Monuments from the inside: the case of the Irish megalithic tombs, *World Archaeology* 22: 168–78.

THOMAS, J. 1991a. *Rethinking the Neolithic*. Cambridge: Cambridge University Press.

THOMAS, J. 1991b. The hollow men? A reply to Steven Mithen, *Proceedings of the Prehistoric Society* 57: 15–20.

THOMAS, J. 1994. The hermeneutics of megalithic space, in C. Tilley (ed.), *Interpretative archaeologies:*. Oxford: Berg.

THOMAS, J. & C. TILLEY. 1994. The axe and the torso: symbolic structures in the Neolithic of Brittany, in C. Tilley (ed.), *Interpretative archaeologies*: 225–327. Berg.

THORPE, R. S. & O. WILLIAMS-THORPE. 1991. The myth of long-distance megalith transport, *Antiquity* 65: 64–73, 297–8.

TILLEY, C. 1984. Ideology and the legitimation of power in the middle Neolithic of Sweden, in D. Miller & C. Tilley (ed.), *Ideology, power and prehistory*: 111–46. Cambridge: Cambridge University Press.

TILLEY, C. (ed.). 1990. *Reading material culture: structuralism, hermeneutics and post-structuralism*. Oxford: Basil Blackwell.

TILLEY, C. 1991. Michel Foucault: towards an archaeology of archaeology, in C. Tilley (ed.), *Reading material culture*: 281–348. Oxford: Blackwell.

TILLEY, C. (ed.). 1994. *Interpretive archaeologies*. Oxford: Berg.

TOGANIVALU, D. 1912. Ratu Cakobau, *Transactions of the Fijian Society*: 1–12.

TRIGGER, B. G. 1989. *A history of archaeological thought*. Cambridge University Press.

TRIGGER, B. G. 1990. Monumental architecture – a thermodynamic explanation of symbolic behaviour, *World Archaeology* 22: 119–32.

TYLOR, E. B. 1871. *Primitive culture*. New York (NY): Harper and Row.

VAN DER LEEUW, S. E. & R. TORRENCE (ed.). 1989. *What's new?: a closer look at the innovation process*. London: Unwin Hyman.

WAINRIGHT, G. J. 1969. A review of henge monuments in light of recent research, *Proceedings of the Prehistoric Society* 35: 112–33.

WALLACE, A. R. 1889. *Darwinism: an exposition of the theory of natural selection*. London: MacMillan.

WALLIS, M. D. 1851 [1967]. *Life in Feejee*. Ridgewood (NJ): Gregg Press.

WATSON, R. A. & P. J. WATSON. 1969. *Man and nature: an anthropological essay in human ecology*. San Francisco (CA): Harcourt, Brace and World.

WHITE, D. 1989. Demonstration diskette for Maptab, *World Cultures Forum* 1(1).

WHITE, J. P. & J. F. O'CONNELL. 1982. *A prehistory of Australia, New Guinea and Sahul*. Sydney: Academic Press.

WHITE, L. 1949. *The science of culture*. New York (NY): Grove Press.

WHITE, L. 1959a. *The evolution of culture*. New York (NY): McGraw Hill.

WHITE, L. 1959b. The concept of evolution in anthropology, in B. J. Meggers (ed.), *Evolution and anthropology: a centenial appraisal*: 106–24. Washington (DC): Anthropoligcal Socioety of Washington.

WHITEHOUSE, H. 1996. Jungles and computers: Neuronal Group Selection and the epidemiology of representations, *Journal of the Royal Anthropological Institute* 1: 1–18.

WHITLEY, D. S. 1992. Prehistory and post-positivist science: a prolegomenon to cognitive archaeology. *Archaeological Method and Theory* 4: 58–100.

WHITTLE, A. 1985. *Neolithic Europe: a survey*. Cambridge : Cambridge University Press.

WHITTLE, A. 1988. *Problems in Neolithic archaeology*. Cambridge: Cambridge University Press.

WHITTLE, A. 1994. The first farmers, in B. Cunliffe, *The Oxford illustrated prehistory of Europe*: 134–67. Oxford: Oxford University Press.

WILLIAMS, T. 1884. *Fiji and the Fikians*. London: Hodder and Stoughton.

WILSON, E. O. 1971. *The insect societies*. Cambridge (MA): Belknap Press of Harvard University Press.

WILSON, E. O. 1975. *Sociobiology: the new synthesis*. Cambridge: Cambridge University Press.

WRIGHT, R. V. S. 1977. Introduction and two studies, in R. V. S. Wright (ed.), *Stone tools as cultural markers: change, evolution, complexity*: 1–4. Canberra: Australian Institute of Aboriginal Studies.

WRIGHT, R. V. S. 1989. *Doing multivariate archaeology and prehistory: handling large data sets with MV-Arch*. Sydney: Department of Anthropology, University of Sydney.

WYLIE, A. 1989. Archaeological cables and tacking: the implications of practice for Bernstein's 'options beyond objectivism and relativism', *Philosophy of the Social Sciences* 19: 1–18.

YOFFEE, N. 1979. The decline and rise of Mesopotamian civilisation: an ethnoarchaeological perspective in the evolution of social complexity, *American Antiquity* 44: 5–36.

YOFFEE, N. 1980. Reply to Dunnell and Wenke: Do you see yonder cloud that looks like a camel?, *American Antiquity* 45: 615–19.

YOFFEE, N. 1985. Perspectives on trends toward social complexity in prehistoric Australia and Papua New Guinea, *Archaeology in Oceania* 20: 41–8.

ZUBROW, E. B. W. 1993. Comment: on 'The Darwinian resurgence and the Cultural Virus critique', *Cambridge Archaeological Journal* 3: 195–7.

Index

This index points to the beginnings of sections discussing ideas rather than to every occurence of a word or name.